Davidson
2004

WORDS THAT COUNT

MacDonald P. Jackson. Godfrey Boehnke, photographer.

WORDS THAT COUNT

Essays on Early Modern Authorship in Honor of MacDonald P. Jackson

Edited by Brian Boyd

Newark: University of Delaware Press

Associated University Presses
2010 Eastpark Boulevard
Cranbury, NJ 08512

The paper used in this publication meets the requirements of the American National Standard for Permanence of Paper for Printed Library Materials Z39.48-1984.

Library of Congress Cataloging-in-Publication Data

Words that count : essays on early modern authorship in honor of Macdonald P. Jackson / edited by Brian Boyd.
p. cm.
Includes bibliographical references and index.
ISBN 0-87413-868-X (alk. paper)
1. English drama—Early modern and Elizabethan, 1500–1600—History and criticism. 2. English drama—17th century—History and criticism. 3. Shakespeare, William, 1564–1616. Lover's complaint. 4. Shakespeare, William, 1564–1616—Authorship. 5. Playwriting—History—16th century. 6. Playwriting—History—17th century. 7. Authorship—History—16th century. 8. Authorship—History—17th century. I. Boyd, Brian, 1952– II. Jackson, MacDonald P. (MacDonald Pairman)

PR658.A9W67 2004
822′.309—dc22

2003025954

PRINTED IN THE UNITED STATES OF AMERICA

Contents

1610s–1620s: Webster and Heywood

1620s: Middleton, Rowley, Ford, and Dekker

WORDS THAT COUNT

Introductions

"A Green Bay-Tree": Tribute to MacDonald P. Jackson

John Kerrigan

SEVERAL VOLUMES WOULD BE NEEDED TO CELEBRATE ADEQUATELY MACDonald P. Jackson's achievements. The focus of this Festschrift on Renaissance poetry and drama reflects his enormous contribution to the study of authorship, chronology, textual bibliography, and performance in that period. But another side of Jackson can be seen in his work on New Zealand verse—reviews, editions, interviews, and authoritative critical analysis. His interest in theater studies has evolved into work on film. And his statistically driven curiosity has taken him into some remarkable areas. Few readers of his work on Peele or Webster will be aware of his 1979 article in *The Journal of Psychology* that tests Eysenck's findings about the calendrical distribution of extraversion and neuroticism. The minute attention to detail, the tenacious pursuit of evidence, that is a hallmark of his best-known scholarship is but one facet of a complex sensibility and wide-ranging intellect.

I first encountered Jackson in the early 1980s, in the bookstacks of Cambridge University Library—not in person (I've never met him) but through the steadily reasoned pages of his booklet on *Shakespeare's "A Lover's Complaint"* (1965). A mundane sort of encounter, but hugely important for me, because at the time I was contracted to edit Shakespeare's *Sonnets* and had reason to believe that my brief should be extended to the complaint. Jackson's multidimensional argument for Shakespeare's authorship of the poem went far toward confirming my impulse to follow the lead of the 1609 quarto and print it after the sonnets. But his booklet set a larger example: it showed a trainee editor how literary and textual analysis could work together to innovative ends. In that sense, it set the standard. Jackson's claims for *A Lover's Complaint* are now widely accepted, and the poem has kept its place in key editions of the *Sonnets*. There are dissenting voices even in the present volume. Yet the strength of Jackson's scholarship is that he always sees problems in the round, and his interlocking of evidence from vocabulary, imagery, stylistic devices, and situational parallels with the plays produces a case that has staying power because it is more than the sum of its parts.

From his booklet on the complaint I turned to his article on "Punctuation and the Compositors of Shakespeare's *Sonnets,* 1609." It proved equally encouraging. Characteristically, Jackson started from a literary question, about how the poems should be read: is there a Shakespearean relationship between verse rhythm and the 1609 punctuation? His analysis showed that different patterns of accidentals can be identified in the quarto, and that the pointing of individual poems is partly a consequence of compositorial habits. This pioneering discussion (1975) set the editing of the sonnets on the same sort of footing as had been achieved for Shakespeare's plays, by scholars who had labored for decades to establish compositor stints in the Folio. Jackson has continued to add to our understanding of the *Sonnets.* He recently clarified their chronology, and his dating of the sonnets about the "rival poet" led him to some brilliant insights into Shakespeare's authorial anxiety—partly triggered by Francis Meres's *Palladis Tamia,* and involving Marlowe, Chapman, and Jonson—in the late 1590s. The *Sonnets* have also been caught up in his commitment to New Zealand literature: in 2000 he published a foreword to a Maori translation, by a University of Auckland colleague and kuia, *Nga Waiata Aroha a Hekepia: Love Sonnets by Shakespeare,* and he followed that with an interview, published in *Shakespeare Quarterly,* with the translator.

The core of Jackson's research lies in early modern drama. From his Oxford thesis on *Arden of Faversham* (1963), through his fundamental *Studies in Attribution: Middleton and Shakespeare* (1979), and the dozens of notes and articles he published on the Shakespeare canon in the 1980s and 1990s, the record has been unbroken. In the field of textual scholarship he now stands next to W. W. Greg, Fredson Bowers, and few others. Rigor he has in abundance, yet the humanity and eye for nuance that make his interventions in textual studies so satisfying only make sense when these arduous researches are placed in the context of the other critical work that he was doing at the time: his review of Lauris Edmond in the *New Zealand Listener,* for example; his notice of a National Theatre (London) production of *The Duchess of Malfi;* and his entries in *The Oxford Companion to Twentieth-Century Poetry.* Jackson's scholarly career is just now peaking, in the long-awaited appearance of the Oxford Middleton, and his volume on that most exhilaratingly theatrical and textually messy play, *Pericles.*

Although they do not constitute the main planks of his output, the reviews of "Editions and Textual Studies" that he undertook for *Shakespeare Survey* (1984–91) show the consort of his gifts most fully singing together. His term in the job included two of the toughest assignments a scholar could be given: assessing the Oxford Shakespeare, and Donald Foster's *Elegy by W.S.: A Study in Attribution.* And although, as Jackson would be the first to point out, there is always room for disagreement, it is hard to see that he put a foot wrong. Stringent about methodological weakness, or anything that looked likely to pollute the springs of the Shakespearean text, he was hospitable to fresh inquiry, however startling its implications, and always careful to point up the capacity of deficient work to provoke new thought. Eric Sams's edition of *Shakespeare's Lost Play: Edmund Ironside,* for example, walks away from the reviewer in shreds but with the proper comment that "it raises vital questions." In these review articles one sees the importance to a textual scholar of thinking about the stage ("This is all perfectly obvious in the theater . . . "), and of having an enormous knowledge of plays beyond Shakespeare if local observations about the canon are to be sustainable. Above all, one senses the weight that modesty can bring to judgment, a modesty that is no doubt temperamental but also comes, paradoxically, from Jackson knowing so much about his subject that he realizes how unwise assurance can be.

Because Jackson's work on New Zealand poetry is not represented in this Festschrift, though it has evidently been important in sustaining his imagination and his Renaissance scholarship, I want to finish with a lyric by Ursula Bethell (1874–1945) that he discusses in *The Oxford History of New Zealand Literature in English.* The poem highlights the love of particularity that has been indispensable to Jackson's own research, while gradually showing us what significance detail can acquire:

Detail

My garage is a structure of excessive plainness,
It springs from a dry bank in the back garden,
It is made of corrugated iron,
And painted all over with brick-red.

But beside it I have planted a green Bay-tree,
—A sweet Bay, an Olive, and a Turkey Fig,
—A Fig, an Olive, and a Bay.

Jackson rightly notes that "'Detail' seems so matter-of-fact as hardly to be a poem at all—until one ponders the repetition, with variations, of the last line." Reading the lyric as a shorthand account of the cultural inheritance of pakeha New Zealand, he interprets the bay, the olive, and the fig as "living insignia for a whole Christian, humanist, and classical tradition. The poet's garage is totally utilitarian. The planting of the saplings of trees that flourished in ancient Greece and Palestine is emblematic of the other side of the colonial enterprise."

These comments are acute, but looking over the reader's shoulder one can also deduce what attracted Jackson to the poem, and thus how it reflects his own qualities. The functionality of the garage, with its acceptable simplicity of means, catches something of the practical, direct candor of Jackson's intelligence, and it is apt that the poem should then develop a counting routine, a regime of repetition. Just where the lyric appears most prosaically "matter-of-fact," numbering the trees, first one way, then another, it becomes most symbolically resonant but also intimately poetic. We might find in this weighing of words a modulated version of the thought processes of an editor who turns readings around in his head, assessing what terms mean and in which order they should appear on the page, but the routine also relates to an innate attraction to numbers (statistics as well as prosodic numbers) in Jackson's psyche. Like Brian Vickers, who uses the comment as epigraph to his essay below, I was struck, when I read the preface to *Studies in Attribution,* by the remark, "I quite enjoy counting things—when some form of demonstration is a likely outcome."

And this points to a subtle dynamic, within the repetitions of the poem, beyond accumulation into sifting and demonstrating relative importance. For it becomes clear as the lyric evolves that, out of the apparently level presentation of detail, the "green Bay-tree" claims priority. We hear of it more often than the olive and the fig, it comes both first and last in the two lines of enumeration, and in its terminal position "a Bay" provides a truncated perfect rhyme (in this unrhymed poem) with "a green Bay-tree" two lines back. It is understandable that, for Bethell, as for Petrarch centuries earlier, the laurels of achievement should have an insistent allure. What should be apparent from this Festschrift is how confident the scholarly community is that Jackson's own contribution, as a textual editor, to the fabric of poetry and drama, and as an expert in attribution, performance, and so on to the air that literature breathes, has earned a similar tribute.

Words That Count: Introduction

Brian Boyd

MAC JACKSON IS NOT THE SORT OF PERSON WHO SPEAKS AS IF HE THINKS his words particularly count. He will often hold back in conversation—though in one of his many moments of enthusiasm, he can turn tense with excitement, he seems almost to jump out of his skin with delight, his voice creaks and cracks with pleasure, his hands swivel up from the elbow like pincers as he appears to grip with his fingertips whatever it is he has just found to like so much. But he always makes his written words count; when he recites the works of others, he makes *them* tell from the start; and his own most important work has relied on counting lines, words, syllables, characters, even though he is so superbly sensitive to the uncountable quiddities and the innumerable nuances of words.

At a time when research is assessed by adding up publications, totaling grants, and tallying the size of research teams, MacDonald P. Jackson, whose retirement from the University of Auckland this volume commemorates, exemplifies a different kind of scholarship, distinguished by quality, consequence, and disinterested curiosity. His painstaking and penetrating work has helped us to discover, in the uncertain data of the greatest age of English drama, just who wrote what and when.

An Auckland native, Mac studied in what was then Auckland University College of the University of New Zealand, coming top of English nationwide, before heading to Oxford, where he wrote a BLitt thesis on *Arden of Faversham* that remains indispensable to scholars of the play.[1] In his publications he would retain a close association with Oxford, but from 1964, his first year as a full lecturer, until his retirement in 2003, he taught in the English Department of what had already become the University of Auckland.

Generations of Auckland students have been enthralled by Mac Jackson, not because they had any idea he was a great scholar, but because he seemed so far from that august aura; because he appeared so approachable and so full of generous enthusiasm and warm amusement at anything absurd in life, literature, and criticism. Like Marcus Aurelius in Gibbon's judgment, he is easy on others but demanding of himself. With a confidence that derives from having worked to meet his own high standards of scholarship, he has never needed to impress others, to seek praise (he would rather change the subject), or to display his erudition. Rather than wanting to stand tall, he sits back and sets others at their ease. At the beginning of a course he sometimes dispelled any nervousness his students might have brought to the first class by confessing, and almost reliving, how moved he had been as a child by *Bambi*.

But although so undaunting and outwardly relaxed, Mac can suddenly tighten with energy as he prepares to hurl himself into reciting from a poem or a play. This quiet man with no liking for the limelight can explode as if suddenly *possessed* by a poem, so that every ear in the room hears every word, and every spine tingles.

Mac's love of verse, like his curiosity, is wide and deep. He has edited an Oxford anthology of New Zealand poetry and prose and the selected poems of A. R. D. Fairburn, and, as John Kerrigan shows, has written superbly about New Zealand poetry for the *Oxford History of New Zealand Literature*. A passionate reader of late nineteenth-century English verse, this "hero of [Shakespearean] Sonnets scholarship"[2] has also rediscovered, revived, and edited the sonnets of Eugene Lee-Hamilton. Writing about Shakespeare's relations to his poetic rivals, he can effortlessly adduce just the right evidence and counterevidence from William Blake, W. B. Yeats, and Theodore Roethke.

Although especially an investigator of verse, Jackson has regularly taught a highly successful Shakespeare on Screen course and has occasionally written evocatively about theatrical and film performances of Shakespeare, most recently about the outstanding film version of *The Merchant of Venice* in Maori translation. Merely by watching a Shakespeare or Pinter play or a Woody Allen or Baz Luhrmann movie with Mac at one's elbow, one reacts differently, primed by a fellow spectator set to a higher level of attention and a lower threshold for laughter than anyone else in the audience.

Reluctant to settle for the deceptive light of common knowledge or the pall of common ignorance, Mac will search for any glimmer of evidence, especially if statistics can amplify the illumination. Even as Head of Department, he would not accept the assumptions or approximations everyone else was ready to make, but would research and report exact figures, standard deviations, margins of error. In matters more congenial to him than administration, he has mined poetry, or birth dates, or the elusive inscriptions on the Phaistos Disk, for prosaic numbers that he could turn into the subprose of statistical tables, and in most cases not just out of raw curiosity but also out of a refined passion for poetry. Counting words in the works of Shakespeare and his contemporaries, treating one expletive or contraction as statistically identical to another, could seem unliterary, insensitive, immune to difference. But his readers, like his students, know better.

Jackson's most influential work has involved the counting of verbal and metrical patterns that can provide clues to authorship and dating. A champion of such internal evidence in practice and in theory—in the course of another recent demonstration of its power, he comments "how ill-informed and unjustified" is Leeds Barroll's dismissal of the very concept of internal evidence as "most often an oxymoron"—he nevertheless always integrates internal evidence with the full range of the relevant external evidence obvious on title pages or hidden in unpublished contemporary records.[3]

But perhaps no one alive has a better grasp of the minutiae of English theatrical records of the 1580s and 1590s than another graduate of the Auckland English Department, a year ahead of Jackson, Andrew Gurr, whose essay on Marlowe opens this collection, arranged chronologically from the 1580s through to the 1620s.

Gurr's discussion begins by invoking Jackson's precision, and it is noteworthy that despite his fellow Aucklander's reputation for illuminating so much through internal evidence, Gurr in discussing the date of *Doctor Faustus* cites Jackson's *external* evidence as "the most tangible" and precise, since it indicates a *terminus ad quem* for the play of February 1589.[4] Gurr steps his way through what he stresses are the murky waters of Marlowe's relations to the constantly shifting theater companies of the late 1580s and early 1590s. Where much of this volume investigates the elusive authorial ownership of early modern texts, Gurr focuses on the theatrical ownership of texts, a matter often intimately related to authorship within the stage practices of the time. He shows reasons for believing that Marlowe wrote at least the first part of *Tamburlaine* while at Cambridge before selling it not, as might be expected, to the dominant Queen's Men—perhaps because of his antipathy to Tarlton as clown—but to the leading player of the Lord Admiral's Men, Edward Alleyn. Although Alleyn bought both parts of *Tamburlaine* and *Doctor Faustus* in 1587–88 and became famous in both lead roles, the plays do not appear in the repertory of the so-called amalgamated company of Strange's and the Admiral's in 1592–93. Gurr suggests that the amalgamation was an illusion, that only Alleyn himself of the Admiral's Men belonged to Strange's, that he lost his right to play Marlowe's great overreachers when he left the Admiral's Men for Strange's, and that Marlowe also switched allegiance, selling Strange's Men *The Jew of Malta* and *The Massacre at Paris.* Meanwhile the residual Admiral's Men, without their star, quit London to tour the country with *Tamburlaine* and *Doctor Faustus,* leaving Marlowe's most popular plays absent from capital and court between 1591 and 1594.

Gurr concludes that when in mid-1594 the Lord Chamberlain and his son-in-law the Lord Admiral reassigned players from all the major existing companies into two new companies, the Lord Chamberlain's Men, including Shakespeare, and the Lord Admiral's Men, including Alleyn, and assigned the Shakespeare corpus to the Chamberlain's Men and perhaps all of the Marlowe corpus to the Admiral's, it seems that they "recognized Marlowe and Shakespeare as the time's two great assets as playwrights." "History," he observes, "has not devalued the judgement made in 1594."

Gurr's conclusion connects with what promises to be one of Jackson's most influential recent papers, demonstrating Shakespeare's alertness to another judgment of the time, that of Francis Meres, who in his *Palladis Tamia* (1598) famously compared Shakespeare with Marlowe and other contemporaries. Through internal evidence, Jackson has been able to date Sonnets 78–86 to 1598–1600, and now uses that knowledge to reinterpret the external evidence, showing that Shakespeare has carefully constructed a composite image of the rival poet "in a general sense of rivalry fueled by [and echoing] Francis Meres's glib inventory of England's top poets and playwrights and exacerbated by the publication of Marlowe's 'Come live with me and be my love' as Shakespeare's, of Marlowe and Chapman's *Hero and Leander,* and of Chapman's *Seven Books of the Iliad,* and the emergence of a brashly confident Jonson as new challenger to Shakespeare's preeminence in the theatre."[5] In much of his work Jackson has confirmed Shakespeare's collaboration with other writers of his time; here he reveals him in assured, almost playful, competition with them.

Brian Boyd joined the Auckland English Department a quarter-century after Gurr and Jackson arrived as students. His essay illustrates the critical consequences that can flow from clarifying authorship. He draws on a recent paper where he shows that George Peele added Titus's killing of Mutius as an afterthought to his share of *Titus Andronicus,* and that Shakespeare discloses no awareness of the addition as he composed his own, much the larger, share of the play. It now becomes possible, Boyd argues, to see that Shakespeare has not only adapted the opening that Kyd's *Spanish Tragedy* provides for his story, and the conclusion that Ovid offers in the rape of Philomela, but has done so to focus on a theme he was developing in his own most recent works, the *Henry VI* plays, and hitherto obscured by Titus's apparent killing of his son: pity for one's own and pitilessness toward others. Aaron, with his sudden unexpected concern for his black babe, now emerges as a key variation on the theme, one that Shakespeare prepares for from his first scene in the play, no matter how much the babe's birth takes the audience by surprise.

Although also a literary critic and theorist of note, Brian Vickers characterizes himself as simply a historical scholar. Among the many things he appreciates in Jackson's work is his awareness of the insights buried in past scholarship: as Jackson writes about the relationship of the *King Lear* Quarto and Folio, "The Shakespearean scholar who looks back beyond current orthodoxies will often enough light upon forgotten truths in need of rediscovery and new formulation."[6] Vickers's own command of over two centuries of authorship debate is one of the things that makes his *Shakespeare, Co-Author* so compelling, and allows him there to place Jackson's scholarship in firm historical perspective. Yet even he could not know the manuscripts of another great investigator of authorship, E. H. C. Oliphant, which Jackson recently examined in the State Library of Victoria in Melbourne, Australia, thrilling at Oliphant's unpublished descriptions of Middleton's style, plunging into the notebooks that showed how much Oliphant had patiently counted, and exclaiming with delight as he resurfaced: "I recognize a kindred spirit!"

In his contribution here, Vickers picks up on Jackson's and Boyd's revival of old claims for Peele's role in *Titus Andronicus* to revive and confirm other old claims for Peele's authorship of *The Troublesome Raigne of King John.* Surveying previous evidence in support of this largely unremarked attribution, especially patterns of repetition and particulars of vocabulary, Vickers adds telling new proof, with exhaustive examples from the established Peele canon and *The Troublesome Raigne:* the mannered use of vocatives and self-address; simple and compound alliterations; macaronic Latin in anti-clerical satire. He concludes by considering the consequences for the relationship of *The Troublesome Raigne* and Shakespeare's *King John.* Adducing Jackson's compelling vocabulary evidence for placing *King John* after *Richard II,* he rightly rules out Boyd's conjecture that Shakespeare not only planned the theatrical plot of the play—from which, Boyd and others argue, the author of *The Troublesome Raigne* had written up *his* play[7]—but presumably also wrote his own version at that time, in 1590–91.

Jackson concludes a recent paper that offers new evidence for the sequence of the Shakespearean canon: "The one play capable of upsetting all orthodox accounts of the dating of Shakespeare's early plays is *King John.* . . . Establishing the relationship between the two King John plays lies well outside the scope of the present enquiry, but the precise dating of Shakespeare's first dozen or so plays depends on the successful accomplishment of that difficult task."[8] Vickers's demonstration in this volume that Peele wrote *The Troublesome Raigne,* and his confirmation in *Shakespeare, Co-Author* of the work of John Dover Wilson, Jackson, Boyd, and others that Peele wrote the first three scenes of *Titus Andronicus* and the first scene of act 4, may offer a quite unexpected new solution, which both extends what Jackson calls the "strong arguments"[9] recently advanced in favor of Shakespeare as the writer responsible for the shape of both King John plays, and yet keeps *King John* in the traditional sequence that his own essay strengthens: immediately after *Richard II.*

Interested in turning to tragedy to develop a theme of his increasingly tragic *Henry VI* plays, and seeking to steep his story in the *gravitas* of Rome, Shakespeare appears to have turned to Peele, a Latin scholar, to establish the Roman atmosphere of the beginning of *Titus Andronicus.* Now that we know of both his close professional contact with Shakespeare at the beginning of the 1590s and his authorship of *The Troublesome Raigne* in 1591, we can see that after contributing to *Titus,* or even as his fee for the task, Peele could have asked the young playwright so successfully adapting Holinshed to the stage to provide the plot of a play based on the life of King John, whose defiance of the Pope made him a hero for an anti-papist like Peele.[10] If Shakespeare drew up the plot, it would explain how Holinshed could have been radically reworked in *The Troublesome Raigne* with a dramaturgical skill beyond that of Peele or any other dramatist of the time, and why the play distorts history to refocus John's reign so intently on the killing of Arthur in a fashion quite at odds with Peele's anti-Catholic purpose.

Timing increases the likelihood of some *quid pro quo* between the two dramatists. Both the play Shakespeare wrote *with* Peele and the plot he may have drawn up *for* him appear to follow closely on *3 Henry VI:* Boyd observes (in this volume) that Shakespeare was continually thinking ahead to *Titus Andronicus* while writing *3 Henry VI,* for the tragedy's plot and characters seep again and again into the history's imagery, while E. A. J. Honigmann has shown that *3 Henry VI* had a major role in shaping the sequence of episodes in *King John.*[11]

In the mid-1590s, several years after Peele had written and published *his* play about King John, Shakespeare, inspired by having just written the story of Richard II's fall, could have returned to the plot he had already worked out for another play about a king whose reign calamitously collapses. Perhaps he had agreed to let Peele have several uninterrupted years at the King John theme. Almost certainly, he had found Peele's treatment of the King John story uncongenial and incompetent, and if he had drawn up the plot would have judged *The Troublesome Raigne* particularly galling for making so little of its opportunities. Peele's death in 1596 may also account for Shakespeare's turning to *King John* in that year. The overall scenario, though speculative, and with details unlikely to be resolved, seems much more likely than the alternative: first, that Peele rearranged the events in Holinshed with a craft he never achieved elsewhere, and for ends utterly opposed to his own; second, that Shakespeare then took this plot over with a meekness he never demonstrated in adapting any other source; and third, that he there discovered a masterly structure, present in Peele's unhistorical sequence of events but quite obscured by Peele's mismanagement, that just happened already to reflect his own unique habits of construction and to serve *his* purposes but not Peele's.[12]

In his second year as a teacher Jackson published through the University of Auckland another outstanding work to add to his unpublished *Arden* dissertation, his pamphlet *Shakespeare's "A Lover's Complaint": Its Date and Authenticity* (1965). Along with the independent findings of Kenneth Muir (1964), Jackson's classic study, completed in 1963, convinced scholars and editors such as Kerrigan that this poem, ascribed to Shakespeare in the 1609 edition of his *Sonnets* but long supposed apocryphal, *did* deserve a place with the sonnets.

But scholarship does not stand still. Ward Elliott, a professor of government, and his mathematician colleague Robert C. Valenza, have been working for some time with Jackson and other leading attribution scholars, advising student research teams from the Claremont Shakespeare Clinic how to assess authorship claims through increasingly versatile and sensitive computer tests. Elliott and Valenza report their amazement on first discovering Jackson's *A Lover's Complaint* pamphlet, since so many of its methods anticipated what they had thought to be recent methodological breakthroughs or possibilities opened up only by new advances in computing. In the early 1960s, nevertheless, Jackson's statistics were necessarily confined to comparisons of *A Lover's Complaint* with the accepted Shakespeare canon, because there were so few concordances and computer-searchable databases for other authors. Without computers and e-text archives, scholars had to rely on similarities to "prove" common authorship. With computers, it became possible to use dissimilarities to disprove common authorship.

In line with Popper's stress as a philosopher of science on the strength of falsification and the weakness of apparent confirmation, Elliott and Valenza argue that disproof is vastly more powerful than proof: if the slipper fits, this *may* be Cinderella; if not, she *cannot* be. Comparing *A Lover's Complaint* with the Shakespeare canon, they show five strong dissimilarities between the poem and Shakespeare's normal patterns. None of these tests was available to Jackson in 1963; together, by Valenza's new calculations, they make the odds of Shakespeare's authorship of the *Complaint* a thousand times worse than for the most discrepant three-thousand-word block in the accepted Shakespeare canon. On the other hand, the same process of comparison shows that the odds that George Chapman could have written *A Lover's Complaint* are even lower. No other plausible candidate for authorship of the poem has yet been advanced.

As someone with great respect for statistical evidence, and for the arguments of others, and with a great inventiveness in devising new ways to test attribution claims, Jackson will no doubt welcome the Elliott and Valenza findings, although they challenge his own. Another contributor, Marina Tarlinskaja, trained in the sophisticated Russian school of metrics, has herself invented a sensitive test for the authorship and dating of verse, the ratio of "proclitics" and "enclitics" (positions of potentially stressed monosyllables to the right or left from their accentual and syntactic hosts), a test that still requires the painstaking manual counting that was once the only way open to Jackson himself. Here she applies this and two other verse tests to show that *A Lover's Complaint,* which Jackson had assumed must be Shakespeare's mature work, stands in many ways outside Shakespearean verse norms altogether, but is at least less distant from early Shakespeare. Since however the poem echoes works written after Shakespeare's early career, she concludes, his authorship of *A Lover's Complaint* appears unlikely.

Michael Neill joined the Auckland English Department three years after Jackson, co-taught early modern drama with him for almost four decades, and co-edited with him the Cambridge *Selected Plays of John Marston.* In the main undergraduate early modern drama paper, Neill normally taught *Othello,* which he is now editing for the Oxford Shakespeare; Jackson would teach *King Lear,* whose Folio text he made a particularly compelling case for reading as an authorial revision of the Quarto in the influential 1983 Oxford volume on the two *Lears.*

If Jackson counts words, Neill here shows with characteristic intensity how Shakespeare makes words count, especially words that we might filter out as so much period background noise. Where much of this volume focuses on shared authorship, Neill's "'Servile Ministers': *Othello, King Lear* and the Sacralization of Service" offers an intricate, nuanced examination of the way a single author rethinks and reworks the words and assumptions he shares with his society. Neill considers notions of service and mastery, slavery and freedom, bonds and obligations in Shakespeare's time, looking at the shifting ironies the playwright generates, especially in *Othello* and *Lear,* by probing the contradictions inherent in early modern notions of service: the dangers, in a world where service *defined* social identity, of being constitutionally or conscientiously no longer able to serve; the acceptance of limits to obedience, yet the risk to the soul of rejecting service in a world where it still had an element of the sacral.

Although Shakespeare appears to have initiated both *Titus Andronicus* and *Timon of Athens,* the role of his collaborators is quite different in each play. In *Titus,* Peele and Shakespeare seem to have worked on their separate blocks independently, and the most discordant discrepancies that result arise from Peele's adding a subscene without Shakespeare's knowledge. In examining *Timon,* John Jowett considers a much more intimate and intricate collaboration. Passing beyond the attribution by David Lake, Mac Jackson and Roger Holdsworth of parts of *Timon* to Middleton, and declaring the time for agnosticism about Middleton's role is past, Jowett tries to identify the precise contributions of each collaborator and the "authorial dialogism" of their interaction.

He opens with a compelling theoretical defense of the importance of determining attribution, against the attack of Jeffrey Masten, who stresses "that language is 'socially produced' and that the language one uses is not 'one's own,'" so that assigning one part of a collaborative text to one author is inappropriate "policing." Jowett notes that to the extent that Masten's premise that a text, as a piece of language, has a fundamentally nonauthorial determination, this "must be true of any text, irrespective of the structure of its authorship. To the extent that [Masten's premise] collapses the author, it collapses the collaborator too." He assumes instead that "the people who write play an overwhelmingly important role in the social production of the written word," and warns that the "anti-authorial critique of attribution study" might actually, through the easy assumption that one need not try to find out who wrote what, perpetuate the treatment of the collaborative works in the Shakespeare canon as if they were one author's alone.

Jowett considers authorial collaboration as a general process before examining in detail Middleton and Shakespeare at work together on *Timon.* After Shakespeare provided the base, Middleton added whole scenes but also modified some of Shakespeare's. Through examining parallel passages in the two authors—as the basis not for *establishing* collaboration, but for assigning passages to authors already identified—Jowett can show Middleton at work especially at the beginnings and endings of scenes, often to prepare for his own ensuing scenes, or establishing stage groupings or silent roles that serve as ironic commentary. Jowett draws attention to the artistic consequences of Middleton's most important addition to a Shakespearean passage, identified by Roger Holdsworth: the encounter with Flavius in the long final movement from 4.3 to 5.2, which adds a "recognition of human worth" otherwise missing from Timon's denunciations in the woods. The dialogism creates loose ends, he suggests, that critics have tried to tie together, but that can start to make sense only once the play is viewed as a collaboration.

David Gunby, a lifelong champion of Webster and general editor of the ongoing Cambridge *Works of John Webster,* sought out Jackson as textual editor for the edition's second and third volumes. Here he answers criticisms of Webster's structural craft by showing a pattern of deliberate situational and verbal repetitions as the playwright's unique authorial signature in the three plays he wrote without collaborators, *The White Devil, The Duchess of Malfi* and *The Devil's Law-Case.* Each of the three reveals a two-part structure, with situations and events in the second part, beginning in act 3, "paralleling those in the first act of the play, and forming ironic variants on their earlier counterparts." Webster establishes this characteristic structure in its most "rigorous and complete" form in *The White Devil,* but redeploys it with increasing freedom in the two subsequent solo plays.

If Gunby is the Webster specialist in the new Cambridge Webster, and Jackson the textual expert, a third New Zealander, David Carnegie, is the theater historian. In his essay Carnegie discusses two particular problems the trio solved in editing the stage directions of *Appius and Virginia,* a play whose attribution to Webster and Heywood Jackson had confirmed in 1985. In his textual introduction to *Appius and Virginia,* Jackson identifies the "clarification of the characters' comings and goings and their interactions on stage" as the edition's "main contribution"; here, Carnegie discusses both how the editorial team tackled key problems in the play's staging and the wider implications of their solutions for editing and understanding the dramaturgy of the early modern stage.

In determining the problem of the identity and movements of the "mutinous soldiers," they needed to draw on the emerging consensus about casting practices on the London stage of the 1620s. In order to decide whether the soldiers in 2.2 remained on stage at the end of the scene, or their shout occurs off stage, the editors could draw on Dessen and Thomson's recent *Dictionary of Stage Directions in English Drama 1580–1642* (1999) and especially on Literature Online (1994), the Chadwyck-Healey electronic database to which Jackson was an adviser and which he, along with Taylor and others, has used so inventively in resolving problems of attribution with a newly possible precision and range. In this case, Literature Online allowed the Webster team to discover an infrequent but recurrent early modern practice of shouts in which a crowd offstage responds at once to an onstage event before it could realistically know what has happened, according to what Carnegie calls "a presentational dramaturgy which compresses cause and effect into a nonrealist amplification of the immediate dramatic moment." Solving the problem clarified the powerful theatrical logic of the particular scene, Carnegie notes, but also reminds us to guard against conclusions about early modern dramaturgy derived from inappropriate naturalistic assumptions.

Gary Taylor is, among other roles, the leading figure in early modern dramatic attribution in the generation after Jackson, with whom he has frequently collaborated. Here he investigates the problems of collaborative authorship that arise from his need to decide on the inclusion of *The Spanish Gypsy* in the Oxford *Collected Works of Thomas Middleton,* of which he is general editor. The play was attributed to Middleton and Rowley on first publication, but after showing the detailed evidence that neither they nor Ford and Dekker, who have been counterproposed as authors, can account for the pattern of linguistic idiosyncrasies in the play, Taylor suggests all four as co-authors. On the basis of detailed internal evidence of the kind Lake and Jackson used to redraw the boundaries of the Middleton canon in the 1970s, he attributes three passages to Ford and one to Middleton, and finds one striking line elsewhere that contains the unique mark of Dekker. Most individual scenes and subscenes, however, especially by Dekker and Rowley, will be difficult to distinguish without the kinds of systematic testing of verbal parallels against the Literature Online database that Jackson proposed in 1998, that Taylor has since refined, and that both are now collaborating on for this play.

Throughout, Taylor pays attention to the minute details of authors' linguistic habits, but with a constant concern for "the broader issues about the nature of authorship and the logic of attribution" that he notes Jackson has always shown. Taylor stresses the shakiness of generalizations about the reliability of external versus internal evidence, the error of presuming in advance the numbers of authors in a given text ("any number between one and five is historically plausible"), the need for different kinds of internal evidence at different stages of determining attribution, and the need now to pay attention to the least important authors in a collaboration to resolve "the few remaining problems" in the canon of Shakespeare, Middleton, and Fletcher.

Like much of the work in this volume, Taylor's contribution testifies to the impact of technologies and techniques that developed after Jackson first entered the field but that he has since pioneered in applying to problems of attribution. And like so many of the essays, Taylor's testifies to the inspiration of Jackson's example on scholars older and younger, and to Jackson's own ongoing efforts, often in conjunction with others, to discover who wrote what and when in the greatest days of English drama.

Neither writers nor scholars work in isolation from their peers, but they nevertheless remain individuals. More than anyone, MacDonald P. Jackson has shown us how even as singular a writer as Shakespeare can work alongside others. As a scholar he has himself cooperated and collaborated widely with others—and it would be hard for the teachers, scholars and editors who have worked with him to imagine a finer colleague and friend—but it is as an irreplaceable individual he has made the most lasting difference.

Those of us who know Mac Jackson will miss him—but we know he will keep on counting.

NOTES

1. For a chronological list of Jackson's main works, see the bibliography.

2. John Kerrigan, in his edition of *The Sonnets and A Lover's Complaint* (London: Penguin, 1986), 66.

3. "Pause Patterns in Shakespeare's Verse: Canon and Chronology," *Literary and Linguistic Computing* 17(2002), 37–46.

4. Detailed references to works by Jackson and others mentioned in this introduction will be found in the contributions under discussion.

5. "Francis Meres and the Cultural Contexts of Shakespeare's Rival Poet Sonnets," *Review of English Studies* (forthcoming).

6. "Fluctuating Variation: Author, Annotator, or Actor?," in *The Division of the Kingdoms: The Two Texts of "King Lear,"* ed. Gary Taylor and Michael B. Warren (Oxford: Clarendon Press), 313–49: 340.

7. Suzanne Tumblin Gary, "The Relationship Between *The Troublesome Reign of King John of England* and Shakespeare's *King John,*" unpub. doctoral diss., Univ. of Arizona, 1971, 13–28; L. A. Beaurline, ed., *King John* (Cambridge: Cambridge Univ. Press, 1990; New Cambridge Shakespeare), 207–9; Brian Boyd, "*King John* and *The Troublesome Raigne:* Sources, Structure, Sequence," *Philological Quarterly* 74 (1995): 37–56. The idea that *The Troublesome Raigne of King John* somehow derives from *King John,* rather than vice versa, began with A. S. Cairncross (1936) and Peter Alexander (1939) and has been championed by E. A. J. Honigmann from his second Arden *King John* (London: Methuen, 1954) to "Self-Repetitions and *King John,*" *Shakespeare Survey* 53 (2000): 175–83.

8. Jackson, "Pause Patterns," 45.

9. "Pause Patterns," 41.

10. Honigmann, *King John,* xlvi–xlvii, and "Self-Repetitions," 178–79, shows the topicality of the play for an anti-Catholic in 1590.

11. "Self-Repetitions," 176–78.

12. For the mismanagement, see L. A. Beaurline, ed., *King John* (New Cambridge Shakespeare, Cambridge: Cambridge Univ. Press, 1990), 201–2; for the Shakespearean construction, see Honigmann, "Self-Repetitions"; for the conflict with Peele's purposes, see Boyd, "Sources."

1580s–Early 1590s: Marlowe

The Great Divide of 1594

Andrew Gurr

STEPPING STONES ARE A HELP WHEN YOU NEED TO TRACK YOUR WAY through muddy waters, and there are not many areas of Shakespeare studies muddier than his relations with Marlowe. Too much of it is lit by the confusing glare of the misleading lights of academic journalism. It needs the careful and measured steps of a Mac Jackson to identify good pathways through the glare and the mud.

Besides the evident reprises of Marlowe's *Jew of Malta* and *Edward II* in *The Merchant of Venice* and *Richard II,* and the allusions in *As You Like It,* theories about interaction between Marlowe and Shakespeare have even extended to finding Marlovian echoes in the *Henry VI* plays, *Titus,* and *Henry V.*[1] There is, however, another association to be made. During his lifetime, Marlowe sold his best-known plays to as many as four different companies of players. In May 1594 they were all put into the hands of a single customer, the Admiral's Men, in a deal that seems to have involved an exchange with some of the existing Shakespeare plays. That was an early testimony to Marlowe's power as a playwright in his own time, and especially his influence with the two great lords, Henry Carey and Charles Howard, who were the government's chief controllers of London's theater in 1594.[2] Much more remarkably, it appears to show that the organizers of the two officially recognized acting companies set up in 1594, the Lord Chamberlain's and the Lord Admiral's, recognized Marlowe and Shakespeare as the time's two great assets as playwrights. Tracing such an idea demands a positively Jacksonian pathway through the mud.

Shakespeare's early career as an actor and playwright will be dealt with here only in the context of Marlowe's activities. Marlowe, the more colorful character, whose university degree gave him the ostensible social status of a gentleman, had much more note taken of him in these early years than the countryman Shakespeare. His constant changes of mode in his playwriting—from classical tragedy in *Dido* to heroic tragedy in *Tamburlaine,* religious morality in *Faustus,* satire in *The Jew of Malta,* contemporary political drama in *The Massacre at Paris,* and English history in *Edward II*—seem to have been matched by the frequent changes in his allegiance to the playing companies who bought them. It is as much the story of changing fortunes amongst the playing companies through a turbulent time as of Marlowe's impact on the theater of his time. Working this story out entails settling, sometimes provisionally, the dates and the sequence of writing for Marlowe's plays, for which the evidence, like so much else about this time, is imperfect, so some of the details offered here are necessarily conjectural. In such mazy marshes tiny details sprout large implications. The plausibility of the story needs to be judged as a whole, in the hope that it will ease the reception of the more speculative parts. The ultimate speculation is just what status Marlowe and Shakespeare had as playwrights a year after Marlowe's hugely sensationalized murder in 1593.

We know that up to his death at the age of twenty-nine Marlowe wrote seven plays and sold them to four different acting companies. On the evidence of its title page and its staging, *Dido Queen of Carthage* was almost certainly the only play that Marlowe wrote for a boy company.[3] A quarto was printed in 1594 as "Played by the Children of her Majesties Chappell. Written by Christopher Marlowe, and Thomas Nash. Gent." Given that the title page credits Nashe with a share in its composition, it could date from as late as 1592, when Nashe wrote *Summer's Last Will and Testament* for a boy company. But *Summer's Last Will* was performed for Archbishop Whitgift at Croydon by a boy group who Nashe said had not played for the last year. This must mean that it was a special occasion, and does not suggest that any other play would have been performed then under similar circumstances. The better and more usual assumption is that *Dido* was written much earlier, before the joint Paul's/Chapel boy company was suppressed in 1590, and possibly even before the Chapel Children closed down in 1584. Nashe was at Cambridge from early in 1582 until 1588, when he left for London. In those years he could have collaborated with Marlowe, who graduated BA in 1584 and MA in 1587. Most critics prefer to see *Dido* as a play closely related to Marlowe's university translations of the *Amores.* It has some verbal resemblances to *Faustus,* and may be one of the plays the *Faustus* prologue cites. I am inclined to regard it as Marlowe's first known play, and his only collaboration.

Dido's subsequent history, after its early performance by the Chapel Children, is obscure. It could have joined all the other Marlowe plays in the hands of the Admiral's Men in 1594. The 1594 quarto could have supplied the text for the "playe of dido & eneus" which the Admiral's Men staged in January 1598, although since no text survives from that performance it is only conjecture that it was Marlowe's. A case might be made for Marlowe's play being on stage in the late 1590s from the faint echoes of it (notably the whiff and wind of Pyrrhus's sword, and the Hyrcanian beast) that occur in Hamlet's recollections of a play of Aeneas's tale to Dido, but no subsequent edition of the play says that it was performed by the Admiral's. Henslowe paid 29 shillings on 3 January 1598 for boys' costumes, and loaned the players another thirty on 8 January "when they fyrst played dido at nyght." The inventory of 10 March 1598 mentions a robe for Dido, but also "i tome of Dido," which would not belong in Marlowe's play as the quarto printed it. At the risk of circular argument (that the post-1594 Admiral's had all of Marlowe's plays including a *Dido* and therefore must have had Marlowe's *Dido*) I would say that the 1598 performance most likely was of Marlowe's play. The performance at night must indicate a special winter showing, possibly at court.

The Admiral's Men were clearly not bothered about having authority to play this *Dido.* Nor did Henslowe pay any money to its author or authors. That may be an important consideration given the strong concern about company ownership of playbooks, and does imply that the Admiral's thought they had the right to play it. A related question is whether they acquired the manuscript from the defunct boy company at some time before 1598 or whether they used the 1594 edition for their script on the grounds that by then they had the right to perform all of Marlowe's plays. The second possibility gains some support from the evidence about the other plays to be considered below.

1 & 2 Tamburlaine were recorded for printing in the Stationers' Register on 14 August 1590. The Register calls them "twooe commicall discourses," but they were printed in 1590 in octavo as "Devided into two Tragicall Discourses," and "sundry times shewed upon Stages in the Citie of London, By the right honorable the Lord Admyrall, his servantes." Marlowe's name did not appear on either title page. The plays were famous on stage in London from the beginning of 1588. Greene's reference in his preface to *Perimedes the Blacke-Smith* about Tamburlaine "daring God out of heaven," almost certainly a reference to the end of part 2, indicates that both plays were on stage some time before 29 March of that year, when *Perimedes* was entered in the Stationers' Register. The many references to Tamburlaine in the following years show how famous he became as a stage character. We know that Edward Alleyn, the leading player of the Admiral's Men in the late 1580s, made it his most famous role. And that raises a large question about its early history. Alleyn clearly made the title roles both of the two *Tamburlaine* plays and of *Faustus* his own. But what did he do with them between 1590 and 1594 when he re-formed the Admiral's Men?

On the evidence of the title page for the 1590 printing, the two parts of *Tamburlaine* must have been sold to Alleyn and the Admiral's Men in 1587–88. Marlowe must have written the first part in the years between 1580 and 1587 when he was, however intermittently, at Cambridge. In its way *Tamburlaine* was a Cambridge subject. A number of Cambridge scholars showed interest in the all-conquering Scythian shepherd before Marlowe reached the university. Gabriel Harvey has notes in his copious marginalia which include several indications that Tamburlaine caught his attention. They date from 1566 to about 1590.[4] In 1576 Harvey acquired a copy of a book first printed in 1538, A. P. Gasser's *Historiarum et Chronicorum totius Mundi epitome,* a synoptic history of the world. Harvey wrote the date 1576 on the title page, 1575 at the end of the dedication, February 1577 on page 277, and 1577 at the end, after the colophon. He annotated the text extensively, most especially against the book's account of Tamburlaine.

Not all of his marginal notes are in the same kind of ink, but they would most likely have been made around 1576 at about the time of his first reading. On page 256, where the text refers to Tamburlaine in the year 1386, "Tamberlanes Tartarorum Cesar belicossisimus, qui Turcas vicit, & Aegyptum" ("Tamberlane the most belligerent king of the Tartars, who conquered the Turks and Egypt"), Harvey wrote "Tamerlane oft a Lusty Heardman, A most valiant & invincible Prynce. His tents ye first day whyte: ye 2 redd: ye 3 black. Bajazetem Turcarum Imp. in cavea ferrea circumfet, ludibrii causa" ("Bajazeth Emperor of the Turks carried in an iron cage, an object of mockery"). There could hardly be a more succinct summary of the most prominent features of Tamburlaine's story that Marlowe subsequently put on stage, the rise from Scythian shepherd, the three colors of his tents, and the humiliation of Bajazeth. Harvey even seems to have corrected Gasser's spellings into the forms that Marlowe used. On the page before the marginal note on Tamburlaine, by Gasser's "Paiazites" Harvey noted "Baiazets, A. Turcarum Imp.," and below the note about Tamburlaine he wrote "Baiazetes," as a reminder of the account on the previous page. Marlowe followed the Harvey spelling rather than Gasser's. Against 1394 in Gasser Harvey corrected "Celapinus" to "Calapinus," the spelling preferred in Marlowe's text. It may of course be coincidence that in the same book Harvey has a marginal note about another of Marlowe's subjects: "Joannes Faustius . . . artem imprimendi libros" ("John Faust, very learned in books"). The book was Harvey's property, and the notes are simply indications of his personal interests. Gasser was not one of Marlowe's sources for *Tamburlaine.* But Harvey's notes do make it clear that both Tamburlaine and Faustus were talking-points in the Cambridge of the 1570s and 1580s.

So the composition of at least the first *Tamburlaine* play came directly out of Marlowe's time at Cambridge. He sold it to the Lord Admiral's Men in 1587 or so, and they performed it in London and around the country for the next few years. The same thing happened to *Faustus.* Where, though, if he was at Cambridge, did Marlowe first meet the plays and the playing companies that set him on the path of writing for the popular players? Cambridge had a long tradition of academic playwriting and performance, including plays about Dido,[5] but Marlowe's were not conceived for the same venue as Legge's *Ricardus Tertius.* The roads Marlowe took between Canterbury and Cambridge and between Cambridge and Paris run through London. It is much more likely that he found his first customers there, and certainly there that he must have seen the plays that stirred him to improve on them. The company that bought his next three plays was there too. It is unlikely that he met the Admiral's Men in Cambridge, though he may have seen them there. Despite the chronic opposition of the university authorities to allowing any performances in the town by professional players, the Town Treasurers' Books show that the Queen's Men played in Cambridge in 1584–85, when they received 24s.8d, but the Admiral's Men are not in the town records till they received 10s in 1588–89.[6] The Queen's Men received 30s from Trinity College for a midsummer show "by appoinctment" in 1586, a visit that probably coincided with a town performance, when an unnamed company of players "yat plaid before Master Maior" got the exceptionally handsome reward of 30s.[7] The surviving evidence indicates that through Marlowe's years the Mayor of Cambridge welcomed the Queen's Men but not the Admiral's. So the first question about Marlowe's customers for his plays is why he sold his *Tamburlaines* to the Admiral's and not the Queen's.

In 1586 the Queen's Men were the outstanding company of their time, with unique privileges. Formed by royal decree in 1583, the company was set up with the best two or three players from each of the companies of the great lords, Leicester's, Warwick's, Oxford's, and Sussex's. They took Richard Tarlton, the most famous clown, and the most famous tragedians, Knell and Bentley. Their supreme status was unchallenged for most of the decade. Town records consistently show them being paid more than the other companies. In 1584, on the grounds that they had been formed to entertain the Queen, the Lord Chamberlain secured special and unique access from the Lord Mayor for them to play in London, making them the only company officially permitted to act in the city.[8]

It is tempting to speculate why Marlowe chose to sell the two *Tamburlaines* to the Admiral's rather than the Queen's. The latter might have rejected his offering, though if so it was a commercial misjudgment of some size. On the other hand it is possible that the prologue's loud scorn of the "jigging veins of rhyming mother-wits" was partly a crack at the Queen's performing practices with its clown Tarlton, famous for his doggerel song-and-dance acts at the end of his company's plays, and partly a signal of approval for the Admiral's practices. Marlowe's friend Nashe reports a brush with Tarlton in the mid-1580s, boasting in *Strange News* that Tarlton had deferred to his "simple judgement" in "matters of wit."[9] Tarlton died in September 1588. Marlowe might have had a firsthand encounter to warrant his objection to jigging moitherers of wit. But that is hardly the best basis for concluding that Marlowe chose to avoid the Queen's Men as his customers. Every adult company had a clown and offered jigs. Since the prologue's distaste is echoed by the printer, who in his address to the reader claimed to have omitted "some fond and frivolous jestures," the octavo's prologue may have been addressed to the reader rather than to the theater audience. Yet it does sound like a Marlovian play-opening. It is similar to the prologue to *Faustus,* which celebrates other stage successes. The Admiral's had no clown so famous as Tarlton. We should acknowledge the possibility that Marlowe opted to sell his plays to the Admiral's Company rather than the Queen's, and that the prologue to *Tamburlaine* indicates the main reason. What negotiations there were before the sale we do not know. A faint whiff of sour grapes rises from the prologue.

Marlowe must have met the Admiral's Men during one of their stays in London. In the 1580s the professional companies were still accustomed to spend most of their time traveling, playing for fairly brief periods in the London playhouses. Not until 1594 did any base themselves permanently there and travel only when they had to. On their travels they rarely spent more than a couple of days in each town or great house before moving on. Since Marlowe could hardly have pursued his first customers around the country, London, the location for their longest runs, was by far the likeliest meeting-place. The better companies tended to work near London through the autumn, visiting the rich East Anglia towns or Kent and Sussex instead of the more remote parts of the country, because it kept them within reach of the Master of the Revels, who had to see their plays before choosing which of them would entertain the Court over the long Christmas season. The Admiral's are recorded at Dover in June 1585 and at Leicester that autumn, but they performed at Court on 27 December 1585 and 6 January 1586. In 1586–87 they visited Coventry, Bath, York, Norwich, Ipswich, Exeter, Southampton, and Leicester. They did not perform at Court that winter, but are nonetheless reported as being in London in a letter of 25 January 1587. The letter, addressed to Walsingham, complains that the playhouses are full and the churches empty because "the players billes are sett up in sondry places of the cittie, some in the name of her Majesties menne, some the Earl of Leicester, some the Earl of Oxford, the Lord Admyralles, and dyvers others."[10]

The most likely time for Marlowe to meet the Admiral's Men would have been during their stay in London in and after January 1587. A letter by Philip Gawdy dated 16 November suggests that by then Marlowe had made his bargain with his first customers for both *Tamburlaine* plays. Gawdy describes how a play suspiciously like *2 Tamburlaine* with its execution of the Governor of Babylon caused an accident when staged in London by the Admiral's Men:

> My L. Admyrall his men and players having a devyse in ther playe to tye one of their fellowes to a poste and so to shoote him to deathe, having borrowed their

> callyvers one of the players handes swerved his peece being charged with bullett missed the fellowe he aymed at and killed a chyld, and a woman great with chyld forthwith, and hurt an other man in the head very soore.[11]

Even if the play was not *2 Tamburlaine,* the letter shows that the Admiral's were in London that autumn, a likely time for Marlowe to sell them at least the first of his two plays, and possibly *Faustus* soon after.[12] The similarity of its subsequent history to that of the two *Tamburlaine* plays supports the view that it was written at broadly the same time, near the commonly accepted date of 1588.

If Alleyn, as chief player for the Admiral's Men, bought the two *Tamburlaines* and *Faustus* for them to perform in 1587–88, a deep puzzle remains. Why did the three plays never appear thereafter with Alleyn in the repertory of Strange's Men, the so-called amalgamated company of Strange's and the Admiral's, while they played at the Rose in 1592 and 1593? Who performed these notorious plays between their first celebrity with the early company of Admiral's Men and their reappearance in Henslowe's lists for the new Admiral's Men after May 1594? Alleyn himself was certainly with Henslowe at the Rose from early 1592—he married Henslowe's stepdaughter that October. But he was then a member of Strange's, not the Admiral's, and Henslowe made no record of *Tamburlaine* being performed at the Rose before 30 August 1594, nor of *Faustus* before the end of September 1594. It was not because they were considered old or undesirable stuff: they were and remained for decades the company's favorite plays. *Tamburlaine* appeared fourteen times at the Rose in the fifteen months from mid-1594, and *Faustus* twenty-four times over the next three years. They became the defining features of the Admiral's company repertory. So who had these three plays through the years from before February 1592, when Henslowe's records begin, up to August 1594?

References from the period are distinctly patchy, but the timing of allusions to *Tamburlaine* suggests that there may well have been an interim between 1591 and 1594 when the *Tamburlaines* and *Faustus* were off the London stage. *Tamburlaine* was spoken of with unique frequency, and yet no reference appeared for three years, from 1593 to 1596. After Greene first named it late in 1587, he renewed the allusion in 1587–88, 1589 and 1591. Peele named the play in 1588–89 and 1589, and Nashe named the character in 1592. Three anonymous plays mentioned him in c.1590, 1591, and c.1592. In 1593 Nashe, Drayton and Harvey named him, Harvey in connection with Marlowe's death, when a libel pinned on a church door on 5 May 1593 was signed "*Per.* Tamburlaine." Then there is a notable gap up to 1596, when Nashe again referred to him, and four mentions in 1597, by Shakespeare, Donne, Joseph Hall, and "E.S.," a satirist. Jonson cited him in 1598, Marston in 1599 and c.1599, Dekker twice in 1599 and twice again in 1601, and an anonymous play cited him in 1600. Thereafter there were regular references, especially in plays in 1605 and 1606, and later in other contexts. *Faustus* was almost equally celebrated, but its earliest mention is in 1596.[13] In all that noise the silence from 1593 to 1596 is remarkable.

Both roles were tied to Alleyn.[14] Yet Nashe's praise of Alleyn in *Pierce Penilesse* in 1592 makes no mention of any specific role he played, unless he was the Talbot of *1 Henry VI* that Nashe praises in an adjacent passage. Thomas Heywood's prologue to *The Jew of Malta* as late as 1633 remembered Alleyn as the creator of both Tamburlaine and Barabas, but that was long after, and presumably recalls the years from 1594 when Heywood himself was playing and writing for the Henslowe team. Alleyn was the leading player in the earlier Admiral's Men, in 1588–91, and that was the company that owned the *Tamburlaine* plays when they were printed in 1590. But what happened to them between 1591 and their resurfacing in the new Admiral's Men's repertory in 1594?

The absence of any mention in 1594 and 1595 needs explanation, and one is to hand. Allowing for a little time lag for writing and printing, the gap matches their even stranger absence from Henslowe's *Diary* up to mid-1594. The silence through 1594–95 fits quite closely with the absence of either play from Henslowe's lists between 1592 and 1594. If the lapse into silence was because the plays were not being performed in London, it suggests that they were in the hands of the residual Admiral's company traveling around the country while Alleyn was in London with Strange's and Henslowe. The old Admiral's and its plays did not return to the London stage until some of its members joined Alleyn in the new Admiral's Company in May 1594, which reunited Alleyn with his old roles. Such a reading of the evidence is supported by the fact that Marlowe's last three plays went through different hands from the famous three that followed *Dido.*

The Jew of Malta and *The Massacre at Paris* took a quite different path from the *Tamburlaines* and *Faustus.*[15] Machevil's reference in his prologue to the Guise being dead fixes *The Jew of Malta*'s writing to a time soon after December 1588, when the notorious French Duke died. *The Massacre* is the story of his death. Both *The Jew* and the play about the Guise must postdate the two *Tamburlaines* and *Faustus,* if only because the history of their ownership was different. What happened to *The Jew* in its first years is unknown, and the date of *The Massacre* is uncertain, though it was certainly written at the beginning of the 1590s. Their difference from the three previous plays is that both were in the hands of Strange's Men at the Rose by 1593. *The Massacre at Paris,* or "the tragedey of the guyes" as Henslowe more commonly called it, is first recorded with excellent takings as a "ne" play, performed by Strange's during their brief return to London in January 1593. Its next appearance in Henslowe was as an Admiral's play in June 1594. Henslowe's records position it with *The Jew of Malta,* well apart from the *Tamburlaines* and *Faustus.*

Henslowe records several performances of *The Jew of Malta* at the Rose by Strange's Men between February 1592 and February 1593, when the plague caused a long break. It reappeared in February 1594, now performed by Sussex's Men. It was staged again in the joint or alternate performances by Sussex's and the Queen's Men in April 1594, but the next month it was an Admiral's play. It reappeared in the joint or alternate season of the Admiral's and Chamberlain's Men in May 1594, and thereafter with some frequency exclusively as an Admiral's play. The conclusion normally drawn from these records is that the playbook was owned by Henslowe himself, who loaned it out to whichever company was playing at his Rose. That may well be the case. If so, it makes *The Jew* unique among Marlowe's plays as a book sold to an impresario, not to a company. It seems not to have followed quite the same track as *The Massacre at Paris,* since although the later play was, like *The Jew,* performed by Strange's Men, it has links with Pembroke's, who also had Marlowe's last play, *Edward II.*

There is an alternative reading of these hints, though. Alleyn was the player who first made *Tamburlaine* famous. If he lost the early Marlowe plays when he transferred his allegiance to Strange's Men and Henslowe, Strange's acquisition of the next two Marlowe plays may indicate that Marlowe stayed loyal to Alleyn with his new company, and that it was Alleyn who secured *The Jew of Malta* for Henslowe. That embeds it in the muddy issue of the so-called "amalgamation" of Alleyn with Strange's Men, which needs some careful washing. It relates to the ownership both of *The Jew* and *The Massacre at Paris.* Alleyn may have secured *The Massacre* either for Henslowe the playhouse owner or for Strange's the playing company. That possibility, however, depends on yet another teasing question to which there is no clear answer.

The last purchasers of a Marlowe play were a new company, Pembroke's Men. *Edward II,* written in 1592, was printed in 1594 as Pembroke's. They were a mysterious grouping of players, coming to prominence suddenly at the beginning of 1592, and "breaking" for lack of money, according to a letter from Henslowe to Alleyn, on their travels in the late summer of 1593. Marlowe's play must have been sold to them while they enjoyed their brief London eminence in 1592–93. Recollections of other Pembroke Men's plays, *2* and *3 Henry VI* and *Edward II* itself, can be found in the only existing text of *The Massacre.*[16] So was *The Massacre* a Pembroke's play before Strange's played it at the Rose in January 1593? Or did it go to them afterwards? There is no sign that, unlike *The Massacre, Edward II* was ever a Strange's play. The *Diary*'s records for this time are detailed, and are unlikely to have omitted a mention if *Edward II* had been played by Strange's along with *The Massacre* in January 1593. We must assume either that Strange's for some reason passed *The Massacre* on to Pembroke's after January 1593, or that Pembroke's had it up to 1593 and then passed it to Strange's. It is also possible that one or more of the players who wrote out the text of *The Massacre* for its printing in 1594 had at some point switched allegiance between the two companies. The player John Holland was in both, and might have had knowledge of plays from the two repertories.[17]

Any of these explanations would add to the evidence that Marlowe switched his allegiance between 1588 and 1589 from Alleyn and the Admiral's to Strange's with Alleyn, and then moved on to Pembroke's in 1592 or so. That broadly fits the other evidence of Marlowe's writing career at this time. It is certain that he was in London for some part of 1589 when he was writing *The Jew of Malta,* because he was arrested and imprisoned in Shoreditch that September along with Thomas Watson for his part in a street affray and murder. Shoreditch, besides being a suburb noted for its thieves and whorehouses, was the location of the other two playhouses of the time. Marlowe was also in London in January 1592 in the wake of his difficulties at Flushing over counterfeiting, and in Shoreditch that May, when the Constable and Sub-Constable had him bound over to keep the peace.[18] In Shoreditch Marlowe was near the Theatre, not in Southwark near the Rose. That fits his *Edward II* going to Pembroke's Men, who most likely played at the Theatre through 1592. It was also the year when he claimed the familiar acquaintance of two noble enthusiasts of the theater, Thomas Percy, Earl of Northumberland and Lord Strange. The records of the case in which Marlowe was involved with Richard Baines over counterfeiting at Flushing include a statement that "The scholar [Marlowe] sais himself to be very wel known to the Earle of Northumberland and my lord Strang."[19] Lord Strange's Men were at the Rose with *The Jew of Malta* from the beginning of 1592. Some time in that year his loyalty switched from Bankside and Strange's to Shoreditch and Pembroke's.

Kyd's letters to the Privy Council in 1593 about his contacts with Marlowe also mention a noble patron: "My first acquaintance with this Marlowe, rose upon his bearing name to serve my Lord although his Lordship never knewe his service, but in writing for his plaiers, ffor never cold my Lord endure his name, or sight, when he had heard of his conditions." Kyd's lord may have been either Strange or Pembroke. Later Kyd claims "I have served [my Lord] almost theis vi yeres nowe,"[20] i.e., 1587–1593, which would make Pembroke more likely than Strange. A switch of Marlowe's allegiance in the course of 1592 from Strange and Strange's Men to Pembroke and Pembroke's Men fits these testimonies. Marlowe certainly had connections with three different companies, the Admiral's, Strange's, and Pembroke's, up to 1593, and with one or more of their patrons. Which company had which plays, and what transfers there may have been subsequently, are questions that need to be disentangled by looking at the history of these companies, and particularly at what is still commonly called the "amalgamated company" of the Admiral's and Strange's, that played at the Rose from 1591 to 1594.[21]

That the Admiral's and Strange's Men were separate companies at the end of 1589 is testified by a letter from the Lord Mayor of London, Sir John Harte, to Burghley, written on 6 November of that year. In it he reports his latest attempt to close the playhouses the day before. He "sent for suche players as I could here of," who turned out to be "the L. Admeralles and the L. Straunges players." They responded in radically different ways to his order to stop playing. "The L. Admeralles players very dutifullie obeyed, but the others in very Contemptuous manner departing from me, went to the Crosse keys and played that afternoon."[22] That variation in the behavior of the two companies provides a date when they were clearly not yet merged or amalgamated. The chief evidence for a subsequent "amalgamation" is based on two pieces of evidence: the record of Court performances, and the theater "plot" of *2 The Seven Deadly Sins.* The latter is a tiring-house paper outlining the scenes of the play, and containing the names of most of the players in the cast. It provides some very specific evidence for the membership of the company performing the play. But what company, and when the play was performed, are not as clear as we might wish.

Sorting out the evidence about playing companies and their membership in these changeable years is a tortuous exercise in the kaleidoscope principle. Shake the fragments of evidence and you make one pattern, then shake them up again and you see a different pattern. The old pattern found in *2 Seven Deadly Sins* indicated a company membership amalgamated from two former companies, the Admiral's and Strange's. This and the inclusion of Richard Burbage's name led to the conclusion that it was written in the period up to May 1591, when Alleyn had a sharp quarrel with Burbage's father. Scott McMillin more recently shook the kaleidoscope to dislodge that pattern, suggesting that a better date might be either 1593 or June 1594.[23] Shaken again, the fragments make a different and prettier pattern. There are some items of evidence that seem misplaced in both patterns.

The company's name came from its patron, Lord Strange, but with one player who insisted on wearing a different livery. Having two liveries in one group is what made commentators label them a joint company. When performing in London they were invariably Lord Strange's Men to their contemporaries. Henslowe called the group with Alleyn in it that played at the Rose in 1592–93 "my lord stranges mene" on and after 19 February 1592. At Court, where the patron's name was most likely to be known, they were also called Strange's: "George Ottewell and his Companye the Lorde Straunge his players," on 27 December 1590 and 16 February 1591.[24] In the 1591–92 season for their six performances they were again Strange's ("ye

Servauntes of ye Lo. Strange"), and again for their three in 1592–93. A Privy Council license dated 6 May 1593 permitting the group to play in spite of the plague in places not less than seven miles from London, names "Edward Allen, servaunt to the right honorable the Lord Highe Admiral, William Kemp, Thomas Pope, John Heminges, Augustine Phillipes and George Brian, being al one companie, servauntes to our verie good the lord Strainge." The note specifically says that Alleyn is the Lord Admiral's servant, but that he is part of "al one companie," the company known as Strange's.[25]

The plot of *2 The Seven Deadly Sins* contains an exceptionally large number of players' names. Some of the major players like George Attewell, named in Court records as leader of Strange's in 1591, and the clown Will Kemp are not specified. Nor is Alleyn. This may be because the main speaking parts were self-evident, so that only the lesser players needed naming. Pope, Bryan, and Phillips, all on the Privy Council license of 6 May 1593 as Strange's, are there, as is Richard Cowley, who is mentioned in a letter of Alleyn's in 1593. Other names are Richard Burbage, Will Sly, John Duke, Thomas Goodall, John Holland, Robert Pallant, John Sincler, a "Kitt" and a "Harry" who may have been Christopher Beeston and Henry Condell, and a "Vincent." Eight of these, Burbage, Sly, Duke, Goodall, Holland, Sincler, Beeston, and Condell, later became members of the Chamberlain's Men with Shakespeare, along with the Strange's men of 1593, Pope, Bryan, and Phillips. Several of them, including Holland and Sincler, seem to have belonged to Pembroke's in 1592–93. Judging from their absence from the names specified as Strange's Men in the 1593 Privy Council license, Burbage, Sly and others may have been in Pembroke's too.

The chief uncertainty is whether Alleyn was one of the leading players omitted from the plot list. Other Admiral's men such as James Tunstall and Richard Jones are not listed either. I think this makes it unlikely that Alleyn was with the group when the plot was made up. If so, the presence of men later associated with Pembroke's fits it to before May 1591 when Alleyn split from Burbage's father James and his Theatre. Pembroke's Company first appeared some time after that date, most likely as a new company set up to occupy the vacated Theatre. Alleyn could therefore have been absent from the *Seven Deadly Sins* list because he had not yet joined Strange's at the Rose, suggesting that the manuscript must have been made for performance in 1590–91. Its presence in the Henslowe papers would thus be a consequence of Strange's long stay at the Rose, and the new Admiral's Men's inheritance of the demised Strange's property in 1594.

The records of Court performances set out the bones of this history. The Admiral's, strong with Alleyn and his Marlowe plays, played once at Court at the end of the winter revels, on 3 March 1590. In the next Christmas season their only appearances were joint ones with Strange's, on 27 December 1590 and 16 February 1591, whereas the Queen's Men played five times. After that came Alleyn's quarrel with Burbage and his transfer to Strange's. The residual Admiral's then disappeared into the country until 1594. Alleyn's presence strengthened Strange's considerably, because in the 1591–92 season at Court they were clearly the top company. They appeared six times to one by the Queen's, one by Sussex's and one by Hertford's. In 1592–93 they appeared three times to Pembroke's twice and the Queen's once. There is no doubt that through the two seasons from late 1591 the Master of the Revels considered Strange's Men to be the strongest of all the companies, largely thanks to the presence of Alleyn with his Admiral's livery. The earlier Marlowe plays were off with the residual Admiral's in the country, but by then the Court could have seen them already.

The following winter, 1593–94, saw only one Court performance, by the Queen's Men. Pembroke's had broken up, Strange's did not appear, and Sussex's, then occupying the Rose, were not used either. The residual Admiral's was nothing without Alleyn, and did not appear in London or at Court until it was reconstituted in May 1594 with Alleyn once again as its leader. It was that season's paucity of Christmas shows, the Lord Chamberlain's chief duty to his ruler, that prompted him with his son-in-law the Lord Admiral to set up the new companies in May 1594.

Evidence from the provincial records of the companies supports this reading of the runes.[26] It is possible that on tour the "amalgamation" at the Rose could have split into its component parts, with Alleyn taking his patent along with some of Strange's to travel as the Admiral's Men while the others toured as Strange's. Unfortunately no names of players are supplied in guildhall records to help this supposition. I think that it is in any case a misconception. An Admiral's company is recorded as touring consistently throughout 1591–93. The Admiral's who visited New Romney on 26 June 1590, Faversham in the same year (*MSC* VII.140, 62), and Gloucester in 1590–91 (*REED* 312), must have been the group including Alleyn before he left to join Strange's. After that the remnant Admiral's company touring from 1591 to early 1594 generally received far less in payment than Lord Strange's. It is recorded at Bath (*ES* II.120n) and Folkestone (*MSC* VII.71) in 1591–92, Norwich (*REED,* Norwich, 103), Faversham and Folkestone in 1592–93, and Lydd in 1593–94 (*MSC* VII.63, 71, 110). Whereas Strange's at Faversham in 1592–93 received twenty shillings, the Admiral's received only ten. As the remnant company it was evidently less highly regarded. But without Alleyn did the old Admiral's keep the early Marlowe playbooks? The two companies were not entirely separated, possibly because of their plays. The merger at Court in the 1591–92 season seems to have continued occasionally in the country too. Two records exist indicating that both companies did play at the same town, possibly in a shared performance, at Shrewsbury after Michaelmas 1591 (*ES* II.120n) and at Ipswich on 7 August 1592 (*MSC* II.3 277). It is a great pity that the guildhall accountants were more concerned with the name of the company's patron than those of the players or the plays performed.

In the absence of an "amalgamation" between the Admiral's with their *Tamburlaine* plays and Strange's with *The Jew of Malta,* I would argue that Alleyn lost his right to play Tamburlaine and Faustus when he left the Admiral's to join Strange's, and that in consequence Marlowe's earlier plays were not seen on the London stages between late 1591 and 1594. Why though did Alleyn keep his livery as an Admiral's man while he worked consistently for three years with Strange's? In the 1580s and 1590s, as government regulation tightened, town authorities insisted on seeing the players' patents before giving them leave to play. The names inscribed for each company in guildhall records confirm that. So the possession of the right to wear a great lord's livery was a prerequisite for traveling. That may explain why Alleyn kept his Admiral's livery while playing in Strange's company. It gave him an insurance, a license to work separately if need be. And need there eventually was. In the event it gave him the right to renew his service for the Lord Admiral by forming a new company under his name in May 1594. And that is where we finally meet the great divide and the lumping together of all Marlowe's and all Shakespeare's plays written up to 1594 in spite of the different companies that owned them.

There is no evidence about who played in the remnant Admiral's group in the traveling years. The membership of the Admiral's up to May 1591 amounted in identifiable names only to Alleyn, Richard Jones, and James Tunstall. Tunstall reappeared in the new Admiral's after May 1594, and probably led the remnant company through the intervening years. Richard Jones traveled on the continent in 1592–93, returning to rejoin the new Admiral's in 1594. The others in the new company were drawn from a variety of groups. Thomas Downton came from Derby's, John Singer probably from the Queen's, of which he had been a founder member in 1583 and which he was still with in 1588. Richard Alleyn, Edward's brother, who was also in the Admiral's by 1597, was probably a Queen's man in 1594 (*ES* II.115). Of the other new Admiral's Men, Edward Dutton, Edward Juby, Martin Slater, and Thomas Towne, there is no earlier record. They may have been members of the touring group through 1591–94.

All this has a strong bearing on the ownership of Marlowe's plays. The Admiral's Men's plays that were in Alleyn's hands up to 1591 ought to have gone with him into the re-ordered Strange's had it really been an amalgamation, but they did not. The appearance of playbooks for the two *Tamburlaines* and *Faustus* in the resources of the 1594 Admiral's indicates that they came into the new group with the leading tourers and their playbooks. The only other explanation is that Alleyn himself kept his most valuable playbooks for nearly three years unused while he played in the other company. That is unlikely. At the Rose Strange's company had its own resources, including two new Marlowe plays. *The Jew of Malta* and *The Massacre at Paris,* along with Talbot in *1 Henry VI* and *Titus Andronicus,* might have given Strange's enough resources to warrant Alleyn withholding his most famous plays from them, but I suspect that they remained with the touring Admiral's Men. We conclude that Alleyn took advantage of the reshuffle of May 1594 to draw the residual Admiral's company into the new Admiral's group so that he could renew his famous roles in the early Marlowe plays.

Marlowe's change of allegiance between the companies is worthy of note for two reasons. The exceptional range of subjects and genres Marlowe chose for his plays does suggest some variety in the companies he wrote for. That point has been submerged by the fact that the whole Marlowe corpus of plays ended up in the hands of the Rose company and its successors. Their later ownership by the one company has been projected backwards to iron out the discrepancies in their earlier history. Clarifying Marlowe's career is one reason for carefully tracking the customers for the plays. The other is to explain how they could all have ended up in the hands of the new Admiral's.

The Lord Chamberlain's action in setting up a new company in May 1594 with Shakespeare in it is well known, but his motives are not. The recent deaths of some major patrons (Sussex on 14 December 1593 and more significantly Carey's relative Ferdinando Strange, now Earl of Derby, on 16 April), and the trouble he had setting up the Queen's Christmas entertainment through the previous season, led Lord Chamberlain Carey to set up what Richard Dutton has called a duopoly,[27] modeled on the Queen's Men's monopoly of eleven years before. With his son-in-law the Lord Admiral he set up a pair of new companies,[28] with players drawn from all the major groups: Strange's, the Admiral's, Pembroke's, Sussex's, the Queen's Men, and possibly others. Carey used as his precedent the establishment of the Queen's Men eleven years before, when the best players were taken from each of the leading companies of the time. He set his own company at the Theatre, whose owner had worn his own livery since the 1580s, with the owner's son as its chief player. His son-in-law Charles Howard set up the other company led by the player who still wore his livery, Alleyn, at Alleyn's father-in-law's playhouse the Rose.[29]

The performances and play titles noted in Henslowe's *Diary* for the first half of 1594 give some indication of the companies drawn on for the new set-up. In those months four companies used the Rose. Between 27 December 1593 and 6 February 1594 Sussex's performed nine plays that appear in the *Diary* only for that run, including *George a Greene,* printed in 1599 as a Sussex's play, and *Friar Francis,* which Heywood in his *Apology* reported as belonging to Sussex's. *Titus Andronicus* also appeared for the first time, if the earlier "*Titus*" that Henslowe records for Strange's was

Titus and Vespasian. The Fair Maid of Italy also appears for the first time as a Sussex's play. Only *The Jew of Malta,* a regular in the *Diary* since the first Strange's entries at the beginning of 1592, seems not to have been a play of Sussex's own. Then in the brief run when Sussex's joined up with the Queen's Men at Easter 1594, they performed five plays. Two of these, *The Jew* and *Friar Bacon and Friar Bungay,* had been at the Rose before, one was a Sussex's title, *The Fair Maid,* and one other, *King Leir,* later appeared in print as a Queen's Men's play. A further play, *The Ranger's Comedy,* also appeared for the first time. It reappeared after May in the Admiral's repertory.[30]

From then on the new Admiral's ran everything theatrical in London. For their first three-day run between 14 and 16 May 1594 they offered one play that was definitely Henslowe's, *The Jew of Malta,* plus *The Ranger's Comedy,* and a new title, *Cutlack,* which Everard Guilpin later identified as an Alleyn role. The most intriguing and possibly most revealing list of plays is the subsequent one, where Henslowe recorded a brief run of joint or alternate performances by the new Admiral's and the new Chamberlain's at Newington Butts. It is the only evidence there is for the original playstock of the Chamberlain's Men before Shakespeare started adding to it. The two companies offered seven plays between 3 and 13 June 1594. They included *The Jew of Malta,* which they may have thought worth a special staging in that month because of the Lopez trial.[31] The others almost certainly came from the companies of the new players. Besides Alleyn's Cutlack, *Titus Andronicus* reappeared, most likely thanks to some players from Sussex's, who were the last of its three owners listed on its 1594 title page. Four new plays appear, *Hester and Ahasuerus, Bellendon, Hamlet,* and *The Taming of A Shrew.* The last of these had been a Pembroke's play, like *Titus.* Where the *Hamlet* came from is uncertain. It may have been a Queen's Men's play like *King Leir* and *The Troublesome Reign of King John,* both of which Shakespeare was later to rewrite.

The subsequent history of the seven titles indicates that in May 1594 three of the seven belonged to the new Admiral's and four to the Chamberlain's, a reasonable divide if they played them on alternate days. *Bellendon, Cutlack* and *The Jew of Malta* appear subsequently in the Admiral's lists, while *Titus* and *The Shrew* became part of the Chamberlain's playstock since they reappear in the First Folio. *Hamlet* and *Hester* may have been theirs too, since they never reappear in the Admiral's lists. By tracking the previous ownership of these playbooks we can deduce that besides the five men from Strange's some players came to the Chamberlain's Men from the Queen's and some from Pembroke's, the latter arriving via Sussex's if the title page of the 1594 *Titus* is to be believed. None of the Sussex's plays in Henslowe's lists for early 1594 and none of the Queen's

Men plays brought to their sojourn with Sussex's at the Rose ever reappear in the *Diary.* Nor, of course, does "harey the vj."

This alliance of Sussex's, Pembroke's and the Queen's Men along with Strange's may help to explain how all of Shakespeare's early plays were taken into the one company in 1594, but it does not tell the whole story. The sequence of *Titus* owners described on the title page of the 1594 quarto, Strange's, Pembroke's and Sussex's, might explain its arrival in the new Chamberlain's along with some of Sussex's Men.[32] The Strange's Men's inclusion in the Chamberlain's new company might explain the arrival of *1 Henry VI,* just as the Pembroke's membership explains *2* and *3 Henry VI* and *The Shrew.* But it does not say why the other Strange's plays, including the Marlowe plays and especially *The Massacre at Paris,* went to the other new company.

All of Shakespeare's earlier plays, formerly performed by Strange's, Sussex's, and Pembroke's, went into the new Chamberlain's. I used to think that such retentiveness on the part of one humble writer indicated a remarkably, indeed uniquely strong possessiveness over his products for their financial value, and that he used his plays to buy his place in the new Chamberlain's. But no playwright other than Ben Jonson ever retained ownership of his plays once he had he sold them to the players. The track through the mud traced to here makes me wonder if there was not some higher agency that gathered the playbooks together for the new companies and enlisted the players who had been acting them to form the duopoly.

The Admiral's, so far as we know, took all the available Marlowe corpus. To the staples used by pretty well every Rose company, such as *The Jew of Malta* and *Friar Bacon,* they added the old Admiral's stock, notably *Tamburlaine* and *Faustus.* They had some plays formerly performed at the Rose by Strange's and some by the Queen's. That gave them five of Marlowe's plays. To these they probably added *Dido,* and possibly also *Edward II* from Pembroke's. This last Marlowe play does not reappear in Henslowe's records after May 1594, but its 1622 reprinting gave it to a later Henslowe company, Queen's Anne's Men.[33] If it did not go with the others it was the only play not gathered up in the two otherwise clean sweeps. If it did go to the Rose, then the Chamberlain's got all of the Shakespeare corpus and the Admiral's secured all Marlowe. One wonders how precisely in May 1594 the Lord Chamberlain and his son-in-law and their advisers knew what they were doing when they divided these spoils. If they did, as I believe, settle all of Marlowe's plays on one company and all of the early Shakespeares on the other, it suggests that someone held a strikingly equal esteem for the two writers. Neither had yet got their name into print on their title pages, but somebody reckoned that bundling together Marlowe's plays for the one and Shakespeare's for the other would be the best guarantee of the duopoly's future. In that calculation, it was a convenient bonus that one of the two was still working and was himself a player. History has not devalued the judgment made in 1594.

Notes

1. The Marlovian echoes in Shakespeare secured some of Mac's reputation for making the most careful measurements in the arcane practices of language analysis.

2. For an account of Henry Carey, Lord Hunsdon the Lord Chamberlain, and Charles Howard, his son-in-law the Lord Admiral, and their dealings with the playing companies of the 1580s and 1590s, see Gurr, "Three Reluctant Patrons and Early Shakespeare," *Shakespeare Quarterly* 44 (1993): 159–74.

3. In his Revels edition of *Dido Queen of Carthage* and *The Massacre at Paris* (Methuen: London, 1968), H. J. Oliver suggests that the play was written for staging with the actors entering from mansions on each side like the university plays (xxx–xxxi). See also Mary E. Smith, "Staging Marlowe's *Dido Queen of Carthage,*" *Studies in English Literature* 17 (1977): 177–90.

4. G. C. Moore Smith, *Gabriel Harvey's Marginalia* (Stratford: 1913).

5. A play about Dido by a Cambridge Fellow, Edward Halliwell, was acted before the Queen there in 1564. William Gager's *Dido* was at Oxford in 1583. See Oliver, *Dido,* xxxix.

6. See Records of Early English Drama (REED) *Cambridge,* ed. Alan Nelson, 2 vols. (Toronto: Univ. of Toronto Press, 1989), 1:313, 323. E. K. Chambers, *The Elizabethan Stage,* 4 vols. (Oxford: Oxford Univ. Press: 1923), 2:135 says that the Admiral's went to Cambridge in 1586–87, information he derived from J. T. Murray, *English Dramatic Companies,* 2 vols. (London: 1910), who notes them as playing there in 1586. But Nelson has no record of any visit before 1588–89.

7. Nelson, *Cambridge,* I.319.

8. Scott McMillin and Sally-Beth MacLean, *The Queen's Men and their Plays* (Cambridge: Cambridge Univ. Press, 1999).

9. Nashe, Thomas, *Works,* ed. R. B. McKerrow, 5 vols. (Oxford: Clarendon Press, 1958), 1:319.

10. *The Elizabethan Stage,* 4:303–4.

11. Ibid., 2:135.

12. The date of *Faustus* is normally set at 1588, although W. W. Greg made a case for 1592 in his parallel texts edition (Oxford: 1950). The most tangible evidence is in MacD. P. Jackson's "Three Old Ballads and the Date of *Doctor Faustus,*" *Journal of the Australasian Universities Language and Literature Association* 36 (1971): 187–200, which argues for a date before 28 February 1589.

13. See Richard Levin, "The Contemporary Perception of Marlowe's *Tamburlaine,*" *Medieval and Renaissance Drama in England* 1 (1984): 51–70. The earliest references are: 1587 Robert Greene, *Perimedes;* 1587–88 Greene, *Alphonsus of Aragon* 4.3 (G2v); 1588–89 George Peele, *Battle of Alcazar* (1.2.214–15); 1589 Greene, *Menaphon,* (F2r); 1589 Peele, *Farewell to Norris and Drake* (A3r); c. 1590 *George a Greene* (1.1.46–49); 1591 *The Troublesome Raigne of King John* (A2r); 1591 Greene, *Farewell to Folly* (A4r); 1592 Thomas Nashe, *Strange News* (F4r); c. 1592 *Selimus* (2344–46); 5 May 1593 "Dutch Church libel"; 1593 Gabriel Harvey, *A New Letter of Notable Contents* (D3r, D4r); 1593 Nashe, *Christ's Tears over Jerusalem* (A4r); 1593 Michael Drayton, *Idea* (172–73); 1596 Nashe, *Have With You to Saffron Walden* (S4v); 1597 Joseph Hall, *Virgidemiarum;* 1597 Pistol in *2 Henry IV,* 2.4.164–65; 1597 E.S., *The Discovery of the Knights of the Post* (C2v); 1597 Donne, *The*

Calme (33); 1598 Jonson, *Every Man In his Humour* (3.2.16–22); c. 1599 Marston, *Histriomastix* (act 5); 1599 Dekker, *Shoemaker's Holiday* (5.4.51–54); 1599 Dekker, *Old Fortunatus* (1.1.187–95); 1599 Marston, *Antonio and Mellida* (Induction); 1600 *The Blind Beggar of Bednal Green* (G2r); 1601 Dekker, *Satiromastix* (4.2.28–89, 4.3.169–71); 1601 Dekker, *Blurt Master Constable* (A3r).

14. See Samuel Rowlands, *The Knave of Clubs* (London: 1609), 29.

15. *The Jew of Malta* was entered for printing in the Stationers' Register on 17 May 1594, but was not printed. A second Register entry dated 20 November 1632 preceded its publication in 1633. The title page for that printing says it was played "by her Majesties Servants at the Cock-pit." *Henslowe's Diary,* eds. R. A. Foakes and R. T. Rickert (Cambridge: Cambridge Univ. Press, 1962), lists Strange's playing it seventeen times between 26 February 1592 and 1 February 1593, Sussex's playing it with the Queen's on 3 and 8 April 1594, the Admiral's on 14 May 1594, with the Chamberlain's on 6 and 15 June 1594, then thirteen times on their own from 25 June 1594 to 23 June 1596. The 1598 inventory lists a "cauderm" for the final scene. *The Massacre at Paris* was printed in an undated octavo as "The Massacre at Paris: With the Death of the Duke of Guise. As it was plaide by the right honourable the Lord high Admirall his Servants. Written by Christopher Marlow," the first time his name was used. Its allocation to the Admiral's Men probably fixes its printing to between 1594 and 1596, when the Lord Admiral became the Earl of Nottingham. The Admiral's Men performed it on 19 June 1594, and nine more times that year.

16. Oliver, *Massacre,* lv–lvii.

17. John Holland is named as a player in *John of Bordeaux,* a Strange's play, and also in the Folio version of *2 Henry VI,* a Pembroke's play.

18. Mark Eccles, *Christopher Marlowe in London* (Cambridge, Mass.: Harvard Univ. Press, 1934), 179.

19. R. B. Wernham, "Christopher Marlowe at Flushing in 1592," *ELR* 6 (1976): 344–45.

20. Millar McLure, *Marlowe. The Critical Heritage* (Routledge: London, 1979), 34. Kyd's patronage for the six years 1587–93 is thought to have come from the Pembroke circle and especially Mary Herbert, who in 1591–92 was translating a closet play by Garnier, and commissioned Daniel to write its sequel. What that suggests about Marlowe's relations with the Earl of Pembroke and his company of players is unclear. Kyd seems never to have written a play for either Pembroke's or Strange's Men.

21. Andrew Gurr, "The Chimera of Amalgamation," *Theatre Research International* 18 (1993): 85–93.

22. *The Elizabethan Stage,* 4:305.

23. McMillin Scott, "Building Stories: Greg, Fleay, and the Plot of *2 Seven Deadly Sins,*" *MRDE* 4 (1989): 53–56.

24. *Malone Society Collections* 6 (1961): 27.

25. Other references confirm the company's patent. *Henslowe's Diary* has (276) a letter from Alleyn to his wife dated 1 August, almost certainly in 1593, from Bristol. It mentions Richard Cowley as deliverer of a letter from his wife, and Thomas Pope's kinsman as bearer of his letter. Both Cowley and Pope are named in the *2 Seven Deadly Sins* plot. Alleyn asks for further letters to be sent "by the cariers of shrowsbery or to west chester or to york to be keptt till my lord stranges players com." Joan Alleyn and Henslowe wrote to him as "one of my lorde Stranges Players" probably in the same month of 1593, and again to the same address on 14 August, having heard that he had been too sick to play at Bath. On 28 September Joan and her stepfather wrote again, chiefly about the plague and household matters, and with news of the impoverished return of Pembroke's Men to London. This too was addressed "unto my welbeloved husband mr edward allen one of my lord stranges players."

26. The evidence about the companies touring is far from complete. Nearly half of the planned volumes of the Records of Early English Drama (*REED*) are now out, but many

counties, towns and great houses are still unrecorded. *Malone Society Collections* (*MSC*) have some records, and J. T. Murray's two-volume work published in 1910 still gives some usefully broad coverage. Chambers, *The Elizabethan Stage,* has some summary notes. The notes supplied in the text here refer to the *REED* volumes for particular towns and counties, *MSC* covering Ipswich and Kent. It might be added that where Chambers states that "therlle of Darbys players and . . . the Lorde Admirals players, the ij amongste" were together at Ipswich 7 March 1594 (*Elizabethan Stage* 2:120n), this entry is not in *MSC*.

27. Dutton, *Mastering the Revels: The Regulation and Censorship of English Renaissance Drama* (Basingstoke: Macmillan, 1991), 111.

28. See Gurr, *The Shakespearian Playing Companies* (Oxford: Clarendon Press, 1996), 65–73.

29. This story is told in more detail in Gurr, "Patrons." James Burbage was wearing Carey's livery in 1584, when the Privy Council tried to have his Theatre pulled down.

30. There is an intriguing question of why some plays, especially *The Jew of Malta* and *Friar Bacon and Friar Bungay,* appear in Henslowe's records at the Rose with different companies. Conceivably they were left behind when the companies went on tour because of the heavy demands they made on staging. A company did not need to take more than four or five plays on tour.

31. For the theory that Henslowe staged *The Jew* in 1594 to coincide with the two trials of the Jewish Lopez, see Margaret Hotine, "The Politics of Anti-Semitism: *The Jew of Malta* and *The Merchant of Venice,*" *Notes and Queries* 236 (1991): 35–38.

32. The 1594 quarto of *Titus* lists Strange's, Pembroke's and Sussex's as its performers. In his Arden 2 edition (London: Routledge, 1995) Jonathan Bate suggested that the three companies may have combined for a first performance in 1594, the one recorded by Henslowe. I doubt this, since Henslowe was usually quite specific about his performers, naming both of the companies involved in any run of joint performances. The *Titus* title page must rather indicate the sequence of Shakespeare's own company membership: first Strange's, then Pembroke's, then Sussex's, before he joined the Chamberlain's, which the 1600 title page added to the first three.

33. Roslyn L. Knutson offers as a possible though unsubstantiatable explanation for the absence of *Edward II* from the Henslowe records the possibility that it went from Pembroke's to the Chamberlain's. She suggests, though without any supporting evidence, that it could have been taken from them later by Christopher Beeston when he left the Chamberlain's in 1600 for Worcester's, which in 1603 became the Queen Anne's Men, who performed it subsequently. See *The Repertory of Shakespeare's Company, 1594–1613* (Fayetteville: Univ. of Arkansas Press, 1991), 230. If *Edward II* really was a Chamberlain's play in 1594 it would have stirred the writing of *Richard II* in 1595.

1590s: Shakespeare and Peele

Kind and Unkindness: Aaron in *Titus Andronicus*

Brian Boyd

AFTER WRESTLING A SLIPPERY PROBLEM INTO WHAT YOU TAKE TO BE submission, the last thing you want to hear is that you have been tackling the wrong task and need to start all over again. I vividly recall meeting Mac Jackson on the University of Auckland library steps late one summer vacation. He asked me how I had spent the summer so far. When I said I had been writing on *Titus Andronicus,* his eyes lit up as he told me that he thought he had just proven that Shakespeare co-authored the play with George Peele. I winced, since I had assumed from the published scholarship that any doubts about Shakespeare's sole authorship of *Titus Andronicus* had long since been dispelled. Valuing Mac's work as I did and do, I had no choice but to look at his arguments. Convinced by them at once,[1] I was soon able to confirm his findings with new evidence, to which still more has since been added by Mac himself and others.

To understand the structure of a play, we can try to reverse engineer it, to reconstruct, from the finished artifact, how and why it was made. It helps if the raw materials are known, as the key components of *Titus Andronicus* are: Kyd, Ovid, Marlowe, and the matter of Rome and Troy.[2] But if two authors have collaborated, yet have composed largely on their own, reverse engineering can be more than doubly difficult.

For a long time some readers supposed that Shakespeare's hand could not be responsible for all the severed hands and heads in *Titus Andronicus,* while others simply felt that the style of act 1 in particular could not be his and sounds suspiciously like Peele's. Today the extreme violence of the action seems all too accurate an image of humanity at its worst, and no grounds for denying Shakespeare authorship. Yet several recent articles and Brian Vickers's magisterial survey of the collaboration controversy, *Shakespeare, Co-Author,* demonstrate that *Titus* has two very dissimilar strata, one that falls within Shakespearean norms, one that falls far outside them.[3] Many independent indices in *Titus Andronicus* 1.1, 2.1, 2.2, and 4.1—scenic construction, staging, stage directions (phrasing and format), speech construction, line construction, phrase construction, figures of speech, habits of collocation, modes of repetition, diction (rare, common, and function words), syntax, and meter—add to the evidence of words and phrases in these four scenes that are elsewhere uniquely favored by Peele and point straight to the conclusion that Peele wrote these four scenes, in Gary Taylor's terms, the first three scenes of the play and the first of the counteraction.[4]

Whether or not they suspected the presence of Peele, some readers who have noticed sharp dislocations of continuity in the long first scene have also wondered whether Titus's killing of his son Mutius was a late addition. I have recently shown the high likelihood that not only did Peele add the killing of Mutius after first composing the rest of the scene, but that he seems to have done so without Shakespeare's awareness of the addition at the time that he was writing *his* share. Indeed, as I sum up, "Titus's killing of Mutius is inconsistent in detail and in design with the Shakespearean part of the play. There, Titus implores mercy for two other sons even when he supposes they may be guilty of murder, and sacrifices his own hand to save them. This makes neither psychological nor dramatic sense if he has just killed Mutius without hesitation or remorse for a minor transgression. Shakespeare's Titus is Roman, but not heartless, not casually unfeeling toward any in his family. Remove the inconsistency caused by Peele's late addition, and *Titus Andronicus* loses what such a staunch advocate of the play as Marco Mincoff has to admit is the received text's 'chief weakness.'"[5]

Even those who see Peele as Shakespeare's collaborator agree that Shakespeare is responsible for the play's overall design. Nevertheless the effort to explain the killing of Mutius as part of Shakespeare's plans has obscured the Shakespearean shape of the play, its intimate relation to his other work of this time, and its anticipation of his future work. Once we dismiss the notion that Shakespeare intended Titus casually to kill one of the last of his twenty-five sons, we can appreciate the key role of the Moor who leaps into full Shakespearean life when he suddenly does all he can to save his one son.

While many have seen Aaron as the most Shakespearean aspect of *Titus Andronicus,* others consider him one of the play's "unexplained ingredients," offering no more than "diversionary horrors" but "never functionally made a part of the plot."[6] I will argue that Aaron is the first of a long line of Shakespearean contrast characters I call his "versos," whom he invents as a key to play after play, as a contrast to the main characters his story requires, and a focus for the ideas that have made him dramatize one story rather than another.[7]

Why did Shakespeare write his first tragedy, and why did he choose the elements he did? Evidence of vocabulary and style places the composition of *Titus Andronicus* immediately after *3 Henry VI* and before its sequel, *Richard III.*[8] At the time he began *Titus,* Shakespeare would have written two comedies and three serious plays, the first three in his first historical tetralogy. Although his most recent play, *3 Henry VI,* naturally joins with the histories before and after, it also has affinities with *Titus Andronicus* as striking as those that would later link *Romeo and Juliet* and *A Midsummer Night's Dream.*

Shakespeare in fact seems to have broken off his history cycle to develop still further, in the mode of pure tragedy, the tragic ideas evolving within the first three plays of the tetralogy: the losses families must endure once the wheel of retribution begins to roll, and the paradox of the pity people can feel toward their own kin while showing pitilessness to their enemies.

In a scene that sums up the cost of the Wars of the Roses, Shakespeare juxtaposes a son who has unwittingly killed his father and a father who has killed his son. Enfolding his son's body, the father declares:

> My sighing breast shall be thy funeral bell;
> And so obsequious will thy father be,
> Mere[9] for the loss of thee, having no more,
> As Priam was for all his valiant sons.[10]

The fall of Troy, as Mincoff notes, Shakespeare would more than once invoke as "a symbol of the utmost in human grief," and in *Titus Andronicus* he would pointedly assign his hero "five-and-twenty valiant sons, / Half of the number that King Priam had" (1.1.79–80).[11]

Verbal parallels suggest that Shakespeare began *Titus* under the strong influence of *3 Henry VI,* and even that he completed the history while thinking ahead to the tragedy. When Shakespeare came to write *his* share of *Titus,* he began with 2.3. The scene's climax, Lavinia's pleas to Tamora and her sons to be spared the rape they have threatened—

> O Tamora, thou *bearest a woman's face*—
> *Demetrius.* Listen, fair madam, let it be your glory
> To see her *tears,* but be your *heart* to them
> As unrelenting *flint* to drops of rain.
> *Lavinia.* When did the *tiger's* young ones teach the dam? . . .
> The milk thou suck'st from her did turn to *marble.* . . .
> Do thou entreat her show a *woman's pity*
>
> (2.3.136–47)

—echoes two passages from *3 Henry VI.*[12] York reproaches Queen Margaret before his death:

> O *tiger's heart* wrapped in a woman's hide,
> How couldst thou drain the life-blood of the child

To bid the father wipe his eyes withal
And yet be seen to *bear a woman's face?*
Women are soft, mild, *pitiful,* and flexible:
Thou stern, obdurate and *flinty,* rough, remorseless.

(1.4.137–42)

Later Henry VI will assess Margaret's chances in appealing for the French king's aid:

For she's a *woman* to be *pitied* much:
Her sighs will make a batt'ry in his breast;
Her *tears* will pierce into a *marble heart;*
The *tiger* will be mild whiles she doth mourn.

(3.1.36–39)

Details of the plot that Shakespeare was brewing for *Titus* filter into the language of *3 Henry VI.* Just after the "drain the life-blood of the child" speech above, with its fore-image of the draining of the blood of Tamora's children to make the paste in their mother's pie, York refers to "That face of his the hungry cannibals / Would not have touched, would not have stained with blood." Disappointed that the dead Clifford cannot hear his mockery, Richard Crookback declares:

If this right hand would buy but two hours' life,
That I in all despite might rail at him,
This hand should chop it off and, with the issuing blood,
Stifle the villain whose unstanchèd thirst
York and young Rutland could not satisfy

(2.6.80–84)

—and so anticipates not only the scene of Titus chopping off his hand to buy his sons' pardon, but Aaron's parting from Lucius with the wish that he might "burn in everlasting fire, / So I might have your company in hell, / But to torment you with my bitter tongue" (5.1.148–50). When Warwick, asked to kneel to acknowledge Edward IV as king, snarls "I had rather chop this hand off at a blow" and Edward retorts,

This hand, fast wound about thy coal-black hair,
Shall, whiles thy head is warm and new cut off,
Write in the dust this sentence with thy blood: . . .

(5.1.50–55)

they prefigure not only the "coal-black Moor" who induces Titus to chop off his hand, and the heads of Titus's sons that Aaron sends back to him, but also the handless Lavinia writing the name of her rapists in the sand.[13]

If *3 Henry VI* suggests that Shakespeare had at least begun to plan *Titus Andronicus* as he was writing its predecessor, it still does not explain how the plan took shape.

The intensifying tragedy of his histories presumably induced Shakespeare to take on the most prestigious dramatic genre of his day. By turning to tragedy proper he could compact into one self-contained play the cycle of retribution that required four plays in the histories.[14] Besides, revenge tragedy was the most fashionable tragic mode of the moment, and Kyd's recent *Spanish Tragedy* the most popular play of its time, with Marlowe's *Jew of Malta* close behind. Shakespeare could in one move capitalize as Marlowe had on Kyd's success, extend the themes of his own histories, and challenge Kyd at his own game.

As Mincoff shows, Shakespeare follows then outpaces Kyd, opening with a return from war more triumphant than Kyd's (not just a prince, but three princes and a queen as prisoners) and more tightly plotted: the hero is not a mere onlooker but the victorious general himself, and the dispute over the prisoners, resulting here in the sacrifice of Alarbus, provides the motive for revenge against the hero and will lead directly to the still more horrible revenge he eventually exacts.[15] Where Kyd compounds ironies of justice by making Hieronimo the country's highest court officer, Shakespeare outdoes him again. Like Kyd he places his hero in an initial position of power that will contrast with the ultimate sense of powerlessness that impels him to seek revenge. But to further compound the tragic irony, he also makes Titus's selfless integrity the very cause of his forfeiting the security he could have had as emperor, and he makes the prisoner whom Titus brings back in triumph the very person who by the end of the first scene has power over him and revenge against him in her heart.

That person, of course, is Tamora, and for her role Shakespeare adds to his refinements of Kyd suggestions from *3 Henry VI.* There Edward IV, newly installed on the throne, plans to shore up his position by a diplomatic marriage with the King of France's daughter, but before the marriage can be arranged, succumbs to his desire for Lady Elizabeth Grey and marries her instead. In *Titus Andronicus,* Saturninus, after being elected emperor on Titus's own recommendation, asks for the hand of this king-maker's daughter, but before the matter is settled, finds himself smitten with Tamora's looks ("A goodly lady, trust me, of the hue / That I would choose, were I to choose anew," 1.1.261–62), and when Bassianus claims Lavinia as already his, swiftly follows his inclination and marries Tamora.[16]

Above all Tamora, "with her fierce vengefulness . . . and her adulterous passion," replays Queen Margaret, the woman who dominates Shakespeare's whole tetralogy.[17] We have already noted the elaborate echoes, in Shakespeare's own first scene in *Titus,* of lines devoted to Margaret in *3*

Henry VI; the tension in Margaret between her pity toward her own and her pitilessness to her foes becomes even more explicit in Tamora as Lavinia's pleas persist:

> *Lavinia.* The lion, moved with pity, did endure
> To have his princely paws pared all away. . . .
> O, be to me, though thy hard heart say no,
> Nothing so kind, but something pitiful.
> *Tamora.* I know not what it means; away with her!
> *Lavinia.* O, let me teach thee for my father's sake,
> That gave thee life when well he might have slain thee,
> Be not obdurate; open thy deaf ears.
> *Tamora.* Hadst thou in person ne'er offended me.
> Even for his sake am I pitiless.
> Remember, boys, I poured forth tears in vain
> To save your brother from the sacrifice,
> But fierce Andronicus would not relent.
>
> (2.3.151–65)

Though the beginning of his story and its protagonist carry on from Kyd, and his subject and antagonist develop from his own *Henry VI* plays, Shakespeare turns back for the middle and end of his story to Rome. As the play repeatedly proclaims, the rape and silencing of Lavinia and Titus's revenge by feeding a parent the flesh of her own offspring rework the story of Philomela in Shakespeare's favorite poet, Ovid[18]—with perhaps, as Hunter suggests, some echoes of the political situation surrounding the rape of Lucrece in Livy.[19]

As so often when he takes over a source, Shakespeare immediately identifies and eliminates a human difficulty there. In Ovid, a mother sacrifices her *own* child to feed him in revenge to the husband who has raped her sister. Shakespeare wants the horror of parent eating child, but creates a revenger who feeds not his own innocent child, but the guilty children of his enemy, to their mother.

As Hunter suggests, Shakespeare also conflates—in a way that anticipates the fusion of ancient Roman virtue and modern Italian vice in *Cymbeline*—two ends of Roman history, the harsh rectitude of the early republic and the decadence of the late empire in which the story is nominally set.[20] Another strand of classical allusion running throughout the play connects the founding and the foundering of classical Rome through its links with Troy: Shakespeare systematically compares the rape of Lavinia and the assault on the whole Andronici family with the fall of Troy.

He gives Titus twenty-five sons, "half of the number that King Priam had." He names Titus's daughter Lavinia, after the Latin princess Aeneas marries, to found, from the remnants of Troy, the settlement of Lavinium that would one day give rise to Rome, the second Troy. Lavinia is raped by the Goths, as Rome itself would be, and as Mincoff notes, in act 3, "Titus's woes are twice, at their very summit, compared to the burning of Troy."[21] The lewd Tamora, brought into Rome behind Titus's chariot but soon made Empress, only to destroy Rome's best hopes, combines the whorish Helen and the Trojan horse, dragged into the citadel of Troy only to violate its population, as the barbarians Chiron and Demetrius who have sprung from Tamora's womb desecrate Lavinia and all but destroy Rome.[22] Marcus makes the comparison explicit at the end when he calls on Lucius to recount the agonies of the Andronici:

> Speak, Rome's dear friend, as erst our ancestor,
> When with his solemn tongue he did discourse
> To lovesick Dido's sad attending ear
> The story of that baleful burning night
> When subtle Greeks surprised King Priam's Troy.
> Tell us what Sinon hath bewitched our ears,
> Or who hath brought the fatal engine in
> That gives our Troy, our Rome, the civil wound.[23]
>
> (5.3.79–86)

Shakespeare now has the ingredients for a hugely ambitious tragedy that can extend the thrust of his own histories at the same time as it assimilates and outdoes Kyd, Ovid, and Seneca.[24] Intensifying Kyd, he begins with a returning hero, a semi-Priam who will soon have all his children to mourn. Because of his piety—his respect for the gods, his concern for his family—Titus sacrifices the son of the enemy queen he has brought to Rome in captivity, but by the end of the scene this queen, now bride of the man he has named emperor, is his empress and committed to revenge.

For the mode of vengeance that results, Shakespeare selects the Philomela story for the horrific impact of its rape and mutilation. To perpetrate the rape, he needs the male kin of the sacrifice victim to assault the daughter of the hero, and to confirm that the rape is an act of vengeance rather than lone Tarquinian lust, he chooses two rapists rather than one. By having the victim plead in vain to the rapists' mother, he can make a mother's pitilessness toward another woman, even when she asks to be saved from rape, still more chilling and unnatural than Queen Margaret's rabid retribution.

But to maximize the ironies of justice, as Kyd had done, Shakespeare also devises a murder for which the hero's innocent offspring will be summarily executed. Since the offspring cannot be the rape victim—who has to remain in the play for the pathos of her presence, and to be there at the moment of the final revenge—Shakespeare needs someone else. To match the two rapists, the two sons of the enemy, he chooses two sons of the hero.

It would also tighten the story if the murder victim had some link to the emperor, so that the emperor's indignation at the crime makes it all the harder for the hero to obtain redress.[25] And if the victim of the murder for which Titus's sons are framed is related to his daughter, if in fact the murder itself is part of the plan of rape and revenge, so much the better. Shakespeare therefore makes the murder victim both the brother of the emperor and the husband of the hero's daughter. But to add a motive of vengeance against the victim in his own right, Shakespeare arranges that Bassianus should abduct Lavinia after Titus has promised her to Saturninus, so that Tamora's status as Saturninus's second choice seems a public humiliation to the Gothic camp.

The play now requires two rapists, brothers; two falsely accused of murder, also brothers; the emperor and his brother; and to match this, Shakespeare gives the hero a brother who can act throughout as Titus's confidant in a Rome that he sees as otherwise "but a wilderness of tigers" (3.1.54). With all the major characters of the first act now in place, Shakespeare has established a brilliant and complex structure for his play, that will lead smoothly from the first-act sacrifice to the disproportionate and foully misdirected vengeance—rape, mutilation, murder, and unjust execution—that will in turn provoke the ultimate, ugly but understandable retribution that at last restores calm.[26]

And for the sacrifice of Alarbus and the atmosphere of Rome at the opening of the play, Shakespeare turned to the Latinist George Peele, who would supply him with the *romanitas* he needed, and who, ever since translating Erasmus's Latin version of Euripides' *Iphigenia,* had had a peculiar penchant for the theme of sacrifice.[27] Unknown to Shakespeare, though, Peele, with his predilection for exaggerated symmetries and repetitions, added the killing of Mutius to the killing of Alarbus.

By the time Shakespeare had steeped Kyd's Hieronimo in Rome and Troy to form Titus, and drawn on Ovid's Philomela and his own Queen Margaret for Lavinia and Tamora, he had a perfectly self-contained plot. But although the play could now run from the sacrifice of Alarbus through the revenge of the Goths to the counter-revenge of the Andronici, he then added another major character that his plot did not need: Aaron the Moor, the second longest part in the play.

In later plays when Shakespeare added a verso[28] to a story that had substantially taken shape, he would construct the character entirely from the play's own structural needs, to contrast and clarify what was already there. In the case of Aaron, he may simply have been attracted at first to the dramatic energy of an out-and-out villain: Barabas in Marlowe's *Jew of Malta,* his own Richard of Gloucester, and the Vice tradition behind them both.

In *The Spanish Tragedy* the insipid Lorenzo seems less a compelling stage presence than a sour, scheming neighbor we would rather avoid than watch. In *The Jew of Malta,* by contrast, we cannot take our eyes off Barabas. If Aaron owes his existence to the energy of evil in Barabas, he owes his color and probably his name to Barabas's buoyantly villainous accomplice, the Moor Ithamore, for in naming his own Moor, Shakespeare's imagination seems to been primed by the recollection that the Bible's Ithamar is "son to Aaron the priest" (Exodus 38:21).[29] Barabas, as Jew, is the Marlovian exotic and outsider. As Moor, Aaron can stand even more strikingly aside from those around him.

But Aaron's immediate forebear is the Richard of Gloucester who gradually steps to the fore in *3 Henry VI,* and who in *Richard III* will become Shakespeare's most vivid villain before Iago. Just as Richard's physical deformity sets him apart and helps propel him toward evil, so Aaron's race distances him from his world to the point where he can gloat that he will make "his soul black like his face" (3.1.204).

Though Aaron has no necessary part in the plot of *Titus,* Shakespeare easily attaches him to the action by borrowing again from the *Henry VI* plays.[30] As queen and pitiless avenger, as a former enemy whose ambition undermines the stability of her new country, Tamora derives from Margaret. To connect Aaron to the story, Shakespeare simply draws on Suffolk's affair with Margaret, an adulterous relationship with a queen, like Aaron's with Tamora, that starts even before she mounts her new throne.

But it is not enough to connect Aaron to his plot. How does Shakespeare harness Aaron's energies to the needs of a play that could work without him? His answer—perhaps even his first aim in constructing Aaron—is contrast.

The transition between the first two scenes, continuous in action in the Quarto text, is an extraordinary *coup de théatre.* Through the almost five hundred lines of 1.1, Aaron has been speechless and unmentioned amid a crowd of prisoners, but a striking enigma to an Elizabethan audience by his black presence, as the Peacham drawing—the only contemporary drawing of the staging of a Shakespearean scene—attests by placing him at the margin of the image but at the center of attention.[31] Now, suddenly, he is alone and voluble, and the enigma can be answered. Someone who had seemed a prisoner, powerless, too insignificant to speak, turns out to be the new empress's longtime lover.

This newly dominant Aaron stands as a theatrical contrast not only to his own previous silence but also to Titus. Titus is the most Roman of Romans; his family monument enshrines forebears who for half a millennium have died in the service of Rome; more than a score of his own sons have offered their lives in Rome's defense. A victorious general, Titus could be emperor on his triumphal return were he not too much the old Roman to lift the prize for himself. Throughout the long 1.1 Aaron, by contrast, has been a nameless Moor, an outsider even among Rome's enemies and prisoners, the Goths. But by the end of 1.1, Titus's very integrity has left him at the mercy of an erstwhile enemy, while Aaron's depravity has earned him a place and power at the intimate heart of Rome.

As 2.1 unfolds, the contrast continues. 1.1 had begun with a dispute between two brothers over which of them should have Rome, but the intervention of the Andronici had resolved the dispute without the force that Saturninus and Bassianus were ready to pit against each other. Now comes a strangely debased recapitulation, as another pair of brothers argue about their respective rights to a Lavinia, who is in any case just married and quite unavailable; they too argue whether the seniority of one brother gives him an automatic preference; but Aaron resolves the dispute by *suggesting* force, turning them from what had seemed protestations of love, albeit crude, to heartless plans for "rape and villainy" (2.1.117). Where the noble Andronici raise the level of Rome's political debate, Aaron rapidly lowers the level even of an unseemly private squabble and suggests the rape of a woman who in a sense herself represents Rome.

In the next phase of the action, from 2.2 to 3.1, Aaron shows himself as the "chief architect and plotter" (5.3.121) of the woes that befall the Andronici. Swiftly and without prompting, he arranges not only the rape of Lavinia but also the murder of Bassianus, the framing of Martius and Quintus, and the chopping off of Titus's hand.

Shakespeare draws here on the tradition of the Vice, transformed—as so often since the old moral plays began to be literalized and secularized in the course of the sixteenth century—from allegorical figure into individual villain.[32] A defect common to many of the so-called hybrid plays of the 1560s and 1570s that mix the Vice figure with particularized characters is that the other evil characters are already "sufficiently motivated not to need the temptation of a Vice."[33] Though *Titus Andronicus* is no hybrid, the weakness shows here too: through the sacrifice of Alarbus, Shakespeare has amply aroused the vengeance of Tamora and her sons before he lets Aaron speak. And Aaron, despite urging the empress and her sons to a vengeance they have already committed themselves to but half forgotten, has himself no motive for revenge.[34] As Bernard Spivack points out, this motiveless malignity in the villain reflects the old Vice rather than the individual psychology of the nonallegorical drama.[35]

No doubt these relics of the Vice convention are flaws. The Vice tradition guarantees Shakespeare the impact of Aaron's evil, but unbalances his accounts: too much motivation for Tamora and her sons, too little for

Aaron. But he quickly recoups his losses when he turns Aaron from formula to foil by adjusting his character—his evil, his blackness, his isolation—to serve the structure of the play.

In her first Shakespearean speech in the play, Tamora invites Aaron to lie with her in the woods, and Aaron in reply insists on his blackness and his desire for vengeance:

> Madam, though Venus govern your desires,
> Saturn is dominator over mine.
> What signifies my deadly-standing eye,
> My silence, and my cloudy melancholy,
> My fleece of woolly hair that now uncurls,
> Even as an adder when she doth unroll
> To do some fatal execution?
> No, madam, these are no venereal signs;
> Vengeance is in my heart, death in my hand,
> Blood and revenge are hammering in my head.
>
> (2.3.30–39)

Nowhere previously has Aaron's race—not even the word "Moor"—been even obliquely referred to in the dialogue. Suddenly, it is everywhere—his "deadly-standing eye" (Lucius will later call him "wall-eyed slave," 5.1.44), his "cloudy melancholy" (here with the full force of the Greek *melas,* "black"), his "fleece of woolly hair"—and it will remain prominent, in his own unabashed voice and in those who reject his blackness. We can probably conclude that, unlike Peele, the Shakespeare who planned Aaron as a Moor had good reasons for doing so, and intended to make the most of it, in imagery, in symbolism (Bassianus, for instance, a few lines hence: "Believe me, Queen, your swarthy Cimmerian / Doth make your honour of his body's hue, / Spotted, detested and abominable"),[36] and in psychology (the revulsion against the black babe, and Aaron's proudly defiant affirmation of his own kind).

At this point, however, we have no idea that Aaron will have a child by Tamora. In this phase of the play, in fact, what sets him apart is that unlike every other major character he has no family ties.[37] Nothing surprises us more on our first encounter with *Titus Andronicus* than its plethora of brothers, in obvious intensification of the pattern of the *Henry VI* plays: Saturninus versus his brother in the opening lines, Marcus supporting his brother in the next sequence, Lucius and his surviving brothers wanting to commemorate their score and more of fallen brothers in the sequence that follows, and the resultant sacrifice of Alarbus that draws protests from *his* two brothers. But Aaron stands alone.

Here we see the ironic wit of Shakespeare's choice of name for his villain, for the biblical Aaron is from the first, and insistently thereafter, the brother of Moses: "Is not Aaron, the Levite, thy brother?" (Exodus 4:14); "Aaron, thy brother, shall be thy prophet. Thou shalt speak all that I command thee: and Aaron, thy brother, shall speak unto Pharaoh" (Exodus 7:1–2)—and so on through the rest of the Pentateuch.

The first act of vengeance in the play—for a supposed threat to Tamora's life, for the real sacrifice of Alarbus—is the stabbing of Bassianus, which Demetrius prefaces with a boast to his mother: "This is a witness that I am thy son" (2.3.116). But if family impels others to revenge, no such impulse drives Aaron. Of course he exhorts Tamora to vengeance when she had in fact had love on her mind, and he turns Chiron and Demetrius from love to rape and revenge (once Aaron makes his suggestion, they never again let slip even the least hint of attraction to Lavinia),[38] but he never articulates a reason for wanting revenge himself. Demetrius by contrast had hoped for "opportunity of sharp revenge" (1.1.137) at the very moment of Alarbus's death, and Tamora vowed later in the scene:

> I'll find a day to massacre them all,
> And raze their faction and their family,
> The cruel father and his traitorous sons,
> To whom I suèd for my dear son's life. . . .
> (1.1.450–53)

Aaron, now advanced through his captivity to the position of the favorite of Rome's empress, has no reason to complain. His opening speech is one of exultation ("Then, Aaron, . . . fit thy thoughts / To mount aloft with thy imperial mistress"), and he sustains that note in the midst of his villainies ("was't not a happy star / Led us to Rome, strangers, and more than so, / Captives, to be advanced to this height?" 4.2.32–34). Though he steadily incites Tamora to vengeance, knowing her indignation at the death of Alarbus, he seems stirred not by any sense of injustice to be redressed but by the potential for villainy:

> This is the day of doom for Bassianus;
> His Philomel must lose her tongue today,
> Thy sons make pillage of her chastity,
> And wash their hands in Bassianus' blood.
> (2.3.42–45)

That becomes even more apparent in his gratuitous mockery of family loyalty, when he cajoles the Andronici into fighting for the honor of sacrificing a hand to save Quintus and Martius. In contrast to *their* stress on family (Lucius: "Sweet father, if I shall be thought thy son, / Let me redeem my brothers both from death"; Marcus: "And for our father's sake, and mother's care, / Now let me show a brother's love to thee," 3.1.179–82), Aaron revels in his remoteness from such concern:

> I go, Andronicus; and for thy hand
> Look by and by to have thy sons with thee.
> (*Aside*) Their heads, I mean. O, how this villainy
> Doth fat me with the very thoughts of it!

At this point, as we know from his later account in 5.1.112–13, he laughs to himself, in as chilling tones as an actor can manage, and concludes: "Let fools do good, and fair men call for grace; / Aaron will have his soul black like his face" (3.1.199–204). Here, he combines several images of evil: the Vice as deceiver and double-dealer, a demi-devil entirely apart from the feelings of men; the Machiavellian knave who thinks himself superior to the naïve folly of doing good; and the black marked by his very color as of the devil's party.

Standing aside from human feelings, Aaron mocks those who have them. He has no kin: he genuinely occupies the position that Shakespeare's previous villain had only imagined. After killing Henry VI, Richard of Gloucester glories in his evil:

> Then, since the heavens have shaped my body so,
> Let hell make crook'd my mind to answer it.
> I had no father, I am like no father;
> I have no brother, I am like no brother;
> And this word "love," which graybeards call divine
> Be resident in men like one another
> And not in me: I am myself alone.
>
> (*3 Henry VI,* 5.6.78–84)

But Richard of Gloucester does in fact have kin, including both a father and a brother whose death he has wanted sorely to avenge. In *Titus Andronicus* Aaron, precisely because he is black, visibly stands on his own, unconnected by blood with anyone else in the play. He starts from the place Richard reaches by the end of *3 Henry VI:* he indulges in evil purely for its own sake, and he proves by contrast, by his exultant inhumanity, that to be human is at the very least to situate oneself in relation to one's kin.

And to be more than minimally human is to be capable of a compassion that extends beyond one's immediate family, a capacity all the more precious in *Titus Andronicus* because so rare. Molly Mahood brilliantly identifies the telling role of bit parts in every play in the Folio but *Titus Andronicus.*[39] She might have noted the messenger who at 3.1.233–39 brings

Titus his sons' heads and prefigures the servant of Cornwall who kills his master—and forfeits his own life—for blinding Gloucester in another frequently heartless tragic world. The Messenger deplores his message ("ill art thou repaid. . . . Thy grief their sports") and commiserates with more sorrow for Titus than even for his own family's loss: "woe is me to think upon thy woes, / More than remembrance of my father's death." This incidental messenger, unwillingly delivering to Titus the punchline of Aaron's most gratuitously cruel joke, represents the play's fleeting norm of human decency and stands in pointed antithesis to the Aaron whose inhumanity he reluctantly serves.

When Titus receives only his sons' heads in exchange for his hand, Marcus expects from him an aria of despair, but, strained beyond breaking point, Titus can utter only a spine-tingling laugh that unexpectedly echoes Aaron's grim guffaw as he tricked Titus of his hand. As Muriel Bradbrook notes, this is the turning point of the play, for Titus now asks: "which way shall I find Revenge's cave?" (3.1.269).[40] Seeking retribution for his family, the man of integrity will now descend into deeds as cruel as those of the man of iniquity who can laugh so heartlessly because he remains so free from human bonds.

Until, that is, the surprise of Aaron's third phase in the play, when he discovers Tamora has given birth to his black babe.[41]

He had been the intimate of the empress and the adviser of Chiron and Demetrius. Suddenly all three stress their distance from him in their eagerness to dissociate themselves from and obliterate the evidence of Tamora's black child. Suddenly, for the first time, Aaron knows what human closeness means, and how little he had had of it even in the pleasures he had shared with Tamora:

> My mistress is my mistress, this myself,
> The vigour and the picture of my youth:
> This before all the world do I prefer;
> This maugre all the world will I keep safe.
>
> (4.2.107–10)

By unexpectedly switching Aaron from contrast to parallel, Shakespeare both expands and tightens the play's focus at a single stroke.

As a variation on Tamora's response to the sacrifice of her "first-born son" (1.1.120) and Titus's to the suffering of his children, Aaron's utter and utterly unexpected concern for *his* "first-born son and heir" (4.2.92) fixes the theme of parental protectiveness. The very universality of that impulse had of course made Titus's plight in 3.1 so powerful, as he has to bear the calamities that befall first two of his sons, then another, then his daughter, and then the two sons again, and all the more disquieting because in mocking his grief Aaron had seemed so diabolically distant from human sympathy. Now he has become as committed to guarding his child as Titus has been to saving his adult sons.[42]

To protect her own, Tamora wants the babe put to death at once. She is as unconcerned about Aaron's son as Titus had been about hers when he ordered the sacrifice of Alarbus. To the Andronici, Alarbus had been only a prisoner, an enemy of Rome, a barbarian; to the Goths, Aaron's son—they cannot think of the babe as kin—is only black, "as loathsome as a toad / Among the fair-faced breeders of our clime" (4.2.67–68). Indignant when the Romans killed her son, Tamora now coolly expects Aaron to kill his own. If Alarbus was a mere Goth to the Romans, Aaron's child seems to the Goths not one of theirs—in fact only a threat to them all—and as remote from them as if he belonged to another species, a mere "tadpole" for Demetrius to "broach . . . on my rapier's point" (4.2.85).

Defending "my flesh and blood," Aaron taunts Tamora's sons with their kinship with the babe:

> Stay, murderous villains; will you kill your brother?
> . . . .
> Look how the black slave smiles upon the father,
> As who should say, "Old lad, I am thine own."
> He is your brother, lords, sensibly fed
> Of that self blood that first gave life to you,
> And from that womb where you imprisoned were
> He is enfranchisèd and come to light.
> Nay, he is your brother by the surer side,
> Although my seal be stampèd in his face.
>
> (4.2.88, 120–27)

Yet for all the tenderness of the father doting on his newborn babe, Aaron is not softened in the least by his child. In a superb theatrical moment, Shakespeare has him hold his babe in his arms as he kills the nurse whose garrulousness might endanger the boy; he even mocks her as she dies. The solicitude of parent for child that had seemed so poignant in 3.1 need have nothing to do with tenderness: it can be the rawest of animal instincts, the tiger ferociously guarding her cubs.

Shakespeare treats parental protectiveness as the primal impulse of concern toward another. And in evolutionary terms that have been clarified only over the last forty years, this is precisely true: altruism, which is difficult to explain in evolutionary terms (how would an organism thrive by serving another's genes at the expense of its own?)[43] yet has unquestionably evolved, can get its first foothold only through a strong degree of genetic relatedness.

Admirable though the impulse to protect kin may be in its own way, it is nevertheless a kind of moral minimum, necessary but far from sufficient, potentially little beyond the bestial or the barbarous, since it can allow us, in the need to protect our own, to treat others—a Gothic prince, a blackamoor babe, a nurse—as completely disposable, as if they did not matter to *their* kin. For true human morality to evolve, the sense of kinship had to extend gradually beyond the immediate family but does so very slowly, so that as Richard Alexander expresses it, the great moral problem consequent on humanity's evolved heritage is that in-group amity grows most readily only at the cost of out-group enmity: the "altruistic" urge to protect even an ever-wider group nevertheless means a readiness to attack those who fall outside this circle of allegiance.[44]

Through Aaron's fierce loyalty to his babe, therefore, after his earlier sense of isolation from *all* others, Shakespeare probes the heart of his play and the heart of human morality: the contrast between kindness and unkindness, concern for our kind and unconcern for others. Throughout his three history plays to date, he had explored the tension between the fierce loyalties uniting and the fierce hostilities dividing English and French, red rose and white, Margaret and her kind and Richard of York and his. Now, in Aaron's ruthless defense of his son, he focuses the tensions in *Titus Andronicus* between Titus and Tamora, Romans and Goths, civilized and barbarian, white and black.

When Tamora and Aaron, in their different ways, identify only with their own and think nothing of another's death, their behavior casts a powerful new light back on the sacrifice of Alarbus. At that early point in the play, we could not be sure, despite the protests of Tamora and her sons, whether or not the sacrifice was simply to be accepted as part of the *romanitas* of Titus's world. But seen in the light of Tamora's bidding Aaron to "christen" his son with his "dagger's point" (4.2.70), or Aaron's casually skewering the nurse, the readiness of the Andronici to sacrifice a live Goth in order to secure peace for their own dead kin—and despite the pleas of his mother—looks unmistakably dubious.[45] Solemnly following their Roman rituals, the Andronici implicitly affirm the dignity of their civilization and the barbarity and insignificance of those who stand outside it. But that very dismissal of the other, like Tamora's of the child, or Aaron's of the nurse, is less the sign of civilization they suppose than proof that unthinking barbarity may lurk all too near.[46]

Aaron's blackamoor babe, central though he may be to the play's sense, is a theatrical surprise. But where Peele notoriously can introduce surprises without preparation and forethought, without even much thought for the consequence, as in Titus's killing of Mutius, Shakespeare prepares *his* surprises well. The first clearly Shakespearean speech in the play readies us for the discovery of the love-child by making Tamora's first speech to Aaron so voluptuously amorous, so emphatically venereal. But more than that, Shakespeare shows throughout the language of this, his first scene, that his mind cannot stop racing ahead to Tamora's and Aaron's child. Tamora's speech ends:

> We may, each wreathèd in the other's arms,
> Our pastimes done, posses a golden slumber,
> While hounds and horns and sweet melodious birds
> Be unto us as is a nurse's song
> Of lullaby, to bring her babe asleep.
>
> (2.3.25–29)

Aaron's immediate response is jarring enough ("Madam, though Venus govern your desires, / Saturn is dominator over mine") but nothing compared with his later scimitar-thrust to silence the nurse who has just handed him his baby.

Later in this first Shakespearean scene, Lavinia implores Tamora in vain to save her from rape, then enjoins first Demetrius, then Chiron, to "entreat her show a woman's pity." Chiron retorts: "What, wouldst thou have me prove myself a bastard?" Lavinia responds eloquently and aptly, but we can see Shakespeare's imagination flitting ahead once again to Tamora's black "bastard":

> Tis true, the raven doth not hatch a lark;
> Yet I have heard,—O, could I find it now!—
> The lion, moved with pity, did endure
> To have his princely paws all pared away.
> Some say that ravens foster forlorn children
> The whilst their own birds famish in their nests.
> O, be to me, though thy hard heart say no,
> Nothing so kind, but something pitiful.
>
> (2.3.149–56)

Here Aaron's black babe, his helpfulness toward Chiron and Demetrius *until* he has his own babe to care for, and Tamora's and her sons' utter refusal to foster Aaron's child—their eagerness, indeed, to thrust it at once from the nest—all peep through Shakespeare's images. When Aaron promises to send Martius and Quintus back if one of the Andronici will supply a severed hand in payment, Titus's gleeful response confirms that Lavinia's raven and lark had subliminally aimed at Aaron: "O gentle Aaron! / Did ever raven sing so like a lark . . . ?" (3.1.157–58)

For all the unexpectedness of Aaron's son, then, Shakespeare has him in mind from the first as a focus for the theme of concern for our kind and unconcern for others. But he complicates the issue still further in Aaron's last major scene, his capture by Lucius in 5.1.

Placed in unexpected parallel to Titus and Tamora in his protectiveness of his child in 4.2, Aaron now moves again into ironic contrast. Unlike the Tamora who will soon eat her own children, or the Titus who has buried more than a score of sons and will be driven to kill his one daughter, Aaron manages, through sheer unscrupulousness, to save his child.

Here again Shakespeare shows he has anticipated all along the surprise of Aaron's son and his absolute commitment to preserving it, not only in terms of the imagery above but even in his very choice of his character's name. As we have seen, his Aaron is pointedly contrasted in his isolation, in a play crowded with brothers, with Aaron the brother of Moses. But if the biblical Aaron is a brother, he is also seen again and again in conjunction with his sons, the first lineage of high priests. Where Alarbus is sacrificed, and Titus's children die in retaliation, Aaron keeps his own son alive, unlike his biblical forebear:

> And Moses and Aaron went into the tabernacle of the congregation, and came out, and blessed the people: and the glory of the LORD appeared unto all the people. And there came a fire out from before the LORD, and consumed upon the altar the burnt offering and the fat, *which* when all the people saw, they shouted, and fell on their faces.
>
> And Nadab and Abihu, the sons of Aaron, took either of them his censer, and put fire therein, and put incense thereon, and offered strange fire before the LORD, which he commanded them not. And there went out fire from the LORD, and devoured them, and they died before the LORD. Then Moses said unto Aaron, This *is it* that the LORD spake, saying, I will be sanctified in them that come nigh me, and before all the people I will be glorified. And Aaron held his peace. (Leviticus 9:23–24, 10:1–2))

In 5.1, Lucius orders the babe to be hanged with his father. Caught but not cowed, Aaron commands: "Touch not the boy; he is of royal blood." "Too like the sire for ever being good," rejoins Lucius, ordering: "First hang the child, that he may see it sprawl— / A sight to vex the father's soul withal" (5.1.49–52). As in 1.1, where he requested the sacrifice of Alarbus, Lucius cannot see the rights of those who stand against Rome. But Aaron makes a cynical bargain that relies on Lucius's commitment to his values: he will confess all, though he believes in no gods himself, if Lucius will swear by *his* gods to spare the child's life. (Here in Aaron's defiant atheism is a further irony in his being named after the first of the Israelite high priests: Shakespeare's onomastic wit has still to be appreciated at full value.) Lucius swears, and Aaron, secure in the knowledge that he has saved his son,[47] gleefully runs through the catalog of his crimes, those we have seen and those we had never suspected, reaffirming his commitment to evil: he has done "a thousand dreadful things . . . And nothing grieves me heartily indeed, / But that I cannot do ten thousand more" (5.1.141–44).

Shakespeare builds ambivalence into the survival of Aaron's son. Aaron exults in his own evil even as he proves his commitment to his child; Lucius, on the other hand, precisely because of his revulsion against evil, had been ready to hang the child without hesitation. In Lucius's hostile perspective, as in Aaron's hopeful one, the babe's survival might mean the persistence of evil, but perhaps it could be seen more objectively (and more Shakespeareanly) as innocence given a chance. Even as he glories in his misdeeds, Aaron may actually allow a real good that a good man, in his antipathy toward evil, almost expunges.

Douglas Parker has argued that the survival of Aaron's and Tamora's child is "a symbol of the perpetuation of the evil that the play has dramatized," an interpretation that has been incorporated, in an age that deems pessimism *a priori* profound, into several productions of the play.[48] But there is no textual warrant for this, no guarantee that a black (or a Gothic) child will be evil. Blackness may be vividly associated with *Aaron*'s particular evil, but as should be evident from the Prince of Morocco, Othello, and even Aaron's countryman Muly[49] in *Titus Andronicus,* Shakespeare makes no presumption that blackness of race means vileness of character, and there is no evidence anywhere in his work that he thinks the sins of the parent pass to the newborn child.

And it need hardly be demonstrated that Shakespeare thinks little—and makes much—of the murder of innocent children: Rutland, the princes in the tower, Prince Arthur, all Macduff's little ones, Perdita's narrow escape. Lucius has no more qualms about killing Aaron's son than about sacrificing Tamora's. Neither he nor his father responded to Tamora's plea for Alarbus, but now he needs Aaron's confession. Although reluctant, he at last agrees to swear by his gods—even as Aaron mocks them—that he will spare the child, and he will abide by his oath.[50] His commitment to his beliefs is admirable in its way, as is Aaron's to his son. But Aaron's devotion to his own means little when coupled with his delight in evil and disdain for all Lucius holds good. And even Lucius's commitment to his own values reveals its limitations when it makes him so ready to dispose not only of Aaron but even of an innocent child.

Lucius's earnest belief in his Roman values cannot be compared to Aaron's gleeful evil, but the commitment to one's own *because* one's own, though natural, is not enough, if it means a failure to allow for others.[51] And yet Lucius's position, though not morally impregnable, could not be more different from Aaron's positively reveling in others' woes.

For that reason, although Shakespeare incorporates ambivalence into the survival of Aaron's child, he invites none toward the punishments meted out to Aaron and Tamora and her children: they get what they deserve. The horrors of the revenge Titus and Lavinia exact on Tamora and her sons reflect the horrors they have suffered, and at the end of the play the assembled Romans explicitly approve their response.[52] In sacrificing Alarbus, the Andronici were guilty of a lapse in pity (although as Lavinia points out, Titus would have been within his military rights to put *all* his prisoners to death),[53] but it was of a different order from the willful, mocking pitilessness Aaron and the Goths showed to the innocent Lavinia, Bassianus, Martius, and Quintus. The conduct of Tamora's party has set the standards by which they should be treated. The morality is that of the Good Duke Humphrey in *2 Henry VI,* who when falsely accused of devising "Strange tortures for offenders," replies, with Shakespeare's obvious admiration:

> Why, 'tis well known that, while I was Protector,
> Pity was all the fault that was in me:
> For I should melt at an offender's tears . . .
> Unless it were a bloody murderer
> Or foul felonious thief that fleeced poor passengers . . . .
> Murder indeed, that bloody sin, I tortured
> Above the felon or what trespass else.
>
> (3.1.124–32)[54]

Once Titus completes his revenge, at the cost of his own life, and once Lucius is named emperor, as if to restore a future forfeited at the outset of the play, a coda sums up the action and the principle of contrast by which Shakespeare has shaped Aaron. Lucius and his son ceremoniously kiss the dead Titus, and recall his tenderness; the dead Tamora, with scraps of her sons inside her, will be thrown to the beasts and birds, since "Her life was beastly and devoid of pity" (5.3.198); Aaron, though his child still lives, will never see him again, but be buried breast-deep in the earth and left to starve, and "If anyone relieves or pities him / For the offence he dies."

On hearing the sentence, Aaron bursts forth one last time:

> Ah, why should wrath be mute and fury dumb?
> I am no baby, I, that with base prayers
> I should repent the evils I have done. . . .
>
> (5.3.180–85)

Throughout the last act Shakespeare sets up one final contrast that extends and reverses our first impression of Aaron. In 1.1 he had been prominently present but totally silent, until the end, when, left alone on stage, at the beginning of what we now call 2.1, he disclosed himself as the empress's lover and an eloquent villain, and proposed to the empress's sons the rape that would leave Lavinia as silent as he just had been, for the rest of the play, for the rest of her life. Now, in the final act, Shakespeare returns to the contrast between speechlessness—Aaron's wordless babe, the tongueless Lavinia who cannot charge Aaron with the crimes he controlled—and the Moor's own unstoppable talk. Although Aaron begins the act stubbornly silent ("Say, wall-eyed slave, . . . Why dost not speak? What, deaf? Not a word?" 5.1.44–46), once he agrees to confess he wants no end to his catalog of crimes or his litany of curses: "So I might have your company in hell, / But to torment you with my bitter tongue," 5.1.149–50; "Some devil whisper curses in my ear, / And prompt me that my tongue may utter forth / The venomous malice of my swelling heart," 5.3.11–13; "Ah, why should wrath be mute and fury dumb? / I am no baby, I. . . . " Shakespeare juxtaposes the child Aaron has damaged most, the even more helpless child he has managed to protect, and the voice of his own unrepentant evil.[55]

Shakespeare did not need Aaron for his revenge plot, and he may have added him in the first instance for the shiver of evil a character like Barabas or a role like the Vice could produce. But he soon went far beyond that. By making Aaron black, so visibly without family ties to anyone else in his world, and then by giving him a son, Shakespeare found a way to explore the very basis of the revenge plot—pity for one's own, pitilessness for others—and to probe its implications as searchingly as he could. No other revenge play examines so insistently our human habit of identifying with our own and our human hesitation about seeing others as also, in some measure, our own.

In biological evolution, a secondary and ultimately major function may often develop from a body part that had first evolved for another purpose: vertebrate jaws from gill arches, wings from thermoregulatory flaps. In the same way, a character whom Shakespeare may have sought primarily for his ebullient evil began to serve another function—of contrast, energy, concentration, extension—that the dramatist could consciously develop in future plays. With Aaron, Shakespeare's versos had begun to evolve.

Although through Aaron Shakespeare can at times expand revenge tragedy into a far wider exploration of the human condition than the conventions of the genre usually invite, not all of *Titus Andronicus* transcends its origins. The arrows scenes (4.3–4.4) and the Revenge-disguise scene (5.2) seem designed to fulfill revenge tragedy formulae as rigid as the car chases of Hollywood action movies.

Despite some emblematic aptness, these scenes show Shakespeare relying on external ingredients, classical allusions, and generic devices. But one other emblematic scene reveals a different Shakespeare. 3.2, omitted from the 1594 Quarto, was first published in the Folio. Widely accepted as a later addition, it is likely, according to vocabulary tests, to have been composed by Shakespeare several years after the rest of the play, at approximately the same time as *Richard II* and *Romeo and Juliet.*[56]

In this short scene Shakespeare approaches his mature manner—already anticipated in the Aaron scenes—of concentrating contrasts through what his story already provides. Here he sets up a poignant family banquet in pointed anticipation of and opposition to the banquet in which another kind of family closeness—a mother eating her own children—provides the play's stomach-turning climax. Where at the end of the play Titus will coolly feed Chiron and Demetrius to their mother, here, with his one remaining hand, he tenderly feeds his handless and tongueless daughter.

In the midst of 3.2's banquet, Marcus unexpectedly lunges at a dish with his knife. When the overwrought Titus discovers that Marcus has killed a fly, he cries out against his brother as a murderer. He has seen too much tyranny: "A deed of death done on the innocent / Becomes not Titus' brother. Get thee gone" (3.2.56–57). Marcus points out he has "but killed a fly."

> "But"? How if that fly had a father, brother?[57]
> How would he hang his slender gilded wings,
> And buzz lamenting doings in the air!
> Poor harmless fly. . . .
>
> (3.2.59–63)

Here Titus views the fly as innocent victim, and part of a nexus of concern. Able to see an image of his own plight in that of the fly's imagined father, he can feel affinity with and compassion for even the lowliest of creatures.

To dispel his brother's disapproval, Marcus tells him "it was a black ill-favoured fly, / Like to the Empress' Moor; therefore I killed him." Instantly Titus changes his attitude:

> . . . . pardon me for reprehending thee,
> For thou hast done a charitable deed.
> Give me thy knife; I will insult on him,
> Flattering myself as if it were the Moor
> Come hither purposely to poison me.
>
> (3.2.66–73)

The fly who may have a father earns Titus's pity, but when he imagines it as Aaron, the idea of family connection suddenly disappears. He now sees the fly in terms not of likeness to himself but of the inhuman otherness of the other, as something alien, to be killed without remorse.

Shakespeare appears to have added this scene to rectify a defect in the construction of the play. Although Aaron is the "chief architect and plotter" of Titus's woes, although he is such a dominant presence late in the play, Titus's revenge includes not a single move against him. From the point of view of pure plot, this is hardly surprising: while Aaron's role is apparent to us from the first, and he boasts of his crimes when Lucius captures him, Titus dies before hearing his son's report of Aaron's confession. Indeed, were he to have heard Aaron's confession, he would have far less reason to focus all the fury of his revenge on serving up Chiron and Demetrius to their mother.

But to compensate for this lack of engagement between hero and villain, Shakespeare adds 3.2, immediately after the one scene where the two confront each other. Although he lacks our evidence of Aaron's malice, Titus here at least has strong reason to suspect that Aaron has deliberately tricked him of his hand in exchange for no more than the heads of his sons. Shakespeare therefore sets Titus against Aaron in the next scene in a way that will not require altering the rest of the plot and that can offer a painful image of Titus's advancing madness and a gentle contrast to the play's gruesome final banquet. And in Titus's two reactions to the fly Shakespeare can sum up the clash between concern for one's own and callousness to others that shapes his play. Confident he has constructed Aaron to embody the tension between kind and unkindness, he can now compress his focal function into the minute compass of "a fly / That comes in likeness of a coal-black Moor." (3.2.76–77)

Notes

1. Cf. Emrys Jones: "I have always previously believed in the Shakespearian 'integrity' of *Titus Andronicus,* but in the light of Jackson's coolly measured and implacably rational presentation of different kinds of evidence, I am wholly persuaded" of Peele's authorship of act 1: "Reclaiming Early Shakespeare," *Essays in Criticism* 41 (2001): 35–50: 39.

2. The mid-twentieth-century assumption that either the ballad "Titus Andronicus' Complaint" or the prose *History of Titus Andronicus* was a source for the play has now been shown to be wrong: Shakespeare invented the story, the ballad was composed shortly afterwards, and the prose history then expanded on the ballad. For the decisive recent arguments, see Marco Mincoff, "The Source of *Titus Andronicus,*" *Notes and Queries* 216 (1971): 131–34; G. K. Hunter, "Sources and Meanings in *Titus Andronicus,*" in J. C. Gray, ed., *Mirror up to Shakespeare: Essays in Honour of G. R. Hibbard* (Toronto: Univ. of Toronto Press, 1984), 171–88; MacDonald P. Jackson, "The Year's Contributions to Shakespearian Study: 3. Edition and Textual Studies," *Shakespeare Survey* 38 (1985): 238–54; Jackson, "*Titus Andronicus:* Play, Ballad, And Prose History," *NQ* 234 (1989): 315–17; Jonathan Bate, ed., *Titus Andronicus* (London: Routledge, 1995), 83–85; Brian Boyd, "The Blackamoor Babe: *Titus Andronicus,* Play, Ballad, and History," *NQ* 242 (1997), 492–94.

3. Brian Boyd, "Common Words in *Titus Andronicus:* The Presence of Peele," (*NQ* 240 (1995): 300–07; MacDonald P. Jackson, "Stage Directions and Speech Headings in Act 1 of *Titus Andronicus* Q (1594): Shakespeare or Peele?" *Studies in Bibliography* 49 (1996): 134–48; Ward Elliott and Robert J. Valenza, "And Then There Were None: Winnowing the Shakespeare Claimants," *Computers and the Humanities* 30 (1996): 191–245; Jackson,

"Shakespeare's brothers and Peele's brethren: *Titus Andronicus* again," *NQ* 242 (1997): 494–95; John Jowett, "The Year's Contribution to Shakespeare Studies: Editions and Textual Studies," *Shakespeare Survey* 50 (1997): 267–90; Jackson, "Indefinite Articles in *Titus Andronicus,* Peele, and Shakespeare," *NQ* 243 (1998): 308–10; MacD.P. Jackson, "Determining Authorship: A New Technique," *Research Opportunities in Renaissance Drama* 41 (2002): 1–15; Brian Vickers, *Shakespeare, Co-Author: A History of Five Collaborative Plays* (Oxford: Oxford Univ. Press, 2002), 148–243.

4. "The Canon and Chronology of Shakespeare's Plays," in Stanley Wells and Gary Taylor with John Jowett and William Montgomery, *William Shakespeare: A Textual Companion* (Oxford: Oxford Univ. Press, 1987), 114.

5. I have slightly rephrased the abstract of "Mutius: An Obstacle Removed in *Titus Andronicus,*" *Review of English Studies* 54 (2003), forthcoming.

6. Larry S. Champion, *Shakespeare's Tragic Perspective* (Athens: Univ. of Georgia Press, 1976), 21, 17, 20. Typical of those who consider Aaron "peculiarly Shakespearian" is J. C. Maxwell, ed., *Titus Andronicus* (1953; London: Methuen, 1961), xxx.

7. See Brian Boyd, "*King* John and *The Troublesome* Raigne: Sources, Structure, Sequence," *Philological Quarterly* 74 (1995): 37–56, pp. 50–53. In time between other, non-Shakespearean, projects, I am developing in *Shakespeare Shapes Here* the evidence for this new kind of character, who owes much to Elizabethan patterns of multiple plotting, but is usually not part of a separable plot. Shakespeare constructs this "verso" (the reverse, as it were, of the characters on the "recto" of the source's *Dramatis Personae,* and a descendant of the Vice) as a deliberate simultaneous contrast to all the characters of his base story, in order to focus, condense, and enliven a source, to define by contrast its usually bland characters, to concentrate key ideas implicit in the story, and to inject theatrical energy. Versos run from Aaron and the Bastard to Bottom, Falstaff, Shallow (since Falstaff is a given by the time Shakespeare starts thinking of *2 Henry IV*), Jaques, Polonius, Malvolio, Parolles, Lucio, Cloten, Autolycus, and Caliban.

8. See Taylor, 114.

9. The Folio text reads "Men"; though the overall sense is clear, emendation is necessary. "Even," "E'en," "Mean," and "Meet" have been proposed; I suggest "Mere" as being orthographically more plausible, more appropriate in sense (the adjective for the adverb, in the sense of "purely," "entirely," as in *All's Well That Ends Well,* 3.5.54: "Ay, surely, mere the truth"; cf OED "mere *adv.*"), and all the likelier for the "Mere . . . more" play that would frame the line.

10. Michael Hattaway, ed., *The Third Part of King Henry VI* (Cambridge: Cambridge Univ. Press, 1993), 2.5.117–20.

11. Mincoff, *Shakespeare: The First Steps* (Sofia: Bulgarian Academy of Sciences, 1976), 133. All quotations from *Titus Andronicus* are from the Oxford edition, ed. Eugene Waith (Oxford: Oxford Univ. Press, 1984). Although the Priam reference comes from Peele's 1.1, Shakespeare as author of the plot must have decided on the size of Titus's family and explained to Peele its rationale.

12. See John Dover Wilson, ed., *Titus Andronicus* (Cambridge: Cambridge Univ. Press, 1948), 118.

13. Though this phrase comes from 3.2, a scene Shakespeare wrote some years later than the rest of the play (see below), the original scenes also refer to Aaron's "coal-black" hue at 4.2.99 and 5.1.32.

14. Mincoff even says: "*Titus Andronicus* was the substitute for the conclusion to *Henry VI* that Shakespeare was, for the time, prevented from writing" (*First Steps,* 121).

15. Mincoff, *First Steps,* 116–17. Bate, *Titus Andronicus,* 85–86, provides an even more elaborate list of parallels.

16. Saturninus asks of Titus, whose sons have helped Bassianus abduct Lavinia, "Was *none* in Rome *to make a stale but* Saturnine?" in close echo of Warwick's lament after his

arranging Edward's marriage to the Lady Bona comes to naught: "Had he *none* else *to make a stale but* me?" Peele, as Dover Wilson comments (*Titus Andronicus,* xxx), frequently borrowed lines from others.

17. Mincoff, *First Steps,* 121.

18. In Arthur Golding's translation, as Anthony Brian Taylor shows in "Shakespeare's Use of Golding's Ovid as Source for *Titus Andronicus,*" *NQ* 233 (1988): 449–51; see also Bate, *Shakespeare and Ovid.*

19. Hunter, "Sources," 184.

20. Hunter, "Sources," 182–88. Hunter's discovery (186) of the source (in Herodian) and implications (in Holinshed) of the coupling of Saturninus and Bassianus is particularly telling.

21. *First Steps,* 132.

22. Notice that Chiron and Demetrius, though barbarians, alone in the play have Greek names, as if in echo of the "subtle Greeks [who] surprised Priam's Troy" (5.3.83).

23. Richard of Gloucester, in the soliloquy that first discloses his intent to snatch the crown, explains that he will "like a Sinon, take another Troy. . . . And set the murderous Machiavel to school" (*3 Henry VI,* 3.3.190, 193). Aaron, the Machiavel in Shakespeare's next play, also sneaks into Rome with the Roman equivalent of the Trojan whore.

24. Many commentators have noted the ambitiousness of Shakespeare's competitive imitation in *Titus Andronicus:* see for instance A. C. Hamilton, in 1963, who comments that Shakespeare "seeks to overgo Ovid" (and Seneca and Kyd), "*Titus Andronicus:* The Form of Shakespearian Tragedy," *Shakespeare Quarterly* 14 (1963): 201–13, p. 207; Leonard Barkan, "*Craftier* than Tereus, *worse* than Philomel, *better* than Philomel, *worse* than Procne: this is mythology viewed in the competitive mode. And the author is the most avid competitor," in *The Gods Made Flesh: Metamorphosis & the Pursuit of Paganism* (New Haven: Yale Univ. Press, 1986), 244.

25. Though sorely irked when Bassianus takes the Lavinia he has claimed for himself, Saturninus later becomes inflamed with anger at his brother's death (2.3.281–85) and at Titus's protests against the execution of Martius and Quintus (4.4.52–56).

26. This is not to deny that, as written by Peele, 1.1 is often less an enactment than a catalog of events, with a "tableau-like grouping of characters" (Mincoff, *First Steps,* 124) that bears out one of Peele's editor's comments: "Peele's genius is not essentially dramatic; he seems generally to conceive his scenes as spectacles" (Frank S. Hook, ed., *The Dramatic Works of George Peele* [New Haven: Yale Univ. Press, 1961], 46).

27. See Boyd, "Mutius," (forthcoming); and see Vickers, *Shakespeare, Co-Author,* ch. 3, for the role Peele's Latin scholarship may have played in shaping some of the details of act 1, scene 1.

28. See n. 6 and text.

29. As noted by Wolfgang Keller, "*Titus Andronicus,*" *Shakespeare Jahrbuch* 74 (1938): 137–62: 140.

30. Aaron has no necessary part in that there is already a tight chain of revenge cause and effect: after the sacrifice of Alarbus, Tamora and her sons have motive and character to exact gruesomely disproportionate revenges on the Andronici, who then have motive to exact grisly but perhaps not disproportionate revenges on the Goths. See n. 5 and text, and below.

31. For reproductions of the drawing, see Waith (Oxford *Titus*), 21, or Bate (Arden *Titus*), 39. June Schlueter has recently proposed that Henry Peacham's drawing represents not Shakespeare's *Titus Andronicus* but a sequence in *Ein sehr klägkliche Tragœdia von Tito Andronico und der hoffertigen Käyserin* (*A Very Lamentable Tragedy of Titus Andronicus and the Haughty Empress*), which, she suggests, may be the German version of the lost "tittus & vespacia" recorded in Henslowe's diary in 1592 ("Rereading the Peacham Drawing," *Shakespeare Quarterly* 50 [1999]: 171–84). But although the drawing *could* represent the

Tragædia von Tito Andronico, it still seems more likely to be a stylized composite of scenes from *Titus Andronicus,* whose text, after all, has been excerpted to provide an extended "caption."

32. This is the burden of Bernard Spivack's *Shakespeare and the Allegory of Evil: The History of a Metaphor in Relation to His Major Villains* (New York: Columbia Univ. Press, 1958); see esp. 303. For a more recent study of Shakespeare and the Vice tradition, see Alan C. Dessen, *Shakespeare and the Late Moral Plays* (Lincoln: Univ. of Nebraska Press, 1986).

33. Lois Potter, "The Plays and the Playwrights," in Norman Sanders et al., *Revels History of Drama in English, II: 1500–1576* (London: Methuen, 1980), 247.

34. See Fredson Bowers, *Elizabethan Revenge Tragedy, 1587–1642* (1940; rpt. Gloucester, Mass.: Peter Smith, 1959), 117–18; Kristian Smidt, *Unconformities in Shakespeare's Tragedies* (London: Macmillan, 1989), 25.

35. Spivack, *Evil,* 57–59, 383–84.

36. Aaron himself finds his race much more amusing: when the nurse asks has anyone seen Aaron the Moor he replies "Well, more or less, or ne'er a whit at all" (4.2.52–53), punning on *white* as well as *Moor,* as Alan Hughes, ed., *Titus Andronicus* (Cambridge: Cambridge Univ. Press, 1994), notes, 111.

37. A point made by Eldred Jones ("his complete isolation," *Othello's Countrymen,* Oxford: Oxford Univ. Press, 1965, 57) and Jacques Berthoud ("The one figure of the play who seems entirely to have evaded emotional dependence on others is Aaron," introduction to *Titus Andronicus,* ed. Sonia Massai, London: Penguin, 2001, 40).

38. Cf. for instance Demetrius, less than two hundred lines after he had protested his love for Lavinia, urging his mother not to kill her before they rape her: "First thresh the corn, then after burn the straw. / This minion stood upon her chastity" (2.3.123–24).

39. *Bit Parts in Shakespeare's Plays* (Cambridge: Cambridge Univ. Press, 1992), 223 n. 2.

40. *Shakespeare and Elizabethan Poetry* (New York: Oxford Univ. Press, 1952), 105–6.

41. Champion sees the babe as no more than "a deus ex machina maneuver to separate [Tamora and Aaron] and thus prepare the empress for what we later learn will be her fate" (*Perspective,* 23).

42. Berthoud also stresses the force of the contrast: "the autonomous Aaron is turned inside-out by the upsurge of the instinct of paternity" (in Massai, Penguin *Titus,* 53).

43. The technical biological definition of altruism is a benefit delivered to another's genes at a cost to one's own.

44. Alexander, *Darwinism and Human Affairs* (Seattle: Univ. of Washington Press, 1979), 17. See also Leonard D. Katz, ed., *Evolutionary Origins of Morality: Cross-Disciplinary Perspectives* (Thorverton: Imprint Academic, 2000).

45. Eugene Waith argues: "We must sympathize, though we are given very little time to do so, with [Tamora's] protest against Titus's inflexibility: 'O cruel, irreligious piety!'" ("The Metamorphosis of Violence in *Titus Andronicus,*" *Shakespeare Survey* 10 [1957]: 44). In 1984, he adds that "The Peacham drawing is evidence that her prayer was, not only verbally but visually, an arresting moment" ("The Ceremonies of *Titus Andronicus,*" in Gray, *Mirror,* 161). Champion comments: "The human sacrifice is never justified; the occasional comments that these are rites enacted to appease the dead simply fail to provide the rationale so distinctly needed when the action has been openly challenged; no god's name is invoked, no spiritual efficacy described" (*Perspective,* 11). Mincoff disagrees: "the blood-sacrifice of the opening was never presented as a crime, except by the Goths, but as an ancient and hallowed ritual" (*First Steps,* 116 n.). But Robert S. Miola observes that "The placing of the blunt and vivid English, 'hew his limbs and on a pile,' next to the formal Latinate phrase, '*Ad manes fratrum,*' exposes a fundamental tension in the proceedings: It suggests that Roman ritual is barbaric savagery and blood lust. . . . Tamora challenges Roman *pietas* to encompass those brothers outside the immediate family, to recognize the human identity

that transcends national disputes" ("*Titus Andronicus:* Rome and the Family," *Shakespeare's Rome* [Cambridge: Cambridge Univ. Press], 42–75, cited from 47–48), while Berthoud comments: "Tamora's passionate maternal pleas, inviting the patristic Titus to share her perception of her child's fate, and concluding with the very argument which Portia would use to launch her appeal to Shylock's mercy . . . makes [*sic*] any identification of Titus's perspective with Shakespeare's impossible to sustain. . . . one family's piety is another's atrocity" (Penguin *Titus,* 33).

46. Including, as we shall see, the barbarity of those unthinkingly ready to dismiss Aaron's child's right to life. Vivian Thomas also stresses "the gap between Roman belief in their civilized values and the barbarous action of the sacrifice" (*Shakespeare's Roman Worlds* [London: Routledge, 1989], 31).

47. Aaron, therefore, wins redemption for *his* son through the very piety that led Titus's son to ask for the sacrifice of Tamora's.

48. Douglas H. Parker, "Shakespeare's Use of Comic Conventions in *Titus Andronicus,*" *University of Toronto Quarterly* 56 (1987): 486–97.

49. Muly may be Aaron's invention, a lie that we, if not Chiron and Demetrius, are to see through (Eldred Jones, *Countrymen,* 56–57). I accept J. C. Maxwell's Arden edition reading (after George Steevens) of 4.2.153 as "Muly lives," rather than the Folio and Quarto "Muliteus."

50. There is no textual warrant for Jane Howell in her 1985 BBC television production to stress that Lucius breaks his promise. Shakespeare's Lucius, both admirable, the best man left, and still severely limited, is far more interesting than the BBC's Roman barbarian.

51. For two other recent judgments of Lucius, see Robert S. Miola's and Vivian Thomas's response, in Thomas, *Roman Worlds,* 38.

52. Waith ("Metamorphosis," 46) notes that "Titus, unlike Tamora, is not finally shown as bestial or degenerate. . . . The final comments on his character are all praise and pity," and Mincoff (*First Steps,* 120) rightly stresses that we are invited to root for Titus. But though our attitude toward the revenge may be that it is justified or at least thoroughly understandable in the circumstances, the sacrifice of Alarbus and the readiness to kill Aaron's child must be meant to complicate our responses to the Andronici.

53. He "gave thee life when well he might have slain thee," 2.3.159.

54. Michael Hattaway, ed., *The Second Part of King Henry VI* (Cambridge: Cambridge Univ. Press, 1991).

55. Spivack, *Evil,* 196–97 shows this cocky unrepentance in the face of death to be part of the Vice tradition.

56. Waith, Oxford *Titus,* 41; Gary Taylor, in Taylor and Michael Warren, eds., *The Division of the Kingdom: Shakespeare's Two Versions of King Lear* (Oxford: Clarendon, 1983), 463, 468.

57. Most editors accept this emendation of the F "father and mother."

The Troublesome Raigne, George Peele, and the Date of *King John*

Brian Vickers

> For my own part, I quite enjoy counting things—when some form of demonstration is a likely outcome.[1]

IN 1591 SAMPSON CLARKE PUBLISHED, IN TWO QUARTO VOLUMES, A SUPposedly two-part play, *The Troublesome Raigne of King John, King of England, with the discoverie of King Richard Cordelions Base sonne (vulgarly named, The Bastard Fawconbridge): also the death of King John at Swinstead Abbey,*[2] no author given. Scholars have long observed that it is not really a two-part play, being only 2,936 lines long and consisting of a single dramatic action. Indeed, *Part One* claims to include the death of King John, which does not take place until the final scene in *Part Two.* It seems reasonable to suppose that Clarke was attempting to cash in on the recent success of a genuine two-part play, *Tamburlaine the Great . . . Deuided into two Tragicall Discourses* (1590). The most substantial argument for its authorship was provided in 1919 by H. Dugdale Sykes,[3] who ascribed it to George Peele. In this essay I shall support that ascription, applying some new linguistic tests, and shall take up again the question of priority, arguing that this play does indeed antedate Shakespeare's *King John,* and provided its main source.

I

In arguing that Peele wrote *The Troublesome Raigne,* I must first report that his canon has recently been enlarged by the addition of four scenes in *Titus Andronicus:* Act 1; Act 2, scenes 1 and 2; Act 4, scene 1. Peele's authorship of these scenes, first suggested by T. M. Parrott in 1919, has been confirmed (or so I believe) by a series of scholars, notably P. W. Timberlake, John Dover Wilson, J. C. Maxwell, MacDonald Jackson, and Brian Boyd.[4] Elsewhere I have reviewed the twenty-one separate tests that, so far, have identified Peele as the author of these scenes,[5] and until someone manages to refute all of them he must be granted the status of Shakespeare's first co-author.

It is important to establish this addition to the Peele canon, since one of the determining features in identifying Peele's hand in *Titus Andronicus* was his remarkable liking for self-repetition. As Wilson and Boyd showed, Peele made use of a limited number of formulaic expressions and verbal mannerisms, which he repeated over and over within the same scene, and from one play to the next. The web of intertextual relationships between his four scenes for *Titus Andronicus* and his acknowledged poems and plays is so dense that it more than satisfies the stringent requirements that modern attribution scholars have laid down for the citation of parallel passages.[6] A pioneer in using such evidence to identify the authorship of anonymous Elizabethan plays was H. Dugdale Sykes, and although his work had obvious failings, it was based on an enormous knowledge of the drama. His case for Peele's authorship of *The Troublesome Raigne* rested mainly on verbal parallels. Its weakest part concerned "the more characteristic words of Peele's vocabulary" (108–9), for the dangers of basing an authorship attribution on single words, such as "doom," "sacrifice," or "flatly," were well demonstrated by A. M. Sampley.[7] Nonetheless, while endorsing Sampley's *caveat,* some of these favorite Peele words are unusual, and I suggest that here the collective argument—that he is the only dramatist known to have used all of them—does carry some weight. The word "remunerate" was one of Peele's favorites:[8]

Nobles strive who shall remunerate (*Ed. I,* 140)
We will remunerate his resolution (2036)
To gratifie and to remunerate / Thy love (*Alc.,* 77–78)
to remunerate / Thy worthiness and magnanimitie (352–53)
and will nobly him remunerate (*Titus,* 1.1.398)
thy forwardnes to fight for Holy Rome
Shall be remunerated to the full (*2 T. R.,* 657–58)

Peele was also fond of "gratifie":

To gratifie and to remunerate / Thy love (*Alc.,* 77–78)
To gratify the good Andronicus
And gratulate his safe return to Rome (*Titus,* 1.1.220)
He is in person come at your commaunds
To undertake and gratifie withall
The fulnesse of your favours proffred him (*2 T. R.,* 587)

In each of these instances, "gratify" is doubled up with a verb having a similar meaning: "to gratifie and . . . remunerate," "To gratify . . . And gratulate," "To undertake and gratifie." This verbal habit surely points to a single hand, one given to repetitious writing.

Another favourite Peele word was "pheere" or "fere," a husband or spouse:

> the woeful fere
> And father of that chaste dishonoured dame (*Titus,* 4.1.88–89)
> Fight not in feare as traitors and their pheres (*Alcazar,* 112)
> A lovely Damsel is the Ladie Blanche,
> Worthie the heire of Europe for her Pheere (*1 T. R.,* 777–78)

In his poetry Peele also favored the term "pheere":

> She dreames, and gives her pheere to understand (*Tale of Troy,* 43)
> And Prince Achilles was her fere misnamed (245)
> How when the King her pheere was absent thence (488)

If the Chadwyck-Healey databases are to be trusted, while other Elizabethan dramatists used "gratify" (Greene, Heywood, Marlowe, the author of *Locrine*), "remunerate" (the author of *Locrine,* Yarington), and "pheere" (Gascoigne, Greene, and Lodge, the author of *The Warres of Cyrus*), George Peele was the only one to use all three. As MacDonald Jackson has recently taught us, electronic databases can serve a useful function in narrowing the focus of authorship debates.[9]

Sykes also cited a number of convincing parallels between *The Troublesome Raigne* and Peele's works involving longer sequences of thought and language, such as that presenting the dying words of Arthur, killed in trying to leap down from the castle walls, who seems more concerned "with the grief that his death will cause his mother, rather than his own sensations or sufferings" (Sykes 1919, 107):

> My fall, my fall, hath kilde my Mothers Sonne.
> How will she weepe at tidings of my death? . . .
> Sweet Jesu save my soule, forgive my rash attempt,
> Comfort my Mother, shield her from despaire.
> (*2 T. R.,* 17–21)

Very similarly Absalom, in Peele's biblical tragedy *David and Bethsabe,* "in his dying speech, harps upon the thought of the sorrow that his death will bring to David":

> O my deere father, that thy melting eyes
> Might pierce this thicket to behold thy sonne,
> Thy deerest sonne gor'de with a mortall dart:
> Yet Joab pittie me, pittie my father, Joab,

Pittie his soules distresse that mournes my life,
And will be dead I know to heare my death

(*D&B*, 1533–38)

Sykes instanced several other cases where distinctive phraseology is shared between *The Troublesome Raigne* and Peele's poems and plays. I select three:

(1) Though God and Fortune have bereft from us
Victorious Richard scourge of Infidels,
And clad this Land in stole of dismall hieu [hue] (*1 T. R.*, 2–5)
Melpomene, the muse of tragicke songes,
With moornefull tunes in stole of dismall hue (*AP*, 610–11)
(2) Or if thou knewest what sutes, what threates, what feares,
To moove by love, or massacre by death (*1 T. R.*, 395–96)
What joy, what ease, what rest can lodge in me,
With whom all hope and hap doth disagree? (*1 T. R.*, 870–71)
What tunes, what words, what looks, what wonders pierce
My soule, incensed with a suddaine fire?
What tree, what shade, what spring, what paradise
Enjoyes the beautie of so faire a dame? (*D&B*, 49–52)
(3) lo Lords the withered flowre
Who in his life shinde like the Mornings blush
Cast out of a doore, denide his buriall right (*2 T. R.*, 83–85)
Loe now at last the Greekes have home againe,
With losse of manie a Greeke and Troyans life
Their wither'd flower, King Menelaus' wife.

(*The Tale of Troy*, 475–78)

That third parallel, between Pembroke's exclamation over Arthur's corpse and Peele's conclusion to his brief poetic digest of the Trojan war, comes from the second (1604) edition of the poem, the 1589 Quarto having read "Unhappy Helen, Menelaus's wife." Further, as Sykes pointed out, line 188 of the poem's revised text—"As blithe as bird of morning's light in May"—echoes line 127 of Peele's *Polyhymnia* ("as blithe, as bird of mornings light"), written after November 1590. These two self-borrowings, Sykes argued, "fix the date of *The Troublesome Reign* between April 1589 and 1591, the latter being the year of publication" (120). The recent discussions by Arthur Freeman[10] and Ernst Honigmann also point to "a date of composition for *TR* very close to 1591, its date of publication."[11]

Further verbal resemblances between Peele's dramas and *The Troublesome Raigne* were collected by Rupert Taylor, in a pioneering essay attempting to establish the chronology of five anonymous Elizabethan plays (*The Troublesome Raigne of King John; Arden of Feversham; Soliman and Perseda; The First Part of the Contention between the Houses of York and*

Lancaster; The True Tragedy of Richard Duke of York), and their individual relations to Marlowe's *Edward II* and *The Massacre at Paris.*[12] Taylor was well aware of the objections regularly raised against the use of parallel passages, but his response remains true to this day: "The very words *parallel passages* provoke controversy. The truth, cynically stated, is that everybody uses parallel passages but mistrusts them in the hands of others" (Taylor 1936, 643). Accordingly Taylor refrained from attempting to assign authorship to these anonymous plays. His goal being simply to establish an internal chronology, he assembled lists of close verbal parallels, *inter alia,* between *The Troublesome Raigne* and seven plays: *Edward II* (644–47), Peele's *Edward I* (649–50), *The Jew of Malta* (659), *Dido* (660), *Arden of Feversham* (668–70), *Soliman and Perseda* (674–76), *The True Tragedy* (685–87), and between many of the other plays. No scholar today would attempt to settle chronology on the evidence of parallel passages alone, without an intensive analysis of the plays' language in as many independent tests as can be devised. In fact, Taylor only established that these plays either imitated each other or shared a common language, and scholarship in the intervening sixty-six years has done little to settle that question either way.

But Taylor's data may be reinterpreted to a different purpose. Having accumulated "32 parallels between *The Troublesome Raigne* and *Edward II* and 22 between it and *The Massacre at Paris,*" he reasoned that "the anonymous author was the borrower," which would mean that *The Troublesome Raigne* (1591) would have to postdate Marlowe's plays (648), a not entirely convincing argument.[13] Convinced that "the author of *The Troublesome Raigne* was a chronic imitator," when Taylor found "many similarities between *The Troublesome Raigne* and Peele's *Edward I*" he reasoned that "Peele is the creditor" (648–49). My deduction, however, is that Peele wrote both plays. Taylor's parallels included the phrase "Mother Queen" (*1 T. R.*, 9), which Peele had used in *The Tale of Troy* in 1589 (1.323; Prouty 1.196), the names "*Acon* (instead of the usual form *Acre*), *Palestine, Albion* (all three of which might derive from a common source), . . . and the opening of both plays with the Queen Mother's welcome to her returning son" (649). Taylor then appended a list of verbal parallels between the two plays:[14]

1 T. R., 209–10	This is my doome, and this my doome shall stand Irrevocable, as I am king of England
Ed. I, 668	Since what I do shall rest inrevocable
1852	And this sentence is irrevocable
1 T. R., 515	Misgovern'd Gossip, staine to this resort
Ed. I, 2148–50	and receave the reward of monstruous treasons and villanye, staine to the name and honor of his noble countrey

1 T. R., 876	Send fell contagion to infect this Clyme
Ed. I, 1040–42	This climat orelowring with blacke congealed clouds, That takes their swelling from the marrish soile, Fraught with infectious fogges and mistie dampes
1 T. R., 1056	And leave thy bodie to the fowles for food
Ed. I, 2066	Hang in the aire for fowles to feed uppon
1 T. R., 1254	Come on sir Frier, pick this lock, this geere doth cotton handsome[15]
Ed. I, 1385	Why so, now it cottens, now the game beginnes
1 T. R., 1303	How now, a Prophet? Sir prophet whence are ye?
Ed. I, 469	What? not Morgain Pigot, our good welsh prophet[16]
1 T. R., 1567	My word is past, receive your boone my Lords
Ed. I, 1656	My word is past, I am well agreede
1 T. R., 1598	The heavens frowne upon the sinfull earth
Ed. I, 2109	The angry Heavens frowne on Brittains face
1 T. R., 1611–12	Decide in cyphering what these five Moones Portend this Clyme
Ed. I, 2321	O Heavens, what maie these miracles portend?
2 T. R., 113	Confound my wits, and dull my senses so
Ed. I, 1886	Halloe Edward how are thy senses confounded
2 T. R., 132	To make thee great, and greatest of thy kin,
Ed. I, 269	Followe the man that meanes to make you great
554–55	must needes bee advaunced to bee highest of your kinne
2386	And be the highest of his kinne
2 T. R., 165	There let him hang, and be the Ravens food
Ed. I, 2066	Hang in the aire for fowles to feed uppon
2 T. R., 658	Shall be remunerated to the full
Ed. I, 140–41	That Nobles strive who shall remunerate
2036	We will remunerate his resolution
2 T. R., 888	And seek some meanes for to pastime the King
Ed. I, 311	Let us like friends pastime us on the sands
2 T. R., 1074	My tongue doth falter
Ed. I, 2400	That while this faultring engine of my speach

These parallels are too frequent, and too ordinary in their phraseology, to be dismissed as imitations. On their own, they would be suggestive of common authorship: taken together with the other evidence I shall present, their significance is much greater.

Returning to the parallels adduced by H. Dugdale Sykes between *The Troublesome Raigne* and Peele's poems and plays,[17] these ranged from echoes involving longer sequences of thought and language to distinctive verbal preferences and general characteristics of style, such as a recurring tendency to self-repetition. Sykes (100) pointed out that the author of *Part 1* "omits the pronoun 'I' before 'dare' in the present tense:"

> Dare lay my hand that Elinor can gesse
> Whereto this weighty Embassade doth tend
>
> (*1 T. R.*, 19–20)

So also the author of *Part 2:*

> Dare lay my life heel kill me for my place
>
> (*2 T. R.*, 892)

This mannerism was "evidently a mark of Peele's early work, for we find it repeatedly in *The Arraignment of Paris* alone of his acknowledged plays" (112):

> Thou hast a sort of prettie tales in stoore,
> Dare say no Nymphs in Ida woods hath more (236–37)
> For thou hast harde my stoore long since, dare say (251)
> Dare saie for him, a never strayed so wyde (333)
> Dare wage my winges, the lasse doth love, she lookes so bleak and thin (605)

Another characteristic Peele verbal mannerism to which Sykes drew attention was a liking—as I would describe it—for symmetrical phrases in the form *aba.* Sykes cited King John's exclamations,

> Griefe upon griefe, yet none so great a griefe . . .
> As I, poore I, a triumph for despight
>
> (*2 T. R.*, 839, 843),

and pointed out two further parallels in Peele:

> Then had not I, poor I, bin unhappie (*AP,* 657).
> Dead, ay me dead! Ay me, my life is dead! . . .
> And I, poor, I, am comforted in nothing
>
> (*Alphonsus, Emperor of Germany,*[18] 1.2.241–43)

Attention was drawn to this Peelean mannerism subsequently by R. F. Hill, in a useful contribution to the scholarly debate that has identified Peele as the co-author of *Titus Andronicus.*[19] Invoking the general rule that "peculiarities of style" can "possess great evidential value" in authorship studies, since "they may constitute the special 'tricks' of a writer," Hill instanced the fact that *Titus* contains forty-five examples of the rhetorical figure *epizeuxis* (repeating a word with no other word intervening, as in "come, come"), and that in sixteen cases a vocative was placed between the repeated words, as in "Help, grandsire, help"—in fact, this would be an instance of *ploké,* repetition of a word with other words intervening. Hill noted that "the trick is most apparent in the often suspected Act 1, where it occurs five times in one hundred and sixty-eight lines" (Hill 1957, 68). Hill pointed out another "unusual feature" of the play's diction, "the repetition of a clause with an inversion in the order of its grammatical parts," as in

> Hear me, grave fathers! noble tribunes, stay! (3.1.1)
> My lord, look here: look here, Lavinia. (4.1.68)

Hill counted eleven instances of this stylistic mannerism in *Titus,* and five in Peele's *Battle of Alcazar* (by no means a full listing). For examples of this construction we could cite the following, from Peele's scenes[20] for *Titus Andronicus:*

> Rise, Marcus, rise (1.1.383)
> Rise, Titus, rise (459)
> I care not, I (2.1.71)
> Help, grandsire, help! (4.1.1)
> I know not, I (16)
> See, brother, see (50).

Peele's *The Battle of Alcazar* includes other instances of this *aba* pattern: "come bishop come" (447); "Tell me Lord Bishop, Captaines tell me all" (713); "death, pale death" (1227). So does *David and Bethsabe:* "see Cusay see" (74); "Go madame goe" (318); "No Cusay no" (1092); as does *Edward I:* "Edward o Edward" (574); "come Potter come" (1287). Verbal patterning in the form *aba* is plentiful in *The Troublesome Raigne:*

> This Madame, this, hath drove me from myselfe (*1 T. R.,* 368–69)
> Come Madame come, you neede not be so lothe (385)
> Yes (false intruder) if that just be just (510)
> England is England, yeelding good and bad (466)
> Peace Arthur peace (528)
> I tell thee, I (544)
> A boone O Kings, a boone doth Philip beg (918)
> True or not true (1647)
> Hence traytor hence (*2 T. R.,* 76)
> Well Meloun well (592)
> Back warmen, back (758)

We also find longer instances of this pattern, with the same word occurring at the beginning and ending of a clause or verse line (the figure *epanalepsis*):

Kings if you wilbe Kings (939)
O helpe me Hubert, gentle keeper helpe (1338)
Hell, Hubert, trust me, all the plagues of hell (1379)

R. F. Hill noted in passing the great number of vocatives in Peele's share of *Titus Andronicus,* another verbal detail that links *The Troublesome Raigne* to Peele's canon. This feature of Peele's style was first noticed in an earlier study identifying him as the co-author of *Titus Andronicus,* having contributed Act 1, 2.1, 2.2, and 4.1. In his edition of that play John Dover Wilson drew attention to the remarkable monotony of the verse in the opening Act, in which

> all the characters speak with the same voice, frame their sentences after similar patterns, and even borrow words and phrases from each other. Almost every speech, for instance, during the first half of the act, i. e. for some 240 lines, begins with a vocative and continues with a verb in the imperative mood. Saturninus opens the play with
>
> Noble patricians. Patrons of my right.
>
> And when Bassianus follows on, seven lines later, like this:
>
> Romans, friends, followers, favourers of my right,
>
> he seems an auctioneer, outbidding his rival by one alliterative word. The speech he then delivers is, moreover, a bag of tricks, some of which are used several times in other parts of the act. (Wilson 1948, xxvii)

In that speech, Wilson noted, Bassianus also uses "the tiresome rhetorical device" of referring to himself in the third person, which "occurs more than a dozen times elsewhere in this act."

Wilson's insight can be endorsed statistically. A computation of the use of vocatives in the two sections of the play ascribed to Peele and Shakespeare yielded the following results:[21]

Table 1. Vocatives in *Titus Andronicus*

Share of play	Total lines	Vocatives alone	Vocatives and imperatives	Total vocatives
Peele	785	118	68	186
Frequency every x lines		6.7	11.5	4.2
Shakespeare	1732	143	56	199
Frequency every x lines		12.1	30.9	8.7

The same test applied to *Edward I* yielded strikingly similar figures to Peele's share in *Titus:*

Table 2. Vocatives in Peele's *Edward I*

Total lines	Vocatives alone	Vocatives and imperatives	Total vocatives
2685	526	102	628
Frequency every x lines	5.1	26.3	4.3

The Troublesome Raigne yielded figures not quite as high as those for *Titus Andronicus* and *Edward I,* but still far higher than for any other Elizabethan text I have tested. I give data for both parts; no individual scene departs significantly from the norm.

Table 3. Vocatives in *The Troublesome Raigne of King John*

Part One	Total lines	Vocatives alone	Vocatives and Imperatives	Total vocatives
Totals	1740	225	90	315
Frequencies: every x lines		7.7	19.3	5.5
Part Two				
Totals	1196	147	50	197
Frequencies: every x lines		8.1	23.9	6.1
Both parts	2936	372	140	512
Frequencies: every x lines		7.9	21.0	5.7

The overall figures for *The Troublesome Raigne* may also be compared to those for Peele's *Battle of Alcazar* (a theatrical abridgement, mangled in several respects):

Table 4. Vocatives in *The Battle of Alcazar*

Total lines	Vocatives alone	Vocatives and imperatives	Total vocatives
1278[22]	111	78	189
Frequencies: every x lines	11.5	16.4	6.8

The similarity between the use of vocatives in Peele's scenes in *Titus Andronicus* and in *The Troublesome Raigne* will be immediately visible by simply quoting some speeches from the first 150 lines of each play (omitting the speakers' names):

The Troublesome Raigne, Part 1

Barons of England, and my noble Lords[23] (1)
My gracious mother Queene, and Barons all (9)
Pembroke, convay him safely to the sea (61)
Wil them come neere, and while we hear the cause,
Goe Salsbury and make provision (70–71)
My Lord of Essex, wil the offenders to stand foorth (83)
My gracious Lord, & you thrice reverend Dame (135)
Ladie, stand up, be patient for a while (143)[24]

Titus Andronicus

Noble patricians, patrons of my right,
Defend the justice of my cause with arms (1–2)
Romans, friends, followers, favourers of my right . . .
Keep then this passage to the Capitol (9, 12)
Stay, Roman brethren, gracious conqueror,
Victorious Titus, rue the tears I shed (104–5)
Patient yourself, madam, and pardon me (121)
See, lord and father, how we have performed
Our Roman rites (142–43)
In peace and honour live lord Titus long;
My noble lord and father, live in fame! (157–58)[25]

Further quotation would be needed to convey the actual density of this "vocative (plus imperative)" formula for beginning a speech.

A closer examination of the language of the plays will bring out another peculiarity of Peele's use of the vocative together with the imperative, the fact that his characters frequently name themselves when communicating orders or exhortations. In *The Battle of Alcazar* Abdelmelec gives himself an order:

Abdelmelec here
Throw up thy trembling hands to heavens throne
(56–57)

So does the Bassa (indulging in a typically Peelean piece of functionless repetition):

Ride Bassa now, bold Bassa homeward ride
(382)

King Sebastian of Portugal urges himself:

> Now breath Sebastian, and in breathing blow
> Some gentle gale of thy new formed joyes
>
> (626–67; also 801)

Zareo appeals to Abdelmelec:

> Great soveraigne, vouchsafe to heare me speak,
> And let Zareos counsell now prevaile
>
> (1037–38)

The dying Abdelmelec reproaches himself with proof of his declining force:

> Ah Abdelmelec doost thou live to heare
> This bitter processe of this first attempt?

Even the adventurer Tom Stukley addressed himself, with more repetitious padding:

> Seest thou not Stukley, O Stukley sees thou not
> The great dishonour done to Christendome?
>
> (1251–52)

The use of vocatives in Peele's share of *Titus Andronicus* is quite extraordinary in its density. In the opening scene virtually every speech begins with a vocative, and many of them include several more (quite unnecessary) instances, sometimes repeating the name of the person being addressed. Self-address, a feature of dramatic language that has attracted little attention so far,[26] is especially prominent in Peele's opening scene. Titus Andronicus, returning victorious to Rome, announces that here "Cometh Andronicus, bound with laurel boughs" (1.1.74). Having described his public triumph and losses in battle he rounds on himself:

> Titus, unkind and careless of thine own,
> Why suffer'st thou thy sons, unburied yet
>
> (86–87)

Alarbus having been sacrificed, Titus again urges himself, "Andronicus," to carry out the act he is about to perform (148–49). Saturninus, likewise, refers to himself by name:

> Patricians, draw your swords and sheathe them not
> Till Saturninus be Rome's emperor.
>
> (204–5; also 304–5, 333–35)

When Saturninus has taken Tamora off to be married, having broken the contract he had made with Lavinia and Titus, Andronicus rebukes himself:

> Titus, when wert thou wont to walk alone,
> Dishonoured thus and challenged of wrongs?
>
> (339–40)

After their wedding, Tamora asks Saturninus leave to speak, appealing:

> My worthy lord, if ever Tamora
> Were gracious in those princely eyes of thine
>
> (428–29)

In the following scene, also by Peele, Aaron urges himself on to new heights of ambition:

> Then, Aaron, arm thy heart, and fit thy thoughts
> To mount aloft with thy imperial mistress
>
> (2.1.12–13)

Peele frequently used the vocative plus imperative for self address in *Edward I.* Queen Elinor urges herself:

> Then Elinor bethinke thee of a gift
> Worthie the King of Englandes wife
>
> (166–67)

Left alone with her daughter, Joan of Acone, Elinor continues to address herself with imperative vocatives, including even praise which would be far more appropriate coming from someone else:

> Now Elinor, now Englands lovely Queene,
> Bethinke thee of the greatnes of thy state
>
> (229–30)

Elinor makes a real feast of self-reference, both in the high style and in the lower, slightly incongruous use of the familiar abbreviation "Nell."[27] Elinor's frequent self-address is not an attempt by Peele to individualize her stylistically, rather the consequence of her role being longer than most others. In fact, at one time or other, almost all the characters in the play address themselves by their own name:

> *Jone.* Madam, if Jone thy daughter may advise (245)
> *Lluel.* Owen ap Rice, tis that Lluellen fears (300; also 769–71, 1255, 2112)
> *[King Edward]* . . . this daies gentle princelie service done,

To Edward Englands king and Scotlands lord (632–33; also 640, 739, 744, 842, 2348, 2573)
David. David must die say thou a shamefull death (819)
Gloster. Shee riseth earelie Jone, that beguileth thee of a Gloster (1707)
Versses. Versses my Lord in tearmes like to himselfe (2046)
Edmund. Edmund thou maist not goe although thou die (2354).

While a degree of self-naming may be useful in drama, especially when introducing a new character, Peele seems to need a character's name to mark and identify each utterance, even if it is the speaker's own. Mortimer, left alone onstage, begins his soliloquy with self-address:

> Mortimer, a brable ill begunne for thee (1005),

a trick he repeats later (1219, 1229, 2154), and again urging himself: "Goe Mortimer and make their love holidaies" (1244). He addresses himself with the second person pronoun, "O Mortimer were it for thy sake" (1313), as if looking in a mirror, and, left alone, roundly rebukes himself:

> Why Mortimer, why doest thou not discover,
> Thy selfe her knight her liegeman and her lover?
> (1487–88)

To modern eyes this repeated signal is as if one were standing outside oneself, looking on, telling oneself what one has just seen: "*Mort.* But Mortimer this sight is strange" (1869). He is not alone in this mannerism. The Friar also exhorts himself: "Then Friar lie thee downe and die" (1161), and repeatedly identifies himself as "the Frier" (1306, 1399, 1725, 1800, 1813, 2145, 2162), an unusually superfluous act given that he is dressed as one. Joan of Acon, informed by her mother that she is a bastard, utters her last words: "Die wretch, haste death, for Joan hath lived too long" (2607)—at which follows the stage direction: "*Shee sodainely dies at the Queenes beds feete.*" Gloster, her widowed husband, appropriately enough, urges himself to "Sigh hapless Gloster for thy sodaine losse" (2671). This excessive use of the vocative and self-address by name must surely mark off Peele's style from all his contemporaries.

Characters in *The Troublesome Raigne of King John* use the same mannerisms equally intensively. Philip, who claims to be the natural son of Richard Coeur-de-lion, addresses himself as "Philip sprung of ancient Kings" (*1 T. R.,* 242), regularly speaks of himself in the third person—"Be Philip Philip and no Fauconbridge, / His Father doubtles was as brave a man" (336; also 247, 283, 292, 302, 360), and rounds upon himself: "Philip, that Fauconbridge cleaves to thy jawes" (271). His rival, Robert Fauconbridge, appeals to the King, "let Fauconbrige enjoy / The living that belongs to Fauconbridge" (127–28), and exhorts himself, "Robert revive thy heart, let sorrow die" (280). Elinor, too, swears to perform something "As long as Elinor hath foote of land" (295). In a later scene Philip (sometimes identified as "Bastard" in the speech headings), reports the urging of Alecto in his ears: "Delay not Philip, kill the villaine straight" (562), and affirms "Philip hath sworne" (578). The author of *The Troublesome Raigne* consistently makes Philip use his own name when describing his thoughts or intentions, a curiously self-reifying form of utterance (700, 709, 722, 799, 918). Lymoges identifies himself as "the Austrich Duke" (945); Constance affirms that "Constance doth live to tame thine insolence" (1060), and asks "Must Constance speak? let teares prevent her talke" (1160); Arthur, captured by Hubert, enjoins himself: "Then Arthur yeeld" (1342).

In *Part Two* minor and major characters continually address themselves by their own names:

Arthur. Ay me poore Arthur, I am here alone. (*2 T. R.,* 15)
Salsbury. And Salsbury will not gainsay the same (94)
Bastard. Now Philip, hadst thou Tullys eloquence
Then mightst thou hope to plead with good successe (256–57)
Salsbury. As Pembrooke sayth, affirmeth Salisburie (435)
Lewes. But al's not done that Lewes came to doo (665)

The Monk who plans to poison John rouses himself to action twice with the self-addressed pronoun "thou" (879–83). But the most frequent user of this mannerism is King John, in whose mouth it marks every stage of his decline, from a false sense of security, through the recognition of his psychological collapse before Pandulph, on to his death agonies:

John. Ascension day is come, John feare not then
The prodigies this pratling Prophet threates. (*2 T. R.,* 116–17)
John. Now John, thy feares are vanisht into smoake (155)
John. There let him hang, and be the Ravens food
While John triumphs in spight of Prophecies (165–66)
John. And John of England now is quite undone (224)
John. Though John be faultie, yet let subjects beare (246)
John. Now John be thinke thee how thou maist resolve (263)
John. Then John there is no way to keepe thy Crowne (274)
John. Peace John, here comes the Legate of the Pope (282)
John. No John, submit again, dissemble yet (304)
John. Absolve me then, and John doth sweare to doo
The uttermost what ever thou demaundst (308–9)
John. O John, these troubles tyre thy wearyed soule (336)
John. John will not spurne against thy sound advice (346)
John. Accursed John, the divell owes thee shame (704)
John. Nor health nor happiness hath John at all (852)

John. Help God, O payne! dye John, O plague
Inflicted on thee for thy grievous sinnes (1040–41)
John. Or who will say that John diceasd too soone? (1064)
John. Since John did yeeld unto the Priest of Rome,
Nor he nor his have prospred on the earth (1075–76)
John. And in the faith of Jesu John doth dye (1090)

II

The strong similarity between *The Troublesome Raigne* and Peele's extant dramatic works can be established by a complementary linguistic test, examining the use of alliteration. Here again H. Dugdale Sykes adduced some convincing verbal parallels, although not recognizing that they also involved alliteration (Sykes 1910, 116–19). Sykes pointed out Peele's liking for alliteratively paired words, often an epithet and a noun, such as "mounting mind," a liking shared by the author of the anonymous play:

Strike on, strike downe this body to the earth
Whose mounting minde stoopes to no feeble stroke (*Alc.,* 1319–20)
sweete Nell thou shouldst not be thy selfe, did not with
thy mounting minde, thy gift surmount the rest (*Ed. 1,* 175–77)
for why this mounting minde
Doth soare too high to stoope to Fauconbridge (*1 T. R.,* 261–62)

Both dramatists reuse the idea, together with the alliteration, but with a present-tense verb:

But man, her minde above her fortune mounts (*Ed. I,* 1449)
My brothers minde is base, and too too dull
To mount where Philip lodgeth his affects (*1 T. R.,* 359–60)

Another alliterative pair used by both Peele and the author of *The Troublesome Raigne* is "damned deed":

With thousand deaths for thousand damned deeds (*Alc.,* 852)
Maie never good betide my life my Lord,
If once I dreamde uppon this damned deede (*Ed. I,* 2525–26)
Hath Alexander done this damned deed? (*Alphonsus,* 5.1.351)
trust me, all the plagues of hell
Hangs on performance of this damned deed (*1 T. R.,* 1379–80)
It was a damned execrable deede (1718)
O ruthful spectacle! O damned deed! (*2 T. R.,* 37)

Another alliterative word pair used by both dramatists, but now combining a verb and noun, is "to wreak wrongs":

To wreake the wrongs and murthers thou hast done (*Alc.,* 306)
And he shall wreake the traitrous wrongs of Saule (*D&B,* 1302)
To wreak my wrong upon the murtherers (*1 T. R.,* 1420)

As with the use of rare or idiosyncratic words, discussed above, Peele was not the only Elizabethan dramatist to relish these alliterative doublets. According to the Chadwyck-Healey database of English verse drama (to 1603), the phrase "mounting mind" also appears in *The Misfortunes of Arthur* (1588), and in *Love's Labour's Lost* (4.1.4). The pair "wreak wrong" appears in *Tancred and Gismund* (1566), in Thomas Newton's *Thebais* (1581), in *The Rare Triumphs of Love and Fortune* (1582), *The Misfortunes of Arthur* (1588), and in a scene of *Titus Andronicus* ascribed to Shakespeare, where Titus has his friends and kinsmen shoot arrows at heaven in order to "move the gods / To send down justice for to wreak our wrongs" (4.3.51–52). Interestingly, in his edition (1948), John Dover Wilson identified Peele's "cadence and diction" in a preceding passage in this scene, where Marcus calls the others to "Take wreak on Rome" (4.3.34). Finally, the alliterative phrase "damned deed" also figures in *Gorboduc* (1562), *Tancred and Gismund* (1566), *The Spanish Tragedy* (1587), Yarington's *Two Lamentable Tragedies* (1594), Chapman's *The Blind Beggar of Alexandria* (1596), Heywood's *Edward IV* and *A Warning for Fair Women* (both 1599). Once again, Peele is the only dramatist to have used all three phrases. (Incidentally, that list shows his affinity to Latinate and academic drama.)

Dugdale Sykes's wide knowledge of Elizabethan drama enabled him to cite many relevant parallels, but he seldom performed any linguistic analysis, either qualitative or quantitative. Fortunately, Peele's fondness for alliteration had already been documented by Erna Landsberg in 1910, in a dissertation supervised by Gregor Sarrazin.[28] Landsberg discussed alliteration in the plays then accepted as Peele's (Landsberg 1910, 51–54), counting 207 instances in *The Araygnment of Paris,* 100 instances in *David and Bethsabe,* and 110 instances in *Edward I.* Of the other plays she discussed which were then ascribed to Peele, only *The Battle of Alcazar* has been admitted to the Peele canon,[29] although it survives in an abridgment "which has affected the style for the worst."[30] Landsberg computed alliteration as occurring once in every eight lines of this play (94–96). Analyzing the degrees of alliteration found in Peele, Landsberg showed that (like other users of this device) he mostly used alliteration for the initial consonants, this basic doubling pattern (*aa*) amounting to half of the total occurrences in the three canonic plays—that is, about 200 instances, according to her count. But Peele also used triple alliteration (*aaa*) within a line no less than 158 times in these three plays, quadruple (*aaaa*) some 29 times, and quintuple (*aaaaa*) 6 times. These are all remakably high figures. Landberg also noted that Peele was fond of alliterative patterns involving two different consonants in one line, either in parallel (*aabb:* 16 times; *aabbb:* 4; *aaabb:* 4) or alternating (*abba:* 7: *aabba:* 1; *aabcbc:* 1). In *The Battle of Alcazar* (total length: 1452 lines), two thirds of the instances of alliteration (about 120 in all), she found, were of the basic double form (*aa*), 37 were of the triple (*aaa*), and four of the quadruple (*aaaa*). Several lines contained alliteration on two distinct consonants (*aabb:* 10; *aaabb:* 1; *abab:* 1; *aabbc:* 2; *abbba:* 1). Elsewhere, I have shown that Landsberg underestimated the amount of alliteration in Peele's plays by treating the rhetorical figures separately, many of which repeat a word and therefore alliterate as well.[31] At least her pioneering work deserves recognition for having documented Peele's exceptional fondness for alliteration.

The author of *The Troublesome Raigne of King John* was evidently fond of alliteration, as the following table shows. (I give totals for both parts; no scene departs significantly from these averages.)

Table 5. Alliteration in *The Troublesome Raigne of King John*

	Total lines	Alliteration	Frequency every *x* lines
Part 1	1740	494	3.5
Part 2	1196	1410	2.9
Both parts	2936	904	3.2

Those figures are strikingly similar to the results I obtained when computing alliteration in *The Battle of Alcazar* and in Peele's scenes (1.1; 2.1; 2.2; 4.1) for *Titus Andronicus:*

Table 6. Alliteration in *The Battle of Alcazar* and *Titus Andronicus*

Play	Total lines	Total alliteration	Frequency every x lines
Battle of Alcazar	1452	507	3.9
Titus Andronicus	785	294	2.7

Source: Vickers 2002, 220–26

The author of *The Troublesome Raigne* produced whole sequences of alliteration for purposes of emphasis, as to express Constance's concern for Arthur's future:

> But I, who see the poyse that *w*eigheth downe
> Thy *w*eale, my *w*ish, and all the *w*illing meanes
> *W*herewith thy *f*ortune and thy *f*ame should mount,

> *W*hat joy, *w*hat ease, *w*hat rest can lodge in me,
> *W*ith *wh*om all *h*ope and *h*ap doth disagree?
>
> (*1 T. R.*, 867–71)

The multiple alliteration there on the letters *w, f,* and *h* well conveys Constance's unease. The dramatist used this linguistic resource to create a more powerful, not to say melodramatic mood when Hubert warns Arthur of the sentence he has been ordered to perform:

> Patience yong Lord, and listen *w*ords of *w*oe,
> *H*armful and *h*arsh, *h*ells *h*orror to be *h*eard:
> A dismall tale *fit f*or a *f*uries tongue.
> I *f*aint to tell, deep *s*orrow is the *s*ound. . . .
> *D*eaths *d*ish were *d*aintie at so *f*ell a *f*east,
> Be *d*eafe, *h*eare not, its *h*ell to tell the rest.
>
> (1344–47, 1351–52)

But the author of *The Troublesome Raigne* also used multiple alliteration for satiric effects, as in the denunciation of monastic corruption. The Bastard refers to the Franciscan monastery at Bungay, Suffolk, and looks forward to hanging the "*b*alde and *b*arefoote *B*ungie *b*irds" (1192), such as the Friar, with his secret wealth and mistress:

> yee *sh*amelesse *sh*aven crowne,
> Is this the chest that *h*eld a *h*oard, at least a thousand pound?
> And is the *h*oard a *h*oly *wh*ore? Wel be the *h*angman nimble,
> *H*ee'le *t*ake the *p*ain *t*o *p*ay you *h*ome, and *t*each you *t*o dissemble.
>
> (1230–33; also 1497–99)

The frequent presence of such alliterative clusters give the play's language a curiously clotted quality, exacting from the actors a stiff and forceful delivery that destroys any hope of free-flowing dramatic verse. At times, indeed, what we hear sounds more like medieval alliterative poetry, surely an archaic medium on the Elizabethan stage in the early 1590s.[32] At present we know very little about stylistic norms in the first twenty years of the Elizabethan theatre, but my reading experience suggests that alliteration of this intensity soon went out of fashion, so that Pistol's "affecting the letter" already seemed archaic by the time of *2 Henry IV* (1597–98).[33] The most common form of alliteration thereafter was the doubling of a consonant within a line—"A little more than *k*in and less than *k*ind." Peele used double alliteration so often that counting occurrences would produce unmanageably high figures. To give a taste of the intensity of his alliterative bent, here are two instances where he managed to produce a double alliteration three times over within a line:

*Sh*ould *sh*ine *d*iscreet *d*esire and *l*awless *l*ust (*Ed. I,* 2517)
*Th*at *th*ey *m*ay *m*arch in number like *s*ea *s*ands (*D&B,* 1228)

In the following discussion I shall consider only instance of three-, four-, and five-fold alliteration within a verse line or semantic unit.

The author of *The Troublesome Raigne* shared with George Peele a fondness for such elaborate effects. We have already seen several examples of triple alliterations, but this chronicle play contains many others:[34]

Who *t*empred *t*error with his wanton *t*alke (*1 T. R.,* 399)
There to *cons*ult, *cons*pire, and *con*clude (*2 T. R.,* 195)
Confound their *d*ivelish plots, and *d*amned *d*evices (255)
The *f*earefull object of *f*ell *f*rowning warre (525)
Was *f*aine to *f*lie before the eager *f*oe (826)

Peele's liking for triple alliteration often lighted on the letters *f* and *s:*

The *f*attest *f*airest *f*awne in all the chace[35] (*AP,* 36)
For *s*ervice done to *S*ultan *S*olimon (*Alc.,* 45)
To *s*ettle and to *s*eate you in the *s*ame (83)
And as this *f*lame doth *f*asten on this *f*lesh (602)
*F*iftie *f*aire *f*ootmen by my chariot run (*D&B,* 1160)

The author of *The Troublesome Raigne* was exceptionally fond of triple alliteration. On my count (which is probably not exhaustive) he used it 50 times in *Part One,* 59 times in *Part Two,* together 109 times in 2936 lines, or once every 26.9 lines. In *Edward I* Peele used triple alliteration 96 times in 2,685 lines, or once every 27.9 lines. In *David and Bethsabe* he used it 69 times in 1,920 lines, or once every 27.8 lines. The amazing coincidence of the results in these three plays (surely among the highest for Elizabethan drama)—26.9, 27.9, 27.8—is almost enough to place *The Troublesome Raigne* firmly in Peele's canon. The only Peele play to score less was the clumsily-abridged *The Battle of Alcazar,* in the surviving text of which Peele used triple alliteration 69 times in 1452 lines, or once every 21 lines. Even this score belongs within Peele's range, and sets him apart from any other Elizabethan dramatist known to me.

The author of *The Troublesome Raigne* also liked quadruple alliteration:[36]

*B*ase *b*orne, and *b*ase *b*egot, no Fauconbridge. (*1 T. R.,* 120)
*F*rom him whose *f*orme was *f*igured in his *f*ace (354)
Why *th*ats to *th*ee if *th*ou as *th*ey proceede (1403)
And *m*ore to *m*ake the *m*atter to our *m*inde (*2 T. R.,* 422)
I so escapt *t*o *t*ell this *t*ragic *t*ale (662)
Who *d*are? why I my lord *d*are *d*o the *d*eede (920)

Peele, too, frequently indulged in fourfold repetition:[37]

For *l*ims, you shall have *l*ivings, *l*ordships, *l*ands (*Ed. 1,* 98)
And *s*able *s*ailes he *s*aw, and *s*o maist thou (572)
*Th*ey *f*eare, they *f*lie, they *f*aint, *th*ey *f*ight in vaine (828)
O *n*o *N*urse, the Babe *n*eedes *n*o great rockeing (2090)
*Th*y sinne, *th*y *sh*ame, *th*e sorrow of *th*y soule.
*S*inne, *s*hame, and *s*orrow *s*warme about thy *s*oule (*D&B,* 576–77)
*F*landers I *f*eare shall *f*eele the *f*orce of Spaine (*Alc.,* 818)
*D*e*s*troy, *diss*olve, *dis*turbe, and *diss*ipate[38] (1284)

These multiple alliterations pose problems to the player: lines such as "A *sh*ell of *s*alte will *s*erve a *sh*eepeherde *s*wayne" (*AP,* 935) or "To *sh*ew how *s*adly his poore *sh*eppeheard *s*ings" (*D&B,* 1826) sound uncomfortably like pronunciation games ("Peter Piper picked . . . "). The anonymous author even carried his liking for multiple alliteration to the fifth degree:

*H*armful and *h*arsh, *h*ells *h*orror to be *h*eard (*1 T. R.,* 1345)
*Gr*ief upon *gr*iefe, yet none so *gr*eat a *gr*iefe
To end this life, and thereby rid my *gr*iefe (*2 T. R.,* 839–40)

Peele, too, used quintuple alliteration:

To *l*oose his *l*ife, his *l*ife and many *l*ives
Of *l*ustie men (*Alc.,* 986–87)
*R*ice shall *r*emaine with me, make *th*ou *th*y boade,
In *r*esolution to *r*evenge *th*ese w*r*onges (*Ed. 1,* 618–19)
And *h*ere *h*e comes, *h*is *h*alter makes *h*im *h*ast (2042)

—unlike the actor speaking that line! *David and Bethsabe* also has instances of multiple alliteration:[39]

O my deere father, *th*at *th*y melting eyes
Might pierce *th*is thicket to behold *th*y sonne (1533–34)
Here end *w*e this, and *w*hat here *w*ants to please
*W*e *w*ill supplie *w*ith treble *w*illingnesse. (1584–85)

The author of *The Troublesome Raigne* made great use of an even more elaborate form of alliteration, which repeats the first two consonants of a word, especially where the second consonant was an *r* or an *l,* and sometimes echoing the initial consonant also within the same line or clause. His favorite combination was *tr,* as the following instances show:

*Tr*eading my Confines with thy armed *Tr*oupes (*1 T. R.,* 498)
*T*o sound *t*he *tr*omp *th*at causeth hell *tr*iumph (1374)

A *tr*oupe of *tr*aytors, *f*ood for hellish *f*eends
If you desist, then *f*ollow me as *fr*iends (*2 T. R.,* 478–79)
I came not Lords to *tr*oup as *tr*aytors doo,
Nor will I *c*ounsaile in so bad a *c*ause. (485–86)[40]

These instances of alliteration on words beginning *tr* may be paralleled with similar instances from Peele's acknowledged plays:

Make me beginne the *Tr*agedie of *Tr*oie (*AP,* 29)
Her *tr*ailing *tr*esses that hang *fl*aring round
Of July *fl*owers so *gr*affed in the *gr*ound (112–13)
Of *tr*agedies, and *tr*agic tyrannies (*Alc.,* 281)
And let me *tr*iumph in the *tr*agedie (1140)
*The tr*ophies and *the tr*iumphs of *th*y men (1379)
To armes *tr*ue Britaines sprong of *Tr*ojans seede (*Ed. I,* 610)
*To tr*emble under Titus' *th*reat'ning look (*Titus,* 1.1.134)
Heaven guide thy *p*en to *p*rint thy sorrows *p*lain
*Th*at we may know *the tr*aitors and *the tr*uth! (4.1.74–75)

The author of *The Troublesome Raigne* showed a similar liking for alliteration based on the consonants *fr:*

But let the *fr*olicke[41] *Fr*enchman take no scorne,
If Philip *fr*ont him with an English horne. (*1 T. R.,* 798–99)
*Fr*owne *fr*iends, *f*aile *f*aith, the divell goe with all (1652)
The smiles of *Fr*aunce shade in the *fr*ownes of death (*2 T. R.,* 755)

In Peele's plays we find the same consonantal combination:

Let us like *fr*iends pastime us on the sands
Our *fr*olike mindes are ominous for good (*Ed. I,* 311–12)
And for distressed *fr*anke and *fr*ee relieve (*Alc.,* 652)

Peele and the author of *The Troublesome Raigne* enjoyed alliterating on the consonantal pair *pr:*[42]

Honor *the* spurre *that pr*ickes *the pr*incely minde (*Alc.,* 1)
I will *pr*ovide thee of a *pr*incely osprie (554)
And Englands *pr*omise *pr*incely to thy Wailes (*Ed. I,* 987)
This Spanish *pr*ide grees not with Englands *pr*ince (1626)
And Cusaies pollicie with *pr*aise *pr*eferd (*D&B,* 1364)
With *pr*actise of such sacred *pr*inciples 1706)
*G*ive us the *pr*oudest *pr*isoner of the *G*oths (*Titus,* 1.1.96)
And all this *Pr*incely[43] *pr*esence shall confesse (*1 T. R.,* 170)
Which in S. Maries Chapell *pr*esently
Shalbe *p*erformed ere this *Pr*esence *p*art (856–57)

The Princely promise that revives my soule (929)
The prodigies this pratling Prophet threates (*2 T. R.,* 117)
And doth a *Pope,* a *Priest,* a man of *Pride* (468)

Another consonantal combination both dramatists favored was *gr,* which could result in extremely graphic growling:[44]

The *gr*ownde whereon it *gr*owes, the *gr*asse, the roote of golde (*AP,* 457)
That you so well have *g*overned your *gr*eefes,
As being *gr*owne unto a *g*enerall *i*arre (*Ed. I,* 639–40)
The *gr*eenest *gr*asse *d*oth *d*roupe and turn to hay (1071)
From heavens *thr*one doth David *thr*ow himselfe,
And *gr*one and *gr*ovell to the gates of hell (*D&B,* 658–59)
And that these haires shall *gr*eet my *gr*ave in peace (1024)
There was I *gr*ac'd by *Gr*egory the *gr*eat (*Alc.,* 1348)
To *gr*atify the good Andronicus
And *gr*atulate his safe *r*eturn to *R*ome (*Titus,* 1.1.220–21)
The *P*opes and *P*opelings shall not *gr*ease themselves
With *g*olde and *gr*oates (*1 T. R.,* 311–12)
A *gr*eater *gr*iefe *gr*owes now than earst hath been (*2 T. R.,* 770)

Finally, the author of *The Troublesome Raigne,* like Peele, enjoyed alliterating on words beginning with *br:*[45]

*Br*andishing *br*ight the blade of Adamant (*Ed. 1,* 846)
A gallant *br*idegrome and a princely *br*ide (1507)
*Br*ed up in court of pride, *br*ought up in Spaine (1690)
. . . now like a *br*ave *Br*idegrome *m*arshall this *m*anie (1961)
Thrice happe is the *Br*idegroome and the *Br*ide
From whose sweete *Br*idal such a concord springs (*1 T. R.,* 907–8)
*Y*our seate, *y*our nurse, *y*our *b*irthdayes *br*eathing place,
That *br*ed you, *b*eares you, *br*ought you up in armes (*2 T. R.,* 759–60)

III

My new evidence for Peele's authorship of *The Troublesome Raigne of King John,* the play's use of vocatives, frequently involving self-naming, and its elaborate deployment of complex alliteration, complements that adduced by H. Dugdale Sykes, and makes a very strong case for Peele's authorship. But there are further links between *The Troublesome Raigne* and Peele's work, involving language and metrics. The language concerned is not English but Latin—or rather, a mixture of the two, especially in the satiric presentation of monastic abuses. Anti-Catholicism is a well-known attitude in Peele,[46] also, and in *Edward I* he exposed such abuses in a similar way, showing friars and nuns who break their vows of poverty, chastity, and obedience without compunction. An amusing exposure of such abuses in *The Troublesome Raigne* is the scene where Fauconbridge, searching a monastery for hidden treasure, opens a coffer supposedly containing money only to find "faire Alice the Nun" sheltering there (*1 T. R.*, 1221–33). He then pries open a Nun's "presse" or cupboard, said to contain "much money," only to find Friar Laurence in hiding (1249–72). Peele was not the only Elizabethan playwright to satirize monastic corruption, but one individual linguistic detail linking *The Troublesome Raigne* to *Edward I* is the citation of Latin texts by a monk or friar for sophistic, nonreligious purposes. When Friar Laurence emerges, in embarrassment, from the Nun's cupboard he attempts to excuse himself with a familiar Latin tag:

> *Amor vincit omnia,* so Cato affirmeth,
> And therefore a Frier whose fancie soon burneth.
>
> (1262–63)

Some members of the audience will have noticed the Friar's error,[47] since this famous phrase actually comes from Virgil (*Ecl.* 10.69)—it was also the motto on the brooch worn by Chaucer's Prioress.[48] In the parallel scenes in *Edward I* we meet "Friar Hugh ap David, Guenthian his wench in Flannell, and Jack his Novice" (*s. d.,* 312). The Novice, being brought up in monastic learning, reminds his master of an important lesson:

> O sweare not maister, flesh is fraile,
> Wenche when the signe is in the taile,
> Mightie is love and will prevaile.
>
> (327–29)

If Jack can English the same verse in Virgil that had served Friar Laurence, Friar Hugh can perform the same *translatio* to a verse from Ovid often cited in the literature endorsing love:

> Then my Guenthian to begin,
> Since idleness in love is sinne
>
> (342–43)

In his *Ars amatoria* Ovid gave the famous rule, *amor odit inertes* (2.229: "Love detests laggards"). The Novice chimes in with another famous rule for lovers:

> For long agoe I learned in schole,
> That lovers desire, and pleasurs coole

Sans Ceres wheat and Bacchus vine,
Now maister for the Cakes and Wine.

(353–56)

This line from Terence's *Eunuchus* (732), "*Sine Cerere et Libero* [or *Baccho*] *friget Venus,*" familiar in libertine literature, sums up Friar Hugh's shameless apologias for the flesh ("I love a wench as a wench should be loved"; 384–90). In both plays, then, representatives of the clergy cite well-known classical tags from the libertine or voluptuarian tradition.

Another linguistic detail linking the two plays is that both mingle English and Latin in the burlesque style known as "macaronic." The (too many) scenes in *Edward I* involving this monastic trio abound in Latin tags,[49] a curious jumble of classical and medieval phrases from poetry, the Mass, and legal jargon: *in secula seculorum; non ego; ab ovo usque ad mala* (Horace, *Satires* 1.3.6); *plena est curia; nolens volens; in numeratis pecuniis legem pone; per misericordiam.* At one point Peele seems to be echoing medieval Latin verse, with its "Gothic" rhymes, jumbling sacred and profane:

And make him sing a dastards note,
And crie *Peccavi miserere David.*
In amo amavi.

(1375–77)

The comparable scene in *The Troublesome Raigne* involving a Friar deliberately uses internal rhyming to convey the curious bilingualism of monastic culture:

Benedicamus Domini, was ever such an injurie (1183)
In nomini Domini, make I my homilie (1186)
Sancte Benedicite, pardon my simplicitie (1224)
Haud credo Laurentius, that thou shouldest be pend thus
In the presse of a Nun. We are all undon.

(1259–60)

Friar Laurence, when he emerges from the Nun's cupboard, starts with perhaps the most famous line in Ovid (*Metamorphoses,* 15.234), for which he then provides an English rhyme before switching to the opening of Ecclesiastes:

O tempus edax rerum,
Geve children bookes, they teare them.
O vanitas vanitatis, in this waning *aetatis*

(1280–82)

His final words juxtapose sacred and profane even more ludicrously, moving from the Psalmist's frequent appeal ("O Lord, hear my prayer") to offering a bribe:

Exaudi me domine, si vis me parce
Dabo pecuniam, si habeo veniam.
To go and fetch it, I will despatch it,
A hundred pounds sterling for my lives sparing.
(1285–88)

The lively, witty language of this scene makes it worth more than Tillyard's dismissive phrase, "a competent scene of knockabout."[50] In *The Troublesome Raigne,* as in *Edward I,* Peele's skills in Latin were well applied to satiric purposes, making good-natured fun of the monasteries' all too human sins of the flesh.

Critical judgments of Peele's verse have also been dismissive, most commentators being content to criticize its plodding quality, its rant, or its repetitiveness, from a no doubt well-informed general knowledge of Elizabethan drama. But one scholar who took the trouble to analyze its verse found that the use of feminine endings in *The Troublesome Raigne* strikingly resembled that of George Peele. P. W. Timberlake's study, belatedly recognized as one of the most reliable stylometric studies of Elizabethan drama,[51] noted that discussion of *The Troublesome Raigne* had linked the date of composition with the question of authorship, and summarized

> the evidence offered by H. D. Sykes to prove that Peele wrote the work. His arguments, which are practically conclusive, are based upon (1) the general style, (2) similarity in subject to Peele's *Edward I,* (3) admixture of rimed fourteeners and short riming lines as in Peele's *Arraignment of Paris* and *Edward I* respectively, (4) a strong anti-papal feeling, notable in almost all of Peele's signed works, (5) parallels in thought and expression to Peele's known work. (Timberlake 1931, 58–59)

Assembling into one table Timberlake's statistical data[52] for Peele's plays (18–24) and those for *The Troublesome Raigne* (59–61) gives the following result:

Table 7. Feminine Endings in Peele and *The Troublesome Raigne*

Work	Blank verse lines	Feminine endings	Percentage
Araygnement	189	1	0.5
Alcazar	1,404	22	1.5
Edward I	1, 390	25	1.8
David and Bethsabe	1,822	15	0.8
1 Troublesome Raigne	1,286	25	1.9
2 Troublesome Raigne	1,107	14	1.2

For comparative purposes, Timberlake's figures for the percentage of feminine endings in *King Leir* were 10.8 percent (61)—any claims for Peele's authorship of this play may be dismissed; *Arden of Feversham* 6.2 percent (52); the three Shakespearean scenes in *Edward III* (1, 2; 2.1, 2) between 8.6 and 10.6 percent (78); *Richard III* 16.8 percent (103); *Richard II* 8.2 percent (107); and *King John* 4.9 percent (109).

Another little-known metrical study which has come to be recognized as having great value for authorship studies was produced by Ants Oras in 1960,[53] who analyzed over seven hundred English plays produced between the 1590s and the 1640s, looking at the placing of pauses within the verse line. Oras provided statistics for over a million lines of verse, counting "the incidence of internal pauses in each of the nine positions within an iambic pentameter line in relation to the totals of such pauses . . . " (Oras 1960, 2). For every play studied, Oras gave the raw figures for the number of internal pauses at each metrical position from 1 to 9, followed by two percentage figures. These indicate respectively (a) "the ratio of such pauses before the fifth position, i. e. in the first half of the line, to pauses after that position (under 'First Half')—that is, comparing positions 1–4, 6–9; and (b) a figure showing the percentage of pauses in even positions, that is, pauses after an even-numbered syllable (under 'Even')" (4). In the following table I give Oras's figures for four Peele plays, followed by my own computations for each part of *The Troublesome Raigne* (I add Oras's results for *King John*).

Table 8. Pause patterns in Peele, *The Troublesome Raigne*, and Shakespeare, *King John*

	1st Half	Even	1	2	3	4	5	6	7	8	9
AP	70.7	67.6	4.7	14.6	11.0	32.1	11.8	17.3	4.7	3.6	0.3
Alc	74.2	72.8	2.0	13.2	8.8	40.1	13.7	18.7	2.6	0.9	-
Ed I	76.5	70.2	1.9	11.8	6.7	43.5	16.4	13.7	3.8	1.1	1.1
D&B	68.6	65.0	1.6	9.7	4.7	35.8	24.5	16.8	4.7	2.2	-
1TR	85.3	72.2	3.0	14.7	6.5	48.4	14.9	8.6	2.9	0.5	0.5
2TR	82.1	76.7	2.7	13.8	3.8	51.7	12.5	10.2	3.7	1.0	0.6
King John	58.7	60.3	4.9	9.2	3.6	28.7	20.9	18.3	8.7	4.1	1.5

These results show a satisfying homogeneity in quantifiable features of the blank verse in four plays by Peele and *The Troublesome Raigne.*

IV

If my case for Peele's authorship of *The Troublesome Raigne* holds water, it will have repercussions on the controversy concerning the play's relationship to Shakespeare's *King John.* For over two and a half centuries, as we can see from Joseph Candido's excellent selection of early criticism,[54] Shakespeare scholars regarded *The Troublesome Raigne* as the undisputed source for *King John.* But in 1954 Ernst Honigmann, inspired by his teacher Peter Alexander, attempted to invert this tradition: *King John* preceded the anonymous chronicle play, and its dating must be revised back from 1595–96 to 1590, so disrupting the agreed chronology of Shakespeare's earlier plays.[55] Honigmann reiterated his thesis in 1982 and 2000; W. S. Matchett accepted it in his Signet edition, as did L. A. Beaurline in his New Cambridge edition, while Brian Boyd supported it in an article published in 1995.[56] But whoever wishes to dislodge *King John* from its position in 1595–96 is going to have to do the same with *Richard II,* for many scholars have commented on the close links between these two history plays.[57] *Richard II,* entered in the Stationers' Register on 29 August 1597, was published in 1597 and was listed by Meres in 1598. Since George Logan published his study,[58] it seems almost certain that Shakespeare made use of Samuel Daniel's *The First Four Books of the Civil Wars* (SR, 11 Oct. 1594; published 1595), which would date the play in 1595. In the Oxford *Textual Companion* Gary Taylor assigns *Richard II* to 1595, *King John* to 1596.[59] However, in his essay supporting Honigmann's thesis Boyd (1995b, 54, n. 10) suggested the following sequence (I omit the narrative poems): *Richard III* (1590–91); *King John* (1591); *Comedy of Errors* (1592); *Love's Labour's Lost* (1592); *Richard II* (1594); *Romeo and Juliet* (1594–95); *Midsummer Night's Dream* (1595); *1 Henry IV* (1595–96); *Merchant of Venice* (1596). I imagine that few Shakespeareans could accept a re-dating that would put *King John* before *Comedy of Errors* and *Love's Labour's Lost,* but for the present purposes it is enough to note the improbability of separating it from *Richard II* by three full years. I am not persuaded by the case for re-dating *King John* so as to make it the precursor of *The Troublesome Raigne,* and I have elsewhere addressed that aspect of the Honigmann thesis that attempts to deny Peele competence in dramaturgy.[60] Here I should like to discuss the general issue of precedence, and draw on a recent essay by MacDonald Jackson validating the accepted chronology of Shakespeare's plays from the mid-1590s.

On the second issue, the empirical and quantitative approaches that I have been using in this essay can also be applied to the study of Shakespeare's chronology. Ever since Capell and Malone scholarly discussions of Shakespeare's chronology have collated several types of information. External evidence includes the date of a play's first performance, the date of its entry in the Stationers' Register, the date of its first printing, and any contemporary allusions. While we know the printing date of *The Troublesome Raigne, King John* was not printed until the 1623 Folio. However, Francis Meres listed it in 1598 among the comedies and tragedies for which

"*Shakespeare* among the English is the most excellent in both kinds."[61] Internal evidence includes Shakespeare's use of published books, whether as source material or for incidental allusions; reference to external events, English or European; linguistic evidence of changes in Shakespeare's grammatical preferences, or choice of vocabulary; and metrical evidence, the proportion within a play's verse of run-on lines, internal pauses, split lines, rhyme, and feminine endings. Although some scholars used to dismiss all internal evidence as "subjective" or "impressionistic,"[62] mere "guesswork" (Sider 1990, xxviii), the history of attribution studies in the second half of the twentieth century showed that, when properly executed, studies using internal evidence were empirically sound, based on the careful collection and evaluation of data, and using computing processes that could be replicated by other researchers—all attributes of a scientific methodology. The work of Cyrus Hoy, David Lake, and MacDonald Jackson, to name only three, has triumphantly validated quantitative linguistic studies as reliable authorship tools.

MacDonald Jackson, the most continuously inventive and innovative scholar in this field, has also shown how these approaches can be applied to establishing a writer's chronology. Once the appropriate parameters have been established and sound methods applied, an accurate chronology enables us to place individual works in sequence and to evaluate a new attribution according to whether its linguistic make-up fits the steady evolution that is one of the major characteristics of Shakespeare's style. Applying these methods, it can be shown that the first two Acts of *Pericles* do not fit into the chronological sequence, whereas acts 3–5 do, and that the anonymous *Funerall Elegye* (1612) corresponds in no way to the ascertainable characteristics of Shakespeare's writing in that period.[63] Jackson devised (to my knowledge) three separate linguistic tests for Shakespeare's chronology. The first, in 1979, used Gregor Sarrazin's "rare word" methods[64] to check the chronology proposed by Karl Wentersdorf;[65] the second (1994), used Marina Tarlinskaja's analyses of Shakespeare's prosody;[66] and the third, recently published, used Ants Oras's work on pause patterns.[67]

The relevance of these tests here is that they may shed light on the dating of *King John,* and especially in relationship to *Richard II.* Jackson's first test used Wentersdorf's chronology, which assigns *Richard II* to the acting season 1594–95, while placing *King John* in 1595–96. Wentersdorf compiled a "metrical index" for each Shakespeare play by combining the results of four separate verse tests ("extra syllables"; "overflows" or "run-on lines"; "pauses in split lines"; and "split lines"). Wentersdorf arranged the plays in sequence according to their metrical index, from the smallest value (7) to the largest (38), discovering a gradual progression which mostly coincided with the chronological order established by other means.

Jackson then compared Wentersdorf's results with the evidence that could be derived from the rare word tests of Gregor Sarrazin. In the 1890s Sarrazin compiled lists for every Shakespeare play of rare words, those which occurred elsewhere in Shakespeare only once ("dislegomena") or twice ("trislegomena"), establishing statistically what any well-practiced reader might have expected, namely that Shakespeare was more likely to reuse the same words in plays chronologically near to each other than in those separated by fifteen or twenty years. Jackson, following Sarrazin, divided Shakespeare's plays into four chronologically arranged groups (respectively, of ten, ten, eight, and nine plays), each containing roughly the same number of "rare" words (Jackson 1979, 148–49). His computation of the word links suggested that "for almost every play the greatest number of links were with the group to which it rightly belongs" (211; Table 19). Wanting to go beyond a simple grouping, Jackson then compiled a "vocabulary index" for each play by working out its "percentage of links . . . with the third and fourth groups," that is, with plays in the second half of Shakespeare's career, presenting his findings in a separate table (212; Table 20). Here, however, the correlation was less successful. *The Taming of the Shrew,* placed sixth in Wentersdorf's chronology (1591–92) emerged in twelfth place according to its "vocabulary index"; *Hamlet* shifted from twenty-third (1600–01) to thirtieth (1605–6); while *The Tempest* moved back from thirty-sixth (1610–11) to twenty-sixth (1603–4), before *Hamlet.* Not surprisingly, perhaps, although *King John* retained both its chronological position and dating (thirteenth; 1595–96), its links with *Richard II* were severed, for that play was moved back from twelfth place to fifth, following *Richard III,* and dated 1590–91. One must reluctantly judge that, despite Jackson's ingenuity and computational skill in devising this test, the results were hardly satisfactory.

Jackson's second essay in testing the chronology of Shakespeare's plays against independent linguistic evidence used Marina Tarlinskaja's computation of prosodic stress patterns in Shakespeare. Tarlinskaja applied the Russian linguistic-statistical method for studying poetic rhythm (as demonstrated in her essay in this volume). Jackson recomputed Tarlinskaja's data and produced a metrical index according to "the total percentage of syllables stressed in positions one and four of the standard ten-position blank verse line minus the total percentage of syllables stressed in positions three, six, and nine" (Jackson 1994, 454). The results turned out to be most valuable in confirming the presence of two authors in *Titus Andronicus* and *Pericles* (455–6), and proved quite reliable for the chronology of Shakespeare's third and fourth periods, from *Twelfth Night* to *The Tempest.* The metrical index was less successful, however, for the chronology of plays generally dated between 1595 and 1599, for it produced a sequence in which *King John* followed *The Two Gentlemen of Verona,* and preceded *A Midsummer Night's Dream, Julius Caesar, Love's Labour's Lost,* and *Richard II,* in that order. Evidently Shakespeare's prosody did not develop in a sufficiently clear-cut manner for Tarlinskaja's data to provide a reliable chronology for this second period, although it was certainly more accurate overall than Sarrazin's rare-word test.

Jackson's third attempt to use quantitative linguistic evidence to establish Shakespeare's chronology, using the painstaking analysis by Ants Oras of the pause patterns within Shakespeare's iambic pentameters, is the most successful yet. Uniting data from all three of Oras's tests (for all pauses; for "heavy pauses," those marked in the original printed texts by a punctuation mark heavier than a comma; and for "line-split" pauses, when a verse line is shared between two or more speakers), Jackson used a software program to correlate each play with every other. The resulting figures, he claimed, were "astonishing," providing "an objective, mathematical measure of similarity; the higher the correlation between two plays the more alike their pause patterns are."[68] Jackson presented his findings in a table giving for each play the five highest correlations with other Shakespeare plays, listed in the chronology as proposed by the Oxford *Textual Companion.* From this table I select the four plays preceding, and the four following, *King John* (decimal points have been omitted).

Table 9. Correlation Coefficients Between Shakespeare Plays

LLL 1594-95	*Rom* 9965	*R2* 9928	*Shr* 9921	*Jn* 9870	*Tit* 9853
MND 1595	*Jn* 9957	*Rom* 9820	*LLL* 9774	*1H6* 9746	*Err* 9721
Rom 1595	*LLL* 9965	*R2* 9947	*Shr* 9911	*Jn* 9872	*R3* 9860
R2 1595	*Rom* 9947	*LLL* 9928	*Err* 9924	*R3* 9906	*2H4* 9898
Jn 1596	*MND* 9957	*Rom* 9872	*LLL* 9870	*Err* 9840	*R2* 9814
MV 1596-97	*1H4* 9940	*Ado* 9894	*H5* 9894	*JC* 9887	*AYL* 9700
1H4 1596-97	*MV* 9940	*Ado* 9935	*H5* 9902	*JC* 9872	*2H4* 9785
Wiv 1597-98	*Tro* 9906	*R2* 9820	*AYL* 9759	*2H6* 9754	*LLL* 9725
2H4 1597-98	*Err* 9908	*R2* 9898	*R3* 9844	*Ado* 9807	*Tro* 9803

(Jackson, "Pause Patterns," 39)

As can be seen, demonstrable correlations exist between *King John* and *Love's Labour's Lost* (fourth highest correlation), *Midsummer Night's Dream* (highest), and *Romeo and Juliet* (fourth highest). Strong links exist between *Richard II* and *Romeo and Juliet* (highest correlation), *King John* (fifth highest), *The Merry Wives of Windsor* (second highest), and *2 Henry IV* (also second highest). Given the close links between this group of plays, any readjustment of chronology which would "sliver and disbranch"

Richard II, as well as *King John,* from their position would need very strong evidence to support it.

The recent attempts to re-date *King John* to the early 1590s, in order to facilitate a scenario in which Peele could be seen as deriving his plot structure from Shakespeare, rather than the other way round, has in fact cited no external or empirically derived internal evidence. It is mostly based on an intuitive aesthetic argument, namely that the dramatic structure of *The Troublesome Raigne,* its rearranging of historical sources into a unified whole is so good, its execution (in terms of characterization and language) so poor, that we cannot imagine Shakespeare using it as a model. I have argued elsewhere that this thesis is based on an inadequate knowledge of Peele's dramaturgy, which, as several scholars have shown, regularly displays just this combination of careful plotting and clumsy or shoddy execution. Accepting *The Troublesome Raigne* as Peele's first attempt to write a chronicle play, followed shortly by *Edward I,* allows us to think again about the relation between an older and a younger dramatist. Shakespeare was not much younger in years, of course, but—in the light of present knowledge—he seems to have started his career a decade or more later than Peele. We now know that they collaborated on *Titus Andronicus* (c. 1593), and with that tragedy as with this history, Shakespeare could have learned much from an older, well-established and more experienced dramatist. Peele had shown his competence in three different theatrical contexts, being more versatile than any of his contemporaries. He had taken an active part in university (Latin) drama during his time at Oxford (1572–1581), with a now-lost translation of one of Euripides' *Iphigeneia* plays (from Latin into English) to his credit (Prouty 1.41–46, 57–64); he had contributed to the court theater, his *Araygnement of Paris* (the first surviving English pastoral play) having been "Presented before the Queenes Maiestie, by the Children of her Chappell," as the 1584 Quarto declared (Prouty, 1.61, 70–71), probably in 1582;[69] and he played an important pioneering role in the City of London's dramatic activities, writing, and probably producing, three pageants for the Lord Mayor's show between 1585 and 1591, two of which survive (Prouty 1.71–76, 154–60). When Peele arrived in London in 1581 he joined several other university graduates attempting to make a literary career in the capital. In his excellent account, "The Emergence of the University Wits,"[70] G. K. Hunter has clearly distinguished the common inheritance of Lyly, Greene, Peele, Lodge, Marlowe, and Nashe. A humanist training at Grammar School and University gave them access to the standard Latin texts, with a good grounding in the *trivium* (grammar, logic, rhetoric); their expectations of a university career or a post serving the commonwealth (the classical ideal of a *vita activa*) being disappointed, they channeled their energy into writing pamphlets, novels, plays and translations; but their short, Bohemian careers ended in penury (Greene, Peele), premature death (Marlowe), or the abandonment of literature for some other career (Lodge to medicine, Gabriel Harvey and Joseph Hall a generation later to the church).

On the other side of a social divide were professional actors, such as Robert Wilson, author of *The Three Ladies of London* (c. 1581), "one of the 'twelve of the best' chosen in 1583 to be players for the Queen" (Hunter 1997, 34–36), and Shakespeare. The existence of a gap between these two groups is testified by many contemporary sources, nowhere more pointedly than in Robert Greene's supposed deathbed confession, *Groatsworth of witte, bought with a million of Repentance* (1592), now known to be the work of Henry Chettle.[71] In it Peele, Marlowe, and Nashe are grouped together as three "*Gentlemen . . . that spend their wits in making plaies,*" who are urged to desist writing for the common actors, "those Puppets . . . that spake from our mouths, those Anticks garnisht in our colours." Chettle is especially contemptuous about "an upstart Crow, beautified with our feathers, that with his *Tygers hart wrapt in a Players hyde,* supposes he is as well able to bombast out a blanke verse as the best of you: and beeing an absolute *Iohannes fac totum,* is in his owne conceit the only Shake-scene in a countrey" (Chambers 1930, ii.188). Chettle's gibe implies that Shakespeare is a new and illegitimate aspirant to the role of playwright. In his own pamphlet later that year, *Kind-Harts Dreame,* Chettle attempted to placate one of the "divers play-makers" among the University wits who had taken offence at the earlier pamphlet, one noted for "his uprightness of dealing . . . and his facetious grace in writing." As Lukas Erne (following F. G. Fleay and Gregor Sarrazin) has shown, Chettle was referring not to Shakespeare but to Peele.[72] The same distinction, between "schollers" or "the university" dramatists on the one hand, and "these mimick apes" or actors on the other, can be found in the *Parnassus* plays written and acted around Cambridge in 1600 (Erne 1998, 433). The actor William Kempe, a character in one of the plays, twice refers to "our fellow Shakespeare" (Chambers 1930, ii.201), as if being an actor would deny him the status of playwright. Chettle's contemptuous dismissal of Shakespeare registers him as a newcomer to the writers' craft, attempting to ascend from the lower social group to which he belonged.

But Shakespeare was not to be kept down by the protests of disgruntled and unsuccessful university graduates. He partly learned his craft from the generation of Marlowe, Lyly, and Peele, but he carried it to heights they never dreamed of. All historically aware studies of Shakespeare testify to his magpie-like ability to pick out structural elements, language, and theatrical effects from his predecessors,[73] and to transform and enlarge them. This is the well-established sequence, from *imitatio* to *aemulatio,* that was basic to classical and Renaissance literary theory and compositional practices.[74] On the other hand, Peele had nothing to learn from Shakespeare. This is true chronologically, in that Peele's London career extended from the early 1580s to the mid-1590s, before Shakespeare had shown the full range of his talents. But it is also true absolutely: Peele had nothing to learn from Shakespeare because he was incapable of learning from him. His dramatic structure, his characterization (or lack of it), his language—a curious mixture of the matter-of-fact (using little imagery) with vapid mythological allusions, pseudo-Marlovian exoticism, and Senecan rant—all these elements were fixed by the time he began writing for the public theater. In the short period between *The Battle of Alcazar* (c. 1588–89) and *David and Bethsabe* (c. 1594–95), although a certain development can be traced in his ability to integrate plot elements,[75] he never shook off his limitations, nor does he show any sign of having seen or read Shakespeare.

Yet the fact that Peele accepted him as a co-author on *Titus Andronicus* in 1593 shows that he, at least, was appreciative of the promise that this new writer showed. Peele died in November 1596, "of the poxe" as Meres alleged, and in great penury. If *King John* may be reliably dated to 1596, then a possible scenario emerges of Shakespeare taking over a structural outline from his former partner, perhaps in emulation, perhaps in tribute, totally transforming its language and characterization, and fully realizing the dramatic potential of the story. Historians attempting to recreate what went on in the Elizabethan theatre sometimes despair of being able to solve old problems unless new material should emerge, perhaps from neglected archives. But MacDonald P. Jackson has shown time and again that the old sources can divulge much more than previous generations realized, when fresh approaches are brought to bear on specific problems, and carried out with care and accuracy. In trying to establish Peele's authorship of *The Troublesome Raigne,* as in other authorship studies, I have been inspired by Mac's ability to design and execute new tests which have established some solid reference points in trying to reconstruct that rich but distant episode in our literary history. This essay aspires to be "some form of demonstration," partly produced by "counting things," in hopeful emulation of and respectful tribute to a master of that art.

Notes

1. MacDonald P. Jackson, *Studies in Attribution. Middleton and Shakespeare,* ed. J. Hogg, Jacobean Drama Studies, 79 (Salzburg: Universität Salzburg, Institut für Anglistik und Amerikanistik, 1979), vii.

2. All quotations from *The Troublesome Raigne* (abbreviated *1* and *2 T. R.,* followed by line numbers) come from the edition by Geoffrey Bullough, in his *Narrative and Dramatic Sources of Shakespeare, Volume Four: Later English History Plays* (London: Routledge and

Kegan Paul; New York: Columbia Univ. Press, 1962), 72–151. In these and other early play texts I have removed italics, reserving them for emphases of my own.

3. Sykes, *Sidelights on Shakespeare* (Stratford-upon-Avon: Shakespeare Head Press, 1919), 99–125. In his edition of *King John* (Cambridge: Cambridge Univ. Press, 1936; 1954) John Dover Wilson linked *The Troublesome Raigne* with Peele's *Edward I,* "a drama almost certainly by the same playwright" (xvii), and described it as "a catch-penny production, possibly of some needy playwright like Peele" (xx). Leonard R. N. Ashley's discussion, in *Authorship and Evidence: A Study of Attribution and the Renaissance Drama Illustrated by the Case of George Peele (1556–1596)* (Geneva: Droz, 1968), 96–102, is worthless.

4. T. M. Parrott, "Shakespeare's Revision of *Titus Andronicus,*" *Modern Language Review* 14 (January 1919): 16–37; P. W. Timberlake, *The Feminine Ending in English Blank Verse: A Study of its Use by Early Writers in the Measure and its Development in the Drama up to the Year 1595* (Menasha, WI: George Banta Publishing Company, 1931); J. D. Wilson (ed.), *Titus Andronicus* (Cambridge: Cambridge Univ. Press, 1948; The New Shakespeare); J. C. Maxwell, "Peele and Shakespeare: A Stylometric Test," *Journal of English and Germanic Philology* 49 (1950): 557–61; B. Boyd, "Common Words in *Titus Andronicus:* The Presence of Peele," *Notes and Queries* 240 (September 1995): 300–07; M. P. Jackson, "Stage Directions and Speech Headings in Act 1 of *Titus Andronicus* Q (1594): Shakespeare or Peele?" *Studies in Bibliography* 49 (1996): 134–48; M. P. Jackson, "Shakespeare's brothers and Peele's brethren: *Titus Andronicus* again," *Notes and Queries* 242 (December 1997): 494–95.

5. Brian Vickers, *Shakespeare, Co-Author* (Oxford: Oxford Univ. Press, 2002), chapter 3. [Editor's note: A twenty-second test has been added in Jackson's "Determining Authorship": see n. 9 below.]

6. See, e.g., M. St. C. Byrne, "Bibliographic Clues in Collaborate Plays," *The Library,* 4th s. 13 (June 1932): 21–48.

7. Sampley, "'Verbal Tests' for Peele's plays," *Studies in Philology* 30 (1933): 473–96.

8. All quotations from Peele's plays and poems derive from C. T. Prouty (ed.), *The Life and Works of George Peele,* 3 vols. (New Haven: Yale Univ. Press, 1952; 1961; 1970). Vol. 1 contains David H. Horne, *The Life and Minor Works of George Peele;* vol. 2 contains *Edward I,* ed. Frank S. Hook, and *The Battle of Alcazar,* ed. John Yoklavich; vol. 3 contains *The Araygnement of Paris,* ed. R. Mark Benbow, *David and Bethsabe,* ed. Elmer M. Blistein, and *The Old Wives Tale,* ed. Frank S. Hook. References to this work in the text will be in the form "Prouty 1.137," etc. Play titles will be abbreviated as follows: *Ed. I; Alc.; AP; D&B; OWT.*

9. See "Determining Authorship: A New Technique," *Research Opportunities in Renaissance Drama* 41 (2002): 1–14."

10. Arthur Freeman, "Shakespeare and *Solyman and Perseda,*" *Modern Language Review* 58 (October 1963): 481–87.

11. E. A. J. Honigmann, *Shakespeare's Impact on his Contemporaries* (London: McMillan, 1982), 133.

12. "A Tentative Chronology of Marlowe's and Some Other Elizabethan Plays," *Publications of the Modern Language Association of America* 51 (September 1936): 643–88.

13. Dates for Elizabethan plays are taken from A. Harbage, rev. S. Schoenbaum, *Annals of English Drama 975–1700* (London: Methuen, 1964), with two *Supplements* (1966, 1970). The *Annals* dates *Edward II* "1591–93," *Massacre* "1593." One must surely allow for mutual influence between Marlowe and Peele. Robert Smith, in "Marlowe and Peele: a further note on the final scholar scene in the *Doctor Faustus* B Text," *Notes and Queries* 245 (March 2000): 40–42, discussing close verbal parallels between *Faustus* and *The Battle of Alcazar,* commented: "As usual it is impossible to say who was the borrower" (41), since both dramatists did so, like all their contemporaries.

14. I have altered both spelling and lineation to correspond to my chosen texts, Bullough's edition of *The Troublesome Raigne* (see note 2) and F. S. Hook's edition of *Edward I* (see note 8).

15. Taylor noted that "cotton" in this sense ("This business prospers admirably," in Bullough's gloss) also occurs in Preston's *Cambyses* (649 n.).

16. Taylor noted that "the resemblance in wording here is strengthened by the general resemblance of the context in both plays, the entrance of the prophet" (649 n.).

17. In all, Sykes cited fifteen parallels between *The Troublesome Raigne* and *The Arraignment of Paris;* fifteen with *The Battle of Alcazar,* eighteen with *Edward I,* thirteen with *David and Bethsabe,* two with *The Tale of Troy,* and one each with *The Old Wives' Tale, The Honour of the Garter,* and *A Farewell.* Having elsewhere ascribed *Alphonsus, Emperor of Germany* to Peele (essays in *Notes and Queries* [1912] collected in *Sidelights on Elizabethan Drama* [Oxford: Oxford Univ. Press, 1924; London: Cass, 1966], 79–98), Sykes noted fourteen parallels between it and *The Troublesome Raigne,* and three with *Jack Straw,* another play he ascribed to Peele. Not all of these parallels convince, but cumulatively they add up to a strong case for Peele's authorship of *The Troublesome Raigne.*

18. Quotations are from T. M. Parrott (ed.), *Chapman's Tragedies* (London: Routledge; New York: Dutton, 1910). This play has since been removed from the Chapman canon.

19. R. F. Hill, "The Composition of Titus Andronicus," *Shakespeare Survey* 10 (1957): 60–70.

20. The habit may have been catching, for in scenes reliably ascribed to Shakespeare we find "Mark, Marcus, mark" (3.1.143); "Fie, brother, fie" (3.2.21); "Fie, Publius, fie!" (5.2.155); "Speak, Romans, speak" (5.3.134). Of course, it is a well-known phenomenon in authorship studies that writers working together influence each other: see R. L. Street and H. Giles, "Speech Accommodation Theory: A Social Cognitive Approach to Language and Speech Behavior," in M. E. Roloff and C. R. Berger (eds.), *Social Cognition and Communication* (Beverly Hills, London, New Delhi: Sage Publications, 1982), 193–226, and Jonathan Hope, *The Authorship of Shakespeare's Plays. A Socio-Linguistic study* (Cambridge: Cambridge Univ. Press, 1994), 79.

21. Cf. Vickers, *Shakespeare, Co-Author,* 226–30.

22. This total omits the Presenter's prologues to each act.

23. Sykes noted some parallel utterances in Peele's *Edward I:* "Princes of Scotland, and my loving friends" (2024); "Lords of Albania, and my peers in France" (1409).

24. For further instances, see ll. 23, 45, 49–50, 108, 110, 119, 131, 155.

25. For further instances, see ll. 18–19, 47, 56, 64, 70.

26. See, e.g., S. K. Viswanathan, "'Illeism With a Difference' in Certain Middle Plays of Shakespeare," *Shakespeare Quarterly* 20 (autumn 1970): 407–15; Deborah T. Curren-Aquino, "Self-naming in Shakespeare's Early Plays," *Names* 35 (September - December 1987): 147–63.

27. For the high style, cf. 1031–32, 2156–57, 2191, 2299; for the low, cf. 721, 1070, 1195–96, 1609, 2078–79.

28. "Der Stil in George Peeles sicheren und zweifelhaften dramatischen Werken," Ph.D. Diss., Univ. of Breslau (Breslau: H. Fleischmann, 1910).

29. Landsberg also discussed *Sir Clyomon and Sir Clamydes,* in which she computed that one verse in every eight displayed alliteration, a proportion similar to *The Arraygnment of Paris* (1910, 56–58, 73–75), and *Locrine,* where she found a lower ratio, once in every fourteen lines (124–25).

30. Wolfgang Clemen, *English Tragedy before Shakespeare. The Development of Dramatic Speech* (London: Methuen, 1961); tr. T. S. Dorsch from *Die Tragödie vor Shakespeare: ihre Entwicklung im Spiegel der dramatischen Rede* (Heidelberg: Quelle und Meyer, 1955), 171 note. Clemen commented that in the many "flights of passion" Peele gave to the Moor, Muly Mahamet, "with the help of such devices as the repetition and sheer accumu-

lation of words, thrown into glaring relief by means of alliteration, a blood-curdling effect is intended to be produced" (172–73).

31. See Vickers 2002, 220–23.

32. Much of Peele's nondramatic poetry reads like the work of a late medieval poet—indeed, as David Horne showed, in his early *Tale of Troy* Peele's "chief debt is to Caxton for narrative material and Chaucer and Spenser for style" (Prouty, 1.149). It is not surprising, then, to find Peele using an archaic form in his poem: "Y-clypped Stately Hecuba was she" (*Tale of Troy,* 11), "Yborne was Piers to be infortunate" (*An Eclogue Gratulatory,* 6), but it is surprising to meet it again in the mouths of the Bastard: "How are thy thoughts ywrapt in Honors heaven?" (*1 T. R.,* 257), and of King John: "Ymixt with death, biding I wot not where" (*2 T. R.,* 798). J. W. Sider, in his useful edition of *The Troublesome Raigne of John, King of England* (New York: Garland, 1979), records the identification by J. F. Dominic (Ph.D. Diss., 1969) of the source for the Bastard's allusion to the statue of Hector erected by the Trojans in order to menace the Greeks (*1 T. R.,* 668–69), in Raoul Le Fèvre's *Recuyell of the Historyes of Troye,* which Caxton translated and published in 1471 (Sider 1979, 195). This work was one of Peele's sources both for *The Tale of Troy* and for *The Araygnement of Paris* (Prouty, 1.149–50; 3.14).

33. "Then *d*eath rock me asleep, abridge my *d*oleful *d*ays! / Why then let *gr*ievous, *g*hastly, *g*aping wounds / Untwin'd the Sisters Three!" (*2 Henry IV,* 2.4.197–99).

34. For other instances of triple alliteration, see *1 T. R.,* 574; *2 T. R.,* 543, 811.

35. In one of his scenes for *Titus Andronicus* Peele has a character promise to "rouse the proudest panther in the chase" (2.2.21).

36. For further instances of quadruple alliteration see *1 T. R.,* 406, 521–22, 1275, 1560, 1653; *2 T. R.,* 17, 422, 838.

37. For further fourfold alliterations see *Ed. I,* 365–66, 1073, 1692; *D&B,* 12–13, 49, 51, 69–70, 213, 327, 455–56, 634, 868, 981–82, 1005, 1010, 1120–21, 1133, 1196, 1317–18, 1402. A surprising number of instances alliterate on "*th*" sounds.

38. Compare alliterations on "*dis-*" in *The Troublesome Raigne:* "*dis*poyled and *dis*possest" (*1 T. R.,* 1640); "*Dis*turbed thoughts, . . . / *Dis*tracted passions" (*2 T. R.,* 110–11).

39. See also, fivefold, *D&B,* 815–18, 1841–42; sixfold: 756–58, 846–50, 1317–18, 1864–65; *Ed. I,* 321–22, 2212–13.

40. For further instances of alliteration on "*tr*" see *1 T. R.,* 576, 888–89.

41. In addition to these occurrences of "frolike" in *1 T. R.* and *Ed. I,* one of the three Pages in *The Old Wives Tale* is called "Frolicke."

42. For further instances of alliteration on "*pr,*" see *Alc.,* 641; *Ed. 1,* 1680; *D&B,* 1030; *1 T. R.,* 1506–7; *2 T. R.,* 168.

43. "Princely" was one of Peele's favorite epithets. According to the Chadwyck-Healey database of English Renaissance drama, Peele used it over thirty times in his plays, twelve of these instances occurring in *The Battle of Alcazar* alone. It also crops up frequently in his poems.

44. For further instances of alliteration on "*gr,*" see *Ed. 1,* 2056, 2203; *D&B,* 1072–79, 1907; *1 T. R.,* 534.

45. For further instances of alliteration on "*br,*" see *Ed. 1,* 881, 1727.

46. See, e.g., Sykes 1919, 104–6; Prouty, 1.75–76, 78–79, 92. In *Descensus Astraeae* (1591) Peele gratuitously introduced "*Superstition. A Friar sitting by the Fountaine,*" who addresses "*Ignorance. A Priest,*" exhorting him to "stirre . . . and with thy beades poyson this spring, / I tell thee all is banefull that I bring" (Prouty, 1.216).

47. A similar deliberate error occurs in Peele's *Edward I,* where the Farmer recalls "an old saide saying, I remember I redde it in *Catoes Pueriles,* that *Cantabit vacuus corame latrone viator.* A man purse pennilesse may sing before a thiefe" (1734–36). As Frank Hook pointed out, the quotation is in fact from Juvenal (*Satires* 10.22), and the Farmer has confused the titles of two elementary Latin texts, the *Sententiae Pueriles* of Leonard Culman

and the *Distichia Moralia* ascribed to Dionysius Cato: "a little joke, the point of which would have been evident to any member of the audience who had gone as far as the second form of a grammar school" (Prouty 2.195).

48. *Canterbury Tales,* General Prologue, 160–62.

49. Cf. lines 367–68, 418–21, 439, 451, 540, 628, 1187, 1291, 1734–35, 1817, 2144.

50. *Shakespeare's History Plays* (London: Chatto and Windus, 1944), 216.

51. For favourable evaluations of Timberlake's work see Gary Taylor, "The Canon and Chronology of Shakespeare's Plays," in S. Wells and G. Taylor, *William Shakespeare. A Textual Companion* (Oxford: Oxford Univ. Press, 1987), 114; Jackson 1979, 151, and Vickers 2002, 163–66.

52. Timberlake counted the number of full blank verse lines in each play, and differentiated feminine endings caused by proper names from "normal" extrasyllabic endings: I omit his data for names, and also those for *The Old Wives Tale,* which contains "no long connected passage of blank verse."

53. *Pause Patterns in Elizabethan and Jacobean Drama. An Experiment in Prosody,* Univ. of Florida Monographs, Humanities, 3 (Gainesville: Univ. of Florida Press, 1960).

54. Joseph Candido (ed.), *King John* (London and Atlantic Heights, NJ: Athlone, 1996): the first volume in a new series, *Shakespeare, the critical tradition,* ed. Brian Vickers.

55. E. A. J. Honigmann (ed.), *King John* (London: Methuen, 1954; the Arden Shakespeare), especially the Introduction, xi–xxxiii, xliii–lix, and Appendix B, "Structural Inconsistencies in *John* and *The Troublesome Raigne of John,*" 167–73. For Honigmann's acknowledgment of the prior formulation of this thesis by A. S. Cairncross and Peter Alexander, see xviii, n. 2.

56. Honigmann 1982, 56–66, 78–88; Honigmann, "Shakespeare's Self-Repetitions and *King John,*" *Shakespeare Survey* 53 (2000): 175–83; W. S. Matchett (ed.), *King John* (New York: The New American Library, 1966; The Signet Classic Shakespeare); L. A. Beaurline (ed.), *King John* (Cambridge: Cambridge Univ. Press, 1990; New Cambridge Shakespeare); Brian Boyd, "*King John* and *The Troublesome Raigne:* Sources, Structure, Sequence," *Philological Quarterly* 74, no. 1 (winter 1995): 37–56.

57. J. Dover Wilson, in his edition of *Richard II* (Cambridge: Cambridge Univ. Press, 1939; 1951), cited and discussed its numerous parallels with *King John* and also with *The Troublesome Raigne* (x, xliv n., lvii–lviii, 119, 132, 133, 142, 151, 154, 150, 157 (twice), 173, 177, 185, 190 (three times), 192, 193, 201, 217 (twice), 230 (twice), 231 (three times), 232, 233. These parallels include many where *King John* draws on *The Troublesome Raigne,* suggesting that Shakespeare knew Peele's play before writing *Richard II.* See also Wilson's edition of *King John,* in which Wilson observed that "*Richard II* . . . seems to be closer to it than any other of his plays" (Cambridge: Cambridge Univ. Press, [1936, 1954] 1969, viii), and added that "most [critics] have found a close connexion between *King John* and *Richard II*" (li).

58. "Lucan-Daniel-Shakespeare: New Light on the Relation Between *The Civil Wars* and *Richard II,*" *Shakespeare Studies* 9 (1976): 121–40.

59. *Textual Companion,* 117–18, 119.

60. See Brian Vickers, "*The Troublesome Raigne* and *King John*: a study in dramaturgy," forthcoming.

61. *Palladis Tamia: Wits Treasury* (1598); repr. E. K. Chambers, *William Shakespeare. A Study of Facts and Problems,* 2 vols. (Oxford: Oxford Univ. Press, 1930), ii. 194.

62. Cf. Vickers, "*Co-Author,*" 132–34, for comments on Samuel Schoenbaum.

63. Jackson, "Pause Patterns in Shakespeare's Verse: Canon and Chronology," *Literary and Linguistic Computing* 17 (2002), 37–46; Vickers, *"Counterfeiting" Shakespeare: Evidence, authorship, and John Ford's* Funerall Elegye (Cambridge: Cambridge Univ. Press, 2002), 156–68.

64. "Wortechos bei Shakespeare," *Shakespeare Jahrbuch* 33 (1897): 121–65; 34 (1898): 119–69.

65. "Shakespearean Chronology and the Metrical Tests," in W. Fischer and K. Wentersdorf (eds.), *Shakespeare-Studien: Festschrift für Heinrich Mutschmann* (Marburg: Elwert Verlag, 1951), 161–93.

66. Jackson, "Another metrical index for Shakespeare's plays," *Neuphilologische Mitteilungen,* 95 (1994): 453–58, drawing on Marina Tarlinskaja, *Shakespeare's Verse. Iambic Pentameter and the Poet's Idiosyncrasies* (New York: Peter Lang, 1987).

67. Jackson, "Pause Patterns," drawing on Oras, *Pause Patterns.*

68. Jackson, "Pause Patterns," 2002, 39.

69. Cf. Carter A. Daniel, "The Date of Peele's *Arraignment of Paris,*" *Notes and Queries* 227 (April 1982): 131–32, citing records of the Revels Office confirming a date of 1582.

70. Hunter, *English Drama 1586–1642, The Age of Shakespeare* (Oxford: Oxford Univ. Press, 1997). Chapter 3 (22–92) is devoted to "Early Tragedy," chapter 4 (93–154) to "Early Comedy," and chapter 5 to "Early History Plays" (155–228). These chapters contain some of the best commentary on Peele's drama. See also Hunter's pamphlet in the British Council's "Writers and their Work" series: *Lyly and Peele* (London: Longman, 1968).

71. See W. B. Austin, "A Computer-Aided Technique for Stylistic Discrimination: The Authorship of *"Greene's Groatsworth of Wit*" (Washington, DC: U.S. Department of Health, Education, and Welfare. Office of Education. Bureau of Research, April 1969), and D. A. Carroll (ed.), *Greene's Groatsworth of Wit* (Binghamton, NY: Medieval and Renaissance Texts and Studies, 1994), 1–31, 105–6 (summarizing Austin's work), and 131–45. John Jowett, in "Johannes Factotum: Henry Chettle and *Greene's Groatsworth of Wit,*" *Proceedings of the Bibliographical Society of America* 87 (1993), 453–86, endorsed Austin's analysis (455–61) and added fresh evidence establishing the *Groatsworth* as a forgery (453, 477), and Chettle as a "fabricator" (473).

72. Lukas Erne, "Biography and Mythography: rereading Chettle's alleged apology to Shakespeare," *Englische Studien* 79 (September 1998): 430–40.

73. For his appropriation of Lyly's use of thematic plot-parallels see, e.g., G. K. Hunter, *John Lyly: The Humanist as Courtier* (London: Methuen, 1962), 298–349.

74. See, e.g., Brian Vickers (ed.), *English Renaissance Literary Criticism* (Oxford: Oxford Univ. Press, 1999), 22–39.

75. See Vickers, "Dramaturgy."

Did Shakespeare Write *A Lover's Complaint?* The Jackson Ascription Revisited

Ward Elliott and Robert J. Valenza

The Great Turnaround

A lover's complaint *(LC)* was printed in the same quarto volume as Shakespeare's *Sonnets* in 1609 (*Q*), with its own title page bearing the name of William Shake-speare. It was also republished as Shakespeare's in John Benson's pirated *Poems: Written by Wil. Shake-speare. Gent.* (1640). But its place in the Shakespeare canon has long been doubted. By 1964 the scholarly consensus ran something like this: *LC* was an "awkward little pastoral," far too clumsy to be Shakespeare's mature work, and probably too clumsy, too ill-matched with the Sonnets, and too full of "non-Shakespearean" language to be Shakespeare's at all. Most likely it was insinuated into *Q* by its unscrupulous publisher, Thomas Thorpe, who had already printed the sonnets without Shakespeare's knowledge or consent and plainly cared more for his own interests than for Shakespeare's. Piracies abound in the Shakespeare record, loaded with false claims of Shakespeare authorship. Benson's collection and Isaac Jaggard's *The Passionate Pilgrim* (1599) are two blatant examples. Who could trust Thorpe's assurance that this dense, ornate little Complaint was actually Shakespeare's?[1]

By the year 2000 this confederacy of doubt was broken, and replaced by a consensus that *LC* was probably a work of Shakespeare's maturity. By then, both external and internal evidence seemed much more favorable to Shakespeare. Thorpe, it appeared, was not a pirate at all, but someone who did business with Shakespeare, had every reason to abide by Shakespeare's preferences, and none to publish his sonnets behind his back, print the Sonnets in the wrong order, or peddle someone else's poem under Shakespeare's name.[2] As for internal evidence, *LC* turned out to be loaded with word links to Shakespeare's late plays and with echoes of late writings by Shakespeare and others, suggesting that it was not only by Shakespeare but by the mature Shakespeare at the peak of his powers, belatedly following a well-established Elizabethan tradition of topping off a sonnet series with a narrative poem.[3]

Almost all the credit for this great turnaround must go to Kenneth Muir and MacDonald Jackson, who in 1964 and 1965, independently of each other, published two landmark studies, both of them *tours de force* of scholarly persuasion.[4] These not only dispelled the old doubts but have also resisted newer ones expressed by Samuel Schoenbaum, M. W. A. Smith, and ourselves in the 1990s. Schoenbaum merely remarked that "the [Shakespeare] ascription would not in general win favour."[5] Smith gave quantitative support to earlier arguments that *LC* was more likely the work of George Chapman than of Shakespeare.[6] Our article was skeptical of both Shakespeare's and Chapman's claims to authorship of *LC*.[7] Here, we revisit both Jackson's original *tour de force* (with occasional reference to Muir) and our first doubts about his central conclusion.

Attribution Evidence, 1965

Our first impression, on tracking down Jackson's 1965 monograph through interlibrary loan, was surprise and pleasure, not that he anticipated the external-evidence rehabilitation of Thomas Thorpe (though he did that, too, and so did Muir),[8] but that his internal evidence was still remarkably fresh, powerful, and still valid, despite the passage of almost four decades of what we had supposed were revolutionary development in authorship studies. Primitive though his resources were then, most of Jackson's evidence and assertions have worn extremely well. No one who has labored through the task of counting distinguishing features of text samples, and entering them on a spreadsheet, again and again in successive modifications, can fail to marvel at the grit, persistence, focus, and accuracy of the iron men of Jackson's generation who had to do it without computers, spreadsheets, word processors, electronic texts, and machine-generated concordances. Not one of the research aids that we take for granted today—personal computers; the Internet; the Oxford Text Archive; the Riverside or Oxford Shakespeares (even in hard copy, let alone e-text); or the Spevack Shakespeare Concordance—was available to Jackson or Muir, or to Alfred Hart, their then-leading model of quantitative analysis.[9]

"New" Thoughts on New Words

The inspiration for our Shakespeare Clinic was the work of two distinguished statisticians, Bradley Efron of Stanford, and Ronald Thisted, of the University of Chicago. Like us, they knew nothing of Jackson's and Muir's work (let alone Hart's), but, like Jackson and Muir, they invoked the work of an earlier master, Sir Ronald Fisher, the greatest statistician of his era. Fisher had been asked to predict the number of new butterfly species that would be discovered if a collection team returned to the Orient for another stint. He studied the previous rate of new discoveries and extrapolated it to the future, publishing his results the same year as Hart.[10] Efron developed Fisher's approach into what is now known as the Bootstrap Method. He encouraged his student, Thisted, to apply it to the then-new Spevack Shakespeare Concordance,[11] substituting words for butterflies. How many "latent" words did Shakespeare know but not write down? How many of these could be expected to appear in a hypothetical, newly discovered Shakespeare poem or play of a given length?

After impressive deployment of high-end numerology, Thisted's answers were something like this: we could expect about 11,000 "new" words if Shakespeare had written double his known output of about 885,000 words, and about as many as appeared in "Shall I Die?" if the text, like "Shall I Die?" were less than 500 words.[12] Even more refined numerology by Robert Valenza indicated that Thisted's and Efron's sample size and Shakespeare poems baselines were both too small to predict reliably a new-word count—but their technique could be made to work by doubling the sample size to at least 1,000 words and the baseline to at least 100,000 words.[13]

After much study, trial, and error, with successive teams of Claremont students and ever-more-potent computers—and still no more than dimly aware of Jackson's pioneering work—we concluded that, in a typical 1,500-word block of Shakespeare play text, Shakespeare would be expected to introduce about twenty to thirty new (to him) words, plus about 320 rare words he had used elsewhere in numbers less than 100. Expected new and rare words should vary somewhat with the sample's vocabulary richness, as measured by type-token ratios. The rare words would also show a "slope" from the rarest of the rare to the most common of the rare, falling within a predictable range of steepness. We found that Shakespeare's poems fitted his play ranges for new words and slope, but had much higher percentages of rare words.[14] This was an important discovery because Shakespeare only wrote about 45,000 words of poems, too few to permit using any of our Thisted-Efron tests with a poems-only baseline. Where observed poem ranges matched observed and validated play ranges, as with new words and slope (but not rare words), it was possible legitimately to apply both tests to poems, and they proved extremely useful to us.

Imagine our surprise, after all this supposedly pathbreaking deployment, when we tracked down Jackson's 1965 monograph and found that, using nothing but Hart, two old concordances, the old OED, and his own wits, he had already done essentially the same thing thirty years earlier. In many respects, as a true literary critic, he had done it better than we or our exemplars, not just because he is a reader and we are only counters, but also because his counting was more literate and more hand-done than ours. He counted not just the word itself, but also some of its roots and kin. For us and our computers, *plat* and *platted* were two different words; so were *scythe* and *scythed.* For Jackson, *plat* and *platted* were one new word, not two, but *scythed* was treated as a new word in *LC* though Shakespeare had used *scythe* (actually *scythe's*) elsewhere (*LLL* 1.01.6), presumably because *scythe* was a noun, *scythed* a verb (p. 12). Our computer was oblivious to such niceties and our calculations were based not on the entire canon, but only on a "core baseline" of Shakespeare plays of undisputed authorship. Our baseline did not include Shakespeare poems because of doubts at the time (since dispelled) that our Thisted-Efron tests were usable for poems. The net result was that our computer was 80 percent more likely than Jackson to count a word as new. Jackson and Muir found about forty-nine new words in *LC;* we found eighty-eight, more loosely defined. Either way of counting is serviceable if used consistently, since both baseline and samples are over- or undercounted in the same way, but, in retrospect, his is the tight, handcrafted, well-explained version. Though inevitably dependent on judgment, his result is almost identical to Muir's "some fifty" (1973, 205–7). Ours is the loose, rough-hewn, machine-made one that has less of one kind of tightness, more of others (we did not count any Shakespeare-Canon passages or plays we thought dubious, and, following Thisted, we calculated expected new words, as well as actual ones, for standard-sized text blocks), plus the large bonuses of extra speed, reach, and uniformity possible from having an e-text archive and machines to do the counting.

Like Muir and Hart, but unlike Mackail, Jackson was well aware that the presence of new "non-Shakespearean" words in a text, far from showing that Shakespeare didn't write it, was an identifying Shakespeare trademark. He noted that Shakespeare introduced a "new word" not found in his concordances every twenty lines in his early plays, every ten lines in *King Lear* and *Hamlet,* and every eleven to twelve lines in *The Rape of Lucrece* and *Venus and Adonis.* He concluded:

> Simple calculation reveals that one word not elsewhere used by Shakespeare occurs in *A Lover's Complaint* for every seven lines. This proportion of once-used words is what we should expect to find in a Shakespearean poem written at about the time of *Hamlet* or *King Lear;* and Hart's studies suggest the improbability that any other writer of the time would have employed so many words of this kind. We should certainly not expect to find even Shakespeare using so large a proportion of once-used words at a date earlier than his writing of *Venus and Adonis.*[15]

OTHER WORD TESTS

The passage is remarkable, not only for grasping and applying the essence of our modern new-word tests—in a much simpler and more comprehensible format than ours—but for seeking to derive from them the now-conventional, but then heretical, conclusion that *A Lover's Complaint* and most of the *Sonnets* were written closer to their actual publication date, 1609, than to the 1590s, when sonnets were most in vogue. In a single, densely researched paragraph on word links he anticipated the work of Kent and Charles Hieatt, dating *LC* and many of the Sonnets in the seventeenth century.[16] He also offered strikingly modern examinations of "coined words" which seemed from the OED to be new, not just to Shakespeare, but to anyone (15–16). He noted that Shakespeare's word-coinage rates rose markedly during his lifetime and were higher than anyone else's, especially Chapman's (18), and he concluded that *LC*'s unusually high word-coinage rate argued against both Chapman and early Shakespeare as author (19). Also modern were his consideration of hyphenated compound words (16); of nouns made into verbs ("sistering," "orbed," "caged," 16–17) of *un-*, *en-*, and *-ing* words; of rare words (pp. 8–12, but for him, "rare" meant five or fewer), and of "twice-used words," an even rarer variant, consisting only of words used in *LC* and once elsewhere in Shakespeare (13). He also discussed Latinisms and Gallicisms (17–18); legalisms and puns (23–25); and "doublets," which he defined as "the combination of two nouns, or, less frequently, two adjectives, to suggest a third or a fourth" (25–26).

In those days many of these could be done by someone who was an inspired counter, making sophisticated and imaginative use of available concordances and dictionaries. But some, such as Latinisms, Gallicisms, legalisms, puns, and doublets, could only be the work of an inspired reader, who knew from direct observation Shakespeare's stylistic peculiarities and how they compared to those of his contemporaries. In general, *Shakespeare's "A Lover's Complaint"* starts with the most countable features (new words and rare words, 8–19), proceeds to the less countable (parallel imagery, Latinisms, puns, doublets, 19–26), and climaxes with the least countable, unabashedly aesthetic judgment of whether the poem is good enough to be Shakespeare, and, if so, whether it is a mature work or an early, unfinished draft (26–39).

This poses a problem for us, radical measurers and counters who admire reading from afar but rarely if ever admit to practicing it ourselves. We admit to being firmly in the tradition of the *Tabellenknechte* so deplored by the elders of the University of Göttingen in the eighteenth century, "slaves of the tables, that bring only the dry bones of Statistics, without clothing them with the flesh of descriptive reality."[17] What, if anything, could we say that would be of value to an audience of readers? That reading, like counting, is an indispensable part of authorship analysis? It is. That, like counting, it can sometimes be inconclusive or wrong? It can be. That it should be cross-checked by counting, where appropriate? It should be, just as counting should be cross-checked by reading. That people like Jackson, who both read and count well and can do their own cross-checking are exceedingly rare and deserve special praise for works like *Shakespeare's "A Lover's Complaint"?* They are, and they do. That Shakespeare must therefore have written *A Lover's Complaint?* Probably not.

How do the countable details of the Jackson monograph look today? The short answer is something like "limited by the resources he had then, but still remarkably sound for Shakespeare." It would not be easy even today to find in the monograph a single statement about Shakespeare that is wrong. But they were probably less reliably sound for non-Shakespeare, for which even the primitive concordances of the day were lacking. We have already seen that introducing new "non-Shakespearean" words is a Shakespeare hallmark, and that *LC* involved a very high rate of such introductions, one every seven lines, much higher than Shakespeare's first ten plays (one every twenty lines), and higher, even than *King Lear* and *Hamlet,* which had a new word every ten lines (12). With computers and databases, we could count such "new words" in 1,500-word blocks, not lines, and cover many more plays and poems than Jackson could in 1965, and it still took us years to do that to our satisfaction. But our evidence is consistent with both of Jackson's propositions: that Shakespeare routinely introduced many words new to him, and that *LC* had more than the normal Shakespeare rate of new-word introductions.

Too Many New Words for Shakespeare?

Is this good evidence that Shakespeare wrote *LC?* The answer depends not just on how they fit with Shakespeare's habits, but on how they compare with those of his contemporaries. In 1965 this was hard to do, even for the most prodigious and retentive reader. A diligent and imaginative scholar could do remarkably well counting new words using one or another of the Shakespeare concordances available then, but concordances for other authors were few and far between, and none of them conveniently identified Shakespeare-new words. Today, with a program like our Intellex, you can fly through all of Shakespeare and whatever other authors you have in a commonized database, and identify introduction rates not only of Shakespeare-new words, but also of Shakespeare-rare words, in baseline text blocks that match, roughly, the size of the sample text in question. Roughly matching block size is important because large blocks can average out more variance than small blocks and hence permit narrower and more useful profiles. Exact matching is not required. The shorter the block, the more important it is to analyze it with its size in mind.

Such analysis says quite clearly that there are upper, as well as lower, limits to Shakespeare's rates of introducing words he hasn't used elsewhere, that it's not at all unusual for other writers to exceed them, and that upper, not lower, limits are the ones which best differentiate between Shakespeare and others. The same new-word profile we set to say "could-be" to 95 percent of Shakespeare's three thousand-word poem and play blocks said "couldn't be" to almost half of non-Shakespeare play blocks tested. Only thirteen of 244 Shakespeare play blocks (5 percent), including three in French from *Henry V,* got a "couldn't be" false rejection, all for having too many new words. Forty-five percent of 443 play blocks by others were rejected, all for having *too many* Shakespeare-new words. The difference was even more pronounced for poems, where none of Shakespeare's fourteen blocks were rejected, but 64 percent of our eighty-four other-authored blocks had too many new words to fit within our Shakespeare profile. (See table 1, below). Not one of our 785 blocks, about 2.4 million words of text by Shakespeare and others, had *too few* "new" words to be Shakespeare's.

How can this be? Wasn't Shakespeare the most flowing fount of new words of his day, the leading OED word-coiner, with a known vocabulary two or three times those of Milton or the King James Bible?[18] One answer is yes, but these don't prove as much as people once thought. One's total known vocabulary and one's coinage of new words are very much a function of how many words one has written down. It is legitimate to compare Shakespeare's vocabulary and word-coinage rates with those of Milton, who, like Shakespeare, wrote hundreds of thousands of words. It is not so legitimate to compare Shakespeare's vocabulary or coinage rates with those of Marlowe, whose output was only a fifth of Shakespeare's. If Shakespeare had written only seven plays, instead of thirty-six, his manifested vocabulary and coinage rates would both be much lower. Had he written seventy-two plays, as Thisted and Efron showed, they would be much higher. There are many ways of measuring verbal inventiveness, some of which make Shakespeare the paragon of his time, some of which do not.[19]

More important, since "new," both for Jackson and for us, normally means "new to Shakespeare," high rates of introduction of "non-Shakespearean" words don't have to mean that the other author has a *greater* inventory of words than Shakespeare, only that he or she has a *different* inventory of favorite words, which show up as Shakespeare-new (or Shakespeare-rare) simply because they were, say, Jonson's or Nashe's favorites, but not Shakespeare's. In this sense, Mackail was probably right, that there *can* be such a thing as too many Shakespeare-new words for a likely Shakespeare ascription. We suspect that this is the case in *LC*. Our computer expected it to have fifty-five new words (loosely defined); it turned out to have eighty-eight (also loosely defined), thirty-three words over its expectation. Thirty-three words over expectation is high for Shakespeare, just over our 95 percent cutoff, but it is not at all unusual for others, being found in almost half the blocks of other-authored plays and almost two-thirds of the blocks of other-authored poems (table 1). On balance, we consider it much stronger evidence against Shakespeare authorship than for it.

Table 1. New-word Rejections, Shakespeare and Others

Category	3,000-Wd. Blocks	Rejections	Percent
Shakespeare			
Plays	244	13	5
Poems	14	0	0
Total	258	13	5
Other			
Plays, other[20]	291	163	56
Plays, Apoc.[21]	152	35	23
Poems, other	84	54	64
Total	527	252	48

Forty-eight percent of other-authored blocks, but only 5 percent of Shakespeare blocks, have too many new words to fit Shakespeare profile. No blocks have too few new words to match Shakespeare.

Two "Hilton-Morton" Tests

LC also falls outside our Shakespeare profiles on four other tests, two of which would be impossibly tedious without computers, two of which, using complex metric tests, are manual (see below). The two computer-intensive tests are *no,* divided by *no plus not,* and *with* as the second-to-last word of a sentence (both ratios are multiplied by a thousand above for greater legibility). After massive validation testing for Shakespeare acceptance and other-rejection in 1993, tying up every PC in our computer lab for three days, our students winnowed them out a battery of sixty tests supplied to us by John Hilton and originally devised by Andrew Morton. No such extravagant, brute-force screening was available to Jackson or Muir. Shakespeare's *no/no+not* ratios for 3,000-word blocks (multiplied by 1,000), ranged from 184 to 536 in his poems, 167 to 400 in his plays. We chose the widest defendable Shakespeare range, including his lowest arguable low, 167, and his highest arguable high, 536, and it still was not wide enough to include *LC,* which had a 120 on this test. Likewise, on *with* as second-to-last word in a sentence, our lowest-low, highest-high Shakespeare range for seventy 3,000-word blocks of poems and play verse was 4–34. *LC* had none at all and scored zero.

Meter Tests

Our final *LC* rejections were for enclitic and proclitic microphrases. These were devised by the "Russian-school" linguist, Marina Tarlinskaja in the 1970s and are best explained in chapter 6 of her *Shakespeare's Verse: Iambic Pentameter and the Poet's Idiosyncrasies.*[22] They have nothing to do with computers, but they were equally remote from anyone's experience when Jackson and Muir were writing. They are slow, manual, complex, require judgment, and are not easy to learn, replicate, or even describe compactly. But, properly done, they are replicable enough, and distinguishing enough, to be one of our most powerful tests.[23] We now use them regularly, though sparingly because they take so much time, on shorter samples where for any reason, we want more resolution than we have reached with other, quicker tests.

A bare-bones description is this: certain "clinging monosyllables," stressed in normal speech, get bent out of stress for metrical reasons in iambic-pentameter verse. Some versifiers, such as Fletcher, were much more inclined than Shakespeare to do such bending; others, such as Marlowe and Peele, were much less inclined. If the stress-losing "clinging monosyllable" precedes the stressed syllable, the microphrase is *proclitic,* "leaning forward." Proclitic microphrases in the passage from Sonnet 29 below are defined by the stress-losing "sings" in "sìngs *hymns*" and "sweet" in "swèet *lóve,*" the italicized second syllable being the stressed one. With *enclitic* microphrases the stress-losing monosyllable follows the stressed syllable, "leaning backward." Example: "wealth" in "*súch* wèalth" in the same passage.

Haply I think on thee, and then my state
(Like to the lark at break of day arising
From sullen earth) sìngs *hymns* at heaven's gate;
For thy swèet *lóve* rememb'red *súch* wèalth brings
That then I scorn to change my state with kings.[24]

In Tarlinskaja's counting rules only "notional" words are counted: nouns, verbs, adjectives, adverbs, impersonal pronouns, "this" as object. "Grammatical" or "form" words that have no stress in common speech—articles, prepositions, personal pronouns, possessives, conjunctions, and indefinite pronouns—are not counted. Only eight kinds of phrase are counted:

1. subject and predicate (love thrives)
2. modifier and modified (sweet heart, love's pains)
3. verb and adverb (sink down)
4. adverb and verb (well said)
5. adverb and adverb or adjective (more strong)
6. verb and object (give ear)
7. adverb modifier not connected with first word (so then)
8. apposition or title (Lord Sands)

And tight links prevail over loose ones. In the phrase "such wealth brings," "such wealth" makes a tighter link than "wealth brings" and thus qualifies as the countable microphrase.

Tarlinskaja's analysis finds that *LC* has only four enclitic and eighty-eight proclitic microphrases. This standardizes to 12 enclitic and 267 proclitic microphrases per 1,000 lines, far below Shakespeare's rates for late poems and plays (respectively, 43 to 87 and 316 to 476). Appendix One gives a complete summary of our every test result on *LC* and every 3,000-word block of Shakespeare's poems. We ran fifteen tests each on fourteen blocks of Shakespeare, for a total of 210 test-runs. Only one of these 210 runs resulted in a single rejection for a Shakespeare block, a narrow, Thisted-Efron rejection. But five of the fifteen test-runs on *LC* produced rejections (shaded in table 2, below).

Table 2. Selected Test Results from *A Lover's Complaint*

	Enclitic (post-1595)	Proclitic (post-1595)	*With* (2lw)	No/no + not	New Words
Sh. Range	43 to 87	316 to 476	4 to 34	167 to 536	-32 to 21
LC	12	267	0	111	-

Table 2. *A Lover's Complaint* falls outside of Shakespeare's range in five of fifteen tests (shaded). Shakespeare's other poems have only one rejection in 210 test runs.

Cautions about our *LC* Rejections

These rejections need to be considered with some caution. Most of our tests are novel; none are perfect; almost all have evolved in the past as we and others have restudied them, refined them, and corrected errors. We would be surprised if this process has come to an end. On the other hand, the mistakes and the corrections have become steadily smaller over the years, and fixing the past mistakes this time has not changed things much. After all the correction to date, *LC* still has five times as many rejections in fifteen test-runs as all the rest of Shakespeare's poems in 210 test runs.

What about our choice to measure *LC* against Shakespeare's *late* range enclitic and proclitic scores? With only twelve enclitics per thousand lines, LC would still have been far outside of Shakespeare's *early* range of thirty-one to sixty-six for enclitics per thousand, but, with 267 proclitics per thousand, it would have fallen (barely) within Shakespeare's early proclitics range of 265 to 388. Thus, moving the poem's date from late to very early would spare it one rejection. But it would also require massive readjustments in the current consensus favoring Shakespeare authorship, and the disavowal of much evidence, such as "echoes" and word links supposedly suggesting that *LC* is not just Shakespeare, but late Shakespeare.[25]

What about the close calls? Our Shakespeare ranges are an analytical convenience, not something that is set in stone. Especially for people like us who define ranges and count rejections, and especially if you are dealing with a small baseline, like our Chapman baseline below, some allowance should be made for margins of error in defining ranges and rejection rates. The smaller the baseline, the looser and more permissive the ranges and rejection criteria should be. Even with a very large baseline, such as Shakespeare's, adding previously unknown or unincluded texts could make some difference. Hence, there are reasonable grounds to distinguish between "firm" rejections and "close calls."[26] For Shakespeare, whose baseline is large, our main mitigation of this problem has been to draw our ranges broadly and conservatively, including play verse as well as poems, and defining ranges by the highest arguable high and the lowest arguable low. This spared *LC* a rejection for its very low slope-test score. A small additional error allowance could also get rid of the new-words rejection.

On the other hand, these "close calls" are still outside of 95 percent of known, tested Shakespeare, and the other four rejections, on today's available evidence, look firm to us. Moreover, however much more deserving it may be, *LC* in recent years hasn't received a twentieth as much attention as say, *Funeral Elegy by W.S.,* even from us. That means that there may be more contrary evidence out there, such as that on stress profiles and word boundaries contributed by Marina Tarlinskaja to this volume, both raising further doubt whether *LC* could be late Shakespeare.[27] Why the neglect? Because the world responds to novelty and *LC*'s ascription was too well settled? Because *FE*'s advocates pushed too hard, claimed too much, scorched too much earth, and goaded too many people into looking for contrary evidence, while *LC*'s careful, gentlemanly advocates did not? Because there still isn't a plausible, testable alternative author for *LC* as there was for *FE* (see below)? Because many still consider *LC* a minor rustic poem? All of the above? We can't say, but, for whatever reasons, few people have been looking hard lately for new reasons to doubt that *LC* is Shakespeare's. We chanced upon ours while looking for something else and couldn't ignore the results. Tarlinskaja chanced on hers while casting about for something suitable to add to this Festschrift, having all but totally ignored *LC* in her otherwise astonishingly compendious *Shakespeare's Verse.* What else might turn up if people were really looking for it?

Using Hyperspheric Analysis to Measure Composite Distance from Shakespeare

Moreover, what can we now say from available evidence about the odds that Shakespeare could have written *LC?* We think they are quantifiable and very low, even if you don't count rejections at all, but simply measure composite distance from Shakespeare's means. We are still trying out names for our methodology but for the moment calling it hyperspheric analysis and would be happy to provide a technical description of it on request.[28] The gist of it is this: For each test of a given sample text block we calculate the block's distance, in standard deviations, from Shakespeare's baseline mean. This is standard practice in dealing with a normally distributed population: you can guess from an observed item's distance from the population's mean the probability that it belongs in the population. If it is only one standard deviation from the population's mean—which by definition encompasses about two-thirds of a normally distributed population—it's hard to reject it as a "couldn't-be" for that population. If it is two or three or five standard deviations from the population's mean, it gets progressively less likely to belong to the population by chance and progressively easier to call a "couldn't-be" for our purposes.

Our practice of defining Shakespeare envelopes to pass at least 95 percent of Shakespeare blocks on a given test amounts to a de facto adoption of something close to a two-standard-deviation cutoff. Then we would count rejections and ask rhetorically, "If a sample text block such as *LC* gets five rejections in fifteen Shakespeare tests, what are the odds that it belongs in Shakespeare's population of poems, compared to those, say, of Shakespeare's most discrepant baseline block?"

It is easy enough to ask such questions of rejection-counting, but not so easy to answer them satisfactorily, since rejection-counting asks only *whether* a sample block is inside or outside of a population's envelope, not *how far* inside or outside, as measured in distance from the population's composite mean.

Hyperspheric analysis attempts to go beyond rejection-counting by considering every Shakespeare distance on every test. For it, we calculate a composite distance from Shakespeare's mean as if each new test provided a new dimension of measurement, the first test a line, the second a circle, the third a sphere, and so on for fourteen or fifteen dimensions for poems, fifty-one for plays. Each test used adds a dimension, and three is not a limit. Any dimension past three is hyper, representing a hypersphere in hyperspace. Not all of us are at home in hyperspace, but a plain old three-dimensional, even two-dimensional, model of the solar system (with different dimensions, of course) may be enough to help explain the idea to nonmathematicians.

The composite of Shakespeare's means would be the sun. For texts of sufficient length, that is, three thousand words or more, everything we have by Shakespeare would be no farther away than, say, Mercury, and almost everything we have by others would fall outside Mercury's orbit. Our investigations are not finished, and we are still experimenting with different ways of aggregating our data, but so far, with whole plays, and with three thousand-word poem blocks, something like 99–100 percent of Shakespeare seems to fall within the orbit, and something like 99 percent of tested non-Shakespeare seems to fall outside. That means we are getting less than one percent false positives or false negatives, a very gratifying result.

For shorter texts we expect more variance, wider Shakespeare profiles, an expanded orbit for Mercury, and more false positives. In limited testing on poems, this is exactly what we have found. For 1,500-word poem blocks, only 85–90 percent of our tested non-Shakespeare seems to fall outside the Shakespeare orbit, meaning that 10–15 percent of the tests give us false positives. Of 750-word and 500-word non-Shakespeare poem blocks only half are rejected. The other half are false positives. We have tested a sampling of 3,000-word play verse blocks and, as with poems, have found extremely low rates of false positives. As with poems, we would expect false positives to increase as block size gets smaller, but we have not yet substantiated this.

Our "composite Shakespeare error (CSE)," or distance from the center of Shakespeare's distribution, corresponds to the sample text's distance from the sun. Shakespeare's CSE's are all low; everyone else's are almost all high. The higher the CSE, the lower the composite Shakespeare probability (CSP), that is, the probability that a random process exhibiting Shakespearean statistics (such as those which define norms and standard deviations for each test recorded) would produce a block of equal or greater CSE. Note that CSP scores are not *absolute* probabilities but a baseline for computing *relative* probabilities that any given text is more or less likely to be Shakespeare's than any other given text.

Consider our Mercury, our Shakespeare poem block farthest from the sun, the one with Shakespeare's own highest CSE and lowest CSP. This least-typical block is the last three thousand-word block of the *Sonnets.* It is called Son3k6 on our charts (appendix One). It has a Shakespeare-high CSE of 4.6 and a Shakespeare-low CSP of about nine percent; that is, 8.9 × 10 to the minus 2 = .089 = 8.9 percent in fourteen tests. Our most "Shakespearean" blocks are Luc3k4 and Son3k4, respectively the fourth blocks of *The Rape of Lucrece* and the *Sonnets.* Both have CSE's of 2.7 or less and CSP's of about 90 percent; they fall much closer to the sun than Son3k6.

When we say that these are not absolute probabilities, it means, in particular, that we do not take them to show the odds that Shakespeare wrote the named *Sonnet* or *Lucrece* blocks are only nine or 90 percent. It would be better to describe them as the odds that a process matching the author's statistical profile could have produced a sample farther from the composite mean than the block in question. Thus, a block with a CSP of 90 percent is not at all exceptional. We would expect that 90 percent of the author's blocks would fall at least as far from the mean as such a block. But a CSP of 0.001 percent is very exceptional indeed. Only 0.001 percent of the author's blocks should fall that far from his mean.

These CSP odds, which can get lower-looking the more strong tests you use, are only the first step toward comparative analysis because, no matter how high or low they may look in absolute terms, they are plainly higher for Shakespeare than the odds of most blocks by *other* poets. Of eighty-six such blocks by other poets, only one has even a hair of overlap with Shakespeare's most discrepant block. Block four of John Ford's *Christ's Bloody Sweat,* has scores identical with Son3k6 to three decimal places, that is, a CSE of 4.6391, compared with 4.6392 for Son3k6, and a CSP of about 9 percent. Hence, it squeezes into the Shakespeare could-be envelope by a ten-thousandth of a point and, by a hair, counts as our one false positive.

Every other block, including the seven others by Ford, have higher CSE's, ranging up to eighteen—that is, longer distances from the sun—and lower CSP's, many so low that they cannot be computed on a computer with standard-issue double-precision arithmetic software. That means that, if we set the boundaries of the Shakespeare envelope at Son3k6 (but not at *A Lover's Complaint,* which tests too far from Shakespeare's other poems to belong in a clean baseline), we get zero false negatives for our fourteen core Shakespeare blocks and only 1 percent false-positive "could-be's" for our eighty-six non-Shakespeare blocks.

Reasonable people could differ as to where to set the boundaries of the authorship envelope, whether right at Mercury's distance, just outside of it, or just inside of it. See section 2.1, of our "Smoking Guns" for our thoughts on "close-calls" and "safety margins" with baselines of various sizes. Maybe there is some way that some errant comet or other could be considered a close call. But it is much harder to argue that Mars, Pluto, or Proxima Centauri, or even Venus, could be close calls because the CSP probabilities fall off so rapidly with increasing CSE distance.

We have been experimenting with different ways of testing *A Lover's Complaint* with this methodology, trying to balance competing objectives of controlling our Shakespeare ranges for date and having a sufficiency of data points. Our safest and most conservative calculation so far has plenty of data points but (unlike brute rejection-counting) lacks some otherwise usable resolution because it does not control for date. It gives *LC* a CSE of 6.44, only 39 percent greater than Son3k6's, but a drastically lower Shakespeare CSP of 8.12×10^{-5}, that is, eighty-one in a million. If you divide the modest 8.9 percent CSP of Shakespeare's most discrepant block by *LC*'s much-lower CSP of $8.12 \times {}^{10-5}$, you find that *LC* is more than a thousand times less likely to be Shakespeare's than the most discrepant of Shakespeare's other blocks. *LC* is much more likely to be to Shakespeare's than, say, the *Funeral Elegy* or the poems of the Earl of Oxford, both of which, by the same computations, are trillions of times more distant from Shakespeare's means than Shakespeare's own most distant block. But a thousand times less likely than Shakespeare's worst block is not good odds for a Shakespeare ascription. Controlling our verse-tests for date, if we can find a proper way to do it, would make the Shakespeare ranges tighter and the odds of his authorship even worse, probably by a factor of ten.

LC WAS NOT BY CHAPMAN

At the same time, however, we should note that, by the same kind of reckoning, the odds for a Chapman ascription are even worse than those for Shakespeare. Table 3 uses Chapman's sestiads from *Hero and Leander* as a baseline, finds that *LC* would get twelve Chapman rejections in fifteen tests and is billions of times more distant from Chapman's composite mean than Chapman's own most distant block. Both by hyperspheric analysis and by simple counting of rejections, John Ford was a highly plausible candidate for the *Funeral Elegy* ascription.[29] The same cannot be said of Chapman and *LC*. Our tests say we haven't a clue who wrote *LC*. But we have what looks like very strong evidence who did *not* write *LC*. It includes both Shakespeare and Chapman, with Chapman by far the more distant of the two.

Table 3. *A Lover's Complaint* Was Not by Chapman

	Chapman Range	*A Lover's Complaint*
Grade Level	14 to 18	13
HCW/20K	37 to 90	109
Relative Clauses	8 to 15	16
Feminine Endings	6 to 10	11
Open Lines	25 to 31	20
Enclitics	46 to 74	12
Proclitics	305 to 384	267
With (2lws)	0 to 24	0
No/No+Not	240 to 400	120
BoB5	-111 to 357	335
BoB7	571 to 818	500
BoB8	-600 to –460	-452
TE Slope	-.17 to -.11	.22
TE NW block	-45 to –23	-33
Sh. Modal Score, Block	622 to 1044	572
Total Rejections		12

Table 3. LC gets twelve Chapman rejections (shaded) in fifteen tests. It is astronomically farther from Chapman than it is from Shakespeare.

Echoes and Parallels

The last two-thirds of Jackson's monograph, twenty pages in all, gets more qualitative, and reflective of the author's command of the literature, which far exceeds ours. Section 3, for example, has to do with parallels between *LC* and other Shakespeare works. Whoever wrote *LC* used language and imagery quite similar and sometimes identical to Shakespeare's, for example, "sleided silk" (line 48; *Pericles,* 4.pro.21), "cold modesty" (293, *Julius Caesar,* 3.01.213), etc. The weeping maid in *LC* applied "wet to wet" to a nearby river (38–42), just as the stag in *As You Like It* "stood on the extremest verge of the swift brook, Augmenting it with tears." (2.01.42–49). Perhaps it is too much to argue that a paragraph or two of such parallels shows common authorship, but who could argue with four pages of such close parallels, plus yet more pages of parallels (many of them the same ones), collected independently by Kenneth Muir?[30] Or with Jackson's later sections (4 and 5) on *LC*'s echoes of Shakespeare's imagery and stylistic devices, or his finding that *LC* also had many and strong echoes of Spenser's *Prothalamion* (1596), and, hence, was unlikely to have been written before that date?[31]

Yet we are among the leading skeptics of echoes and parallels as conclusive proofs of common authorship, and it is not just because we don't consider ourselves particularly good at it. We think there is general truth to the notion that negative evidence is generally stronger than positive evidence. As Karl Popper put it: "No number of sightings of white swans can prove the theory that all swans are white. The sighting of one black swan may disprove it." Fitting the tiny slipper does not prove you are Cinderella nearly as conclusively as *not* fitting the tiny slipper proves you are not Cinderella.

Hence, we normally look for "silver-bullet" evidence tending to disprove common authorship by showing differences, rather than "smoking gun" evidence seeking to prove it with similarities, especially the "uncanny" ones so favored in anti-Stratfordian tracts. We've never found a perfect quantifiable thumbprint for any author. Imperfect ones by definition are not truly peculiar to a single writer; many writers, in fact, shared words and images; and over the years we have grown skeptical that a multitude of imperfect thumbprints can ever add up to a perfect one.[32] One could quibble in detail about individual echoes in Jackson's work, wondering, for example, whether the *LC* maid's extravagant weeping, like a force of nature, was really unique to Shakespeare,[33] but, with limited time, space, and talent for such things, we believe that our attention would be more fruitfully addressed to relatively conclusive differences from Shakespeare, rather than not-so-conclusive similarities.

DOES *LC* SOUND LIKE SHAKESPEARE?

But first, one last round on qualitative similarities. Jackson's crowning sections, 6 and 7, on *LC*'s quality and maturity are as learned, judicious, and persuasive as the rest of his 1965 monograph, well aware of the poem's shortcomings, but equally aware of its merits, its dramatic qualities, its Shakespearean skill in depicting the artifice of seduction: "I am less concerned to list the obvious similarities in the wording with which the almost feminine beauty of the two personages is described than to note the similarities which allow one to speak of the Young Man of *A Lover's Complaint,* the Friend of the Sonnets, Richard Gloucester, Iago, and Hamlet's Player as kindred spirits." (37)

Earlier (and characteristically attentive to opposing views) he had said this: "Even Mackail admits that 'there are more than a few passages in the poem which are like Shakespeare at his best, and of which one would say at first sight that no one but Shakespeare could have written them, so wonderfully do they combine his effortless power and his incomparable sweetness." The two most frequently praised lines in the poem are:

> O father, what a hell of witchcraft lies
> In the small orb of one particular tear!
>
> (288–89)[34]

"There is no point in abstracting all the prize-passages from their context. Mackail selects these three for special commendation:

> Some beauty peep'd through lattice of sear'd age (14)
>
> Threw my affections in his charmed power,
> Reserved the stalk and gave him all my flower (146–47)
>
> But kept cold distance, and did thence remove,
> To spend her living in eternal love. (237–38)"

"But," Jackson continues, "the poem as a whole is, in my opinion, infused with the Shakespearean essence. It is true that some of the verse seems 'flat,' 'poor,' 'ragged,' marred by apparent clumsiness [citing Mackail]. Once again Mackail has no trouble offering examples. This merely means that Shakespeare was human and not perfect. As contemporary scholarship reacts against earlier disintegrationist theories it is becoming more and more obvious that Shakespeare was capable of comparative failure. He could write badly. I find it far easier to believe that Shakespeare wrote the worst lines in *A Lover's Complaint* than that somebody else wrote the best ones."[35]

Jackson's summary is characteristically compact and firm, yet careful not to overstate: "In fact, everything about the poem—vocabulary, phraseology, imagery, stylistic mannerisms, subject matter—confirms the correctness of Thorpe's attribution. [*LC*] deserves to be taken seriously as a product of the latter half of Shakespeare's career."[36]

Magisterial Methods Don't Guarantee Correct Results

It is hardly our part as counters to pass judgment on such magisterial reading, though it is ours to note that magisterial readings disagree with each other, and to wonder in passing whether there is not some way to validate reading in a countable way.[37] Nevertheless, it is hard even for counters to study such work without being impressed. This is the language of a man of unusually broad and deep discernment, who has brought a wealth of learning and judgment, both qualitative and quantitative, to bear on an old and important controversy. His treatment is wide-ranging, yet compact, strikingly gracious and fair to his adversaries (especially so by today's roughhouse standards), attentive to contrary arguments, cautiously presented, yet in the end so powerfully persuasive that it is not surprising that it overturned the old skepticism for almost forty years.

In particular, Jackson's quantitative evidence, on which we *can* reasonably pass judgment, is remarkably modern, solid, and plausible after decades of supposedly revolutionary development in authorship studies—but only as far he could take it with the tools then available. Its three big flaws from our perspective are that it was comparatively blind to non-Shakespeare; it did not lend itself to high-end number crunching or metric tests; and its conclusion, though magisterial, was probably wrong. After ninety years, it appears to us that J. W. Mackail was more likely right after all: the odds are strongly against *LC* being Shakespeare's at all, and especially against it being late Shakespeare.

Cautions and Caveats

The main differences between our approach and Jackson's are that we had many modern research aids that he lacked and could do things that he could not. We had computers and a sizeable archive of commonized texts. He did not. We could divide texts into standardized blocks, profile them quickly, conveniently, and uniformly, and record the results on a handy electronic spreadsheet—and we had much more easily quantifiable access to non-Shakespeare texts than he had. That means that we had what it took to do our trademark silver-bullet, block-and-profile tests. He did not, and was forced to use mostly smoking-guns tests, *faute de mieux,* though he was fully aware of their limitations. We could crunch in fancy ways, with slope tests and modal tests. He could not. We had access to Russian-school metric tests; he did not. In short, we had new resources and tools so powerful that we could take on Shakespeare without being readers or Shakespeare scholars and get away with it. None of our five block-and-profile tests which rejected *LC*—enclitics, proclitics, *with* (2lw), *no/no + not,* not even new words the way we used them—were available to Jackson.

These novel tests had hazards of their own—their very novelty, their complexity, their hidden glitches, their reliance on reasonably uniform, accurate editing, among others. We and our students were sorcerer's apprentices learning from trial and error, and profiting greatly from consultation with whatever mentors we could find—Thisted, Efron, Foster for eight good years, and, later, Brian Vickers and Mac Jackson himself, among others. We made many mistakes, corrected many of them (but probably not all), and, as should be plain to the most casual reader of this chapter, expect to make more mistakes every time we try to push a little farther. We listed two pages of cautions and caveats in our 1996 "Final Report" of the Claremont Shakespeare Clinic[38] and told our readers we did not expect ours to be the last word on the subject.

Six years later, most of the caveats are still valid, and we still don't claim to have the last word on the subject. The same developments which led us to fresh insights have not stopped. Many of them will doubtless continue in the future, supplemented by other developments which none of us has thought of today. We hope and expect that future researchers will have tools and techniques that, together with the old ones, such as reading, will cast new light on areas that for us are still in shadow. Maybe they'll even tell us who did write *A Lover's Complaint.*

We don't know what the light of the future will show, but we do know that much of our past evidence has now been subject to public scrutiny and challenge for many years. It has faced the most strenuous of criticism and, in our estimation, survived it almost without a scratch.[39] We continue to caution our readers about our newest tests, but we can hardly help being a bit less tentative about the older ones than we were in 1996.

Conclusion

We do believe that modern, silver-bullet evidence is much more conclusive than the smoking-gun evidence available to Jackson in 1965, and that it now points away from Shakespeare, rather than toward him, Jackson's still-cogent arguments to the contrary, *LC* seems to get a new look about twice a century, followed by a long interval of neglectful consensus that it is or isn't Shakespeare's. Will ours look as good in forty years as Jackson's and Muir's studies do today? We don't know, but we would be pleased and proud if it did, and we were alive to appreciate it. Will it even produce another great turnaround within our lifetimes? We don't know, though we think the available evidence says that it should.

Will people even care in forty years who wrote *LC?* We don't know, but we think they should and probably will. Not every literature professor today cares what Shakespeare wrote, but many do, and there are few ordinary people who don't. If they do, they could do much worse than go to interlibrary loan and take a look at Jackson's yellowed 1965 monograph which began the great turnaround to today's consensus on who wrote *LC.* Whether or not it came to the correct conclusion, it's still a great piece of work by a man whose erudition, graciousness, versatility, good sense, and attentiveness to the views of others shine from every line. It's well worth reading today, and we would expect it still to be so whenever people think it's time for a new look at *A Lover's Complaint*—or to revisit an exemplary old one.

Appendix One. Available tests on *LC* and 3,000-Word Blocks of Shakespeare Poems

Shakespeare Poem/Block*	Date	Words	Grade Level	HC /20K	Relative Clauses	Fem Endings	Open Lines	Enclitics	Proclitics	of	of /3000	with (2lws)	no /(no+not)	BoB5	BoB7	BoB8	TE Slope alt.	TE NW 3k block	Rej	TE Rej*	Total Rej	Modal raw**	Modal Distance	Composite Score 1***	Composite Score 2 ****
Venus	1593																								
1		3135	10	153	7	15	7	42	270	35	33	6	233	211	826	-593	-0.12	-32	0	0	1	467	-0.67	1.20	
2		3108	10	148	9	25	9	40	317	40	39	6	326	325	579	-536	-0.15	-26	0	0	0	281	-1.35	1.35	
3		3559	12	118	14	14	11	47	317	49	41	34	417	244	542	-419	-0.13	-7	0	0	0	1149	1.82	1.82	
Lucrece	1594																								
1		3013	11	133	11	9	17	34	278	55	55	11	536	556	941	-405	-0.11	-20	0	1	1	358	-1.07	1.47	
2		3015	11	153	12	15	13	42	265	40	40	6	324	270	867	-580	-0.16	-8	0	0	0	535	-0.43	0.43	
3		3018	12	152	11	13	18	31	301	64	64	19	351	538	714	-541	-0.21	-20	0	0	0	969	1.16	1.16	
4		3153	12	133	12	14	10	59	350	55	52	19	391	198	714	-609	-0.10	-2	0	0	0	994	1.26	1.26	
5		2450	11	114	14	13	21	65	338	29	36	17	500	262	529	-625	-0.08	-6	0	0	0	712	0.22	0.22	
Sonnets	1603																								
1		3052	14	98	12	12	19	77	334	57	56	15	184	429	818	-300	0.00	-1	0	0	0	842	0.70	0.70	
2		3225	13	68	9	8	15	61	367	65	60	22	333	282	840	-560	-0.08	7	0	0	0	740	0.33	0.33	
3		3172	13	88	9	3	18	43	316	84	79	7	500	478	944	-510	0.01	9	0	0	0	543	-0.39	0.39	
4		3208	12	50	14	8	15	48	321	80	75	7	333	288	611	-520	-0.14	6	0	0	0	601	-0.18	0.18	
5		3210	12	56	12	12	19	87	360	49	46	7	313	285	818	-560	0.07	-3	0	0	0	331	-1.17	1.17	
6		1729	12	104	16	7	17	81	476	34	59	12	290	116	826	-412	0.06	0	0	0	0	892	0.88	0.88	
Summary Statistics																									
Average			12	112	12	12	15	54	329	53	52	13	359	320	755	-512	-0.08	-7	0	0	0	673	0.08	0.90	
St. Dev.			1	35	2	5	4	17	51	16	14	8	97	126	136	90	0.08	12	0	0	0	261	0.96	0.50	
Min.			10	50	7	3	7	31	265	29	33	6	184	116	529	-625	-0.21	-32	0	0	0	281	-1.35	0.18	
Max.			14	153	16	25	21	87	476	84	79	34	536	556	944	-300	0.07	9	0	1	1	1149	1.82	1.82	
*Shakespeare Profile Boundaries***																									
Poems (3K)			10-14	50-153	7-16	7-25	7-21	31-87	265-476		33-79	6-34	184-536	116-556	529-944	-300- -625	-.21 to .07	-32 to 9	0-1	0-1	0-2	281-	-1.35-	0-1.82	
to 1600						9-25	7-21	31-65	265-350							-405- -625						1149	1.82		
from 1600						7-12	15-19	43-87	316-476							-300- -560									
Plays (3K)			3-8	31-150	7-17	7-25	14-57	34-87	266-388			4-30	167-400	117-466	136-895	-265--867	-.22 to .15	-32 to 21							
to 1600					7-17	7-12	14-53	34-66	266-388																
from 1600					12-17	12-25	17-57	53-87	327-362																
Consolidated			**10-14**	**31-153**	**7-17**	**7-25**	**7-57**	**31-87**	**265-476**		**33-79**	**4-34**	**167-536**	**116-556**	**136-944**	**-265--867**	**-.22 to .15**	**-32 to 21**	**0-1**	**0-1**	**0-2**	**281-**	**-1.35-**	**0-1.82**	
to 1600							**7-53**	**31-66**	**265-388**													**1149**	**1.82**		
from 1600							**15-57**	**43-87**	**316-476**																
Lover's Complaint	1608?	2579	13	109	16	11	20	*12*	*267*	69	*80*	*0*	*120*	335	500	-452	0.22	*-33*	4	0	**5**	572	-0.29	**5.03**	

Notes :

*Composite score averages do not count *A Lover's Complaint* . (LC). See text for discussion of LC's Thisted-Efron (TE) Scores.

The *Phoenix and Turtle* is omitted as too short for meaningful analysis.

**For grade level, the consolidated range is for poems only; in all other cases we take the union of the poem-play range.

For enclitics and proclitics, early means to 1595, late from 1595.

*** Modal-score blocks are exactly 3,000 words long, overlapping, but not identical to otherwise-tested blocks.

Results appear here to show Shakespeare's range, not to show precise modal score of each left-hand block.

****Composite score 1 = Square root of the squares of modal distance and rejections per block.

*****Composite score 2 = Multidimensional distance from Shakespeare's mean. See text.

In 210 total test-runs on fourteen 3,000-word poem blocks, Shakespeare gets one narrow rejection (half a percent).

In 15 total test-runs, *A Lover's Complaint* gets 5 rejections (33 percent).

Notes

1. Oscar James Campbell and Edward Quinn, eds., *The Reader's Encyclopedia of Shakespeare* (New York: Crowell, 1966), 469: "Scholars have all but unanimously rejected any attribution of it to Shakespeare, while conceding that there is an occasional echo in it of Shakespeare's work"; F. E. Halliday, *A Shakespeare Companion, 1550–1950* (London: Duckworth, 1952), 375: "Shakespeare's authorship of *A Lover's Complaint* . . . on the internal evidence is generally rejected, though there are passages that might well be his early work." Among the Shakespeare doubters were William Hazlitt, Sidney Lee, George Saintsbury, G. L. Kittredge, Thomas M. Parrott, C. S. Lewis, Hyder E. Rollins, J. M. Robertson, John Middleton Murry, and J. W. Mackail, probably the leading early-twentieth-century authority on the poem. On the other hand, Edmond Malone, George Rylands, and Charles Algernon Swinburne thought the poem was Shakespeare's. See Kenneth Muir, *Shakespeare the Professional* (Totowa, NJ: Rowman and Littlefield, 1973), 204.

2. Katherine Duncan-Jones, "Was the 1609 *Shake-speare's Sonnets* Really Unauthorized?" *Review of English Studies* 34 (1983): 151–71.

3. Eliot Slater, "Shakespeare: Word Links between Poems and Plays," *Notes and Queries* (1975): 157–63; A. Kent Hieatt, T. G. Bishop, and E. A. Nicholson, "Shakespeare's Rare Words: 'Lover's Complaint,' *Cymbeline,* and *Sonnets,*" *Notes and Queries* (1987): 219–24; MacDonald P. Jackson, "Echoes of Spenser's Prothalamion as Evidence against an Early Date for Shakespeare's *A Lover's Complaint,*" *Notes and Queries* 37 (1990): 180–82; John Kerrigan, ed., *The Sonnets and A Lover's Complaint* (New York: Viking, 1986); Ilona Bell, "'That which thou hast done': Shakespeare's Sonnets and *A Lover's Complaint,*" in James Schiffer, ed., *Shakespeare's Sonnets: Critical Essays* (New York: Garland, 1999): 455–74.

4. Kenneth Muir, "A Lover's Complaint: a Reconsideration," in Edward A. Bloom, ed., *Shakespeare, 1564–1964: A Collection of Modern Essays by Various Hands* (Providence, Rhode Island: Brown Univ. Press, 1964); revised in Muir, *Shakespeare the Professional,* ch. 12; MacDonald P. Jackson, *Shakespeare's "A Lover's Complaint": Its Date and Authenticity* (Auckland, NZ: Univ. of Auckland, 1965).

5. Samuel Schoenbaum, *Shakespeare's Lives: New Edition* (Oxford: Clarendon Press, 1991), 35.

6. M. W. A. Smith, "The Authorship of 'A Lover's Complaint': An Application of Statistical Stylometry to Poetry," *Computers and the Humanities* 18 (1984): 23; see J. M. Robertson, *Shakespeare and Chapman: A Thesis of Chapman's Authorship of "A Lover's Complaint," and His Origination of "Timon of Athens," with Indications of Further Problems* (New York: E. P. Dutton, 1917).

7. Ward E. Y. Elliott and Robert J. Valenza, "Glass Slippers and Seven-League Boots: C-Prompted Doubts About Ascribing *A Funeral Elegy* and *A Lover's Complaint* to Shakespeare," *Shakespeare Quarterly* 48 (summer 1997): 177–207.

8. Jackson, *Complaint,* 31: "It is true that the 1609 Quarto was obviously not seen through to the press by the author, but neither, of course, were any of the plays. . . . No reputable modern critic would deny that all but a handful of the Sonnets are genuine Shakespearean works, and presumably Thorpe included *A Lover's Complaint* because he thought it was also genuine. It is not absolutely certain that the 1609 volume was published without Shakespeare's approval, and there is no reason whatsoever for thinking Thorpe 'unscrupulous'; even if he were so, it is hard to see what he could have hope to gain by adding a poem that he knew to be non-Shakespearean to a collection of Shakespeare's Sonnets which would have sold just as well without it. He must have believed that *A Lover's Complaint* was Shakespeare's, and doubtless his grounds for believing this were that it was supplied him, as were the Sonnets, by someone in a position to know."

9. Jackson, *Complaint,* 8, citing Alfred Hart, "Vocabularies of Shakespeare's Plays and

the Growth of Shakespeare's Vocabulary," *RES* 19 (1943): 128–40, 242–54. Foster resigned as our mentor in February 1996 and has since been our chief critic.

10. Ronald A. Fisher, et al., "The Relation Between the Number of Species and the Number of Individuals in a Random Sample of an Animal Population," *Journal of Animal Ecology* 12 (1943): 42–58.

11. Marvin Spevack, *Complete and Systematic Concordance to the Works of Shakespeare,* vols. 1–6 (1968–70; Hildesheim, Germany: Georg Olms Verlag, 1993).

12. Brad Efron and Ronald Thisted, "Estimating the Number of Unseen Species: How Many Words Did Shakespeare Know?" *Biometrika* 63 (1976): 435–447; Ronald Thisted and Brad Efron, "Did Shakespeare Write a Newly-Discovered Poem?" *Biometrika* 74 (1987): 445–55.

13. Robert J. Valenza, "Are Thisted-Efron Authorship Tests Valid?" *Computers and the Humanities* 25 (1990): 27–46. 100,000 words means total words (tokens), not different words (types).

14. Ward Elliott and Robert J. Valenza, "And Then There Were None: Winnowing the Shakespeare Claimants," *Computers and the Humanities* 30 (1996): 191 (197–98).

15. Jackson, *Complaint,* 13.

16. Jackson, *Complaint,* 13. See Kent Hieatt at al., "Shakespeare's Rare Words" (1987); Kent and Charles Hieatt, 1991, "When did Shakespeare write *Sonnets* (1609)?" *Studies in Philology* 88 (winter 1991): 69–109.

17. Harald Westergaard, *Contributions to the History of Statistics* (London: King, 1932), 14. On the other hand, some say that finding new ways to measure, count, and discover things was the heart and soul of the Renaissance, and who are we to doubt them? See Alfred W. Crosby, *The Measure of Reality: Quantification and Western Society,* 1250–1600, (Cambridge, England: Cambridge Univ. Press, 1997); and Ricardo J. Quinones, *The Renaissance Discovery of Time* (Cambridge: Harvard Univ. Press, 1972).

18. F. Max Müller, *The Science of Language* (New York: Scribners, 1891), 389.

19. J. C. Baker, "Pace: A Test of Authorship Based on the Rate at Which New Words Enter the Author's Text," *Literary and Linguistic Computing* 3 (1988): 136–39; Fiona Tweedie and R. Harald Baayen, "How Variable May a Constant Be? Measures of Lexical Richness in Perspective," *Computers and the Humanities* 32 (1998): 323–51.

20. "Plays, other" includes fifty-one plays by nineteen playwrights other than Shakespeare. They are listed in Appendix Zero (C) of our "None."

21. "Plays, Apoc." refers to twenty-seven plays from the Shakespeare Apocrypha, plays attributed to Shakespeare at one time or another but not included in the canon today. They are listed in Appendix Zero (A) of our "None."

22. New York: Peter Lang, 1987, 203–30.

23. Early Elliott e&p counts were 5–10 percent below Tarlinskaja's counts, close enough to be useful for most comparisons. More recent calibrations are even closer. For *LC,* the Tarlinskaja count was enclitics: 4; proclitics: 88. Elliott counts were: enclitics: 5; proclitics:88. All Shakespeare counts used in this paper, and the counts for *LC,* are Tarlinskaja's.

24. . Sonnet 29, in G. Blakemore Evans and Harry Levin, eds., *The Riverside Shakespeare* (Boston: Houghton Mifflin, 1974), 1754.

25. Note, however, that the baseline for our Shakespeare verse profiles is Tarlinskaja's analysis of all of Shakespeare's poems and only two plays, *Richard II,* and *The Tempest.* Her resulting play and verse ranges are almost identical, but, if more plays were included, the profiles would probably be somewhat wider than the ones we are using.

26. Ward E. Y. Elliott and Robert J. Valenza, "Smoking Guns and Silver Bullets: Could John Ford Have Written the *Funeral Elegy?*" *Literary and Linguistic Computing* 16 (2001): 205–32 (210–15).

27. By the same token, there could well be undiscovered favorable evidence for *LC* as well.

28. Robert J. Valenza, "Reporting from the Hypersphere: A Composite Score for the Shakespeare Clinic Results," Claremont McKenna College manuscript, 14 Sept. 2000.

29. See our "Guns," and our manuscript "Elliott notes on Valenza's hyperspheric analysis," Claremont McKenna College, 4 March 2002.

30. Jackson, *Complaint,* 19–39. See also Muir, *Professional,* 209–19.

31. Jackson, "Echoes," 180.

32. See, for example, our "Guns," 215–17, which finds too many of Donald Foster's supposedly unique Shakespeare "thumbprint" indicators in the poems of John Ford: incongruent *who*'s ("book who"); redundant comparatives and superlatives ("more better," "most unkindest"); noun-plus-noun doublets ("grace and strength"); and hendiadys ("cups and gold"). All of these turned out to be equally or more abundant in Ford. These may be of some use in distinguishing Shakespeare from *other* writers, but they turned out to be useless or worse for distinguishing him from Ford. Jackson presented only one or two of these, noun-plus-noun and/or hendiadys as Shakespeare indicators, and he carefully refrained from calling them "thumbprints" (*Complaint,* 25–26).

33. For example, consider these lines (997–1001) from George Peele's *David and Bethsabe:*

> Season this heavy soil with showers of tears,
> And fill the face of every flower with dew;
> Weep, Israel, for David's soul dissolves,
> Lading the fountains of his drowned eyes,
> And pours her substance on the senseless earth.

34. Jackson, *Complaint,* 26, quoting J. W. Mackail, "*A Lover's Complaint,*" *Essays and Studies* 3 (1912): 51–70 (62).

35. Jackson, *Complaint,* 27. See also Muir, *Professional,* 207: "It is surely easier to believe that Shakespeare wrote a poem with a number of feeble lines—some explicable by textual corruption or lack of revision—than that some other poet, having steeped himself in Shakespeare's poems and sonnets, succeeded at times in equaling his models."

36. Jackson, *Complaint,* 39.

37. One recent experiment on our campus shows that a small panel of undergraduates, from reading alone, can achieve 80–90 percent accuracy in distinguishing sonnet-length Shakespeare passages from non-Shakespeare: Ward Elliott and Robert J. Valenza, "The Shakespeare Golden Ear Test," Claremont McKenna College manuscript, 17 October 2002. Unfortunately, the amateur panel, like many professionals before it, was evenly divided as to whether *LC* is Shakespeare's or not.

38. Elliott and Valenza, "None," 208–10.

39. Ward E. Y. Elliott and Robert J. Valenza, "So Many Hardballs, So few over the plate; Conclusions from our 'Debate' with Donald Foster," *Computers and the Humanities* (forthcoming). In June 2002, Foster conceded that John Ford, not William Shakespeare, is the probable author of the *Funeral Elegy:* Rick Abrams and Donald Foster, "Abrams and Foster on 'A Funeral Elegy'" (online posting, 12 June 2002, *SHAKSPER: The Global Electronic Conference,* SHK 13.1514, 13 June 2002 http://www.shaksper.net/archives/2002/1484.html).

The Verse of *A Lover's Complaint*: Not Shakespeare

Marina Tarlinskaja

Did Shakespeare write *A Lover's Complaint*? And if he did, when? Opinions of the authorship vacillate between a complete rejection[1] and an attribution to a later, "mature" Shakespeare.[2] Most conclusions have been based on word frequency. In addition, MacD. P. Jackson analyzed the phraseology, imagery, stylistic mannerisms, and subject matter of the poem. Surprisingly, however, few have looked at the *verse* of the poem, except for Elliot and Valenza (1996) who used the "proclitic-enclitic" test that I devised in the early nineteen-eighties and reported at an international conference on metrical theory held at Stanford University in 1984.[3] And yet, the poem *is* verse; it is iambic pentameter that should be analyzed and compared to other works by Shakespeare of different periods and genres, and to poetry by other authors. I neglected *A Lover's Complaint* when preparing material for my Shakespeare book of 1987;[4] now is an apt occasion to study the verse of the poem.

Professor MacDonald P. Jackson, for whom I am writing this paper, is a sensitive reader of Shakespeare's poetry, but he also counts what is countable. I try to do the same. I have long admired Mac's achievements. In fact, when I first read his works, back in the 1970s, still living in Moscow, I was so impressed by his scholarship that I believed he had long since died and become a classic. How happy I was, after coming to the United States, to discover that Mac was very much alive! We got in touch; he reviewed my work;[5] I visited Auckland, where I gave several lectures in 1998; Mac and I finally met, talked, and partied together!

Thus, I am going to analyze the iambic pentameter verse of *A Lover's Compaint* and compare it to the iamb of "early" and "mature" Shakespeare: his two long poems, his *Sonnets,* and several plays. I will use three tests. Each type of analysis will be explained in detail. I cannot program them on a computer: the type of work I do, though "objective," finds few formal textual indicators. Therefore all quantitative analyses have been done manually, by "crawling" through every syllable of every line. The simple statistics have been done with the help of a Hewlett-Packard hand calculator.

The bulk of Shakespeare's texts is iambic pentameter verse. The exceptions are longer or shorter iambic lines (Sonnet 145, for example, is iambic tetrameter, and some utterances in the plays are even shorter or longer); certain lines in the plays are hard to assign to a recognizable meter; and the plays occasionally contain inserts of prose.

In iambic poems, their structural particulars can be abstracted from the already written texts. But as a general principle, meter is known to a poet before he begins to compose a text: the author is the child of his, or her, literary tradition and time. Few poets invent a new meter; but they use an already existing form idiosyncratically. A poet's individuality leaves its impact on the texts, and a poetic style may sometimes be recognized, not unlike a handwriting (see an overview of verse analyses used for the purposes of attribution and chronology in Brian Vickers's *Shakespeare, Co-Author*).[6]

The iambic meter requires that the syllables in a line should be stressed with unequal frequency. **Even** syllabic positions ("ictic," or "strong": **S**) tend to be stressed, though different positions with different frequencies. **Odd** syllabic positions ("non-ictic," or "weak": **W**) tend to be unstressed, though "odds" do occasionally permit stresses, and different "odds" accept stresses with unequal frequency. For a recognizable contrast between the "evens" and the "odds," the mean stressing of **S** needs to be considerably higher than that of **W.** To calculate the stressing of each even and each odd syllabic position in a text, we count the number of stressed syllables in each syllabic position (1, 2, 3, 4 . . .) of the text, say, one hundred lines long, and express the number of stresses filling each position as percent from the total number of lines. These strings of numbers are called the **stress profile** of the text. Next, we calculate the mean stressing of all even (**S**) and of all odd (**W**) positions. Different poetic traditions, and different epochs of the same literature, accept a greater or a smaller difference between **S** and **W.** The English iamb, for example, accepts more stresses on **W** than do its Russian or German counterparts. The mean stressing of **S** in the English iambic pentameter varies between 70 percent (Donne's *Satyres*) and 85 percent (Pope's poetry, e.g., *The Rape of the Lock*). The mean stressing of **W** vacillates between 25 percent (the *Satyres,* as loose as the English iamb gets) and 10 percent (*The Rape of the Lock,* as strict as it gets). Thus, the mean difference between **S** and **W** in the English iamb has the following range: 45 percent (Donne)—75 percent (Pope).

The mean numbers are not enough to describe iambic poetry; each syllabic position needs to be specified. The most frequently stressed **S** in the iambic pentameter are syllabic positions 10 (the end of the line) and, less noticeably, four—the end of the first "hemistich" (the hemistich segmentation is created by prevailing word boundaries after positions 4 or 5; these are frequently reinforced by a syntactic break). The least frequently stressed **S** are syllabic position 2, and either 6 (in a stricter verse, such as

English Classicism) or 8 (in looser verse of later Jacobean or postromantic poetry).[7] Here are two lines more typical of Pope:

> A constant Vapour **o'er** the Palace flies;
> Strange Phantoms rising **as** the Mists arise. . .
> (*The Rape of the Lock* 4: 40–41)

And here are two lines more characteristic of Browning:

> I am poor brother Lippo, **by** your leave!
> You need not clap your torches **to** my face . . .
> (*Fra Lippo Lippi:* 1–2).

The verse in Shakespeare's oeuvre evolved during the course of his writing career.[8] It went from the stricter verse of the Elizabethan Renaissance to the looser verse of the Jacobean Baroque. In early Shakespeare (up to *2 Henry IV*), the least frequently stressed midline **S** is position 6. Then, gradually, positions 6 and 8 lose stresses equally often (from *Much Ado About Nothing* to *Troilus and Cressida*), and in "late" Shakespeare, position 8 loses stress more often than 6 (from *Measure for Measure* to the end of Shakespeare's dramatic career). This evolution of stressing is, at least in part, caused by a changing syntactic structuring of the line. At first, a stronger syntactic break occurred particularly often after syllables 4 or 5, marking a "hemistich" segmentation of the line 4 + 6 or 5 + 5. In later Shakespeare, a stronger break gradually shifts to the right, and the line becomes more typically segmented 6 + 4 and even 7 + 3 syllables. Locations of splits in lines divided between two or more characters also evolve: the most numerous breaks occur after position four, or 4 and 5 (the last plays to demonstrate this tendency are *Julius Caesar* and *Troilus and Cressida*), then, gradually, the most frequent location of the split begins to occur after position 6 (the tendency is already displayed in *Henry V* and *Hamlet,* and becomes prevalent after *Measure for Measure*), or after 6 and 7 (*Henry VIII*). Syntactic breaks also occur after positions 8 and even 9 (not shown in table 2):

> Though I am mad, I will not bite him. /// Call . . .
> That we must leave thee to thy striking, /// for
> Thy dearest quit thee.
> (*Antony and Cleopatra* 2.5.80,
> 3.13.64–65).

Here are typical lines of early Shakespeare:

> Thou princely leader / **of** our English strength.
> Never so needful / **on** the earth of France

Spur to the rescue / **of** the noble Talbot,
Who now is girdled / **with** a waist of iron . . .
(*1 Henry VI*, 4.2.6–9)

And here are typical lines of later Shakespeare:

Pisanio, thou that stands so / **for** Posthumus!
He hath a drug of mine, / I pray his absence
Proceed by swallowing that; / **for** he believes
It is a thing most precious. / **But** for her . . .
(*Cymbeline* 3.5.57–60)

Thus, **the first test** that we shall use to diagnose the possible authorship of *A Lover's Complaint* and its chronological place in Shakespeare's oeuvre will be *the geometry of stress profiles.* **The second test** will involve analyzing the *locations of strong syntactic breaks* and *close syntactic links* in the line.

One more aspect of English iambic verse may be used as a diagnostic tool in revealing a poet's idiosyncrasies. This is the number, syntactic functions and location of stressed monosyllables occasionally occupying **W** syllabic positions in the line.[9]

The third test traces the location of stressed monosyllables on **W** in relation to an adjacent word with a stess on **S** and the syntactic link between the two.

Some monosyllables in English speech are usually unstressed (unless emphasized). These are function words (such as articles, prepositions, auxiliary verbs), as well as some words of other grammatical classes, for example, personal, indefinite, and possessive pronouns. An unstressed word tends to cling to the following or preceeding strongly stressed word, its "host,"[10] to "cliticize" with it and even to generate contracted forms.[11] A stressed word with its unstressed clitics constitutes a "clitic group,"[12] or a "phonetic word,"[13] for example: "**Shall** SUM / **my** COUNT / **and** MAKE / **my** OLD / exCUSE" (Son. 2: 11); "**O,** LET **me,** / TRUE / **in** LOVE, / **but** TRUly / WRITE" (Son. 21: 9).Unstressed words are usually syntactically connected with their stressed host. The unstressed clitics preceding their stressed host are called "proclitics," those that follow their host are called "enclitics." In faster, colloquial speech another tendency is also detected: a clitic is sometimes drawn to the preceding word with which it has no grammatical link, rather than to the following word with which it is syntactically connected: "AS-**you** / like it /," " . . .TOLLS-**the** / KNELL-**of** / parting / day."[14] In verse analyses this second possibility is usually disregarded, and a clitic is assumed to be tied to the stressed word with which it has a syntactic link.

Not all clitics are completely unstressed. In connected speech, notional words that are, as a rule, stressed, may get a reduced stressing or fully lose their phrasal accentuation. Particular syntactic patterns seem to have a particularly frequent predisposition for a weakened stressing of one element, for example, attributes in attributive phrases. This seems to explain a frequent placement of monosyllabic modifiers on **W** in iambic verse, while the monosyllabic modified noun (or the first stressed syllable of a polysyllabic modified noun) occupies the following **S:** "And with **old** WOES . . ." (*Son.* 30: 4). There are other syntactic types of two-word phrases in which one, normally stressed, monosyllable regularly stands on **W,** e.g.: "Nor can thy shame / **give** PHYSIC / . . ." (*Son.* 34: 9), "**Sinks** DOWN / to death / . . ." (*Son.* 45: 8), "And yet, / **love** KNOWS / . . ." (*Son.* 40: 11).

Less frequently, the notional word on **W** is linked with the preceding, rather than the following, stressed host: "But thou / the TENTH **Muse** /, TEN **times** / more / in worth" (*Son.* 38: 9). Some grammatical types of two-word phrases with back-to-back stressing fill the **WS** or **SW** positions more readily than others. In my analyses of two-word phrases with adjacent stresses, by way of analogy, I called the phrases with a (theoretically) stressed monosyllable *preceding* the stress on S, "**proclitic,**" as in "**Great**-PRINces' / favourites / . . ." (*Son.* 25: 5), "How can my Muse / **want** SUBject / to invent" (Son. 38: 1). Phrases with a stressed monosyllable *following* the stress on **S,** were called "**enclitic,**" as in "To see / the BRAVE-**day** / sunk / in hideous / night /" (*Son.* 12: 2), "And will, / thy SOUL-**knows,** / is admitted / there" (*Son.* 136: 3). Certain semantic classes of words fill "enclitic" slots more readily than others, for example, nouns referring to notions of space and time, as in " . . . he was but ONE-**hour** mine" (*Son.* 33: 11).[15] In analyzing verse it is helpful to use one more notion: the "**metrical word**":[16] a phonetic word (that is, a clitic group) arranged around a strong stress on **S.** All the lines quoted above are broken into metrical words.

The stresses on **W** in proclitic phrases get resolved on the following **S;** thus, they do not disrupt the iambic rhythm too much. In contrast, enclitics frequently occur before a syntactic break ("And will, /// thy SOUL-**knows,** /// is admitted . . ."), they do not get resolved in the same phrase, and therefore they disrupt the iambic flow of rhythm more than proclitics. Probably therefore they are, on the whole, less frequent in verse. Some poets, such as Chapman and Fletcher, and, later, Browning, and Frost, made use of enclitic phrases relatively often. Fletcher, Browning, and Frost might have done so to reproduce nonpoetic, everyday speech. Shakespeare, however, used enclitics sparingly even in his later works. This, incidentally, gives us one "objective" clue why Shakespeare's poetry has always struck its readers as mellifluous. The use of proclitic and enclitic phrases is indicative of a poet's individual rhythmical style, for example, of Shakespeare's and Fletcher's in *Henry VIII.*[17] Thus, the relative frequency of proclitic and enclitic phrases and the incidence of enclitics per thousand lines will serve as **our third test** of *A Lover's Complaint.*

Table 1. Stress Profiles: Percent of Stresses on Each Syllabic Position from the Total Number of Lines

Works	Dates	Strong Syllabic Positions						Weak Syllabic Positions				
		2	4	6	8	10	Mean	1	3	5	7	9
A Lover's Complaint	?	75.1	87	<u>67.5</u>	76.6	98	80.8	19.1	9.1	4.3	4.5	5.1
Venus and Adonis	1593	66.5	88.9	74.5	72.8	97	80.9	27.9	10.6	9.5	9.3	6
The Rape of Lucrece	1594	72.4	89.2	<u>74.2</u>	78.5	92.7	81.4	22.3	10.8	8.7	8.3	4.9
Sonnets	c1596-1604	66.6	89.1	<u>71.5</u>	75.6	94.3	79.4	23.2	11.2	10.4	9.2	8.6
Taming of the Shrew	1591-92	64.9	87.2	<u>68.6</u>	74.3	88.6	76.7	30.1	9.1	9.1	7.3	3.7
Romeo and Juliet	1594-95	65.7	87.2	<u>68.3</u>	75.6	88.5	77.1	33.2	13.4	13	12.3	7.5
Troilus and Cressida	1601-02	67.6	84.6	<u>72.4</u>	72.7	91.8	77.8	26.4	11.4	10.7	11.5	7.4
King Lear	1605-06	63.9	82	77.6	<u>67.8</u>	95.7	77.4	25.5	11.4	12	<u>14.8</u>	11.7
Antony and Cleopatra	1606-07	62.8	82.3	77.4	<u>69.7</u>	93.6	77	24.4	11.1	10.2	<u>14.1</u>	11
The Tempest	1610-11	67.9	80.1	77.7	<u>70.4</u>	87.6	76.7	20.9	14.8	10.5	12.7	<u>14.1</u>

Test 1. Stress profiles. Table 1 displays the stress profiles of *A Lover's Complaint,* of Shakespeare's poems *Venus and Adonis* and *The Rape of Lucrece,* of the *Sonnets,* and of his five plays: the early *The Taming of the Shrew* (1591–92) and *Romeo and Juliet* (1594–95); one play transitional from "early" to "mature" Shakespeare: *Troilus and Cressida,* 1601–02, two plays of 1605–06 and 1606–07 ("mature Shakespeare," assumed by MacD. Jackson to be of the same period as *A Lover's Complaint*):[18] *King Lear* and *Antony and Cleopatra;* and one of the last plays: *The Tempest,* 1610–11. Both *The Shrew* and *Romeo and Juliet* show a decrease of ictic stresses on position 6: this is the sign of Shakespeare's early dramatic verse. In later years the midline drop on position 6 will gradually rise, and on position 8 gradually decrease: thus, in *Troilus and Cressida* positions 6 and 8 are equally stressed. In later plays, the least often stressed midline position is eight. The "drop" on 8 is already seen in both *King Lear* and *Antony and Cleopatra,* and is very obvious in *The Tempest.* The non-ictic stresssing (on **W**) decreases from the first to the ninth positions in the early plays, but shows a relative increase on position 7 (*King Lear* and *Antony and Cleopatra*), or even 9 (*The Tempest*). As we shall see below, this is the result of a changing location of major syntactic breaks in the line. Thus, stress profiles of "mature" Shakespeare's plays show a decrease in ictic stressing on position 8 and a rise of non-ictic stresses on position 7.

Shakespeare's nondramatic and dramatic verse forms have their own particulars. The mean stressing of **W** is, on the whole, higher in the dramatic verse, particularly so in *Romeo and Juliet,* and the mean stressing of **S** in nondramatic verse is higher than in any drama of any period. Thus, the difference between **S** and **W** is greater in nondramatic poetry. The "dip" on the midline position 6 is obvious in the *Sonnets,* not so noticeable in *Lucrece,* and not found in *Venus and Adonis:* this is the consequence of a frequent tripartite syntactic segmentation of its lines ("she says; he replies"): "'Give me my hand,' / saith he; / why **dost** thou feel it?' 'Give me my heart,' / saith she, / 'and **thou** shalt have it'" (374–375); " 'Nay, then,' quoth Adon, 'you **will** fall again'" (770); but:"Fondling,' / she saith, / 'since **I** have hemmed thee here . . .'" (230): a missing stress here fills position 6. On the whole we may suggest that a drop on position 6 should be expected in earlier Shakespeare, and a drop on position 8—in his mature works.

Let us now look at the stressing of *A Lover's Complaint* (table 1). Its mean ictic stress somewhat resembles Shakespeare's nondramatic verse, but not his dramas. The mean non-ictic stress of the *Complaint* is very low—considerably lower than in any other work by Shakespeare of any period. The geometry of the stress distribution in the line of the *Complaint* and other works analyzed is even more striking. The midline drop on position 6 in the *Complaint* falls lower that in Shakespeare's nondramatic poetry analyzed (table 1). The stress profile of *A Lover's Complaint* looks not unlike *Romeo and Juliet,* but it is certainly different from his plays after 1597. The stress profile of the *Complaint,* with its "dip" on position 6 and too few extrametrical stresses on **W,** points either to a very early Shakespeare, or to a more constrained form, characteristic of earlier Renaissance iambic pentameter.[19]

Here are some consecutive lines from the *Complaint* with a missing stress on syllabic position six:

> . . .Though slackly braided **in** loose negligence.
> A thousand favours **from** a maund she drew
> Of amber, chrystal, **and** of beaded jet,
> Which one by one she **in** a river threw . . .
> I might as yet have **been** a spreading flower,
> Fresh to myself, and **to** no love beside. . . .
> So on the tip of **his** subduing tongue
> All kind of argu**ment** and question deep . . .
>
> (*A Lover's Complaint,* 35–38, 76–77, 120–21)

And here are lines typical of "mature" Shakespeare's dramas, 1600 and later, with a missing stress on syllabic position eight:

> Our potency made good, take **thy** reward.
> Five days we do allot thee **for** provision
> To shield thee from disasters **of** the world . . .
> I have this present evening **from** my sister
> Been well informed of them, and **with** such cautions
> That, if they come to sojourn **at** my house,
> I'll not be there . . .
>
> (*King Lear* 1.1.172–74; 2.1.101–4)

Thus, *A Lover's Complaint* must be either a very early Shakespeare, or—not Shakespeare?

Test 2. Word boundaries in lines; locations of strong syntactic breaks. Lines are composed of words; and the shapes and locations of boundaries between adjacent words are one more feature of verse rhythm.

As words are strung together in speech, there may be no actual articulatory and acoustic boundaries between them;[20] but speakers of a language know, most of the time subconsciously, where one word ends and another begins. I assume that as we read, or hear, verse lines, we segment them into phonetic words: "Which die / for goodness, / who have lived / for crime" (Son. 124: 14), "Where time / and outward / form / would show it / dead" (Son. 108: 14). In my analyses below, all monosyllables on **W,** including the stressed ones, are incorporated into a phonetic word with its stress on

S (thus, the group constitutes a "metrical word"): "***Sweet**-LOVE,* / renew / thy-force" (*Son.* 56: 1), "***Make**-ANSwer,* / Muse / . . ." (*Son.* 101: 5), "And-MORE, / ***much**-MORE* / than-in-my-verse / can-sit" (*Son.* 103: 13), "Resembling / *STRONG*-**youth** / in-his-middle / age" (*Son.* 7: 6). The "ending" of a word is structured by its stressed syllable plus, if any, unstressed syllables (e.g., "im**POSsible**"). A word boundary is generated by the ending of the first word, whose structure very much depends on its part of speech: for example, adjectives, with their long unstressed tails, create "feminine," and longer, word boundaries ("With **UGly** / rack / on his ce**LEStial** / face" (*Son.* 33: 6), while verbs, with their stressed stems and long unstressed necks—the unstressed prefixes—often generate "masculine" word boundaries: " . . . / per**MIT** / the basest / clouds / to **RIDE**" (Son. 33: 5), " . . . / re**TURN** / in happy / plight" (Son. 28: 1). "Masculine" word boundaries, as it were, emphasize the foot structure of the line, and are more numerous in constrained iambic pentameter, while "feminine" and longer word boundaries (the latter may occur only in the lines with missing ictic stresses) are more frequent in a looser variant of iambs.[21] Here are examples of "dactylic" and "hyperdactylic" word boundaries (one stressed syllable plus two or three unstressed ones): "Had tracked / the hosts / in **FEStival** / array" (Shelley, *The Revolt of Islam:* 3914); "And weren't there / special / **CEmetery** / flowers" (Frost, *Place for a Third:* 26).

Two adjacent words may have a different degree of syntactic link; the strength of the link varies within a wide range. Shapir, for example, in his analysis of Russian eighteenth-century odes differentiates twenty-three degrees.[22] To be able to generalize, I consider only three degrees of link. Thus:

1. **A strong link** (marked [/]) exists:

   between a modifier and the modified noun: " . . .a glorious / morning . . ." (*Son.* 33: 1), " . . .what woman's / son" (*Son.* 41: 7);

   between a verb and its objects: "Presents / thy shadow . . ." (Son. 27: 10), "Consumed / with that . . ." (*Son.* 73: 12), or between verbs and other types of complements: "So I return / rebuked . . ." (*Son.* 119: 13);

   between a noun and its complement (e.g., postpositional possessive): "The glory / of our Troy . . ." (*Troilus and Cressida* 4.4: 147), "In praise / of ladies (*Son.* 106: 4);

   between a verb, adverb, or adjective and their specifying qualitative adverb: "Is poorly / imitated . . ." (*Son.* 53: 6), "Accurse me / thus . . ." (*Son.* 117: 1).[23]

2. **A medium link** (marked [//]) is formed:

   between a subject and a predicate: "That Time // will come . . ." (*Son.* 64: 12);

between specifiers of time, location, or cause and the specified word, e.g., " . . .I sometimes // hold / my tongue" (*Son.* 102: 13), "And therefore // art enforced . . ." (*Son.* 82: 7), "Look // in thy glass . . ." (*Son.* 3: 1), " . . .alive // that time" (*Son.* 17: 13);

between coordinated not expanded phrasal elements: "The scope // and tenour . . ." (*Son.* 61: 8), "Make glad // and sorry / seasons . . ." (*Son.* 19: 5);

and between any adjacent words that have no immediate syntactic link: "This silence // for my sin // you did impute" (*Son.* 83: 9),"My heart // mine eye // the freedom / of that right" (*Son.* 46: 4).

3. **Weak syntactic links,** that is, **syntactic breaks** (marked [///]) are found:

at the juncture of sentences and clauses: "My day's / delight // is past, /// my horse // is gone" (*Venus:* 381), " . . .To mend / the hurt /// that his unkindness // marred (*Venus:* 479);

between the author's and direct speech: " 'For shame,' /// he cries, /// 'let go, /// and let me / go" (*Venus:* 380);

between participial, infinitival, absolute or isolated phrases and the main part of the clause: "She sinketh / down, /// still hanging / by his neck" (*Venus:* 594),"Their mistress, /// mounted, /// through the empty / skies . . ." (*Venus:* 1192), "And now // Adonis, /// with a lazy / sprite, /// . . ." (*Venus:* 181);

between phrases with expansion, e.g., an expanded apposition: "When as I met / the boar, /// that bloody / beast . . . (*Venus:* 1000), or between expanded coordinated phrases: "He thought / to kiss him, /// and hath killed him / so" (*Venus:* 1112).

Let us look at table 2. It shows the breaks after positions 2–7 (cf. Tarlinskaja 1984); breaks after positions 8 and 9 will be discussed in the text. The table includes the data on *A Lover's Complaint,* two long poems and the *Sonnets,* and four plays, the early *Romeo and Juliet,* the transitional *Troilus and Cressida,* and the later *King Lear* and *Antony and Cleopatra. Venus and Adonis* is represented by the eighty-four first and forty-five last stanzas, *Lucrece* by stanzas 1–40, 66–93, 98–100, 111–18, 173–232, 246, 247 (two first lines), 248, 262–65; the *Sonnets* by the first forty-seven and the last sixteen texts (excluding 145). In the dramas analyzed, longer and shorter lines, lines of a questionable form, as well as lines split between two or more characters were excluded. The rhythm of the plays is more heterogeneous than that of nondramatic verse, therefore our samples from the dramas are long. Thus: *Romeo and Juliet,* the first three acts; *Troilus and*

Table 2. Locations of Word Boundaries after Positions 2–7 (in percent of total number of lines)

		Total Number of Word Boundaries, after positions:						Strong Syntactic Breaks, after positions:						Lines Analyzed
Works	Dates	2	3	4	5	6	7	2	3	4	5	6	7	
LC	?	48.0	27.7	51.1	36.8	<u>33.4</u>	31.3	7.0	1.2	<u>21.6</u>	10.3	8.2	2.4	329
V&A	1593	43.3	22.5	56.0	32.7	46.4	28.3	6.7	1.9	<u>26.5</u>	10.2	17.7	3.7	774
RL	1594	46.0	31.6	51.5	35.7	46.8	28.2	6.3	1.8	<u>16.6</u>	5.7	10.5	1.4	1010
Sonns	c1596-1604	40.2	26.7	52.8	33.9	50.7	25.0	5.0	1.8	<u>20.1</u>	7.0	<u>14.6</u>	2.5	602
R&J	1594-95	44.9	27.0	<u>53.4</u>	34.6	<u>41.8</u>	31.1	10.6	5.4	<u>28.9</u>	13.6	14.9	4.7	1600
T&C	1601-02	36.0	24.1	41.4	33.1	36.7	27.6	6.9	3.4	<u>15.7</u>	12.4	14.7	7.1	1723
KL	1605-06	38.8	25.8	43.8	37.6	44.2	31.1	7.3	4.2	<u>17.3</u>	16.5	26.9	15.2	1000
A&C	1606-07	39.4	27.6	43.4	38.5	42.3	32.9	5.2	3.8	15.2	16.4	25.7	16.9	1570

Cressida, acts 1–2 and 4–5; *King Lear:* five hundred lines from the beginning and five hundred from the end; *Antony and Cleopatra,* acts 1–3 and 5. The "total number of word boundaries" incorporates the data on initially stressed disyllabic words on positions **WS,** the so-called "rhythmical inversions of stress," e.g., "*Music* to hear, why hear'st thou music sadly?" (Son. 8: 1). The distribution on medium and strong links will be mentioned in the text.

Let us start with **strong breaks:** these are more striking. In early Shakespeare, the maximum of strong syntactic breaks occurs after position 4, thus, emphasizing a 4 + 6 composition of the line. If we also add strong breaks after position 5 (a "feminine" ending of the first half-line), the hemistich structuring of the "early" Shakespeare line into 4 + 6 and 5 + 5 is obvious. In *Lucrece* it is less prominent than in *Venus and Adonis* and the *Sonnets,* while in *Romeo and Juliet* the 4 + 6 segmentation is especially strong. It is particularly noticeable in the utterances and monologues of the two main characters:

> The clock struck nine /// when I did send the nurse;
> In half an hour // she promised to return . . .
> O, she is lame; /// love's heralds should be thoughts. . . .
> It was the lark, /// the herald of the morn,
> No nightingale: /// look, love, what envious streaks . . .
> Let me be ta'en, /// let me be put to death;
> I am content, /// so thou wilt have it so . . .
> It is, it is: /// hie hence, be gone, away!
> It is the lark /// that sings so out of tune . . .
>
> (*Romeo and Juliet* 2, 5.1–2, 4;
> 3.5.6–7, 17–18, 26–27)

Here are typical examples from early Shakespeare's nondramatic verse:

> Hunting he loved, /// but love he laughed to scorn . . .
> Here come and sit, /// where never serpent hisses,
> And being set, /// I'll smother thee with kisses.
> He red for shame, /// but frosty in desire.
>
> (*Venus and Adonis:* 4, 17, 18, 36)

In *Troilus and Cressida* the number of strong breaks after position 4 falls dramatically and stays this way in both later plays. In both *King Lear* and *Antony and Cleopatra* the number of breaks after positions 6, as well as 7, 8 and 9 increases. At the same time, the number of strong syntactic links after position 4 grows. Thus, the segmentation into hemistichs 4 + 6 and 5 + 5 in later dramas becomes effaced, while major syntactic breaks move closer and closer to the end of the line, particularly in *Antony and Cleopa-*

tra which is, in many ways, a turning point in Shakespeare's rhythmical style (including the increased number of "enclitic" phrases; cf. Oras 1953: 212, 1960, and the use of unstressed monosyllables in position 10). Here are typical lines from "mature" dramas:

> Show scarce so gross as beetles. /// Half way down
> Hangs one that gathers samphere ///—dreaded trade!
> Methinks he seems no bigger /// than his head.
>
> (*King Lear* 4.5.14–16)

> . . .Whom these things cannot blemish, /// —yet must Antony
> No way excuse his foils, /// when we do bear
> So great weight in his lightness. /// If he fill'd . . .
>
> (*Antony and Cleopatra* 1.4.24–26)

And now let us look at the data of *A Lover's Complaint*. Even taking into account the genre difference between dramatic and nondramatic verse, the *Complaint* resembles earlier Shakespeare, both nondramatic and dramatic verse, more than his mature plays. But there is a striking difference between *A Lover's Complaint* and early Shakespeare: in no Shakespeare text analyzed is the number of breaks after position 4 so numerous compared to the breaks after position 6 as in the *Complaint*. Let us present the data of strong breaks after position 6 as a percentage of breaks after 4: *A Lover's Complaint:* 37.9; *Venus and Adonis:* 66.8; *The Rape of Lucrece:* 63.2; *Sonnets:* 72.6; *Romeo and Juliet:* 51.6; *Troilus and Cressida:* 93.6; *King Lear:* 155.5; *Antony and Cleopatra:* 169.1. The difference between *A Lover's Complaint* and early Shakespeare is striking, and between the *Complaint* and the later dramas—staggering. The 4 + 6 / 5 +5 segmentation of the *Complaint* is too persistent for even *Romeo and Juliet*. Here are typical lines from the *Compaint:*

> From off a hill /// whose concave womb re-worded (1)
> Tearing of papers, /// breaking rings a-twain (6)
> Nor youth all quit; /// but spite of heaven's fell rage (13)
> Their view right on; /// anon their gazes lend (26)
> For some, untucked, /// descended her sheaved hat (31),

and so on. We may add here lines with "medium breaks" (= "medium links"), particularly if such medium breaks are flanked, in contrast, by tighter links on either side, as in:

> In bloodless / white // and the encrimsoned / mood (201)
> Could scape / the hail // of his all-hurting / aim (310)
> He preached / pure maid // and praised / cold chastity (315)

Such correlations of links and breaks adds to the 4 + 6 (or 5 + 5) half-line segmentation tendency of the poem. The total number of strong plus medium breaks *after position four only* reaches 50 percent of all lines:

> What rocky heart // to water will not wear? (291)
> What breast so cold /// that it is not warm'd here? (292)
> O cleft effect! /// Cold modesty, hot wrath (293)
> Both fire from hence // and chill extincture hath (294),

and so on. Add to these 50 percent another 22.5 percent: lines containing strong and medium breaks after position five. Thus, three-quarters of the poem *A Lover's Complaint* displays a syntactically supported hemistich segmentation 4 + 6 and 5 + 5. This is either a very, *very* early Shakespeare, or, more likely, not Shakespeare at all, but somebody else's earlier Renaissance verse. Compare, for example, with Sir Philip Sidney's:

> In wonted walks, /// since wonted fancies change,
> Some cause there is, /// which of strange cause doth rise;
> For in each thing /// whereto my eye doth range,
> Part of my pain // meseems engraved lies.
> (Sidney, *The Certain Sonnets*, *18:* 1–4)

The geometry of the total number of word boundaries demonstrates the same difference of *A Lover's Complaint* from the rest of Shakespeare's texts analyzed. The somewhat low number of word boundaries after position six brings together the *Complaint* and *Troilus;* and yet, there are some striking differences between the two texts: the number of word boundaries after position 4 in *Troilus and Cressida* has already dropped to the index of "mature" Shakespeare. The number of strong syntactic breaks after position 2 brings together *A Lover's Complaint* and *Romeo and Juliet,* but the total number of word boundaries after position 2 is more frequent in the *Complaint,* whose first hemistich often falls into 2 + 2 syllables, for example:

> Her hair, /// nor loose, /// nor tied in formal plait (29)
> For some, /// untucked, /// descended her sheaved hat (31)
> "Father," /// she says, /// "though in me you behold . . ." (71)
> Ay me, /// I fell, /// and yet do question make
> (321)

This pattern is more indicative of earlier Renaissance verse, illustrated again by Sidney:

> Leave me, /// O Love, /// which reachest but to dust;
> And thou, /// my mind, /// aspire to higher things . . .
> (Sidney *The Certain Sonnets, 32:* 1–2).

The number of strong syntactic breaks after positions 2, 4, and 5 gradually decreases in Shakespeare's oeuvre, and of strong syntactic links after the same positions, on the whole, grows. Syntactic breaks begin to be scattered in the first part of the line more randomly, and they peak after position 6 (and its "feminine" tail, 7), gradually increasing also after 8 and 9. In *Lear,* for example, strong syntactic breaks after position nine occur in only 1.7 percent of lines, and in *Antony and Cleopatra,* in 5.6 percent of lines: three times more often. Thus, the half-line segmentation 4 + 6 and 5 + 5 disappears from later Shakespeare. Here are examples of syntactic structuring of lines in his later works:

> Love not / such nights // as these. /// The wrathful / skies . . .
> (*King Lear* 3.2.42)

> Our great / competitor: /// from Alexandria . . .
> (*Antony and Cleopatra* 1.4.3)

> Perchance // shall dry / your pities: /// but I have . . .
> Hermione // hath suffered / death, /// and that . . .
> (*The Winter's Tale* 2.1.110, 3.3.42)

> From what / a torment // I did free thee?—/// No!
> (*The Tempest* 1.2.252)

A syntactic break occurs after position 6 in the first two examples, and after 7, 8 and 9 in the last three.

The difference between genres needs to be considered; and yet, the syntactic structuring of lines in the *Complaint* deviates from early Shakespeare, and it certainly does not resemble later Shakespeare.

Test 3: the relative frequency of proclitic and enclitic phrases, and their number per thousand lines. For the 329 lines of *A Lover's Complaint,* a theoretical projection had to be calculated.

Recall that **proclitic phrases** are metrical words where the stressed host (or, in case of a polysyllable, the stressed syllable) occupies an **S** syllabic position, and an adjacent notional monosyllable (with a full or possibly reduced stress) occupies the preceding **W** ("***Sweet** LOVE,* renew . . ."). **Enclitic phrases** are metrical words where the stressed host, again, occupies an **S,** while an adjacent notional monosyllable stands not on the preceding but on the following **W** ("To eat *the WORLD'S **due,*** by the grave and thee"). In cases of three adjacent stressed words, the two with a stronger syntactic link are assumed to constitute the metrical word (and create either a proclitic or an enclitic phrase). Thus, "And see / *the BRAVE **day*** / sunk in hideous night" (*Son.* 12: 2): an enclitic phrase, not *"To see the brave / ***day***

SUNK / in hideous night": a proclitic phrase. A strong syntactic break between the elements on **W** and on **S** disallows the formation of proclitic or enclitic phrases; thus, cases like "Lo, in the orient . . ." (Son. 7: 1) were disregarded.

Table 3 shows the proportion and frequency of proclitic and enclitic phrases in *A Lover's Complaint, Venus and Adonis, The Rape of Lucrece* and the *Sonnets,* as well as in five plays: *Romeo and Juliet, Troilus and Cressida*, *King Lear, Antony and Cleopatra,* and *The Winter's Tale.* Even in the early nondramatic poetry by Shakespeare the percent of enclitics (from the total of proclitic and enclitic phrases) is higher than in the plays, except for the last: *The Winter's Tale.*[24] In Shakespeare's non-dramatic poetry analyzed the percent of enclitic phrases vascillates in a narrow range: 14.3–17 percent; a particularly high number of enclitics is displayed by the *Sonnets* (perhaps a shorter lyrical text allows more attention to its rhythmical variety). Among the five plays, the range of variation is from 9.4 percent (*Troilus and Cressida*) to 18 percent *(The Winter's Tale). A Lover's Complaint* is strikingly different: Its amount of enclitic phrases, expressed both as percent from the total of proclitics and enclitics, and as a projected number of enclitic phrases per thousand lines, is two to three times lower than in *Troilus and Cressida,* three to four times lower than in either of Shakespeare's long poems and the *Sonnets,* four and a half times lower than in *Romeo and Juliet,* five times lower than in *Antony and Cleopatra,* and six times lower than in *The Winter's Tale.* The tradition of a "complaint" poem is believed to have been started with Samuel Daniel's *Complaint of Rosamond,* 1592.[25] If this is true, then *A Lover's Complaint* must have been written sometime after 1592, but it shows indices much below the two long poems of 1590s unquestionably attributed to Shakespeare, and much below both the *Sonnets* and the early tragedy. True, the proclitic-enclitic test takes long chunks of text, and the index may vary from one portion of text to another; still, the test speaks against attributing *A Lover's Complaint* to early Shakespeare; and it certainly points away from "mature" Shakespeare.

To conclude. We have looked at the iambic pentameter verse structure of *A Lover's Complaint* from three angles: 1. the distribution of stresses along the even (**S**) and odd (**W**) syllabic positions of its line (the stress profile of its verse); 2. the word boundary structuring of its lines and their syn-

Table 3. Proclitic and Enclitic Phrases

	Non-Dramatic Verse				**Dramatic Verse**				
	L'sC	*V&A*	*RL*	*Sonn*	*R&J*	*T&C*	*KL*	*A&C*	*WT*
Percent Enclitic Phrases (from total procol. & encl.)	4.3	14.3	15.7	17.0	11.3	9.4	10.7	14.3	18.0
"Number of Enclitics," per 1000 lines	12.0	41.0	56.0	68.0	54.4	33.0	37.0	57.3	73.0

tactic segmentation; and 3. the number and proportion of proclitic and enclitic phrases. *A Lover's Complaint* was compared with works by Shakespeare in three genres: two long poems; the short lyrical texts of his *Sonnets;* and six plays. The verse of *A Lover's Complaint* cannot possibly point to "mature" Shakespeare. It also differs from early Shakespeare, both nondramatic and dramatic poetry. I wish I could suggest that *A Lover's Complaint* does belong to Shakespeare, after all, albeit to a very early Shakespeare. But this seems unlikely.[26]

Notes

1. Elliott, Ward E, and Robert J.Valenza, "And Then There Were None: Winnowing the Shakespeare Claimants," *Computers and the Humanities* 30 (1996): 191–245; Elliott and Valenza, this volume, which also contains (n.1) a fuller list of references to *A Lover's Complaint.*
2. MacD. P. Jackson, "Shakespeare's *A Lover's Complaint:* Its Date and Authenticity," *University of Auckland Bulletin 72* (1965): 7–39 (*English Series 13.*)
3. Marina Tarlinskaja, "General and Particular Aspects of Meter: Literatures, Epochs, Poets," *Phonetics and Phonology: Rhythm and Meter,* edited by Paul Kiparsky and Gilbert Youmans (San Diego: Academic Press, 1989) , 121–54.
4. Marina Tarlinskaja, *Shakespeare's Verse: Iambic Pentameter and the Poet's Idiosyncrasies,* (New York: Peter Lang, 1987).
5. MacD. P. Jackson, "Another Metrical Index for Shakespeare's Plays: Evidence for Chronology and Authorship," *Neuphilologische Mitteilungen* 95 (1991): 453–58.
6. *Shakespeare, Co-Author: A Study of Five Collaborative Plays* (Oxford: Oxford Univ. Press, 2002).
7. Marina Tarlinskaja, *English Verse: Theory and Hist*ory (The Hague: Mouton, 1976), table 41.
8. Tarlinskaja, *Shakespeare's Verse.*
9. Ants Oras, "Extra Monosyllables in 'Henry VIII' and the Problem of Authorship," *Journal of English and Germanic Philology* 52 (1953): 198–215: 212, Tarlinskaja, *Shakespeare's Verse,* ch. 6.
10. Bruce Hayes's term, "The Prosodic Hierarchy of Meter," *Phonetics and Phonology: Rhythm and Meter, 1,* ed. Paul Kiparsky and Gilbert Youmans (San Diego: Academic Press, 1989), 201–60: 208.
11. Cf. Andrew Radford's definition of Clitic(ization), in *Syntax: A Minimalist Introduction* (Cambridge: Cambridge Univ. Press, 1997), 256.
12. Hayes, "Hierarchy," 207.
13. M. L. Gasparov, *Sovremennyj Russkij Stikh* (Moscow: Nauka, 1974), 203.
14. David Abercrombie, "A Phonetician's View of Verse Structure," *Linguistics* 6 (1961): 5–13, Elizabeth Selkirk, *Phonology and Syntax: The Relation Between Sound and Structure* (Cambridge: MIT Univ. Press, 1984), 42.
15. Cf. Oras, "Monosyllables," 212.
16. Gasparov, *Stikh.*
17. Tarlinskaja, *Shakespeare's Verse,* table 6.1
18. *Complaint.*
19. Tarlinskaja, *English Verse,* table 41.
20. Ellen Kaisse, *Connected Speech: The Interaction of Syntax and Phonology* (Orlando: Academic Press, 1985).

21. Marina Tarlinskaja, "Rhythm-Morphology-Syntax-Rhythm," *Style* 18 (1984): 1–26.

22. M. I. Shapir, *Universum Versus: Jazyk-stikh-smysl v russkoj poezii XVIII–XX vekov* (Moskcow: Jazyki russkoj kul'tury, 2000), 164–66.

23. In deciding which expansion to a verbal phrase is a complement (complements have a strong link with the verb), and which is an adjunct (adjuncts have a weaker link with the verb), I relied on Radford's classification (Radford 1988: 230–41).

24. The data on *The Winter's Tale* are from Tarlinskaja, *Shakespeare's Verse,* table 6.1.

25. Cf. John Dover Wilson, ed., *The Complete Works of William Shakespeare: The Cambridge Text Established by John Dover Wilson* (London: Octopus, 1980), 1082.

26. I would like to thank Ward Elliott for nudging me in the direction of *A Lover's Complaint,* for his encouragement, and for his unwithering friendship.

1600s: Shakespeare and Middleton

"Servile Ministers": *Othello, King Lear,* and the Sacralization of Service

Michael Neill

IN THE COURSE OF THE GREAT SPEECH OF SELF-JUSTIFICATION WITH WHICH he defends himself to the Venetian Senate, Othello recalls how he was "taken by the insolent foe, / And sold to slavery" (1.3.6–7).[1] But at the end of the play, in an irony that usually passes unnoticed, it is the Moor's triumphant antagonist, Iago, who is branded—not once, but four times—as a "slave" (5.2.241, 275, 289, 338). Iago's brand is not literal, of course; for "slave" had become one of the most common (as well as potent) terms of abuse in the extensive repertory of status-based insult that adorned the early modern lexicon. In *King Lear* it is the word which the King uses to denounce another treacherous subordinate—the compliant Officer who performs his murderous "man's work" on Cordelia: "I killed the *slave* that was a-hanging thee" (5.3.274); it is also the word with which Lear and Kent repeatedly debase Goneril's overweening steward, the "super-serviceable" Oswald (1.4.55, 86; 2.2.17–18, 41–42, 73; 2.4.187, 218); it is the word that concentrates Cornwall's sense of outrage, when his own servant reneges against the blinding of Gloucester: "Throw this slave upon the dunghill" (3.7.95); it is the word that expresses Oswald's disgust when he is overcome by the disguised Edgar: "Slave, thou hast slain me" (4.6.247); and it is the word with which the King describes his own degraded condition on the heath, when exposed to the power of elements that in turn appear to function as "servile ministers" of his daughters' will: "You owe me no subscription: then let fall / Your horrible pleasure; here I stand, your slave" (3.2.19–21) . The very frequency of the term means that modern readers are likely to brush over it as a vague hyperbole—especially as it seems unanchored to a recognizable social context either inside or outside the plays. After all, the institution of slavery had no significant place in the English social order; nor (despite the efforts of John Hawkins in the 1560s) had the Atlantic slave trade yet become a major source of English mercantile wealth.[2] Pre-Roman Britain may have been a slave-owning society, but slavery seems, if anything, even more remote from Lear's Britain than from Othello's Venice. Othello himself may have been "sold to slavery," but that can easily seem part of his exotic "travel's history," along with "Anthropophagi and men whose heads / Do grow beneath their shoulders" (1.3.137).[3] His enslavement hardly seems to impinge on the self-confident character we are shown in the play, nor does it have much to do with the world he presently inhabits: perhaps these Venetians, like Shylock's persecutors, keep amongst them "many a purchased slave";[4] but, if so, we hear nothing of it.

Nevertheless, it is clear that both plays are profoundly concerned with an institution that bore an obvious relation to slavery—namely service. The two terms, one standing for voluntary and the other for involuntary subordination, define two modes of social being, and ultimately two kinds of society. In *Othello,* it is on the "service" that he has done the state that the Moor founds his claim to be "of Venice";[5] just as in *King Lear* it is his commitment to "service" that marks the dual identity of Kent/Caius. By the same token, it is their hypocritical betrayal of the bonds of service that marks the villains of the plays, reducing them to the moral status of slaves. Thus if we want to understand the insulting power that infuses the epithet "slave," it is to the discourse of service that we must turn.

As I have argued elsewhere, "service" in the early modern period was a remarkably inclusive concept, embracing in its most elastic definition virtually all forms of social relationship—since even the bonds between husbands and wives, parents and children involved the same principles of authority and obedience.[6] The ideological reach of the concept was guaranteed by the sacralized authority with which it was invested, in a world where the distinction between the sacred and the secular was by no means as clear as it appears to us. Then as now, of course, the term had a conspicuous application to sacred ritual—as in the description of formal worship as "divine service"; but that expression merely reflects the way in which the Christian subject's duty to God was imagined as the pattern of all servant-master relationships. By invoking God and Christ as the patterns not merely of paternal authority and filial obedience, but of mastery and service, the official voice of early modern culture could present all domestic relationships as profoundly sacralized.[7] We can recognize this when Desdemona, invoking the sacrament of marriage, speaks of her "soul and fortunes" as "consecrate[d]" to her husband;[8] or when Lear humbles himself by kneeling to Cordelia in an inversion of the quotidian ritual of blessing through which fathers acted as the conduit of divine grace for their children. But it can be equally conspicuous in master-servant relationships: the shocking power of the improvised rite in which a kneeling Iago gives up "The execution of his wit, hands, heart, / To wronged Othello's service" (3.3.462–64) depends on its sacrilegious enactment of a sacred bond. In the patriarchal household, Peter Laslett has written, "every relationship could be seen as a love-relationship," and that love, as Iago's parody of nuptial vows suggests, was sacralized.[9]

In this context it is worth noticing that the idea of slavery in *Othello* is dressed with its own theologically weighted language: Othello speaks of his release from enslavement as "my *redemption* thence," while Iago is successively denounced by Montano, Othello, and Lodovico as a "*damned*" and "*cursed* slave." "Redemption," was of course, the usual term for purchasing the freedom of a slave or captive; but the powerful Christian connotations of the word are impossible to ignore when it is applied to the history of a Christianized Moor, just as the literal sense of "damned" inevitably attaches to a self-professed adherent of the "divinity of hell" like Iago (2.3.340), whom Othello half-believes a "devil" (5.2.284, 297). The neatness of this reversal is compromised, however, by the ambiguous reference of Othello's distracted cry, "cursed, cursed slave," which threatens to collapse the distinction between Iago and himself. If slavery is imagined as a reprobate state—the opposite of that "free condition" achieved by Othello's double redemption from slavery and paganism (1.2.26)—then it is into a new and worse slavery that the Moor is betrayed when having "curse[d] his better angel from his side . . . [he] fall[s] to reprobance" (5.2.207–8). For, if the abject condition of the slave could stand for reprobation, the free performance of service, it turns out, could often resemble grace.

The Latin word *servus,* from which *servant* derives—and whose original connotations survive in such denigratory formations as *servile*—did not discriminate between slavery and free service; but Christian doctrine, with its insistence on equality before God and the freedom conferred by Christ, had made the distinction all-important. "Art thou called, being a servant?" writes St Paul. "Care not for it. . . . For he that is called being a servant, is the Lord's freeman; likewise also he that is called, being free, is Christ's servant" (1 Cor: 21–22); "we are not children of the bondwoman, but of the free," he urges. " Stand fast therefore in the liberty wherewith Christ hath made us free, and be not entangled again with the yoke of bondage" (Gal. 4:31–5.1). For the bondage to which humanity was consigned by the ruthless logic of sin and the Law, the new dispensation substituted the reciprocal "bonds in Christ" or "bonds of the Gospel" described in the Epistles (Phil. 1.13; Philem. 13).[10]

Conscious of the subversive potential of such doctrine in the hands of radical sectaries, early theorists of service were quick to adapt its rhetoric to their own autocratic idea of household government. Thus William Gouge set out to rebut the Anabaptists, who, citing St Paul's "be not ye the servants of men" (1 Corinthians 7:23), had proclaimed that all "subiection of seruants to masters is against [Christian] prerogatiue," since "it is the prerogatiue of Xtians to be all one" and "subiection is against the liberty that Christ hath purchased for vs . . . wherewith he hath made vs free."[11] Gouge, following the paradoxical insistence of the *Book of Common Prayer* that God's "service is perfect freedom,"[12] countered by citing an earlier verse in Corinthians and insisting that, since all service belongs to God, the true servant is always free:

> Let there be cheerefulnesse in a seruants minde, and he is as free as his master: for such a seruant is *the Lords freeman* (1 *Cor:* 7.22) . . . and when he cannot be made free of his master, he doth after a manner make his seruice free.[13]

Of course servants are "bound to obedience," indeed "it is their main, and most popular function, to *obey their masters,*" while

> They who are contrary minded, who are rebellious, and disdain to be under the authority of another, and are ready to say of their Master, *We will not have this man to reigne over vs,* are fitter to live among Anabaptists, than orthodoxall Christians. For to what end is the lawfulness of authority acknowledged, if subjection be not yielded unto it?[14]

But such "subjection" is not to be confused with slavish bondage. In language that resonates with *King Lear*'s emphasis on the "bonds" of service and filial duty, Gouge writes of "that neare bond which is betwixt master and seruants":

> *Masters are as well bound to duties as seruants.* Gods law requireth as much. . . . So doth also the law of nature which hath tied master and seruant together by mutuall and reciprocall bond, of doing good, as well as of receiuing good.[15]

The notion of service as a divinely sanctioned institution appeared to be underwritten in scripture not only by a number of parables in which God's relationship with humanity is analogized to that of a master with his servants, but even by the routine deployment of secular honorifics such as "lord" and "master" in religious discourse. As such language suggested, the "mutuall and reciprocall bond" celebrated by Gouge, though founded in "a common equitie betwixt masters and seruants," did not involve any kind of "equalitie."[16] It required instead a quasi-religious "dutie of reuerence" toward masters, since if Christ, by "*[taking] vpon him the forme of a seruant,*" offered the perfect ideal of willing service, he was also the pattern of all masters. Thus service, as St Paul had insisted, must be performed "*with feare and trembling in singlenesse of your heart, as vnto Christ*" (Ephesians 6.5); and although the "*[o]bedience which [servants] yeeld to their master must be such as may stand with their obedience to Christ,*" there should in theory be no conflict between sacred and profane duty. Since God was the supreme master from whom all authority derived, and the rebellious Lucifer the original of all disobedience, the faithful servant's fulfillment of his office was an expression of Christian duty, while any resistance to the master's command must be devilishly inspired; indeed Gouge went so far as to say that

> masters by vertue of their office and place beare Christs image, and stand in his stead, by communication of Christs authority to them they are called *Lords,* yea also *Gods* (for that which a Magistrate is in the Common-wealth a master is in the family). Hence it followeth that seruants in performing duty to their master performe duty to Christ, and in rebelling against their master, they rebell against Christ.[17]

Conservative, even reactionary, as Gouge's arguments may appear, they neverthless chime with the idea of free service that more liberal thinkers, anxious to discard all relics of the "Norman yoke" had begun to develop as part of the myth of the "free-born Englishman." The role of slavery in this discourse was in essence rhetorical: by defining all that the servant was *not,* the abject bondage of the slave helped to sustain the idea of service as a system of voluntary engagement and profoundly naturalized "bonds" that constituted, however paradoxically, an expression of the free condition. Thus William Harrison, in his *Description of England* (1580), proclaimed that: "as for slaves and bondmen, we have none; nay, such is the privilege of our country by the especial grace of God and bounty of our princes, that if any come hither from other realms, so soon as they set foot on land they become so free of condition as their masters, whereby all note of servile bondage is removed from them."[18] In the words of the leveler John Lilburne (writing in 1652, but citing an Elizabethan case) England breathed "too pure an air for slaves to live in."[19] In some cases, of course, the distinction between service and slavery might seem an uncomfortably narrow one; but it was, all commentators agreed, essential. Thus Sir Thomas Smith's *De Republica Anglorum* (1583) acknowledged that "necessitie and want of bondmen hath made men to use free men and bondmen to all servile services: but yet more liberally and freely, and with more equalitie and moderation, than in time of gentilitie [i.e., pre-Christian times] slaves and bondmen were woont to be used" (98).[20]

Shakespeare's own engagement with such paradoxes is conspicuously displayed in the schematic design that underlies the most visionary of his dramas, *The Tempest*—the play with which he seemingly planned to close his London career, and which Heminge and Condell chose to open the First Folio. Crucial to the design of *The Tempest,* with its elaborate variations on the themes of service and freedom, is the contrast between the obedient servant Ariel and the refractory slave Caliban in their struggle to win liberty from their overweening master, Prospero. Far from being inimical to freedom, however, service turns out to be the route to its attainment. At the centre of the play's action is a scene in which the captive Prince Ferdinand transforms his exhibition of "wooden slavery" to Prospero (3.1.62) into a proof of the humble service he vows to Miranda, offering it "with a heart as willing / As bondage e'er of freedom" (ll. 88–89).[21] Like Gouge's servant, whose acceptance of servitude "doth . . . make his service free," Ferdinand discovers freedom (as Ariel, and ultimately Prospero himself, will do) through submission: and this is what it will mean for Caliban (in the theologically loaded language with which he acknowledges Prospero as "my master") to "seek for grace" (5.2.262, 295).

Looking back to *Othello* and *King Lear,* we can see how the action of each of these plays turns on a similar contrast between free service and slavery. These two tragedies, though probably written no more than a year apart, are not often considered together: the narrow domestic focus of the former contrasts so sharply with the visionary grandeur of the latter that they can seem to stand at opposite poles of Shakespeare's tragic range. Yet on one level, of course, *Lear* is a family drama in which the politics of the household are quite as important as those of the state; and in both plays it is the ideology of service that links the two domains. I am not, of course, the first to explore to their common interest in what it means to be a servant. It was Jonas Barish and Marshall Waingrow who, forty years ago, first drew attention to the prominence of service in *Lear:* "Its presence [they wrote] is felt very strongly not only through the steady succession of incidents involving masters and servants, but even more pervasively through . . . reiteration [of the terminology of service]."[22] For all the persuasive detail of their analysis, however, Barish and Waingrow, were troubled by an uneasy sense that "the theme of service is obvious . . . only in its presence, not in its meaning"; any attempt to formulate that meaning, they concluded, tended to stumble on "a number of intersecting paradoxes which effectively demolish a complacent reading."[23] These paradoxes involved both a deeply equivocal attitude toward the significance of rank, and a sense of the disturbing contradictions between socially sanctioned duties and moral obligation.

In a trenchantly argued essay, Richard Strier sought to account for the play's paradoxical attitudes toward rank and authority by linking them to Renaissance arguments about the limits of obedience—and in particular to the views advanced by sixteenth-century Protestant radicals like Ponet and Buchanan, who advocated resistance to tyranny as the path of Christian duty.[24] The servant who refused consent to his master's iniquity, Buchanan had argued—in an image that resonates powerfully with the medical language of Lear's restoration scene (4.7)—was "his master's true physician."[25] Strier traced Shakespeare's interest in "virtuous disobedience" back to Othello, discovering "the very threshold" of *King Lear* in Emilia's renunciation of her wifely duty to Iago: "'Tis proper I obey him, but not now" (5.2.193). From this point onward, Strier argued, "Shakespeare consistently dramatized and espoused the most radical of [Ponet's and Buchanan's] ideas and placed them in a secular context."[26] Much of Strier's argument is entirely persuasive. However, it seems to me that, in his effort to identify Shakespeare with a secularized radicalism, he simplifies the dramatist's treatment of subordination and obedience, whilst largely discounting the social and theological context in which early modern arguments about the nature and limits of true service were conducted. In the process he disguises the extent to which the limits of obedience were a matter of concern not merely for radicals like Buchanan, but for social conservatives like William Gouge. Commenting upon St Paul's "be not ye the servants of men" (*1 Cor: 7.23*), Gouge distinguished between true service and obsequious "excesse," arguing that the former would always place "Gods word and will" above the whims of an earthly master:

> *To be a seruant* in that place is not simply to be in subiection vnder another, and to doe seruice vnto him, but to be obsequious to a man, so addicted to please him, and so subiect to his will, as to doe whatsoeuer he will haue done: to regard nothing but his pleasure: to prefer it before Gods word and will. It is not therefore the thing it selfe, but an excesse therein which is forbidden.[27]

Shakespeare's propensity, in both *Othello* and *King Lear,* to push the paradoxes of obedience precisely to the point of "excesse" no doubt contributed to the gradual desacralization of service that Gouge was resisting. But far from adopting a consistent attitude to this process, the plays use it as an occasion for holding the ideology of service up to question, and for exposing its painful contradictions: as always, Shakespeare seems more interested in questions than in doctrine, more concerned to stretch his audience upon the rack of doubt and uncertainty that to instruct them.

In the case of *Othello,* Emilia's gesture of disobedience cannot be detached from the play's larger treatment of duty and service, on which its theatrical power depends. In Shakespeare's Venice (as I have argued elsewhere)[28] faithful service is imagined as the very ground of social identity: Montano, the governor of Cyprus who yields his office to Othello as a master whom he is proud to have "served" (2.1.35–36), is defined by his role as the "trusty and most valiant servitor" of Venice (1.3.40); while Cassio's self-image is completely inseparable from the "place" secured by "love and service" to his general (3.3.17–18). As "a member of [Othello's] love" (3.4.108), Cassio (like any good servant) imagines himself as an aspect of his master's countenance, a creature whose very being is contingent upon his continued capacity to perform "the *office* of [his] heart (3.4.109).[29] No wonder that his plea for reinstatement is founded on an appeal to "service past" (3.4.117). In much the same way Desdemona sees her identity, formerly expressed in the filial obedience owed to her father, as contained in the wifely "duty . . . Due to the Moor, my lord" (1.3.182–87): what looks to Brabantio like an act of disobedience—something that the Duke sees as having "beguiled your daughter of herself" (1.3.66)—she herself justifies as a due transfer of allegiance, a reconstitution of self in which "My heart's *subdued* / Even to the very quality of my lord" (1.3. 147–48). It is this same sense of her identity as being properly subsumed in that of her husband that informs the paradoxical self-cancellation of Desdemona's last speech in the play, when she nominates herself as her own murderer: "Nobody—I myself . . . Commend me to my kind lord" (5.2.125–26). But it is Othello more than anyone who invests himself in the ideology of service and obedience: on his first appearance in the play, already stigmatized by Roderigo as "an extravagant and wheeling stranger / Of here and everywhere" (1.1.137–38), the Moor asserts his oxymoronic claim to be "of Venice" by appealing to "My *services* which I have done the signiory" (1.2.18); and at the point of death, when his Venetian self seems to have disintegrated into the unbeing of "he that *was* Othello" (5.2.281), he seeks to restore it with a defiant repetition of that claim—"I have done the state some *service,* and they know't" (5.2.335).

At the opposite extreme from those whose identity can be expressed only in the self-effacement of service is Iago, for whom it is egotistically invested in the "power and corrigible authority" of his own will (1.3.322). Where Othello imagines his service to the state (in a secular version of the Christian paradox) as the very ground of his "free condition," Iago regards "service" as the euphemism in which authority cloaks the "obsequious bondage" of subordinate rank. His resentment fired by the inferior "place" to which his general has assigned him, he experiences the performance of any subordinate office as a form of humiliating enslavement. Yet, as his long tirade against "the curse of service" (1.1.35) reveals, service defines his identity as surely as it defines Othello's—if only by embittered negatives:

> We cannot all be masters, nor all masters
> Cannot be truly followed.
> . . . .
> Were I the Moor, I would not be Iago:
> In following him, I follow but myself.
> . . . .
> I am not what I am.
>
> (1.1.43–66)

In this revolutionary deconstruction of official ideology, Iago boasts of serving Othello only "to serve my turn upon him," and of trimming himself "in forms and visages of duty . . . shows of service" only in order to "do himself homage" (ll. 42, 50–54). His "flag and sign of love" (1.1.157) is precisely the diabolical token of hyprocrisy that the handbooks of domestic government taught their readers to expect in false servants, who (according to Gouge) "have *a heart,* and a heart, making show of one heart outwardly, and have another, even a clean contrary heart within them"

(617). Such servile hypocrites, according to Gouge and his fellow propagandist "I.M.," resemble "Judas, that false traitor, [who] . . . betray[ed] his own master, Christ," being "so possessed with a devil, as they will seek all the revenge they can, if they be corrected, [and] secretly endeavour to take away the life of their masters."[30] Just as Doctor Faustus's surrender to the devil was couched in the language of egotistical self-service ("The God thou *servest* is thine own appetite," A-Text, 2.1.11),[31] so Iago's rebellion is characterized as the self-homage of one who acknowledges no "power and corrigible authority" save that of his own "will" (1.3.326–27). The Ensign is someone who, for all his obsession with "place" and "office," is at heart a "masterless man" desiring to live (as the phrase had it) "at his own hand."[32] But to be masterless, in an hierarchical order that defines each individual as somebody's "man," was to be no man at all. Even Caliban's desire for "freedom" and to be "a new man" can be fulfilled only so long as he can claims "a new master" *(Tempest,* 2.1.185–87).

At once envying and detesting what he sees as his master's "free . . . nature" (1.3.393), Iago exploits it in order to enfetter the Moor to his own will. Yet in one of many ironic reversals that characterize the structure of this tragedy, the word "slave," with which Montano, Othello, and Lodovico successively denounce him, symbolically degrades the Ensign to the very condition of "obsequious bondage" (1.1.46) from which his every action in the play was meant to free him. This is the condition he compares to the abject fate of "his master's ass" who "wears out his time . . . for naught but provender, and when he's old—cashier'd!" (1.2.47–48). Iago's figure slyly invokes the biblical type of virtuous disobedience, Balaam's ass, who defied his abusive master by appealing to a lifetime of dutiful service: "Am not I thine ass, upon which thou hast ridden ever since I was thine unto this day? was I ever wont to do so unto thee?" (Numbers 22:30). But where the revolt of Balaam's patient beast was inspired by the angel of the lord, Iago's parodic unspeaking of the name of God ("I am not what I am"),[33] reminds us that *Non serviam* ("I will not serve") was the watchword of the fallen angel Lucifer and his rebellious cohorts. "In heav'n they scorned to *serve,* so now in hell they reign," wrote Phineas Fletcher of the rebel angels (*Purple Island* [1633], vi.10; emphasis added), anticipating the famous defiance of Milton's Satan "Better to reign in hell, than *serve* in heaven" (*Paradise Lost,* i.263).[34] But where Lucifer asserts his independent selfhood by outright opposition to God, Iago's enigmatic taunt ironically betrays the self-undoing nature of his covert defiance.

The opposition between the idealized vision of service espoused by the Moor, and Iago's satanic *non serviam* establishes a complex framework for Emilia's disobedience—the action in which Strier discovers the "threshold" to *Lear.* This is especially so because her defiance extends beyond her husband, to include his (and her) "lord," Othello. Othello himself (like his "obedient" wife) remains a paradigm of honorable obedience: when he is "commanded home," even though it means the surrender of his "place" to his disgraced subordinate Cassio, he is quick to "obey the mandate" (4.1.260–63); but when Emilia receives the same command from her domestic superior, she twice declines: "Perchance, Iago, I will ne'er go home. . . . I will not" (5.2.196, 221)— repeating, in effect, her husband's willful repudiation of "corrigible authority." An act of deliberate self-estrangement from the domestic realm by which she is at once defined and confined, Emilia's refusal to return home constitutes a radical challenge to the very notions of propriety and property on which subordinate identity depends. Of course her disobedience is warranted, like Desdemona's repudiation of filial subservience in 1.3 by a "divided duty" (1.3.179)—"'Tis proper I obey him, but not now" (l. 195); but where Desdemona's allegiance is transferred to a new "lord," Emilia's love for her mistress compels her to defy both of the males who claim authority over her—her husband and her master too.

In the brothel scene, after Othello has redefined his "obedient lady" (4.1.248) as "that cunning whore of Venice" (4.2.88), Desdemona comes close to withdrawing allegiance when she feigns incomprehension of Emilia's reference to their "lord," declaring "I have none" (4.2.101). But the deferential language with which she greets her murderer in 5.2, together with her dying "Commend me to *my kind lord*" (ll. 24–25, 126), patiently reaffirms her subservience—to the point where the repeated "Lord" of her terrified pleading (ll. 57, 85) can seem to be addressed to her husband as much as to God. When Emilia first arrives at the scene of murder, she defers to Othello in the same language as her mistress, calling him "my lord," and "my good lord" (ll. 86, 91, 104, 107, 109,113);[35] but, once he confesses to the murder, she sees him (in language that uncomfortably echoes Iago's slanders at the beginning of the play) only as "black . . . devil," "most filthy bargain," "gull," "dolt as ignorant as dirt," "villain," "dull Moor," "murderous coxcomb," "fool," and "cruel Moor"(ll. 132–247). Reducing her master to "the Moor" and stripping him of the respectful pronouns due from a subordinate, she degrades him with the same contemptuous "thous" (ll. 134–36, 158–64, 197–98, 223, 247) that she uses to unspeak her husband's authority (ll. 171–73).

Emilia's rebellion belongs, then, to a painfully ironic circle, through which the initial contrast between idealized service and diabolical disobedience is acted out in reverse—the vicious *non serviam* of the masterless rebel being replayed as his wife's virtuous repudiation of patriarchal authority: "I will ne'er go home." By a similar inversion, through the cruel metamorphosis that converts the "rites" of matrimony into murder on the bed, Desdemona's desperately preserved allegiance to her "kind lord" produces only an absolute undoing of her identity, in which "nobody" becomes another name for "I myself." In much the same way, Othello's frantic attempt to re-make himself through a re-enactment of past service issues in an act of radical self-cancellation: for what is his suicidal performance of revenge upon the malignant Turk who "Beat a Venetian and traduced the state" (5.2.350) but a brutal literalization of Iago's "I am not what I am"?[36] It is to the extreme contradictions of Othello's last rhetorical performance and its "bloody period" that Gratiano's baffled paradox responds "All that's spoke is marred" (l. 353). It is as if speech—traditionally both the signature of individual identity and the foundation civil life in the *polis*—had learned to unspeak itself . No wonder that Lodovico orders the erasure of the unsettling spectacle on the bed, and, having confirmed Cassio's substitution in Othello's "place," ceremoniously reasserts his own role as official servant of Venice:

> Myself will straight aboard, and *to the state*
> This heavy act, with heavy heart relate.
>
> (5.2.366–67)

If suicide, as Rosalie Colie once wrote, is "the paradox of self-contradiction at its irrevocable extremity,"[37] then Othello's drive to what he calls "my journey's end . . . [the] butt / And sea-mark of my utmost sail" (5.2.265–66) may be said to extend the contradictions of service to their self-cancelling limit. At the end of *King Lear,* the self-annihilating "journey" announced by the dutiful Earl of Kent, as he prepares to follow the dead king, is fraught with similar contradiction. The well-meaning but ineffectual Albany has attempted to restore order with an appeal to public duty that recalls Lodovico's pious invocation of "the state" at the end of *Othello.* In what may seem like a disconcerting recapitulation of Lear's initial division of the kingdom, the Duke summons Edgar and Kent to joint authority in the realm:

> Friends of my soul, you twain
> Rule in this realm, and the gor'd *state* sustain.
>
> (*King Lear,* 5.3.329–30)

But, in contrast to Lodovico's choric couplet, Albany's conspicuously fails to achieve even the rhetorical closure that its form encodes. Edgar, though sounding again "the note of obedience" observed by Barish and Waingrow, does so only by a kind of equivocation that sidesteps the very issues of authority and service with which the tragedy has been so obsessively concerned— "The weight of this *sad time* we must *obey*" (l. 323).[38] The blunt-speaking Kent, by contrast, responds to Albany with an absolute refusal, insisting that his duty lies unanswerably elsewhere.

I have a journey, sir, shortly to go
My master calls me, I must not say no.
(ll. 321–22)

Kent says no by insisting that no is what he must not say. What are we to make of this resolute, but paradoxical demurral—coming as it does from a man whose fortunes in the play have been wholly determined by his defiant negation of his master's will in the opening scene? The answer is to be found partly in the play's larger treatment of service and obedience, and partly in the contradictions that characterize Kent's own performance of his servant role.

King Lear, as Barish and Waingrow showed, is built around a set of oppositions (even more elaborate than those of *Othello*) between the exponents of false and true service—between the mercenary time servers mocked by the fool, who "serve and seek for gain, / And follow but for form" (2.4.72–73, 78–79), and those faithful servants whose willingness, if need be, to "break [their] neck with following" is played out through their physical following of the King in his demented progress through the wasteland of houseless (and therefore masterless) wretches that takes the place of his kingdom. In this scheme it is Edmund, the man with "service" constantly on his lips,[39] who emerges as Iago's most obvious counterpart. Edmund begins the play with a courtly tender of "services" to Kent and a promise to "study deserving" (1.1.29–31). But just as Iago's opening tirade declares his intention to follow Othello only "to serve my turn upon him," so Edmund's first soliloquy announces that his "services are bound" only to "Nature" (1.2.1–2), the "Goddess" who stands (like Faustus's God) only for his own appetite, the egotistic desires licensed by his identity as a "natural son."[40]

Thus the "loyal service" for which Edmund is praised (4.2.7) amounts in the end to no more than the sexual "services" he exchanges with his "mistress," Goneril, and her sister Regan, whose unnatural "lord and master" he becomes (4.2.21–27, 5.3.78–79). Goneril's go-between in this business is another exemplar of false service, her flattering steward Oswald—prophetically identified by Kent as "one that [would] be a bawd in way of good service" (2.2.18–19), and denounced by Edgar as "a serviceable villain, / As duteous to the vices of [his] mistress / As badness would desire" (4.6.254–56). To Goneril, Oswald is her "trusty servant" (4.2.19), but to Kent a mere "slave," one of those abject time servers who "Renege, affirm, and turn their halcyon beaks / With every gale and vary of their masters, / Knowing nought, like dogs, but following" (ll. 73, 79–81). Kent's contemptuous epithets echo the indignant language of the sixteenth-century music teacher, Thomas Whythorne, who, refusing to be a pliant "water-spaniel" to his employer, thought it "a slave-like and servile trade to be a flatterer, for . . . like as the shadow followeth a man continually wheresoever he doth go, so a flatterer applieth to crouch, follow, and please, when he thinketh to gain any good thereby."[41] Such abject, doglike obedience, Kent suggests, is a form of false service that can only destroy the sacred bonds by which the household (and thus the whole social order) is held together: "Such smiling rogues as these, / Like rats, oft bite the holy cords atwain / Which are too intrince t'unloose" (2.2.74–76). Yet Kent himself is a man whose deliberate disobedience at the beginning of the play has, from an orthodox perspective at least, already loosened the "holy cords" that bind servant to master.

Kent is foremost amongst those, like Gloucester, and Cornwall's servant, who discover the moral limits of compliance, and (in contrast to the retinue of "silly-ducking observants" sneered at by Cornwall) insist upon upholding those limits even at the risk of their own lives. It is Cornwall's nameless manservant who, though dismissed by his master as a "slave" or mere chattel ("*My* villain!" 3.7.77), is made to assert the freedom of his conscience by articulating the paradox of "virtuous disobedience" that is central to Strier's account of the play:

> I have serv'd you ever since I was a child,
> But better service have I never done you
> Than now to bid you hold.
>
> (3.7.72–74)

As important as the paradox itself, is the Servant's appeal to the intimacy of early modern service: together with the Messenger's later description of the servant as one that Cornwall himself "bred," this speech acts as a reminder of the naturalized ties that made the words *household* and *family* virtually interchangeable. "Bred," after all, is the same word that Cordelia uses in defining the "bond" between father and child at the moment of her own defiance:

> Good my Lord,
> You have begot me, *bred* me, lov'd me:
> I return those duties back as are right fit,
> Obey you, love you and most honour you.
>
> (1.1.95–98)

In this way the servant's rebellion implicitly invites comparison with the tempestuous confrontation of the opening scene, in which the King's rebellious subordinate unites with his recalcitrant child in opposition to the royal will. There too the close resemblance of filial and servantly bonds is emphasised in the language of Kent's intervention against the King's disinheritance of Cordelia:

Royal Lear,
Whom I have ever honour'd as my King,
Lov'd as my father, as my master follow'd,
As my great patron thought on in my prayers—

(1.1.139–41)

The incantatory syntax of this speech, linking the roles of king, master, patron, and father, is dense with the assumptions of patriarchal thought, which stressed the paternal role of monarchs, even as it insisted on the sovereign authority of heads of household within their domestic realms. The sacralized nature of service, implicit in Kent's deferential honorifics, is underlined by his use of "patron"—literally a surrogate father, but a term with religious connotations that are animated by "thought on in my prayers." Kent, however—by insisting, like Cordelia, that love and duty cannot be coterminous with obedience—invokes the sacredness of service only (it seems) to violate it. Cordelia's conviction that her bond itself defines the exact bounds—"no more nor less"—of obligation (ll. 92–93), is amplified in the Earl's allegory of honorable resistance, where the heavy metrical stress on "falls" identifies Lear's metamorphosis from King to Fool as a virtual deposition:

Think'st thou that Duty shall have dread to speak
When Power to Flattery bows. To Plainness Honour's bound,
When Majesty *falls* to Folly.

(147–49)[42]

It diminishes both the power of this scene and the impact of the whole tragedy to assume, as Strier does, that Kent's revolt must command the immediate and unequivocal endorsement of the audience. The courtier's public defiance, like the daughter's stubborn negatives, is meant to shock. Indeed Kent's own language (together with Lear's response) makes it clear that such resistance, however virtuously motivated, involves a *de facto* repudiation of "allegiance" (l. 167). The man he first addressed with proper deference as "my Liege," "Royal Lear," and "my King" (ll. 120,139–40), is now hailed (as Emilia hailed Othello) with the insulting intimacy of the singular pronoun (ll. 146–81), and (in a rhetorical anticipation of the political and literal divestiture to come) reduced to bare "Lear," and "old man." No wonder, then, that in the King's eyes Kent becomes (in terms suggestive not merely of feudal betrayal, but of religious heresy and apostasy) a "miscreant" or "recreant" (ll. 161, 166)—one whose repudiation of obedience appears almost as monstrous as Cordelia's seeming violation of the filial bond. Just as "paternal care, / Propinquity, and property of blood" are formally withdrawn from the unfilial daughter (ll. 113–14), so the protection of the royal law is withdrawn from the revolted vassal (ll. 176–79).

Each is rendered, in the deepest sense, "a stranger to my heart and me" (l. 115)—a curse that Lear renders "sacred" by calling on the gods, Hecate and Apollo (ll. 110, 159) to endorse his sentence.

The original power of this scene must have depended on its ability to animate the strains and contradictions apparent in early modern attitudes toward service and obedience. On the one hand Kent's resistance to the "excesse" of the King's authority, could capitalize on the radical theories espoused by Buchanan and others, to appeal to the discontents of men like Thomas Whythorne, for whom the obligations of service had begun to feel like tyranny; on the other—as the apocalyptic imagery of Gloucester's ensuing meditation on the cracking of natural "bonds" suggests (1.2.107–23)—the audience were meant to feel the profoundly destructive potential of Kent's violation of deferential taboo. For the vassal's repudiation of service amounts to a desacralization of royal authority—something that, as Shakespeare had already shown in *Richard II,* could not easily be reversed. Indeed, scarcely has the rebellious Kent been banished from the King's retinue, than the bonds of service begin to unravel with Goneril's instructions to Oswald and his fellows to exercise "a weary negligence" toward her father —"If you come slack of former services, / You shall do well" (1.3.10–14). Whatever the motives for Kent's defiance, it visibly initiates the process by which Lear is symbolically denuded of the "train" of followers essential to the preservation of his royal "countenance" and the "authority" it expresses (1.4.29–30, 255–60, 303–4; 2.4.239–65)[43]—to the point where, in the storm scene, the King feels himself in thrall to the those "servile ministers" of his daughters' malign will, the elements, against which he will oppose his desecrated nakedness: "You owe me no subscription: then let fall / Your horrible pleasure; here I stand, your slave" (3.2.18–21).

Thus, however virtuous Kent's disobedience may seem to us, it nonetheless remains a kind of sacrilege for which the play will require him to do penance; and if Lear's progress through the play is often understood as a kind of purgatory, then Kent's journey resembles a penitential pilgrimage, in which the fallen servant is redeemed only by submitting himself to what Edgar will call "service / Improper for a slave" (5.3.220–21), his degradation humiliatingly marked by the acceptance of money from the King as "an earnest of [his] service" (1.2.99). However, whereas Kent's *non serviam* begins to dissolve the familiar hierarchy of obedience, his return as the humble manservant, "Caius," determined to "serve where [he does] stand condemn'd" (1.3.5), introduces what will emerge as an antic double of the royal household: he is joined in succession by the Fool—whose schooling of Kent as he sits in the stocks identifies him as a second avatar of self-sacrificial service (2.4.67–85); by Edgar, who claims to be another disgraced "servingman, proud in heart and mind"—one who (like Oswald or Edmund) "serv'd the lust of my mistress' heart" (3.4.65–66); and finally by Gloucester whose sense of duty to the King compels his fatal disobedience to the "hard commands" of Goneril and Reagan (3.4.152–53).

Kent, whose his disguise enables him to transform his life into a virtual allegory of obedient service, is the key figure in this schema: in "[s]erv[ing] the King" he makes himself once again, as every good servant should, simply part of his presence, so that any assault on himself becomes an attack "Against the grace and person of my master" (2.2.129–32). Challenged by Lear to identify himself, Kent answers simply "a man"—a claim that implicitly links his very humanity to his dependent role as the King's "man": and when Lear asks him what he seeks, Kent answers with the single word, "service," that defines both "what" he is ("who" being no longer of any concern to him) and the limit of all that he could possibly desire. He will "profess" service (ll. 12–15) as another might profess faith. The King, he declares, using a term that will become increasingly resonant as the action unfolds, has "that in [his] countenance that I would fain call *master*"—namely "authority" (ll. 30–32).

"Master" is, of course, the same richly resonant word with which Kent, at last abandoning his base disguise, and coming (as he says) "To bid my King and *master* aye goodnight" (5.2.235), will announce his formal return to the court from which he was expelled in the opening scene; and it is also the word with which he will justify his departure from the play-world. Edgar, similarly stripped of his antic guise and arrayed once more in his true nobility as Gloucester's heir, has praised the constancy with which Kent "Follow'd his enemy king, and did him service / Improper for a slave" (5.3.220–21). However, Kent's decision to shed his servile livery and show himself, as Cordelia urged, "better suited" (4.7.6), hardly confirms Edgar's straightforward understanding of social propriety. Indeed the Earl is at pains to stress the seamless continuity between his base and noble roles: greeting the King not with the flattering honorifics which the fool has mocked as "court holy-water" (3.2.10), but with a repetition of the commonplace term that defines his own humble dependency—"my good master!" (5.3.267)—he insists that "Your servant Kent" and "your servant Caius" are indistinguishable, since "I am the *very man* . . . That from your first of difference and decay, / Have follow'd your sad steps" (ll. 283–89). Kent proclaims himself unchangeably "the same" (l. 283); yet his claim rests on an unsustainable paradox: the very "difference" that he has committed himself to follow (a difference partly of his own making), means that neither he, nor the idea of service for which he stands, can ever be "the same" again. His transformation, whatever Albany may wish, can no more be reversed than Lear can be restored by the "fresh garments" in which his daughter has reinvested him. In his deep conviction of the sacred nature of service, the Earl turns to the unanswerable language of vocation to announce his determination to attend his dead lord on his final progress:

I have a journey, sir, shortly to go;
My *master* calls me, I must not say no.

(5.2.321–22)

Among the scriptural texts remembered in this deceptively bare speech are the scribe's words to Jesus in Matthew 8.19 ("master, I will follow thee whithersoever thou goest"), Martha's to Mary in John 11.28 ("the master is come, and calleth for thee"), and (above all) Jesus' own words in St John's gospel, where he defines true service by the willingness to follow him out of this world: "He that loveth his life shall lose it; and he that hateth his life in this world shall keep it unto life eternal. If any man *serve* me, let him follow me; and where I am there shall also my *servant* be; if any man *serve* me him will my Father honour" (12:25–26; emphasis added). This last echo is made even more powerful by the fact that the passage immediately follows John's account of the resurrection of Lazarus—the episode that is so bleakly deconstructed in Lear's agony over Cordelia's corpse:

she lives! if it be so,
It is a chance which does redeem all sorrows
That ever I have felt

(5.3.265–67)

But the very desolation of this spectacle of failed redemption is a reminder that Kent's appeal to the ethos of sacralized service is made in a desacralized world where no correspondence can be demonstrated between human order and the arbitrary powers that Lear once saw manifested in "the sacred radiance of the sun" (1.1.109). The pious resolution of Kent's "journey" will lead him out of the play-world into a space that seems defined only by the litany of appalled negation that, with unalterable finality, reinstates the sullen "nothing" of the opening scene:

. . . .Thou'lt come no more,
Never, never, never, never, never!

(ll. 307–8)

Notes

1. Unless otherwise indicated, all references to *Othello* are to the Penguin edition, ed. Kenneth Muir (Harmondsworth: Penguin, 1968), while all references to *King Lear* are to the Arden edition, ed. Kenneth Muir (London: Methuen, 1964); emphases, however, are my own.

2. For some discussion of the significance of the term in early modern culture, see Camille Wells Slights, "Slaves and Subjects in *Othello,*" *Shakespeare Quarterly* 48 (1997): 377–90.

3. In fact his slavery belongs not to the mercantile Atlantic triangle, but to the very different institution fostered by the struggle between Christianity and Islam in the Mediterranean—see Michael Neill, "'His Master's Ass': Slavery, Service, and Subordination in *Othello,*" forthcoming in Stanley Wells and Tom Clayton (eds.), *Shakespeare in the Mediterranean* (Newark: Univ. of Delaware Press, 2003).

4. *The Merchant of Venice,* 4.1.90, cited from the edition by W. Moelwyn Merchant (Harmondsworth: Penguin, 1967).

5. Here Shakespeare seems to be remembering Contareni's remarks on service as a route to Venetian citizenship for foreigners: "Yea and some forrain men and strangers haue beene adopted into this number of citizens, eyther in regard of their great nobility, or that they had beene dutifull towardes the state, or els had done unto them some notable seruice," Gasparo Contareni, *The Commonwealth of Venice,* trans. Lewis Lewkenor (1599), 18.

6. See Michael Neill, "Servant Obedience and Master Sins: Shakespeare and the Bonds of Service," in Neill, *Putting History to the Question: Power, Politics, and Society in English Renaissance Drama* (New York: Columbia Univ. Press, 2000), 13–48. The close links between the obedience owed by wives and children is stressed in William Gouge's comprehensive manual of household government, *Of Domesticall Dvties Eight Treatises* (1622): "[although] a seruants place and dutie is of more abiect and inferiour kinde then the place and dutie of a childe or wife: the former word (. . . *obey*) was common to all" (168).

7. For a detailed account of ways in which the idea of divinely sanctioned service was propagated through Cranmer's Anglican liturgy, see David Evett, "Luther, Cranmer, Service, and Shakespeare," forthcoming in Daniel Doerksen and Christopher Hodgkins (eds.), *Centered on the Word: Literature, Scripture, and the Tudor-Stuart Middle Way* (Dover: Univ. of Delaware Press, 2003).

8. It is in this context that Desdemona can properly speak of the "rites" for which she loves her husband—rites that include the performance of all those duties that constituted wifely obedience.

9. Peter Laslett, *The World We Have Lost—Further Explored,* 3rd edn. (London: Methuen, 1983), 5.

10. For other scriptural formulations of the doctrine of free service, and its various elaborations by the Church fathers, medieval theologians, and Protestant reformers, see Evett, "Luther, Cranmer, Service, and Shakespeare" (forthcoming).

11. Gouge, 593.

12. See the Collect for Peace in the service of Morning Prayer. The sources of Cranmer's paradoxical formulation are discussed in Evett, "Luther, Cramer, Service, and Shakespeare" (forthcoming).

13. Gouge, 619.

14. Ibid., 167, 618, 603–4.

15. Ibid., 629, 171–72.

16. Ibid., 173.

17. Ibid., 637, 124, 641.

18. William Harrison, *Description of England* (1580), 118; cited in Robert J. Steinfeld, *The Invention of Free Labor: The Employment Relation in English and American Law and Culture, 1350–1870* (Chapel Hill: Univ. of North Carolina Press, 1991), 97.

19. Cited in Steinfeld, 97.

20. Rather more equivocally, Edward Chamberlayne, in *Angliae Notitia* (1669) described apprentices as "a sort of servants that carry the marks of pure villains or Bond-

slaves," but insisted that they "[differed] however in this, that Apprentices are slaves only for a time and by Covenant"; both cited in Steinfeld, *The Invention of Free Labor,* 98.

21. See Neill, "Servant Obedience and Master Sins," 21–24, and Evett, "Luther, Cranmer, Service, and Shakespeare" (forthcoming). All citations from *The Tempest* are to the Arden edition, ed. Frank Kermode (London: Methuen, 1964).

22. Jonas A. Barish and Marshall Waingrow, "'Service' in *King Lear,*" *Shakespeare Quarterly* 9 (1958): 347–55 (here cited from 348).

23. Barish and Waingrow, *loc. cit.*

24. Richard Strier, "Faithful Servants: Shakespeare's Praise of Disobedience," in Heather Dubrow and Richard Strier (eds.), *The Historical Renaissance: New Essays on Tudor and Stuart Literature and Culture* (Chicago: Univ. of Chicago Press, 1988), 104–33.

25. Ibid., 110.

26. Ibid., 111

27. Gouge, 593–4.

28. See Neill, "Servant Obedience and Master Sins," and "'His Master's Ass,'" cited above, nn. 5, 3.

29. Compare John Dod and Robert Cleaver, *A Godly Forme of Household Government* (London: 1630), Sig. Aa3: "[G]ood and faithful servants, liking and affecting their masters . . . obey them . . . not as a water-spaniel, but as the hand is stirred to obey the mind." On the subsumption of the servant's identity in that of his master, see "Servant Obedience," 20–28.

30. Gouge, 614, 617 and "I.M.," *A Health to the Gentlemanly Profession of Seruingmen* (London, 1598), 148.

31. Cited from Christopher Marlowe, *Doctor Faustus and Other Plays,* ed. David Bevington and David Rasmussen (Oxford: Oxford Univ. Press, 1995).

32. See Paul Griffiths, "Masterless Young People in Norwich, 1560–1645," in Paul Griffiths, Adam Fox, and Steve Hindle (eds.), *The Experience of Authority in Early Modern England* (New York: St Martin's Press, 1996), 146–86 (here cited from 154).

33. Ironically enough the Moor—having killed the wife whose love shaped his Venetian identity, his "occupation gone" and "chaos . . . come again"—at his lowest emotional point in the play, when he feels himself already in hell (5.2.275–78), will offer his own abject paraphrase of Iago's diabolic self-negation: "That's he that *was* Othello: here *I am.*" (l. 281)—where the reference of the final *I am* is confounded in advance by *he that was.*

34. Compare the faithful Abdiel's wish only to "*serve* / In heaven God ever blest, and his divine / Behests *obey*" (*Paradise Lost,* vi. 183–85; emphasis added). Satan's words constitute a diabolical travesty of the traditional formulae which insisted that to serve God was actually to rule (*cui servire regnare est,* in the words of the *Missa pro pacis* from the Sarum rite), and that (as the Benedictine Rule put it) it is "better to serve than to rule"—both cited in Evett, "Luther, Cranmer, Service, and Shakespeare".

35. The point is given particular emphasis in the Q text, where Desdemona's cry of "O Lord, Lord, Lord" mingles with Emilia's offstage "My lord, my lord . . . My lord, my lord" so that Othello seems almost unable to tell them apart: "What voice is this?" (5.2.85–87).

36. I have been anticipated here by Eldred Jones, who notes that the "deliberate antithesis between what Iago is supposed to be and what he is ('I am not what I am') also occurs in Shakespeare's portrayal of Othello" —see Jones, *Othello's Countrymen: Africans in English Renaissance Drama* (Oxford: Oxford Univ. Press, 1965), 109.

37. Rosalie Colie, *Paradoxia Epidemica: The Renaissance Tradition of Paradox* (Princeton, NJ: Princeton Univ. Press, 1966), 486.

38. F, as Muir suggests, is surely right in giving this speech to Edgar, rather than to Albany (as in Q). Richard Strier (123) emphasizes the way in which Edgar's lines, setting

"what we *feel*" against "what we *ought* to say" (l. 324) echo "the paradoxical conception of obedience through breaching normal decorum" that is so recurrent a feature of the play.

39. Barish and Waingrow, 350.

40. See Michael Neill, "'In Everything Illegitimate': Imagining the Bastard in English Renaissance Drama," in *Putting History to the Question,* 127–48 (here cited from 138).

41. James M. Osborn (ed.), *The Autobiography of Thomas Whythorne* (London: Oxford Univ. Press, 1962), 53.

42. I have altered the capitalization in Kent's speech in order to point up the allegorical schema, according to which Kent identifies himself with Duty or Honour, Cordelia with Plainness (or Truth), her sisters with Flattery, and Lear with Power or Majesty turned to Folly.

43. The double sense of "train" makes a king's retinue effectively an extension of royal costume, like the trailing ends of "robes and furred gowns," so that the loss of his servants is quite literally part of the process of reducing Lear to the nakedness of act 4.

The Pattern of Collaboration in *Timon of Athens*

John Jowett

HAVING PIONEERED THE REVIVED CLAIM FOR THE PRESENCE OF THOMAS Middleton's hand in *Timon of Athens,* MacD.P Jackson wrote, with characteristic modesty and respect for the limitations of evidence, "I have no fixed idea about how Middleton's work got there, if it did."[1] Since then the case for Middleton's part-authorship has been considerably developed, most compellingly by R.V. Holdsworth, but the nature of Middleton's role within the jointly authored play has remained unclear.[2] This paper is an exercise in second-stage attribution study, building on foundation laid in the attribution work of David Lake, Jackson, and Holdsworth. The time for assuming that the play is of Shakespeare's sole authorship has gone; so too, I would argue, has the time for agnosticism. The play still awaits adequate presention as a collaboration: the Middleton contribution has yet to be fully placed in the context of that dramatist's work,[3] and critical appraisal of the play might look more closely at how the play reads in the light of its new status. I have considered elsewhere how some aspects of the play can be reinterpreted in the light of a model of authorial dialogism.[4] What remains is to refine and develop the primary attribution work so as to present a fuller model of its interauthorial structure. I will be arguing that all the evidence is compatible with a particular model of collaboration: that Shakespeare initiated the collaboration, perhaps even writing his draft before Middleton put pen to paper, and that Middleton's is the second hand in the collaborative scenes.

Muriel St Clare Byrne's admonitions against gathering "ungraded" parallels between one text and another are well remembered.[5] The project undertaken here is, however, different in kind from work identifying the author or collaborators in anonymous plays: the joint authors of the play as a whole have, for the purpose of this essay, been established already, and the issue to be resolved is the narrower question of which of the two is likely to have written a given phrase or passage. Techniques of attribution study have reached a stage, in the case of writers with readily distinguishable linguistic traits such as Middleton and Shakespeare, where such an investigation can have some hope of success. Recently, the increasing availability of text databases such as Literature Online has made it relatively easy to identify genuinely significant phrases and collocations. The skepticism or even hostility prevailing through the mid-twentieth century toward what E. K. Chambers in 1924 influentially disparaged as "disintegration" has largely been superseded.[6]

These technical developments run in parallel with a more complex set of changes in the way we conceptualize authorship in general and the early modern dramatist in particular. In an influential monograph on collaboration, Jeffrey Masten has argued that language is "socially produced" and that the language one uses is not "one's own."[7] This rejection of the autonomy of the individual subject leads directly to a critique of attribution study: to assign one part of a collaborative text to one particular agent is an inappropriate form of "policing," a coercive and divisive maneuver. By this view, collaborators, even if there are just two of them, seem to constitute a viable unit for the social production of language, and, as long as their endeavors remain packaged together, the text is saved from the perception of asociality. However, a pair of authors does not constitute a society. The initial premise that language is "socially produced" places the writing of a text within the widest cultural environment. It suggests that a text has a fundamentally nonauthorial determination. To the extent that this is true, it must be true of any text, irrespective of the structure of its authorship. To the extent that it collapses the author, it collapses the collaborator too. In this paper I will assume instead that writers play an overwhelmingly important role in the social production of the written word. Sometimes they figure as readers, for intertextuality depends on transmission through human consciousness. As will be seen, Middleton may not have read texts that Shakespeare had read, and *vice versa;* this too is part of the collaborative structure of *Timon of Athens.*

Masten makes an important point in suggesting that a belated ideology of single authorship has distorted our picture of early modern dramatic production. Both single authorship and collaborative authorship were widely prevalent practices. But they are misrepresented in the "external" evidence of title pages and the like. In particular, collaboration is seriously underrepresented. Attribution study is therefore an essential task in the recognition and mapping-out of collaboration, whether within a single text or on a wider scale. In the particular case of Shakespeare, the dramatist's work as a collaborator has been repeatedly minimized or utterly denied, from the publication of the First Folio in 1623 onward. Today there is a risk that, paradoxically, the anti-authorial critique of attribution study might generate a default situation whereby the simplified and rigid authorial boundary that has customarily surrounded Shakespeare will remain undeservedly intact.

Thanks to attribution study we know of about nine Shakespeare collaborations and a further two plays that were adapted by Middleton. We also know something about how these collaborations differ one from another. Gordon McMullan and others have pointed out that attribution study is poorly equipped to deal with local transcription, revision, convergence of style, and other causes of merged collaboration.[8] This is not an incidental issue: merged collaboration poses a challenge to the very epistemological foundations of attribution study. But investigation reveals that whereas some texts are authorially complex and merged, others can be more readily divided into cleanly defined sections. It is a task that attribution study can and does undertake to distinguish between the undistinguishably merged and the distinguishably separate, and to map out, as far as possible, different and varying modes of interaction between dramatists, both within a given text and between different texts.

A feature of Holdsworth's study of *Timon of Athens,* the main prop of the argument for Middleton's hand, is that it reaches beyond the initial two-block analysis and produces a more complex and responsive account of localized authorial patchwork. His attributions contain queries, and they recognize the likelihood or at least the possibility of complications such as McMullan describes.[9] The scenes of mixed and doubtful authorship do not imperil the entire project of describing authorial differentiation in *Timon.* They provide a basis on which to move beyond a demarcation of the textual string into authorial sectors and toward a more process-oriented account of how this play came into being.

Although Holdsworth's analysis builds its case from quantifiable minutiae such as contractions, it produces consistent results that are not counterintuitive in terms of what we understand about Shakespeare's and Middleton's characteristics as dramatic writers. For instance, the representation of Timon and the distinctively Shakespearian poetry of rage and nihilism that goes along with it remain with Shakespeare, while the acerbic city comedy material is supplied by Middleton. Such a claim is, of course, based on a very broadly drawn binary distinction between two writers who in reality display a range of styles. The Shakespeare who had written *Merchant of Venice* and the Middleton who had written the domestic tragedy of *A Yorkshire Tragedy* and was later to write "Fletcherian" tragicomedy are both in evidence as well. Authorship is not demonstrated by broad observation of authorial traits; they add support and plausibility to the more empirical evidence.

At a less impressionistic level, quantifiable features of style that register as unexpected or even corrupt to a reader trained on Shakespeare can be seen to belong to the recognizable texture of Middleton's writing. For instance, the intermixture of prose with verse, some of it in rhyme, within a single speech such as Apemantus's speech at 1.2.37–51 is well instantiated in Middleton's writing. To highlight the point, the verse lines in the following quotation are prefixed with 'V':[10]

> V I scorn thy meat. 'Twould choke me, for I should
> ne'er flatter thee. O you gods, what a number of men eats Timon,
> and he sees 'em not! It grieves me to see so many dip their meat
> in one man's blood; and all the madness is, he cheers them up, too.
> V I wonder men dare trust themselves with men.
> V Methinks they should invite them without knives:
> V Good for their meat, and safer for their lives.
> There's much example for't. The fellow that sits next him, now
> parts bread with him, pledges the breath of him in a divided
> draught, is the readiest man to kill him. 'T'as been proved. If
> I were a huge man, I should fear to drink at meals,
> V Lest they should spy my windpipe's dangerous notes.
> V Great men should drink with harness on their throats.

In numerous other respects too, writing such as this is alien to Shakespeare but at home within the context of Middleton. It remains to be shown that any scene Holdsworth attributes to Middleton can be reattributed to Shakespeare or any other dramatist with any degree of conviction.

Admittedly Jonathan Hope has endorsed the presence of Middleton's hand only with qualification, and M. W. A. Smith has seriously questioned it.[11] But as against the evidence set forward by Holdsworth and others, these scholars run a more limited number of tests, and their counter-indicative results are inconclusive. Smith's findings endorse the presence of non-Shakespearean material, but produce different indications from test to test. For example, in a test based on the first word of speeches, Middleton is the favored author in five out of six comparisons, whereas the same test applied to words that are not first in speeches variously posits Chapman, Dekker, Heywood, Shakespeare, Middleton, and Webster as the most favored author, and a collocation test produces similar results.[12] The tentative hypothesis that emerges is that George Chapman employed a team of dramatists to rough out his plays and acted merely as a coordinating reviser; and that in this case they "collaborated to try to rescue the play before its final abandonment, and the task of creating a fair copy from the ensuing indecipherable foul papers of the part Shakespeare had left least complete fell to Middleton." Despite the model of *Sir Thomas More* for a complex authorial genesis of a vaguely comparable kind, the hypothesis seems a strained attempt to reconcile conflicting outcomes; the division of work between coordinating reviser, multiple contributors, and final transcriber is without example, the collaborators are left in a vacuum as regards their contributions, and the emphatically and consistently Middletonian poetics and ideation in the non-Shakespeare sections remain unexplained.

Smith's investigations might work effectively on *Pericles* but not *Timon* at least in part because the distribution of authorial labor is more complex, indeterminate, and in some sections blended in the latter play—a point on which all investigators agree. But it is the scenes of mixed authorship that can tell us most about how the collaboration proceeded. In investigating these scenes, it will be assumed that Middleton's hand as a collaborator in the play as a whole can be taken as given. The first aim will be to establish whether a particular passage is more plausibly attributed to one of the two dramatists than the other. If the burden of demonstration is reduced by the starting assumption that Middleton's hand is present in the play, the quantity of evidence is also diminished, simply because the passages are far smaller than the monolithic blocks initially tested by Holdsworth and others. In shorter passages the evidence of contractions and grammatical forms is rarely adequate because the occurrences are too few to be statistically significant. Hence it is that parallels between *Timon* and the works of Shakespeare and Middleton become more significant evidence. The point will not be to show that Middleton and only Middleton (or Shakespeare and only Shakespeare) could have written a particular phrase or image. It will be, rather, to determine whether, in the established context of collaboration, Middleton or Shakespeare is more likely to have written it. This highly localized analysis can then be set within the collaborative context of larger passages and scenes. A commitment to the fecundity of collaboration as a mode of playwrighting informs this study, and a commitment to understanding how the dialogic text converses with itself.

In Holdsworth's account, Shakespeare wrote the opening scene and act 5. By far the greater part of 4.3 is also in his hand, though Middleton supplied the episode in which Flavius visits Timon. Middleton supplied the banquet scene (1.2), and also the shorter scenes showing Timon's creditors refusing to lend him financial assistance and Alcibiades' petition to the Senate for clemency toward a friend who has committed murder (most of act 3). The scenes that are considered in the present paper are 1.1, where Middleton evidently added some touches, 2.2, 3.7, and 4.2, which are scenes Holdsworth identified as of joint authorship, and 4.3, where Middleton added a major passage that has implications for the structure of the scene and the significance of the entire play.

1.1

As Holdsworth observed, Middleton seems to have added a passage at 1.1.276–86:

First Lord. . . . Come, shall we in,
 And taste Lord Timon's bounty? He outgoes
 The very heart of kindness.

Second Lord.
He pours it out. Plutus the god of gold
Is but his steward; no meed but he repays
Sevenfold above itself; no gift to him
But breeds the giver a return exceeding
All use of quittance.

First Lord. The noblest mind he carries
That ever governed man.

Second Lord. Long may he live in fortunes! Shall we in?

First Lord. I'll keep you company.

This is the first example of an addition that establishes continuity with Middleton's banquet scene, which follows immediately after. The strongest connection with Middleton lies in the phrase "taste Lord Timon's bounty," which has a parallel in *Roaring Girl* 2.1.83–85 and connects with ideas of bounty and of the consumption of Timon's body that are especially prevalent in Middleton's contributions to *Timon*.

Middleton probably added some other minor details. In the stage direction at 1.1.179 there is an instance of the spelling "Apermantus," which is usually associated with Middleton. The following lines contain Middleton features. "Will you be chid" compares with *Women Beware Women* 1.2.212, "I shall be chid for't." An unusual intransitive use of *bear,* meaning "put up with it," in "We'll bear, with your lordship" (1.1.181) has a parallel in *Lady's Tragedy* 4.2.36, "I'm ashamed of my provision, but a friend will bear."[13] Two lines near the end of the scene, at 1.1.256–57, contain a proverbial idiom, "saved my longing," that is used by Middleton but not Shakespeare.

Early in the scene Middleton evidently filled out the staging by introducing the silent figure of the Mercer into the opening stage direction, where F reads "*Enter Poet, Painter, Ieweller, Merchant, and Mercer, at seuerall doores.*" (TLN 2–3).[14] Some *Timon* editors suppose that the Mercer is merely an accidental duplication of the Merchant, or a "false start,"[15] and so, following Samuel Johnson, they remove him from the text. But it seems clear from Middleton parallels that Middleton added the name, to call for a background presence of a figure who would be identified by his wares and his proverbial book of debts. As Lawrence Stone observes, "Mercers, silkmen, jewellers, and goldsmiths" were favorably placed to act as creditors.[16] Middleton not only mentions mercers on several occasions, but also satirizes their double function as clothes sellers and creditors. *Michaelmas Term* refers to "Master Gum, the mercer" as a possible source for a loan of two or three hundred pound (2.1.85), and to "Master Profit, the mercer" (2.3.152).[17] In *Mad World* 2.1.18 the supposedly rich Lord Owemuch is said to be "free of the mercers," meaning not in debt to them. Elsewhere it is an instance of an unlikelihood that one might "pay his mercer wondrous duly" (*More Dissemblers* 5.1.104). In contrast, in Shakespeare's work the word *mercer* occurs only at *Measure for Measure* 4.3.10—in a passage now identified as a Middleton addition.[18] This Middletonian mercer has evidently sued "one Master Caper" for debt, causing his imprisonment.

Whether the Mercer in *Timon* appears instead of or as well as the Merchant is not entirely clear (the speech prefixes for "*Mer.*" are ambiguous), but there seems, from Middleton's point of view, little point in changing the term in the stage direction for its own sake. The direction can be taken at face value, with the Merchant the speaking character and the Mercer a silent caricature. His presence visually anticipates the themes of conspicuous consumption and debt. If both figures are present on stage, there is added substance to the bustle of gathering clients, described as "all these spirits" at 1.6. There can be little doubt that Middleton annotated the name onto Shakespeare's stage direction.

The Senators at 1.1.38.1–42 appear to be an addition of a similar kind, though here a short exchange between the Poet and Painter is attached to the entry:

Enter certaine Senators.
Pain. How this Lord is followed.
Poet. Happy men.
Pain. Looke moe.
Po. You see this confluence, this great flood of visitors,

(TLN 54–58)

—after which the Poet turns to a self-congratulatory account of the "rough work" he has brought to show Timon, which there is no need to question as Shakespeare's. The effect of the Senators' passage over the stage, as with the Mercer, is to add to the background drift of people toward Timon. The reasons for suspecting that Middleton's hand is present lie again in verbal parallels.[19] The first is not decisive, in that a Shakespeare parallel competes with one from Middleton; but the Middleton parallel is closer. At 1.39 "How this lord is followed" compares with "Behold / How pomp is followed" at *Antony and Cleopatra* 4.2.146–47. But it can also be compared with "That lord has been much followed" at *Mad World* 2.1.16. Here, as in *Timon,* a lord is followed, and significantly he is called Lord Owemuch, a name indicating that he, like Timon, has been overly bounteous to his followers. In other words, the ironization of the utterance is similar in both plays, and that ironization is very much in Middleton's manner. A few lines further on, at 1.42, the visitors are described as "this great flood." The parallel to this is strong, but comes not with Middleton's own works but with a text he read shortly before contributing to *Timon.* As Holdsworth noted, the same phrase occurs in *Two Most Unnatural and Bloody Murders,* which is the source for *A Yorkshire Tragedy,* and which is echoed also at 2.2.1–5 and 3.4.13. In that pamphlet the phrase is found referring to the effect that visitors such as Timon's will have on their hosts: "restrain *this great flood* of your expense, before your house be utterly overthrown."[20] This is again a suggestive indication of Middleton's hand in the Senators' passage over the stage. The idiom may not appear to be distinctive, yet Literature Online identifies no other instance of "this great flood" in literature of the period in any genre, and only one other occurrence of "great flood of" (in Richard Stanyhurst's *Aeneas*).

Holdsworth detects the presence of Middleton's hand once again in the speech that follows the Senators' exeunt. The Poet notes that his "free drift" is such that it "flies an eagle's flight, bold and forth on, / Leaving no tract behind." The image is evidently suggested by the biblical Wisdom of Solomon 5:10–11: "as a bird that flieth through in the air . . . whereas afterward no token of her way can be found."[21] Middleton had a particular interest in this text, for his earliest extant work is a verse elaboration of the Apocryphal book, called *The Wisdom of Solomon Paraphrased.* Holdsworth notes that the passage is closer to Middleton's *Paraphrased* 5.97–108, where the bird is again an eagle: "Or as an eagle with her soaring wings . . ."[22] The conflation of the biblical text and the proverb "The eagle flies alone" stems from Middleton's writing. The passage of the Senators over the stage emphasizes Timon's extraordinary popularity; the Poet's emphasis now on the independent, freestanding nature of his verse separates him from the phenomenon that he is thereby free to criticize.

Nevertheless, whereas the annotation of "Mercer" points to Middleton, the signs of his hand in supplying the Senators' passage over the stage are less distinct. The evidence leans in Middleton's favor. Crucially, it is consistent not only with the addition of the Mercer but also with changes Middleton evidently made to another Shakespeare text. The posited modifications in the staging of the opening passage of the play compare interestingly with the posited addition through adjusted stage directions of Juliet and the two Gentlemen to fill out the scene in adapting *Measure* at 1.2.105.1–2.[23] These Middletonian additions of nonspeaking roles to an expository scene make the action much more a demonstrably public shaming of Claudio, and add Juliet alongside her betrothed lover as the object of shame. The alterations envisaged in the opening scene of *Timon* similarly give visual reinforcement to the thematic statement made in an expository scene, emphasizing the perils of conspicuous consumption just as the alterations in *Measure* emphasize the perils of extramarital sex. Middleton's revision of *Measure* was to come years later in 1621. There is a model for the staging of the first scene of Jonson's *Sejanus* (1603), as is suggested by the word "confluence," which was rarely applied to people and never used elsewhere by either Shakespeare or Middleton; in a later scene Jonson referred to "The multitude of suits, the confluence / Of suitors" (3.605–6), in terms that recall the play's opening.[24] But the elaborate use of separate stage groupings and of silent roles to provide an ironic implied commentary is a persistent characteristic of Middleton's dramaturgy.

Middleton's activities in 1.1 evidently were small enough to have been written as marginal insertions in a Shakespearean draft, though the passage at the end of the scene could have been continuous with his writing of 1.2, either filling the same sheet that Shakespeare had used or beginning a new one.

2.2

Shakespeare is clearly present in this scene. But Holdsworth suggests that Middleton contributed to the Fool and Page episode, and is persistently present in 2.2.121–229, an episode which, like Middleton's probable additions to 4.2 and 4.3, features Flavius. Moreover, the characteristic of calling servants by their masters' names is shared with Middletonian 3.4.

The writing at times may well be an indissoluble mixture of the two authors. Middleton's contribution is immediately suggested by the concentration of contractions associated with his writing: "'em" (2.2.46, 64, 188, and 194), "e'en" (2.2.68 and 86), "Ne'er" (2.2.226), "'ha" (2.2.46), "she's" (2.2.68), and "he's" (2.2.219) are all typical of Middleton's hand, as are the grammatical preferences "has" (2.2.96) and "does" (2.2.66). These forms are not conclusive individually, but collectively they are most unexpected in a passage of this length in Shakespeare's hand, and the cluster of nine of them in 2.2.45–119 particularly stands out from the usual complexion of Shakespeare.

Middleton probably supplied the soliloquy with which Flavius opens the scene, which, as Holdsworth notes, closely echoes another passage in the source for *A Yorkshire Tragedy* and is Middletonian in its repetitions of "Fie, fie, fie, fie" (2.2.9). The addition of this soliloquy can be understood in terms of Middleton's development of the role of the speaker (see below). As with the anticipatory passages at the end of 1.1 and in 2.2.173–95 (see below), it knits the scene into the larger sequence of action, though with different considerations in view. Without it, Caphis leaves at the end of Shakespeare's 2.1 and immediately reenters. There was, then, evidently a temporary and unsustainable problem of continuity in the Shakespearean script.

In the episode beginning with the entry of Apemantus and the Fool and ending with the exit of the Page (2.2.45–86), where many of the contractions already noted occur, there are several other signs of Middleton admixture. At 2.2.53–56 Isidore's Servant taunts Varro's Servant with "There's the fool hangs on your back already," to which Apemantus responds, "No, thou stand'st single: thou'rt not on him yet." The phrase "hangs on your back" has a distinct homosexual overtone, as, less distinctly, might "backwardly" at 3.3.18 and, more certainly, "turn your back to any man living" at *Mad World* 3.1.194–95. "Backward" in the latter play at 3.3.65, at *Nice Valour* 4.1.240, and elsewhere has the same implication; and Easy, in *Michaelmas Term* 2.3.356, says of "Porters' backs and women's bellies" that "they bear men and money."[25] *Stand'st* quibbles on "have an erection," a usage common to both dramatists, but the specific idiom *Stand'st single* is Middletonian: "Let the knave stand single" (*Phoenix* 10.100).[26] "On him yet" is a minor collocation found in Middleton (*Puritan Widow* 2.1.75) but not Shakespeare or any other pre-Caroline dramatist. All this strongly suggests that Middleton may have added some homosexual banter, of a kind more plausible from his pen than Shakespeare's.

Other sexual banter might also be Middleton's. At 2.2.68 the Fool's mistress is "e'en setting on water to scald such chickens as you are." The associations with venereal diseases are in Middleton's manner. *1 Honest Whore* 2.109 refers to fretting "at the loss of a little scald hair," a clear allusion to such ailments, and *Old Law* 3.2.78–79 describes "my three court codlings that look parboiled / As if they came from Cupid's scalding-house."

If there is the Middleton of sexual wordplay, there is also the Middleton of Calvinist mentality. A short exchange combines the latter with a spelling associated with a Middleton section. At 2.2.73 the Page greets Apemantus using, in the Folio, the spelling "Apermantus," the consistent form in 1.2. In reply Apemantus chides "Would I had a rod in my mouth, that I might answer thee profitably." The line alludes to Proverbs 26:3–4, ". . . a rod [belongeth] to the fool's back. Answer not a fool according to his foolishness, lest thou also be like him," and Isaiah 11:4, "he shall smite the earth with the rod of his mouth, and with the breath of his lips he shall slay the wicked." As Literature Online identifies no other text with the word "rod" near the word "mouth," it is especially significant that the second biblical text is quoted in Middleton's *Two Gates of Salvation* at 87.I, and Middleton supplies a marginal note that explains, "Meaning Christ, *the rod of his mouth,* which is his word." The "rod" would enable Apemantus to answer "profitably," and Middleton elsewhere writes "Her rod is profit" (*Wisdom of Solomon Paraphrased* 9.116).

The word "superscription" in the very next speech at 2.2.76, "read me the superscription of these letters," is also a Middleton feature. Elsewhere in Shakespeare it is found only in a scene of *1 Henry VI* that is probably un-Shakespearean (4.1.53).[27] There are at least three instances in Middleton. The closest in phrasing is "Read but the superscription" (*Puritan* 1.1.141).

Middleton may be present locally elsewhere in the first half of this scene. He prefers "has" as against Shakespeare's preference for "hath"; the scene's one instance of "has" occurs in a passage not so far considered: "I think no usurer but has a fool to his servant" (2.2.96). The construction has a definite Middletonian cast; "no [noun] but has a [noun]" is found three times in his works (*Nice Valour, Lady's Tragedy, Your Five Gallants*), but is nowhere in Shakespeare.[28] Furthermore, Literature Online identifies no other example of the construction in the literature of the Elizabethan and Jacobean periods.

The episode of the servants, the Fool, and the Page is a loose end: little happens in it, the plot line apparently initiated by the letters does not seem to be followed through, and the characters of the Fool and the Page appear nowhere else in the play. Shakespeare's hand as well as Middleton's certainly seems to be present. The business of the illiterate servant bearing letters is reminiscent of Peter in *Romeo and Juliet* 1.2, and *OED*'s only earlier instance of the un-Middletonian verb to "dialogue" (2.2.50) is from a work usually though not securely attributed to Shakespeare ("Lover's Complaint" l. 132).[29] The Fool's allusion to Corinth and Apemantus's reply "Good; gramercy" at 2.2.69–70 are also in Shakespeare's manner. "I know not which is which" (2.2.77) has an exact parallel in *Comedy of Errors* 5.1.366. Despite the Middletonian line at 2.2.96 (see previous paragraph), the episode dealing with the Fool, 2.2.86–119, seems to be predominantly Shakespearean. As Holdsworth notes, it includes a Shakespeare parallel: "Thou art not altogether a fool" (2.2.112) is closely echoed in *History of Lear* 4.146, "This is not altogether fool." It is puzzling that both writers should have invested effort on what is perhaps the least satisfactory and least necessary episode in the play.

The second half of the scene, 2.2.120–229, can be set alongside a number of substantial passages involving Flavius that seem to have been supplied by Middleton, though neither his role in the play as a whole nor his presence in this scene are exclusively of Middleton's doing. Holdsworth identifies good Middleton parallels with 2.2.133–45. This passage, like the scene's opening soliloquy, involves Flavius describing Timon's excessive consumption and spending in terms of the same word, "flow." Both speeches, in anticipation of Flavius's concern for Timon in 4.3, express an emotive concern for Timon: he is "so unwise to be so kind" (2.2.6), and Flavius, reluctant to obey his comands to give, has "shook my head and wept, / Yea, 'gainst the authority of manners prayed you / To hold your hand more close" (2.2.133–36). There are signs here of a design that connects the opening of the scene with its second half and looks forward to later episodes.

Elsewhere in the second half of 2.2, Jackson has explained "wasteful cock"(2.2.159) with reference to Middleton. It can be added that "vaults" at 2.2.156—"when our vaults have wept / With drunken spilth of wine"—may be used in the Middletonian sense of "covered drains," as in "destruction's vaults, / Full of old filth, proceeding from new slime" (*Wisdom of Solomon Paraphrased* 18.39–40), as well as or instead of in the more familiar sense of "vaulted cellars." Moreover, at 2.2.187–88 Timon prefers himself to his friends using a Middleton idiom with the message that "my occasions have / Found time to use 'em toward a supply of money." "My occasions" occurs twice elsewhere in Middleton scenes of *Timon* and at least once in his works elsewhere: "It makes me bold to speak my occasions to you" (*Widow* 3.3.205).[30] There are, indeed, four other instances of possessive "my" or "his" followed by "occasion(s)" in *Timon,* all in Middleton scenes. In three of these, the "occasion(s)" are given agency through personification, as here: "If his occasion were not virtuous" (3.2.41), "his occasions might have wooed me first" (3.3.15), "many my near occasions did urge me to put off" (3.7.10–11). A specifically Middletonian dialogue is played out around this expression, its evasive meaning, and its power to command or deny help.

However, Holdsworth also notes a cluster of strikingly Shakespearean idioms: "englutted" (2.2.163), "couched" (2.2.169), and "hard fractions," "half-caps," and "cold moving nods" (2.2.207–8). Further, the "d" spelling of "Ventidius" at 2.2.216 and 218 (here "Ventiddius," in contrast with Middleton's "Ventigius") is evidently Shakespeare's. The most distinctively Shakespearean parts of this second half of the scene are 2.2.160–73 ("Prithee no more . . . lack friends") and 195–225 ("I have been bold . . . talents").

The scene's last couplet is probably by Middleton:

Flavius.
I would I could not think it. That thought is bounty's foe:
Being free itself, it thinks all others so.
(2.2.228–29)

"I would I could not think it" looks at first sight an everyday utterance, but "I would I could" expressing a desire to alter one's thoughts and the phrase "I would I could not" are without example in Shakespeare. Middleton has both: "I would I could persuade my thoughts / From thinking thee a brother" in *Nice Valour* at 4.1.23–24, and "I would I could not" in *Nice Valour* at 5.3.139 and *The Widow* at 1.2.169. "Bounty's foe" compares with "virtue's foe" (*Wisdom of Solomon Paraphrased* 14.183) and as a rhyming phrase it compares with "virtue's foes" rhymed with "close" (*Game at Chess,* Prologue 9). Moreover, the personification of Bounty is found in civic pageants by Middleton such as *The Triumphs of Truth* and *The Triumphs of Honour and Industry.* In *Honourable Entertainments,* the entertainment for Sir William Cockayne ends with "For bounty did intend it always so"; just as Flavius's line about bounty is part of a couplet rhyming "foe" with "so," the entertainment's line with personified bounty rhymes with "flow," "so," "go," and "below" in the previous four lines. A strikingly similar moralizing couplet, again with the rhyme word "so," is to be found at the end of another passage of *Measure for Measure* now understood to have been added by Middleton at the end of a Shakespeare scene:[31]

> Mercy is not itself that oft looks so.
> Pardon is still the nurse of second woe.
>
> (2.1.272–73)

"Mercy" and "bounty" are key words in *Measure* and *Timon* respectively. Both couplets occur at the same stage in the play, the point where the principle in question is beginning to come under extreme pressure. Such moralizing couplets at the end of scenes are especially prevalent in Middleton's writing; one example out of many may be cited because it occurs at a similar stage in the action and involves another key abstraction, here sin:

> Sin tastes at the first draught like wormwood-water,
> But, drunk again, 'tis nectar ever after.
>
> (*Women Beware Women* 2.2.475–76)

At the end of the scene, then, Middleton evidently added a couplet onto a Shakespeare section. And this is probably symptomatic of the situation the second half of the scene as a whole. Holdsworth identifies another sustained section of Middleton at 2.2.173–95. This passage, like Middleton's addition at the end of 1.1, sets up the immediately following action by Middleton, in this case the scenes in which Timon's men visit Lucullus, Lucius, and Sempronius. The first two have already been named in a Middleton scene (1.2), and Sempronius is mentioned for the first time here. The three names are evidently exclusive to Middleton's writing. By the suggested distribution it would be, as Jackson posited was the case elsewhere in the play, Shakespeare who uses the low number of talents ("five" at 2.2.222 and 225) and Middleton who uses high numbers ("fifty" at 2.2.189, "A thousand," no less, at 2.2.195). Shakespeare anticipates a scene in which Ventidius is petitioned for money (2.2.216–26); Middleton was not to supply it, though at 3.3.3–9 he assumes the episode has happened.

Despite the areas of uncertainty, some passages can be claimed to be predominantly by Middleton. They are 2.2.1–9, much of 45–86, 136–45, 173–95, and 228–29. The pattern that applies elsewhere fits this scene best also: namely, that Shakespeare was the initiator. For it appears that Middleton added short passages at both the beginning and the end; it is only a short step to deduce that he worked from a Shakespeare draft that was already extant. Middleton probably transcribed Shakespeare's draft of the entire scene, making alterations as he went. This explanation is conjectural, and it remains the case that the scene is mergedly collaborative to an extent that does not apply to any other part of the play.

3.6

It is only in 3.6 that Alcibiades first takes a positive role in the action, in solo confrontation with the Senate. At first sight there is little reason to review the authorship of the scene. Holdsworth simply assigns it to Middleton, and, as far as authorial inscription is concerned, there is no reason to question or modify that conclusion. But if the writing is so insistently Middletonian, a puzzle arises in terms of the scene's relationship to Plutarch's "Life of Alcibiades" and to Shakespeare's *Coriolanus.* The play's verbal echoes of Plutarch are all in Shakespeare sections apart from some character names that occur in Middleton scenes as well, and they come from the "Life of Marcus Antonius," not the "Life of Alcibiades."

The latter offers a detailed account of the history surrounding the play's events and, potentially at least, a source for the plot line showing Alcibiades' revolt against Athens. In Plutarch, Alcibiades is banished not for overstepping the mark in pleading for clemency to his soldier, but for mocking the holy mysteries of Ceres and Proserpina. Though he attacks Athenian forces, he does not attempt to attack the city of Athens itself. Marginal notes in North's Plutarch provide a cue for the dramatic character's appearance with two prostitutes, one of them called Timandra; they comment on "*Alcibiades dishonestie* [i.e., sexual promiscuity] *& wantõnes*" (T1^{v}; p. 218) and record that "*Timandra the curtisan buried Alcibiades*" after his death (V3^{v}; p. 234).[32] The dramatists (one or both of them) may have done little or no more than merely skim the notes; they may have consulted the rest of the text little if at all.

The account in 3.6 of the soldier and friend who has committed murder, which has no basis in the sources, has been criticized for its lack of connection to the rest of the play. It is often cited as the strongest instance of the embryonic nature of the Alcibiades plot line, engaging as it does with issues of which the audience has no knowledge.

It may be, however, as Karen Newman has suggested, that the disconnected opening of the scene can be understood without reference to collaboration.[33] Instead, the play might be dealing obliquely with the topic of homosexuality. In Plutarch's "Life of Alcibiades," Alcibiades is a young, volatile, beautiful warrior; though a womanizer, he is also the homosexual companion of Socrates, and special friend of Timon, who is said to have "kissed him very gladly" when banqueting him. Plutarch describes him as having spoken with a "fat lisping tongue," in a way that gave him "a certain natural pleasant grace." His homoerotic relationship with Socrates was well known to early modern writers; both Edmund Spenser and Christopher Marlowe refer to it.[34] The play gives only a sketchy impression of such a figure, perhaps not simply because the source was scarcely consulted, but also because the play was to offer no more than oblique hints of his homosexuality.

Hence in 3.6 Alcibiades' plea for his friend comes as it were from nowhere. Some commentators have been confused enough to suppose that the friend is Timon himself. Alcibiades' feelings toward him matter greatly, but are without context. He is insolently passionate about his friend, extravagant and illogical in his arguments extenuating murder, and emotionally excessive in resolving to wage war on Athens in revenge for the Senate's rejection of his plea and banishment of him. The Second Senator's account of the soldier's crime uses some ambiguous language that, notwithstanding its primary sense, might hint at a judicial condemnation of homosexual assaults: "He's a sworn rioter; he has a sin / That often drowns him and takes his valour prisoner . . . In that beastly fury / He has been known to commit outrages" (3.6.66–70).[35] These are mere clues, but they help to explain the text's lack of explanation. In this respect, then, the text may be reticent rather than incomplete or disjunctive.

At all events, the germ of the interest in the banishment of the military leader from the city must surely have come from Shakespeare. If in a certain sense one might speak of the scene providing a non-Shakespearean source for *Coriolanus,* it is no more than the concept intrinsic to the initial plotting of *Timon* that gets developed in *Coriolanus.* The specific details that Middleton supplied are virtually forgotten. The case acts as a reminder that even a thoroughly Middletonian scene can be described as collaborative, in the particular sense that Middleton was developing Shakespearean ideas. Here they derived from Shakespeare's reading of Plutarch and therefore are Shakespearean only, at best, in a weak sense of ideational ownership.

3.7

The "mock banquet" scene, 3.7, provides, like 2.2, a striking example of collaboration between the dramatists within a single scene, and here it is more immediately clear that Shakespeare would have been the originator of writing as well as ideas. Shakespeare probably first drafted the central section of the mock grace, with Middleton subsequently supplying an opening and a conclusion. Shakespeare's contribution might begin at 3.7.25 or 39, and probably ends with Timon's exit at 3.7.104.

The kernel of the scene, by Shakespeare, is the banquet in which Timon serves his guests with steaming water and stones. His act of throwing water and stones on the false friends as a token of violently rejecting Athens and its inhabitants before quitting the city for good is the turning point of the entire drama. Middleton contributed comic and satiric episodes before and after this central element in the scene. They weave Middleton's creditor scenes into the play as it is emerging now that those episodes are over. In the first of these episodes, the opening of 3.7, the creditors assemble at Timon's house, recalling and regretting their heartless responses to Timon's servants when they sought money in Middleton's creditor scenes. After Timon's departure in a rage, they come back to retrieve their caps and gowns; this Middletonian and highly comic passage not only concludes the scene but also, more importantly, forms a little epilogue to the entire sequence dealing with the creditors. These contributions to 3.7 are wrapped around the scene's key and Shakespearean central matter, the mock banquet. Once again we see Middleton establishing connections between an essentially Shakespeare scene and his own more sustained contributions.

4.2

4.2 is another scene of mixed authorship. On the basis of Holdsworth's work, it appears that the short episode showing Flavius parting from the other servants of Timon's household might be of mixed authorship, and that the soliloquy thereafter, beginning "O, the fierce wrechedness that glory brings us," is probably by Middleton. A sequence of composition cannot reliably be deduced, but there is no objection to Middleton revising the first twenty-nine lines then adding the soliloquy, as would accord with his contribution to other scenes. The end of the soliloquy looks forward to Flavius's visit to Timon in the woods (a matter to which I will return below), and so is of a piece with other passages that he supplied at the beginning and end of scenes to tie the play together, and with his augmentation of the role of Flavius in 2.2. It appears, then, that the overall situation in the scenes between the major Middleton section of act 3 and the major Shakespearean scene in the woods was something like this: Middleton expanded some fragmented Shakespeare material so as to forge a more or less coherent section as part of a more or less complete play. As we have seen, much the same applies to the episodes between Middleton's banquet scene (1.2) and his act 3, though Middleton left a more connected and coherent text in the section from 3.7 to 4.2.

4.3, 5.1, and 5.2

The longest scene in the play, 4.3, is supplemented by two other scenes that continue the staging of Timon in the woods to make up a single massive sequence of action. The act division beginning act 5 introduced by editors is a destructive intrusion. This whole sequence is predominantly by Shakespeare. However, as Holdsworth identified, Middleton seems to have made the decisive addition of the Flavius episode (4.3.460–537), a passage whose presence has a strong bearing on the overall meaning of the play. He may also have added a short passage at 4.3.66–69:

Alcibiades.
How came the noble Timon to this change?
Timon.
As the moon does, by wanting light to give.
But then renew I could not like the moon;
There were no suns to borrow of.

Holdsworth cites a number of Middleton parallels. For instance, Tailby in *Your Five Gallants,* when asked, "How cheer you, sir?" replies "Faith, like the moon, more bright; / Decreased in body, but remade in light" (2.1.297–98). Tailby's brightness is his newly acquired money. Holdsworth describes this as "The only occasion where I can find close links with Middleton outside the Middleton sections." Holdsworth also notes *Love's Labour's Lost* 5.2.211–14 as an analogue in Shakespeare, but the parallel is less close than that in *Your Five Gallants.*

Middleton may have supplied other minor touches in the following scenes; there are passing and slight hints at his hand in 5.1, and good evidence for his addition of some crucial lines, the short passage in which Timon contemplates his death:

My long sickness
Of health and living now begins to mend,
And nothing brings me all things.

(5.2.71–73)

The idea compares with *Hengist* 3.1.39–42: "Forgetfulness, / 'Tis the pleasing'st virtue anyone can have / That rises up from nothing, for by the same, / Forgetting all, they forget from whence they came." The idiom "sickness of" followed by an abstraction is in Middleton's vein, as in "sickness of affection" (*Lady's Tragedy* 2.2.96); and there is a similar echoic collocation of "thing," "nothing," and "bring" in *Triumphs of Truth* ll. 303–4. Holdsworth compares Middleton passages such as *Lady's Tragedy*

5.2.89–90, "health / After long sickness," and *The Changeling* 3.4.161–62, "Let me go poor unto my bed with honour, / And I am rich in all things." The tone of the lines attributable to Middleton is far more lyrical and philosophically accepting than anything else Timon utters, and they are the only lines in the scene that can plausibly be taken to be addressed to his steward Flavius. In both respects, this local insertion relates to Middleton's more substantial addition to 4.3.

Middleton's writing of that passage, Flavius's unaccompanied visit to Timon, raises questions relating to the sequence of episodes. He would have had to work out exactly where the Flavius episode should be slotted into this extraordinarily long and abruptly episodic sequence. What I propose is that in the course of inserting his episode into Shakespeare's draft Middleton changed the position of the episode in Shakespeare's hand dealing with the Poet and Painter. The case emerges from a consideration of two kinds of evidence: textual anomalies in the scene as it stands, and fleeting indications of Middleton's adjustments to the material he received from Shakespeare.

The most striking textual anomaly is that the arrival of the Poet and Painter is anticipated long before it happens. At 4.3.353 Apemantus says "Yonder comes a poet and a painter." It is approaching another two hundred lines before they actually arrive. The usual explanation is couched in terms of the text's origination in a rough draft of Shakespeare's sole authorship. The matter needs to be reevaluated in the light of Holdsworth's demonstration that the Flavius episode that falls between Apemantus's announcement and the Poet and Painter's actual arrival is in another hand. If the intervening material were to have been written entirely by Middleton, the theory that Shakespeare changed his mind would collapse entirely. In fact Holdsworth does not attribute to Middleton the second intervening episode, the one dealing with the Thieves. But the possibility arises that Middleton could have transposed a Shakespeare episode, or could have inserted a separately written Shakespeare episode, when he introduced his own material.

It is probable that he did so. The sequence of episodes in F is:

> Alcibiades—Apemantus—Thieves—Flavius—Poet and Painter—Flavius and Senators.

In this sequence, the Poet and Painter episode prevents an exit and immediate reentry by Flavius. Prior to Middleton's addition of the Flavius episode, however, the Poet and Painter episode would not be needed as a spacer. An original Shakespeare sequence that would have been in accordance with Apemantus's statement is therefore possible:

> Alcibiades—Apemantus—Poet and Painter—Thieves—Flavius and Senators.

This posited Shakespeare sequence is entirely coherent, the main phase of it moving from high (Alcibiades) to low (Thieves), and framing the civic visitors (Apemantus, Poet, and Painter) between the military visitors (Alcibiades, Thieves as disaffected soldiers from his army). The details of the text as it is here conjectured to have stood are effective or at least functional. Apemantus's parting shot, "More things like men. Eat, Timon, and abhor them" (4.3.400), would have referred to the Poet and Painter; he has already implied that they are beastlike by mentioning them just after declaring that "The commonwealth of Athens is become a forest of beasts" (4.3.349–50). There would have been an abrupt transition in tone from Timon expelling the Poet and Painter with "Out, rascal dogs" (5.1.114) to the First Thief's "Where should he have this gold?" (4.3.401); it is not inconceivable that Middleton cut a few lines here. At the end of the Thieves episode, Timon's imperative to the Thieves "To Athens, go . . ." (4.3.448) and their parting comment "Let us first see peace in Athens . . ." (4.3.457) would offer a strong lead into the entry of the Senators on their mission to save Athens from the ravages of war by securing help from Timon.

At first sight this theory leaves a difficulty to resolve, which is that the Poet and Painter know that Timon "likewise enriched poor straggling soldiers with great quantity" and that "'Tis said he gave unto his steward a mighty sum" (5.1.6–8). These comments presuppose that the episodes in question have already been seen on stage, and so accord with the arrangement in F. But the statement about Flavius is immediately open as to its authorship simply because it refers to an episode written by Middleton. The language is at least suggestively Middletonian. As Middleton here refers to "poor straggling soldiers," he elsewhere, in *More Dissemblers* 5.2.103, refers to "a poor straggling Gypsy." Shakespeare's only use of "straggling" is in a nondramatic context (*Lucrece* l. 428), and it is not there adjunct with "poor." And it is Middleton rather than Shakespeare who refers to soldiers as "poor" (*Puritan Widow* 3.5.50, *World Tossed at Tennis* l. 600).

The speech referring to the straggling soldiers also contains a textual crux in its radically variant forms for the names Phrynia and Timandra. Elsewhere in the Folio text, variant name forms have proved to be good evidence for divisions in authorship, even when they relate to less extreme alternatives such as "Apermantus" for "Apemantus" and "Ventigius" for "Ventidius." The names "Phrynia" and "Timandra," as used during the episode where Alcibiades makes his visit to Timon, are the correct forms: as has been noted, Timandra is mentioned in Plutarch as a concubine of Alcibiades; Phrynia is based on Phryne, an Athenian courtesan mentioned by Quintillian. But in the allusive mention at 5.1.5–6 they are, in the Folio, "*Phrinica* and *Timandylo*." The double error is highly implausible as a double misreading of the manuscript, and very curious as a double inconsistency on Shakespeare's part. Misrecollection by Middleton offers a better explanation, and is consistent with the suggestion made above that he barely if at all consulted Plutarch in writing his contribution.

Three details in the one speech are therefore well explained by a short Middleton addition: the references to Alcibiades' whores, which misremembers their names, to the straggling soldiers, which presupposes a sequence of episodes incompatible with "Yonder comes a poet and a painter" and uses a Middleton idiom, and to Flavius, which refers to a Middleton episode. Moreover, Jackson has noted Middleton's linguistic preferences in the speeches immediately adjacent to the lines in question, at 5.1.3–9 ("does," "has"), and again at 74–81 (in the Folio spellings, "Y'are . . . Y'haue . . . Y'are," and "E'ne"). Middleton may have transcribed this scene in order to relocate it, in other words the Middletonian forms support the case for a relocation, and he may have supplied the lines in question as part of the same readjustment of the text.[36]

If this theory of transcription is extended back to the episode of the Thieves before the Steward's visit, or at least the end of the episode, this would explain the inconsistency in the stage directions between the entry, "*Enter the Bandetti.,*" and the exit, "*Exit Theeues.*" Again, as Holdsworth suggests, a localized alteration or addition by Middleton provides a better explanation than the usual view that the inconsistency is typical of Shakespeare's foul papers. The entry is Shakespearean, in that Shakespeare elsewhere refers to *bandetti* whereas Middleton does not. But the formula "exit" followed by a collective noun is found elsewhere in *Timon* only in the Middleton scenes: "*Exeunt Lords*" at 1.2.232 and "*Exeunt the Senators*" at 3.7.114. "*Exit Theeues*" comes immediately before Flavius' entry, and so it has obvious potential to be an addition by Middleton, especially if he were writing on the same leaf of paper. There is, moreover, another Middleton marker just seven lines previously in the Thieves episode. The abbreviation "Has" for "he has" at 4.3.452 is taken by Holdsworth to be a sign of Middleton. Here too he was perhaps acting here as transcriber, in which case the exit direction can readily be attributed to him.

Clearly the Flavius scene needs to come before, but not imediately before, his return with the Senators. Yet it also needs to be late in the woods sequence, for logically Timon needs to reject his potentially true friends Alcibiades and Apemantus before recognizing and accepting friendship in his retainer; the rule of his conduct needs establishing before the exception can be registered. The possibilities facing Middleton were therefore limited. It is hard to escape two subsequences:

Alcibiades—Apemantus—Flavius;
Flavius—[another episode]—Flavius and Senators.

Evidently Middleton rejected the least intrusive solution:

Alcibiades—Apemantus—Poet and Painter—Flavius—Thieves—Flavius and Senators.

What is least clear in this hypothesis is why Middleton should not have been satisfied with this arrangement. Perhaps he sought to head off difficulties in doubling parts because he reasonably foresaw that the three speaking Thieves should double with the Senators and Lords, who elsewhere in the play likewise tend to come in threes.

The sequencing is potentially sensitive, for Timon's recognition of humanity in the figure of his Steward is a considerable modification to his remorselessly negative attitude through the rest of the scene. If we take away the episodes involving Flavius that Holdsworth attributes to Middleton, Flavius then appears for the penultimate time in 4.2 (assuming that Shakespeare wrote a first draft of the opening section), where he parts with the servants. Without the Middletonian soliloquy, he says nothing about Timon's predicament in this scene, as is consistent with the pre-Middleton state of the text. His next scene would have been his final appearance in 5.2, where he leads the Senators to Timon's cave. This gives a coherent but different plot line. In the first of the two pre-Middleton episodes, Timon is neither present nor a point of reference; in the second Flavius engages with Timon only by calling him before he enters from his cave. There is thus no personal relationship between the two in either scene. Flavius's final appearance fails to give any indication of his dramatic or personal role, beyond that he has visited Timon previously or perhaps has merely spoken to someone else who has done so.

Middleton made Flavius a far more important and engaged figure in the second half of the play. As we have seen, Middleton added a soliloquy to 4.2 that consolidates the audience's impression of Flavius's personal feelings for Timon and that sets up his visit to Timon in the woods: "I'll follow and enquire him out. / . . . / Whilst I have gold I'll be his steward still" (4.2.49–51). That episode provides one of the most moving moments in the play, decisively altering the plot of Flavius and adding an otherwise missing recognition of human worth to the range of responses to humanity that Timon articulates in the woods. Middleton contributes an exception to Timon's "exceptless" rejection of humanity. This episode, crucial to readings of the play stressing its religious dimension such as those by Wilson Knight and, more recently, Ken Jackson, is an example of interauthorial modification rather than the isolated vision of Shakespeare.[37]

Conclusions

There is a distinction to be drawn between annotations that could have been inserted as interlineations or in the margin of a manuscript and those that would have occupied one or more separate leaves. If one thinks of the Folio copy materially in these terms, discounting for a moment the minor additions that have been considered in this paper, the following broad division of the text between the main hands is suggested:

a) 1.1: Shakespeare (286 lines)
b) 1.2: Middleton (251 lines)
c) 2.1–2: Mixed (263 lines)
d) 3.1–6: Middleton (419 lines)
e) 3.7–4.2: Mixed (205 lines)
f) 4.3–5.5: Shakespeare (802 lines) with Middleton insert (77 lines)

The details reviewed in this paper lead to a picture of how the collaborative text was made. Middleton worked on the play after Shakespeare drafted his contribution. This is not to say that Middleton belatedly adapted or revised Shakespeare. Holdsworth points out that the Middleton parallels indicate a date of around 1605, which is early within the range of possible dates of composition. No matter where one dates the writing of the rest of the play within the usually accepted range of between late 1605 and 1608, it remains unlikely that Middleton picked up a text abandoned by Shakespeare some time earlier. In most of the scenes of mixed authorship it seems clear that Shakespeare supplied the core and Middleton added passages to it. Jackson suggests that Shakespeare might have acted similarly in Middleton scenes, but I have found no particular evidence to support this view.

Shakespeare was senior dramatist, theater company sharer, and the writer with an ongoing interest in North's Plutarch. He was the initiator of the draft, and presumably, in consultation with other members of the King's Men, would have made the first decision about working on the play. He perhaps would have put together a "plot" sketching out the order of scenes in the usual way with dramatists of the period seeking company approval. The Shakespearean context described above for the Middletonian 3.6 suggests that Middleton was here at least writing according to a Shakespearean groundplan,[38] though the two dramatists' apparent uncertainty about the roles of the Fool and the Page suggest a certain amount of improvisation, and some of Middleton's expansions of the role of Flavius may have been on his own initiative.

Whether Middleton was in the picture from the very beginning we can only guess. But he was the obvious choice of dramatist to contribute scenes in a mode that was relatively unfamiliar to Shakespeare, satirical city comedy. He was also one of the few major dramatists other than Shakespeare known to be working for the King's Men in this period, for he is now thought to have written *A Yorkshire Tragedy* and *Revenger's Tragedy* for the same company at about the same time as *Timon; Lady's Tragedy* would follow a few years later. The subversion of tragedy into a satiric and experimental mode that characterizes *Revenger's Tragedy* is displayed to different effect in *Timon.* Middleton was no novice, but an experienced dramatist at the height of his creativity. He was the play's poet of credit and debt—which in the period had a moral dimension that is developed in Alcibiades' language of "purchase," "debt," "security," "pawn," and "returns" when pleading for his friend, and in the idea of the altruistic gift and service without bonds in the Flavius passages. And if one adds to these elements the banquet scene, 1.2, it can be said that Middleton was the preeminent poet of homosociality.

His writing contains ideas about the play that conflicted with Shakespeare's, and the result of their interaction was a play with a peculiar dynamic energy but full of small loose ends. Lacking any secure explanation, critics have focused on the loose ends, finding them symptomatic of a text that does not conform with what they intuitively expect of a Shakespeare play. The intuition is right, but puzzlement and rejection are not the appropriate responses. The loose ends and inconsistencies are merely the key to a door that opens onto the dialogic play. Once *Timon of Athens* is understood as a collaboration, it starts to make sense.

Notes

1. MacD. P. Jackson, *Studies in Attribution: Middleton and Shakespeare* (Salzburg: Universität Salzburg, 1979), 63. See also David Lake, *The Canon of Thomas Middleton's Plays* (Cambridge: Cambridge Univ. Press, 1975). Middleton's hand was first advocated by William Wells, in *"Timon of Athens,"* in *Notes and Queries* 112 (1920): 226–29, part of an earlier and more impressionistic generation of attribution studies rightly castigated by E. K. Chambers (see n. 6).

2. R. V. Holdsworth, "Middleton and Shakespeare: The Case for Middleton's Hand in *Timon of Athens,*" doctoral thesis, Univ. of Manchester, 1982. References to Holdsworth are to this study unless otherwise indicated.

3. *Timon* will, however, appear in Thomas Middleton, *Collected Works,* gen. ed. Gary Taylor (Oxford: Oxford Univ. Press, forthcoming). The present essay feeds into my editing of the play as a collaboration for the Oxford Shakespeare series.

4. John Jowett, "Middleton and Debt in *Timon of Athens,*" *Money and the Age of Shakespeare,* ed. Linda Woodbridge, Palgrave Early Modern Cultural Studies (Basingstoke: Palgrave, (forthcoming).

5. Muriel St Clare Byrne, "Bibliographical Clues in Collaborative Plays," *The Library,* IV, 13 (1920), 364–73. See also S. Schoenbaum, *Internal Evidence and Elizabethan Dramatic Authorship: An Essay in Literary History and Method* (London: Edward Arnold, 1966).

6. E. K. Chambers, "The Disintegration of Shakespeare," British Academy Shakespeare Lecture, 1924, repr. in *Aspects of Shakespeare* (Oxford: Clarendon, 1933), 23–48. On *Timon* specifically, see his *William Shakespeare: A Study of Facts and Problems,* 2 vols. (Oxford: Clarendon, 1930), I:481.

7. Jeffrey Masten, *Textual Intercourse: Collaboration, Authorship, and Sexualities in Renaissance Drama* (Cambridge: Cambridge Univ. Press, 1997), 20.

8. Gordon McMullan, "'Our Whole Life is Like a Play': Collaboration and the Problem of Editing," *Textus* 9 (1996): 437–60.

9. H. J. Oliver makes a case in his Arden 2 ed. (London: Methuen, 1959), xix, for a scribal overlay introduced in a transcript by the scrivener Ralph Crane. This has been dismissed in T. H. Howard-Hill, "Ralph Crane's Parentheses," *Notes and Queries* 210 (1965): 334–40, p. 339; Lake, *Canon,* 284; and Jackson, *Attribution,* 55–56. Folio Compositor B set all the text except one page (Gg3, printing 1.2.10–129). The scope for compositorial variation is therefore limited and the compositorial sections lack correspondence with the authorial stints. But inter-authorial transcription is an issue in *Timon* (see 294–95).

10. All quotations from *Timon of Athens* are based on William Shakespeare, *Complete Works,* gen. eds. Stanley Wells and Gary Taylor (Oxford: Clarendon, 1986).

11. Jonathan Hope, *The Authorship of Shakespeare's Plays: A Socio-Linguistic Study* (Cambridge: Cambridge Univ. Press, 1994); M. W. A. Smith, "The Authorship of *Timon of Athens,*" *Text* 5 (1991): 195–240.

12. Smith, "Authorship," figs. 7a, 8a, and 9a (228–30).

13. The untitled manuscript play is otherwise known as *The Second Maiden's Tragedy* or *The Maiden's Tragedy.*

14. TLNs (through line numbers) from *The Norton Facsimile: The First Folio of Shakespeare,* ed. Charlton Hinman (New York: W. W. Norton, and London: Hamlyn, 1968).

15. G. R. Hibbard, ed., *Timon of Athens* (Harmondsworth, 1970), 146.

16. Lawrence Stone, *Crisis of the Aristocracy, 1558–1641* (Oxford: Clarendon, 1965), 532.

17. All quotations from non-Shakespeare works are from Middleton's works, or sections of collaborative works securely attributed to Middleton, unless otherwise stated. References to Middleton's works are from Middleton, *Collected Works.*

18. See introduction and commentary in Middleton, *Collected Works.*

19. The irregular speech prefix "*Po.*" is not significant, as it occurs in a tightly packed line of type and has been reduced to save space.

20. *Two Most Unnaturall and Bloodie Murthers* (1605), repr. in A. C. Cawley and Barry Gaines, eds., *A Yorkshire Tragedy* (Manchester, 1986), 99.

21. Naseeb Shaheen, *Biblical Reference in Shakespeare's Plays* (Newark: Univ. of Delaware Press, 1999), 672. Biblical quotations are from the Geneva version.

22. R. V. Holdsworth, "Biblical Allusions in *Timon of Athens* and Thomas Middleton," *Notes & Queries* 235 (1990): 188–92.

23. As proposed by Taylor and Jowett in *Shakespeare Reshaped, 1603–1623* (Oxford: Clarendon, 1993), and further substantiated in Middleton, *Collected Works.*

24. Ed. Philip J. Ayers (Manchester: Manchester Univ. Press, 1990).

25. For discussion of the last, and the play's allusions to homosexual acts, see Theodore B. Leinwand, "Redeeming Beggary/Buggery in *Michaelmas Term,*" *English Literary History* 61 (1994): 53–70; see also Herbert Jack Heller, *Penitent Brothellers: Grace, Sexuality, and Genre in Thomas Middleton's City Comedies* (Cranbury, NJ: Associated Univ. Presses, 2000), 125–38.

26. The riposte from Caphis "Where's the fool now?" is possibly also Middletonian, for there is a parallel in a scene that might be by Middleton in *Old Law* 1.1.235, "Where's the fault now?" But this should be discounted as evidence not only on account of the collaborative nature of *Old Law* and uncertainty as to authorship of this particular scene. The exchange appears to be imitated from Marston's *What You Will* (1601; printed 1607), where the same phrase "Where's the fool now" has the same table-turning function.

27. Gary Taylor, "Shakespeare and Others: The Authorship of *Henry the Sixth Part One,*" *Medieval and Renaissance Drama in England* 7 (1995): 145–205.

28. Middleton also uses the same construction with "hath"; this too is unexampled in Shakespeare.

29. Ward E. Y. Elliott and Robert J. Valenza, "Glass Slippers and Seven-League Boots: C-Prompted Doubts about Ascribing *A Funeral Elegy* and *A Lover's Complaint* to Shakespeare," *Shakespeare Quarterly* 48 (1997): 177–207.

30. There is another example in *The Changeling* at 1.1.213, "Did my occasions suit as I could wish," which has a similar conceptual structure to the line in *Timon* but falls in a scene thought to be mostly by Rowley.

31. See Introduction to *Measure for Measure* in Middleton, *Collected Works.*

32. Plutarch, *The Liues of the Noble Grecians and Romanes,* trans. Thomas North (1579).

33. Karen Newman, "Cultural Capital's Gold Standard: Shakespeare and the Critical Apostrophe in Renaissance Studies," in *Discontinuities,* ed. Viviana Comensoli and Paul Steverns (Toronto: Univ. of Toronto Press, 1998): 96–113.

34. Edmund Spenser, denying sexual activity, in *Shepheardes Calender,* in *Minor Poems,* ed. Charles Grosvenor Osgood and Henry Gibbons Lotspeich with Dorothy E. Mason, 2 vols. (Baltimore: John Hopkins Univ. Press, 1943–47), I:18; Christopher Marlowe, affirming that the wisest men had "minions," in *Edward II* 1.4.391–97, in *"Doctor Faustus" and Other Plays,* ed. David Bevington and Eric Rasmussen (Oxford and New York: Oxford Univ. Press, 1995); as noted in Newman, "Gold Standard."

35. In Greg Doran's 1999 production at the Royal Shakespeare Theatre, Stratford-upon-Avon, the soldier was shown onstage killing one of the male dancers in the masque for sexually motivated reasons.

36. He was perhaps aware of Timon's repeated and sarcastic descriptions of the Poet and Painter and "honest men" when writing the previous Flavius episode, where Timon first claims "I never had / Honest man about me" (4.3.478–79) but later acknowledges Flavius as "Thou singly honest man" (4.3.524). Holdsworth demolishes the case made by Oliver, in his ed., xxiv–xxv, to the effect that verbal echoes between putative authorial sections are evidence for actual single authorship.

37. G. Wilson Knight, in various publications including *The Wheel of Fire* (Oxford: Oxford Univ. Press, 1930); Ken Jackson, "Derrida, the Gift, and God in *Timon of Athens,*" *Shakespeare Quarterly* 52 (2001): 34–66.

38. Hence, perhaps, its resemblance to a passage in *Richard III* (2.1.97–100) where Stanley unsuccessfully pleads for mercy for his servant who "slew today a riotous gentleman." In *Timon of Athens,* however, it is the condemned man who is the riotous gentleman.

1610s–1620s: Webster and Heywood

"Strong commanding Art": The Structure of *The White Devil, The Duchess of Malfi,* and *The Devil's Law-Case*

David Gunby

"WHAT IS STRIKING ABOUT DISCUSSION OF THE WORK OF JOHN WEBSTER is the absence of that larger area of agreement within which meaningful arguments about detail can take place. There is not a universally acceptable definition of Webster's peculiar genius." So wrote Neil Carson in 1978.[1] Forty years earlier, however, there had not even been universal acceptance of "Webster's peculiar genius," with Ian Jack and L. G. Salingar, last in a line of dissenters stretching back to HM's 1816 articles in *Blackwood's Magazine* on *The White Devil* and *The Duchess of Malfi,* proclaiming that "in Webster there is no deeper purpose than to make our flesh creep,"[2] and that "Webster is sophisticated; but his sophistication belongs to decadence."[3] Such philippics now seem quaint, and Webster's status secure, but there remains significant critical disagreement about aspects of his dramaturgy, and most notably about meaning, plotting, and structure. It is the last of these I wish to consider here.

Of the three plays I shall discuss, *The White Devil, The Duchess of Malfi,* and *The Devil's Law-Case, The White Devil* has attracted the severest criticism. John Russell Brown, for instance, considers its structure "loose and rambling, a gothic aggregation rather than a steady exposition and development towards a single consummation,"[4] while J. R. Mulryne finds its plot "on any estimate, exceptionally disjointed and difficult to follow,"[5] and Roma Gill declares that "the tragedy is disjointed and seems to have been written in episodes, not as a whole."[6]

Strictures directed at *The Devil's Law-Case* tend to be similar, with Charles Forker concluding that it "gives an impression of having been conceived as a group of separate episodes or emotionally entangling situations that were only later spliced into a play."[7] Gunnar Boklund, earlier, came to much the same conclusion,[8] while Rowland Wymer comments that "Webster has overloaded the narrative complications to the point of incoherence."[9] Criticisms of *The Duchess of Malfi* have, however, focused not on overelaboration but rather on the aspect of the play that led William Archer to declare it "broken-backed":[10] why the Duchess dies during the fourth act. Besides this major critical issue there are others of considerable import also, most notably why (besides allowing the Duchess and Antonio to have two further children) several years elapse between acts 2 and 3.

Criticism of Webster's structural skills is not, of course, universal. Jacqueline Pearson, for instance, writes of Webster's "four perfectly structured plays,[11] while Peter B. Murray, discussing *The Devil's Law-Case,* praises "the nearly perfect order of its plot."[12] Nonetheless, the balance of critical opinion is clearly negative; Webster may be a tragic writer of genius, but his genius does not extend to plotting and structure.

My argument here will be that charges of confused, disjointed and overelaborate plotting and of concomitant structural failures are misplaced: that Webster knew precisely what he was doing in all three plays, and that, moreover, he employs the same structural principles in each. In making this case, I shall discuss at most length *The White Devil,* since it is there that his structural methods are most fully and rigorously deployed. In *The Duchess of Malfi* and *The Devil's Law-Case* the structures are similarly conceived but less complex, perhaps because *The White Devil* met with such incomprehension at its first performance at the Red Bull in 1612.[13]

Emrys Jones contends that "most of Shakespeare's . . . histories and tragedies gain in clarity if they are considered as plays conceived in two unequal movements."[14] So, too, do Webster's three plays, in each of which we find, beginning in the third act, a second movement that constitutes a replaying, with ironic variations, of situations and events in a first. Most fully employed in *The White Devil,* where 3.3 closely echoes and parallels the opening scene of the play, this structure occurs also in *The Duchess of Malfi,* where there is a similar relationship between act 1 and the first two scenes of act 3, and in *The Devil's Law-Case,* where the third act is again where new actions begin, often paralleling those in the first act of the play, and forming ironic variants on earlier counterparts.

This two-movement structure is central to the three plays under discussion, but on it Webster builds cyclically, employing what Jacqueline Pearson has termed an "elaborate and coherent system of parallels and repetitions."[15] This is most comprehensively so in *The White Devil,* which repeats itself in matters large and small, with the repetitions rendering the whole increasingly subtly articulated and significant. In *The Duchess of Malfi* and *The Devil's Law-Case* the pattern of "parallels and repetitions" is less complex and thoroughgoing, but the same structural principles apply.

A characteristic feature of *The White Devil* is, as Susan McLeod has pointed out, a pairing of characters and situations:

> Webster presents us with two ghosts, two mad persons, two malcontents, two sets of lovers, two dumb shows depicting murder, two simultaneous plots to be

rid of Camillo, two books and two letters used as props. Brachiano and Isabella have two divorce scenes, Vittoria two arraignments and two wooing scenes, Monticelso two persuasion scenes regarding revenge for Isabella's death. Brachiano dies of two causes (poison and the rope), while Flamineo has two death scenes.[16]

Taking up one of the pairings to which McLeod draws attention—the two malcontents—we can begin to discern the patterning that underlies *The White Devil,* and its implications.

In all but social status, the Count, Lodovico, and the lowly secretary, Flamineo, are closely paralleled. Both narrowly escape the death penalty for murder, Lodovico, as the play opens, learning that he is banished, and Flamineo being, in effect, released on bail (3.2.253–56).[17] Both acknowledge their crimes in private, but neither is willing to acknowledge his good fortune, each railing at those who have sentenced him. Both, likewise, are re-employed after their "convictions" and both, finally, meet the retribution they deserve.

In developing this parallelism, 3.3 is crucial, since recognition of the relationship of this scene to 1.1 provides an important insight into the structural basis of *The White Devil.* The clash between Flamineo and Lodovico is the dramatic core of the scene, but another significant feature, linking it to 1.1, is the successive entries by the Savoy, French, and English Ambassadors. Peter Thomson cites this as a prime example of Webster's failure in his handling of the Ambassadors, who, he says, "are reduced to acting as feed-men for the 'distracted' Flamineo's bitter wit."[18] But the Ambassadors take on considerable significance if we recognize their part in the process of repetition and parallelism so central to *The White Devil.* In 3.1, before the trial, they processed mutely over the stage to a cynical commentary by Flamineo. Now three reappear, offering brief but pertinent comments on the trial, comments revealing parallels with the opening scene of the play. Thus when the Savoy Ambassador offers Flamineo "comfort" (3.3.10), he echoes Antonelli's more wordy attempt to comfort Lodovico (1.1.44–50), while Flamineo's rejection of these sentiments (3.3.12–14) likewise echoes Lodovico's (1.1.50–52). Equally the French Ambassador's rebuke, "The proofes are evident" (18), echoes Antonelli's assertion that Lodovico was "justly dom'd" (1.1.13), with the English Ambassador's "Fie, fie, *Flamineo*" (28) an equivalent of Gasparo's deprecatory "O Sir" (1.1.52).

There are other significant parallels, too, between 1.1 and 3.3. Thus Flamineo's observation that "your Noblemen are priviledged from the racke" (33) echoes the sentiments of Lodovico when wondering how "some great men scape / This banishment" (1.1.38–39), while the latter's sour comment in I.i. on how "some ready to be executed / Give pleasant lookes, and money, and growe familiar / With the knave hangman" (53–55) is echoed by Flamineo's equally bitter comment to Lodovico: "if you will be merry, / Do it i'th like posture, as if some great man / Sate while his enemy were executed" (3.3.99–101). Likewise, in Antonelli's entrance at 3.3.96–98 with the "good newes" of Lodovico's pardon, there is a clear parallel with his entry in 1.1 as the bearer of the bad news of Lodovico's banishment. Such echoes, constituting a repetition in 3.3 of themes, images, and dramatic situations encountered in 1.1, both enforce the parallelism pervasive in the depiction of Lodovico and Flamineo and mark the beginning of the second half of *The White Devil.*

1.1 and 3.3, then, indicate the larger cyclic structure, but within each half of the play we find smaller-scale, but equally significant, parallelism. One of the most telling examples involves the relationship between 4.3 and 5.5, and once more involves Lodovico, though here in relation to Monticelso and Francisco, revengers who are, like the two malcontents, presented in parallel.

Of 4.3 Lee Bliss has written: "The rather awkward conclave scene . . . provides visual spectacle, but . . . we are largely diverted from our primary interests while tension dissipates in ecclesiastical minutiae."[19] But Webster's often-criticized insistence on presenting in detail aspects of the papal election *has* a function, which relates to the contrast between the reactions of the newly elected Pope and of Francisco to Vittoria's escape from the House of Convertites. From the Monticelso of acts 1 and 2, acting in concert with Francisco, we would have expected delight at an opportunity for revenge. But 4.1 reveals a growing rift between the two, with Francisco convinced that the Cardinal's desire for vengeance is waning (4.1.38–42), so that, in part at least, we are prepared for their different responses to Vittoria's flight. The restraint of Paul IV in merely excommunicating the lovers has, even so, surprised many critics, as have his efforts to dissuade Lodovico from revenge. Yet here lies the point of the conclave. For the accurate and spectacular representation of the process by which the choice is made, reinforced by the conversation of the French and English Ambassadors, and the latter's emphasis (4.3.24–32) on the safeguards against bribery or coercion, demonstrates that the new Pope has been honestly elected. And because this is so, the conclave functions as a symbolic indicator of Monticelso's changed attitude toward revenge. The Pope's blessing, with its *remissio peccatorum,* is not an empty one: Vittoria, Flamineo and Brachiano cannot flout the law with impunity, but Paul IV will not seek their deaths.

The Pope's restraint on hearing of Vittoria's escape contrasts sharply with Francisco's delight at his success in engineering it (4.3.54–58), and the contrast continues as Lodovico talks first with Francisco, then with Monticelso, and finally (through the servant) with Francisco masquerading as Monticelso. Francisco merely wishes to confirm that Lodovico will indeed murder Brachiano, but his inquiry whether Lodovico has "tane the sacrament to prosecute / Th'intended murder" (72–73) contrasts sharpiy with Monticelso's efforts first to establish "what devill [Lodovico and Francisco] were raising" (88–89) and then to dissuade Lodovico from carrying out the murder.

The encounter between Monticelso and Lodovico is noteworthy in two respects. One is the way in which Lodovico confides in Monticelso "as a penitent sinner" (108). Intended as a ploy, since "What I utter / Is in confession meerely; which you know / Must never bee reveal'd" (108–10), the parody of the confessional act gives place to reality, with Monticelso as priest offering unimpeachably good counsel (116–27). The second is that Lodovico's determination to abandon the planned murder derives as much from Monticelso's forbearance as from his denunciation of it:

> I'le give it o're. He saies 'tis damable:
> Besides I did expect his suffrage,
> By reason of *Camillo's* death.
>
> (128–30)

The new Pope has behaved impeccably, and fails in his attempt to avert Brachiano's murder only because Francisco subverts Lodovico's confessional resolve:

> *Francisco.* Do you know that Count?
> *Servant.* Yes, my Lord.
> *Francisco.* Beare him these thousand Duckets to his lodging;
> Tell him the Pope hath sent them. Happily
> That will confirme more then all the rest.
>
> (131–34)

Duped, the cynical Lodovico is "doubly arm'd" to commit the murder. Francisco has won the battle for Lodovico's soul. For that is how the latter part of 4.3 is presented, with Francisco as the tempter, lurking outside the confessional, and Monticelso as the priest. Like the Good and Evil Angels in Marlowe's *Doctor Faustus,* Francisco and Monticelso compete for Lodovico. And as in *Faustus,* evil prevails because the tempter plays so unerringly on the would-be penitent's weaknesses.

Defeated, Monticelso is seen no more, and the revenge action runs its course. Yet what he attempted is recalled when, in 5.5, crucial aspects of 4.3 are echoed as Webster creates yet another pairing—this one of "overhearing scenes." 5.5 is not, at first sight, likely to demonstrate Webster's mastery of plot and structure, his use of a minor court functionary, Hortensio, to discover Francisco's plans appearing clumsy. But it is carefully prepared for, with verbal and situational parallels showing the apparently accidental to possess a kind of inevitability, and to be related, causally, to earlier events.

The verbal parallels Webster employs connect statements in 5.5 with antecedents in 4.3. Thus Lodovico's objection to Francisco's further participation in the revenge (5.5.1–3) echoes his more tentative statement on the subject at 4.3.74–75, while Francisco's reply carries similar echoes. Likewise Hortensio's comment, "These strong Court factions that do brooke no checks, / In the cariere oft breake the Riders neckes" (5.5.14–15), recalls the warning, "Take you heede: / Least the Jade breake your necke," which Monticelso gives Lodovico when the latter tries to avoid revealing the planned revenge by inventing a story about "a restie Barbarie horse" (4.3.93–97).

This last parallel, with its emphasis on the consequences of crime, is reinforced by similarities in situation. Both Monticelso and Hortensio become suspicious upon observing Lodovico and Francisco in conversation. Each discovers what is planned, and each tries to prevent the murders being carried out. There is also a significant difference, however. For Monticelso seeks to save Lodovico's soul, while Hortensio hastens to "raise some force" in order to frustrate the murderers and bring them to book. And it is in the distance between penitence and punishment that a raison d'être for the echoes and parallels on which 5.5 is built may be found. In stressing both the similarities and the differences between this scene and 4.3, Webster is able to emphasize Lodovico's changed circumstances. Lodovico's warning to Francisco applies equally to himself:

> My Lord upon my soule you shall no further:
> You have most ridiculously ingag'd your selfe
> Too far allready
>
> (5.5.1–3).

These three examples of parallelism suffice to illustrate Jacqueline Pearson's point (though in ways that she does not) that in *The White Devil* we find an "elaborate and coherent system of parallels and repetitions."[20] Other examples could be examined to demonstrate how pervasive this structural device is—the close parallels between Vittoria's "dream" in 1.2 and Zanche's in 5.3, for example, or between Brachiano's death and Flamineo's mock death—but they would be superfluous here. What I want to do, rather, is show how similar in construction to *The White Devil* are *The Duchess of Malfi* and *The Devil's Law-Case.*

The most persistent criticism of the structure of *The Duchess of Malfi* has been that first voiced, about 1650, by the clergyman, Abraham Wright. While praising *The Duchess of Malfi* as "a good play," Wright complained that "the business was two years a-doing, as may be perceived by the beginning of the third Act, where Antonio has three children by the Duchess, when in the first Act he had but one [*sic*]."[21] For Wright (subscribing to the doctrine of the unities), the problem is primarily the play's time span, but later critics have been affronted more by the gap in time. Arthur Kirsch, for instance, argues problems of characterization caused when, though "At the end of act 2, after learning that the Duchess has had a child, Ferdinand vows 'not to stir' till he knows 'who leaps my sister,'" "the opening of act 3 reveals that Ferdinand still has not stirred."[22]

How, in motivational terms, Ferdinand's inactivity is to be explained is not an issue that I want to take up here. For more important, structurally, is the point made by John Russell Brown, namely that there are "important time-gaps between each act,"[23] gaps that are in various ways emphasized. The time elapsed between acts 1 and 2, for instance, is stressed when Bosola voices his suspicion that the Duchess is pregnant (2.1.63–68) and then Delio exclaims, in response, clearly, to what Antonio has just revealed: "And so long since married? / You amaze me" (71–72). At the beginning of act 4, likewise, Ferdinand asks Bosola, "How doth our Sister Dutchesse beare her selfe / In her imprisonment?"(1–2), his question and Bosola's answer alike implying that she has been incarcerated for some time, while the conversation of Antonio and Delio about the former's "hope of reconcilement / To the *Aragonian* brethren" (5.1.1–2) performs the same function in act 5.

Of all the time gaps, however, that between acts 2 and 3 is the greatest and most emphasized. For here Webster not only provides a thirty-five-line dialogue between Antonio and Delio in which time is constantly at issue, but also allows the latter to joke about it in consciously theatrical terms (3.1.7–11). And it is with 3.1 that the characteristically Websterian replaying, with ironic variations, of the first act of the play begins.

A first, striking instance of this is the paralleling of the conversation between Delio and the newly-returned Antonio in the opening moments of *The Duchess of Malfi,* and between Antonio and the newly-returned Delio early in 3.1. The conversation with which the play opens has Delio inquiring about the French court, and eliciting from Antonio praise for a King whose reforms are designed to set his kingdom an example, since

> a Prince's court
> Is like a common Fountaine, whence should flow
> Pure silver-droppes in generall: But if't chance
> Some curs'd example poyson't neere the head,
> "Death, and diseases through the whole land spread.
>
> (1.1.11–15)

The conversation in 3.1 forms an ironic counterpart to this, when the newly-returned Delio asks Antonio about the public response to rumors that the Duchess has had children by an unknown father:

Delio. What say the common people?
Antonio. The common-rable, do directly say
She is a Strumpet.
Delio. And your graver heades,
(Which would be pollitique) what censure they?
Antonio. They do observe, I grow to infinite purchase
The leaft-hand way, and all suppose the Duchesse
Would amend it, if she could:

(3.1.24–30)

The point is clear: in France, a ruler is setting his people a positive example, whereas a very different situation obtains in Malfi. Nor is the Duchess the only one affected. For the "graver heades" at Malfi see Antonio as corrupt, and in 3.2 the Duchess is forced to give public credence to this when she covers his sudden departure from court by pretending that "*Antonio* . . . Hath dealt . . . falsely with me, in's accounts" (166–67). In 1.1, by contrast, both Antonio and the Duchess are at pains to stress his probity, the Duchess with her loving jest about his being an "upright treasurer" (367).

These parallels between 1.1 and 3.1 are supported by others. One is the counterpart in 3.1 of Ferdinand's enlistment of Bosola as a spy (1.1.227–87), with Bosola reporting to his master what he has learned (57–92). In each case there is criticism by Bosola of his employer: criticism that Ferdinand rejects. Another parallel is the echoing of the homily that in 1.1 Ferdinand and the Cardinal preach to their sister against remarrying, a homily that includes the warning that "Your darkest actions: nay, your privat'st thoughts, / Will come to light" even though the Duchess may "privately be married / Under the Eves of night" (310–14). In act 3 the warning is borne out, with the Duchess anxious, in the face of widespread rumor, "About a scandalous report, is spread / Touching mine honour" (3.2.47–48). In 1.1, likewise, she avers (under pressure) that "I'll never marry" (298), but privately says, "Let old wives report / I wincked, and chose a husband" (343–44). In 3.1, however, when Ferdinand proposes that she marry Count Malateste, she replies not by repeating the earlier statement, which would involve a lie, but with something more equivocal in "When I choose / A husband, I will marry for your honour" (43–44). Despite these warnings, the Duchess woos Antonio, with her waitingwoman, Cariola, a hidden witness, and 3.2 provides a bitterly ironic counterpointing of this, when Antonio takes the initiative that in 1.1 was perforce the Duchess's, and then Ferdinand reveals a passion to which Antonio and Cariola are hidden witnesses.

As in *The White Devil,* this repetition in act 3 of material in act 1 is part of a larger cyclic design, allied to another structural feature, noted by Jacqueline Pearson: that in *The Duchess of Malfi* "a single incident is repeated and repeated throughout the play; the Duchess's wooing of Antonio."[24] This incident recurs variously in 1.1, 2.1, 3.2, 4.2, and 5.2. Of these,

4.2 is without doubt the most significant and complex, as Inga-Stina Ekeblad first showed,[25] but that in 5.2, where Julia woos Bosola, is closest, situationally, to the Duchess's wooing of Antonio, and most usefully illustrates the cyclic process.

In 2.4 we see Julia in illicit domesticity, the scene a parodic version of the Duchess's happy domesticity in 3.2, prior to the entry of Ferdinand. In 5.2, however, we are presented with an ironic rerunning of the wooing section of 1.1 as Julia boldly declares her attraction to Bosola (5.2.149–56). "This nice modesty, in Ladies / Is but a troublesome familiar, / That haunts them" (165–67), she tells him. "I am sudaine with you," she adds,

> We that are great women of pleasure, use to cut off
> These uncertaine wishes, and unquiet longings,
> And in an instant joyne the sweete delight
> And the pritty excuse together: had you bin i'th'streete,
> Under my chamber window, even there
> I should have courted you.
>
> (5.2.187–93)

The contrast between Julia's blatancy and the Duchess's embarrassment at having to take the lead in wooing Antonio could scarcely be more thoroughgoing.

In the Duchess's wooing, as has been often remarked, references to love and death are juxtaposed. So they are in 5.2, but with this difference: that the language of love employed by Julia contains metaphors involving not only death but also guilt (5.2.185–87) and judgment: "I am like one / That is condemn'd: I have my pardon promis'd, / But I would see it seal'd" (5.2.214–16). Given the different circumstances, it is hardly surprising that, in place of the Duchess's serenity in the face of death, Julia can in dying voice only a spiritual confusion shared with Vittoria, Flamineo, and Bosola: "'Tis weaknesse / Too much to thinke what should have bin done, I go, / I know not whether" (5.2.281–83).

Turning from Webster's tragedies to *The Devil's Law-Case* involves a generic shift, but even so, his tragicomedy can be closely related to his two tragedies, not least structurally. For in *The Devil's Law-Case,* again, there is a two-part structure, the second beginning in act 3, with situations and events paralleling those in the first act of the play, and forming ironic variants on their earlier counterparts. The recasting of the subplot takes place in 3.1, where links are established with 2.1, but the more significant new actions, and parallels, are to be found in 3.2 and particularly 3.3, where much relating to Romelio, Leonora, Contarino, and Jolenta is picked up from act 1, and reformulated.

In this reformulation, 3.2 is important. For it is here that Romelio, "The fortunate Youngman" (1.1.12) of the first half of the play, metamorphoses into a parody of Marlowe's Barabas in attempting to hasten the young nobleman Contarino's death, and thereby sets himself up as the unfortunate young man of the second half. In 3.3 Romelio resumes his customary garb, but he is no longer the supremely confident and successful merchant of act 1. And what happens in 3.3, paralleling the events of act 1 and initiating the second movement in *The Devil's Law-Case,* underlines that fact. In act 1 Romelio pressures his sister Jolenta to marry Ercole, to whom he asserts she is contracted. Jolenta and Contarino see themselves, however, as contracted in the eyes of heaven, while Winifrid's more earthy view is that they should "get . . . instantly to bed together" (1.2.299). They do not, but 3.3 imparts an ironic twist to her suggestion when, reacting to Romelio's urging her to pretend that the child that his mistress, the nun Angiolella, is carrying, is hers by Ercole, Jolenta asserts that she is pregnant by Contarino. Romelio argues that scandal can be avoided by affirming that a precontract between Jolenta and Ercole existed "By the same words usde in the forme of mariage" (3.3.55). Jolenta counters by asserting that a "Precontract shall justifie" (71) her (false) pregnancy. In act 1 Romelio is able, with his mother Leonora's support, to bully Jolenta. In act 3 he is obliged to seek her complicity in his plans, and the strength of her position is emphasized by the way she turns Romelio's words against him.

Another parallel demonstrating Romelio's new vulnerability is pointed up by the use of "picture" in its metaphorical and actual senses. In act 1 Leonora's failure to recognize that by "picture" Contarino means her daughter intensifies her support for Romelio's efforts to force Jolenta to marry Ercole. In 3.3, however, an actual picture features crucially as Leonora plans to disgrace and disinherit her son. Having called for "the picture / Hangs in my inner closet" (3.3.379–80), which the donor bade her "looke upon" "when I was vext" (388–89), she finds "It has furnisht me with mischiefe" (391). And that Leonora is now initiating action rather than reacting to the initiatives of others is another indicator of a turning point in the play. "Here begines / My part i'th play," she comments at 3.3.392–93, and in a sense this is true. Romelio dominates the first half of *The Devil's Law-Case,* but in the second, dominated by Leonora, he becomes the victim.[26]

Yet another parallel, marking the beginning of the second movement in *The Devil's Law-Case,* remains to be noted. In act 1 Contarino is the object of Jolenta's affections, and Ercole is rebuffed, but in 3.3 the situation is reversed when Jolenta says, "Why, I protest / I now affect the Lord *Ercoles* memory, / Better then the others" (3.3.167–69). That the grounds for rejecting Contarino are false does not reduce the significance of this switch of affections, which is proleptic both of the final (and appropriate) pairing of Jolenta and Ercole and, ironically, of that of Leonora and Contarino.

Another indication of the two-part structure of *The Devil's Law-Case* is the fact that several major actions are concluded by act 3. Save in the play's final moments, for instance, Jolenta and Contarino do not meet again after 1.2, nor she and Ercole, while the duel in 2.2 ends the conflict between Ercole and Contarino, and the stabbing in 3.2 Romelio's vengeful pursuit of Contarino. But Webster also uses the first half of the play to prepare the ground for actions largely confined to the second, introducing Ariosto and Crispiano in 2.1, the Capuchin in 2.3 and the Surgeons in 3.2. He also echoes in the second half actions which have taken place in the first, as with the duels of 2.2. and 5.4, where the erstwhile opponents, Contarino and Ercole, become allies, and as with Ariosto, urging Romelio to patience in 2.3 and to anger in 4.2. Likewise, we find Romelio in meditation in both 2.3 and 5.4.

The subplot of *The Devil's Law-Case,* concerning the lawyer, Crispiano, and his scapegrace son, Julio, serves the customary Jacobean purpose of providing comparisons and parallels with the main action. But it also fits the two-movement structure of the play once it is recognized that the key figure in the subplot is not Julio but Crispiano. For where he is concerned, there is a decided shift in act 3 akin to that involving Leonora in the main action. In 2.1 he explains his merchant's disguise as a means of observing his son's profligacy and in 3.1 justifies it as cover for surveillance of Romelio's illegal gold trading. This plot strand, however, is dropped, and Crispiano's real role in the second half of the play is revealed in his vow to "curbe the insolencies / Of . . . women" (3.1.29–30), this presumably being the "other businesse of greater consequence" referred to gnomically at 2.1.10–11.

Clearly, *The Devil's Law-Case* is constructed according to the same principles as *The White Devil* and *The Duchess of Malfi.* But it is also clear that while Webster employed the two-movement structure in all three plays, he did so with increasing freedom. In *The White Devil* the pattern of repetitions, parallels, and echoes is exceptionally rigorous and complete. It is also, at times, highly oblique, as the bafflement of the Red Bull audience and many twentieth-century critics attests. In *The Duchess of Malfi* and *The Devil's Law-Case* the pattern is less thoroughgoing, but present nonetheless. Recognizing its presence in all three plays not only provides a sense of artistic unity and progression, but also supplies important evidence in rebuttal of the charges so often laid: that John Webster had no skill—or no interest—in dramatic structures. The evidence, I suggest, is precisely to the contrary.

Notes

1. Neil Carson, "John Webster: the Apprentice Years," in G. R. Hibbard, ed., *The Elizabethan Theatre VI* (Hamden: Archon Press, 1978), 76.
2. Ian Jack, "The Case of John Webster," *Scrutiny* 16 (March 1949): 43.

3. L. G. Salingar, "Tourneur and the Tragedy of Revenge," in Boris Ford, ed., *A Guide to English Literature 2: The Age of Shakespeare* (Harmondsworth: Penguin, 1955), 349.

4. John Russell Brown, ed., *The White Devil,* Revels Plays Series (London: Methuen, 1960), xliv.

5. J. R. Mulryne, ed., *The White Devil,* Regents Renaissance Drama Series (Lincoln: Univ. of Nebraska Press, 1969), xix.

6. Roma Gill, "'Quaintly Done': A Reading of *The White Devil,*" *Essays and Studies* 19 (1966): 42.

7. Charles R. Forker, *Skull Beneath the Skin: The Achievement of John Webster* (Carbondale: Southern Illinois Univ. Press, 1986), 380.

8. Gunnar Boklund, "*The Devil's Law-Case*—An End or a Beginning?" in Brian Morris, ed., *John Webster* (London: Ernest Benn, 1970), 118.

9. Rowland Wymer, *Webster and Ford* (New York: St. Martin's Press, 1995), 75.

10. William Archer, *The Old Drama and the New* (London: Heinemann, 1923), 55.

11. Jacqueline Pearson, *Tragedy and Tragicomedy in the Plays of John Webster* (Manchester: Univ. of Manchester Press, 1980), 2.

12. Peter B. Murray, *A Study of John Webster* (Philadelphia: Univ. of Pennsylvania Press, 1964), 187.

13. For a discussion of the failure of *The White Devil* at the Red Bull, see Alexander Leggatt, *Jacobean Public Theatre* (London: Routledge, 1992), 123–29.

14. Emrys Jones, *Scenic Form in Shakespeare* (Oxford: Clarendon Press, 1971), 81.

15. Pearson, *Tragedy and Tragicomedy,* 57. Pearson cites some of the parallels discussed here, but to a different purpose, while Christina Luckij, who in *A Winter's Snake: Dramatic Form in the Plays of John Webster* (Athens: Univ. of Georgia Press, 1989) sets out to "explore Webster's use of repetition to relate the passages and scenes of his plays through parallel, contrast, intensification, recapitulation, and reversal" (p. xxv), uses in the main different examples and draws different conclusions.

16. Susan H. McLeod, *Dramatic Imagery in the Plays of John Webster* (Salzburg: Institut für Englische Sprache und Literatur, Universität Salzburg, 1977), 33.

17. *The White Devil, The Duchess of Malfi* and *The Devil's Law-Case* are cited from volume 1, David Gunby, David Carnegie, and Anthony Hammond, eds., and 2, Gunby, Carnegie, and MacDonald P. Jackson, eds., *The Works of John Webster* (Cambridge: Cambridge Univ. Press, 1995, 2003).

18. Peter Thomson, "Webster and the Actor'" in Morris, ed., *John Webster,* 42. For a detailed rebuttal of Thomson's argument see David Gunby and David Carnegie, "Bit Parts in Webster: The Ambassadors in *The White Devil,*" in Greg Waite et al., eds., *World and Stage: Essays for Colin Gibson,* Otago Studies in English 6 (Dunedin: Department of English, Univ. of Otago, 1998), 183–96.

19. Lee Bliss, *The World's Perspective: John Webster and the Jacobean Drama* (Brighton: Harvester Press, 1983), 122.

20. Pearson, *Tragedy and Tragicomedy,* 57.

21. In R. V. Holdsworth, ed., "*The White Devil*" *and* "*The Duchess of Malfi*"*: A Casebook* (London: Macmillan, 1975), 31.

22. Arthur C. Kirsch, *Jacobean Dramatic Perspectives* (Charlottesville: Univ. Press of Virginia, 1972), 106.

23. John Russell Brown, ed., *The Duchess of Malfi,* Revels Plays Series (London: Methuen, 1964), xxiii. Brown does not, however, note the emphasis on these gaps, commenting, without controversion, that "Webster has been particularly criticized for giving only a slight indication in the text of the several years that pass between Acts II and III." It seems almost certain that, as performed at Blackfriars by the King's Men in 1614, *The Duchess of Malfi* would have had act breaks. See Gary Taylor, "The Structure of Perfor-

mance: Act-Intervals in the London Theatres, 1576–1642," in Gary Taylor and John Jowett, *Shakespeare Reshaped, 1606–1623* (Oxford: Clarendon Press, 1993), 3–50. Taylor notes that "no play known to have been written for the King's Men after spring 1608 is undivided" (p. 30). Interestingly, the Queen's Men adopted act breaks later, c. 1614, *The White Devil* showing no evidence of them.

24. Pearson, *Tragedy and Tragicomedy,* 60.

25. Inga-Stina Ekeblad, "The Impure Art of John Webster," *Review of English Studies,* n.s. 9 (August 1958), 253–67.

26. It might be noted in this connection that each of the two movements in *The Devil's Law-Case* is given over to one of the two social ills, dueling and ungovernable women, with which the play concerns itself.

Mutinous Soldiers and Shouts [Within]: Stage Directions and Early Modern Dramaturgy

David Carnegie

MACDONALD P. JACKSON SAYS, IN HIS TEXTUAL INTRODUCTION TO THE Cambridge Webster edition of *Appius and Virginia,* that "the main contribution of the [newly edited] text lies in its clarification of the characters' comings and goings and their interactions on stage."[1] This typically modest statement belies both the sheer extent of the work undertaken and the significant new approaches developed in that work. "Clarification of the characters' comings and goings" demands rigorous attention to stage directions: in particular, determining where the directions in the original early modern printed texts are deficient. Of course all editors of critical editions, whether old-spelling like the Cambridge Webster or modernized like the Oxford Middleton (in which Mac Jackson has also had a significant hand), have the job of considering carefully the stage directions, speech prefixes, and other matter that determines the "interactions on stage" of the actors. But, as our late co-editor Antony Hammond has pointed out, "there has been remarkably little *analytical* discussion of stage-directions, as distinct from pragmatic commentary on where editors have gone wrong."[2]

This essay aims to provide "pragmatic commentary" on some issues in the editing of *Appius and Virginia,* and at the same time to enlarge on some aspects essential to the "*analytical* discussion." The first section, "Mutinous Soldiers," deals with the need for closer attention than has usually been paid in the past to the relationship between entry and exit directions on the one hand and speech prefixes on the other. The editorial solution to the particular problem in *Appius and Virginia* requires a combination of theatrical and historical criticism with the more purely textual.

Growing out of this conjunction of critical approaches, the second section, "Shouts [within]," discusses a previously unconsidered category of stage directions. Close analysis of these directions reveals not only a problem and its solution in *Appius and Virginia* where previous textual and literary criticism has seen nothing amiss, but also contributes to our understanding of the "presentational logic" that is a vital strand in our editorial, critical, and theatrical approaches to early modern dramaturgy.[3]

Mutinous Soldiers

"*Enter the first mutinous Souldier in haste*" reads the quarto stage direction at 4.2.59.1 of Webster and Heywood's Roman tragedy *Appius and Virginia* (1654; probably first performed c. 1625–27).[4] This stage direction forms part of a nexus of entry directions and speech prefixes in the scene that for a textual editor, critic, or actor raise a number of crucial questions. The directions concerned are as follows: at the start of the scene the quarto entry direction reads "*Enter two Souldiers,*" and they are identified in speech prefixes as "1" and "2." At 4.2.32 we have "*Enter Minutius with his souldiers . . .*", followed at line 59 by the "*Enter the first mutinous Souldier in haste*" direction. Immediately upon his entry he speaks, with the speech prefix "1 *Sould,*" to announce that their captain, Virginius, is arriving. Subsequently "2 *Sold*" also speaks (at line 137 and later), and eventually "*Omnes*" (line 156).

For the casual reader these quarto stage directions may be all that is needed: two starving soldiers enter at the start of the scene with comic grumbles about lice, maggots, and a dead cat as a culinary opportunity; they see the general, Minutius, entering with more soldiers, and decide to "give him place" (4.2.33); Minutius, deeply perturbed, reads a letter from the tyrannous Appius in Rome instructing him to arrest the upright old captain, Virginius; then another soldier bursts on the scene to announce the imminent arrival of Virginius himself with a great mass of distracted and threatening citizenry.

For the reader, the text as it stands may be sufficient. But for a textual editor, critic, or actor the following questions arise: who is "*the first mutinous Souldier*" who is then identified in speech prefixes as "1 *Sould*"? Is he one of the "*two Souldiers,*" identified in speech prefixes simply as "1" and "2", who enter at the start of this scene and grumble about the food until line 35? A similar question attaches to "2 *Sold*" who speaks after the "*first mutinous Souldier.*" Is he the "2" identified at the start of the scene? If the answer to either of these questions is affirmative, that poses further uncertainties about both: given that there is no exit direction in quarto for "1" and "2" (the two comic soldiers from the start of the scene), but that "*first mutinous Souldier*" has an entry direction at 4.2.59, how did he get offstage in order to reenter here, and did "2" accompany him in order to become the "2 *Sold*" of line 137?

Further, who are the soldiers who enter with Minutius? How many are there? And what is the relationship of these various soldiers to the "*six Souldiers*" who enter in mutiny at the start of 2.2, and are then brought back to obedience by Virginius? The answers to these questions must be specific and detailed in order to offer a clear picture of what is expected to happen on stage, and also, as we shall see, because they have implications for other decisions about stage directions elsewhere in the play. These answers will also have a more general bearing on a significant thematic issue: whether "*mutinous*" is a concept specific to the soldier so described at the time, or whether the playwrights regarded all the soldiers, throughout the play, as, collectively and generically, mutinous soldiers.

Mac Jackson, David Gunby, and I were faced with these questions in our joint editing of *Appius and Virginia* for the second volume of the Cambridge *Works of John Webster.* We were not, however, the first editors to confront at least some of these questions. Dilke in 1815 provided an "*Exeunt*" after line 35 for "1" and "2," the "*two Souldiers*" who occupy the first thirty-five lines of the scene, a decision that has been followed by all subsequent editors of the play.[5] This decision is presumably based on an apparently common sense assumption that "*the first mutinous Souldier*/1 *Sould*" who enters at 4.2.59 can be the "1" from earlier in the scene, as long as he leaves after line 35 and thereby becomes available to reenter now with his urgent news heralding the arrival of Virginius. Supplying an "*Exeunt*" after line 35 does not, however, solve the problem of "2 *Sold,*" since neither quarto nor any subsequent editor has provided him with an explicit entry direction. Is he, therefore, a new "second soldier" who entered with Minutius's soldiers as 1 and 2 departed? If so, what are the implications for the actors (and the bookholder/prompter) of having two "2"s? Or is he the original "2," in which case perhaps he returned with "*the first mutinous Souldier,*" and therefore needs an entry direction provided? Or is there another explanation?

Our editorial search for an explanation started with two working hypotheses: one theatrical and one critical/historical. The theatrical hypothesis was that the "*six Souldiers*" of 2.2, who actually do mutiny, were likely to be parts for the six hired men who would, in addition to doubling other parts, continue to play all the required soldiers for the rest of the play. Therefore all the soldiers—"1" and "2" at the start of 4.2, Minutius's soldiers, "*the first mutinous Souldier*/1 *Sould,*" and "2 *Sold*" of 4.2.137—would need to be drawn from the same pool of six men. Recent studies of casting and doubling, particularly those of David Bradley and T. J. King, have confirmed an emerging consensus that the norm on the London stage in the 1620s was about ten principal actors taking major male roles (some of the supporting roles doubled), and about six hired men taking more heavily doubled minor male roles such as servants, guards, citizens, and soldiers.[6]

In order to test our working hypothesis about the hired men playing soldiers, however, we needed to apply the general pattern of professional theater casting to the specific play in question. Most of *Appius and Virginia* would be easily accommodated by these numbers, with the usual addition of boys to play the women's roles. But two scenes in particular would create pressure on such resources. The first of these is 2.2, which includes all six soldiers and the minor role of Lieutenant, and is immediately followed by the entry at the start of 2.3 of two petitioners in what look like two more hired men's roles. Much more difficult is the transition at the end of 4.1, the big trial scene with seventeen adult male actors required onstage, into 4.2, with our two soldiers "1" and "2." The trial scene, juxtaposed thus to the requirements of 4.2, is what Bradley usefully calls a "limiting scene," a scene that puts most demands on the company, and therefore allows us to judge the minimum acting resources needed for presenting the play.[7] Nineteen actors may therefore be the minimum needed: seventeen in 4.1 (including "*six Senators*" and at least two "*Lictors,*" identified at 4.1. 48, but no soldiers), and then immediately two more at the start of 4.2 to play the two soldiers.[8]

It is unusual, though, for experienced professional playwrights to write more parts than there are actors, so it may be that this is one of those occasional instances in which a decision was made to bring in extra mute actors (e.g., gatherers, tire-men, or boys) for this scene alone.[9] That would explain the otherwise surprising situation that no more than two of the "*six Senators*" could be played by the usual group of six hired men (who almost certainly play the "*six Souldiers*" of 2.2), since two of those men are needed as soldiers for the start of 4.2, and two more as lictors in 4.1. Whether or not extras were brought in for 4.1, however, it seems clear that pressure on the company's acting resources would be such that any more than the original six soldiers (and their costumes) from 2.2 would be unlikely to appear in 4.2. Such was our theatrical hypothesis.

The critical/historical hypothesis was that, since our first view of the soldiers is the mutiny scene of 2.2, and we next meet two of them grumbling in 4.2, the playwrights might well have regarded all these Roman soldiers (living in appalling conditions, reminiscent of the English expeditionary force, pressed in support of the Elector Palatine, that starved and for the most part died under Count Mansfeld in 1624 and 1625)[10] as generically and essentially "*mutinous.*"

Following from these two hypotheses, it seemed most likely that "1" and "2" from the start of 4.2 would be the same characters (and actors) as "1" and "2" from 2.2, and as "*the first mutinous Souldier*/1 *Sould*" who enters at 4.2.59 and "2 *Sold*" of 4.2.137. We could not achieve this apparently straightforward solution, however, by following the quarto, which has left "1" still on stage when "*the first mutinous Souldier*" enters at 4.2.59; nor by following Dilke and subsequent editors, who take "2" off along with "1" after 4.2.35, and never bring him back on.

Our solution, after extensive debate, and over a table eventually peopled with a small army of coffee mugs, whiteout bottles, and paperclip trays representing all possible combinations of soldiers, was to realise that while an exit must be provided for "1" after 4.2.35 so that he can reenter at 4.2.59, it might be possible for "2" to remain on stage. He could then join the rest of the group of soldiers (the other four hired men who were soldiers in 2.2) who enter with Minutius just prior to the exit of "1." With this possibility in mind, we reexamined the dialogue between the two men, and noticed that two examples of what we had taken to be simply satiric comment on the conditions for soldiers might actually support an anticipated exit by "1" alone. At 4.2.25 "1" says he "must have some strong water"—an opportunity for a pun on "strong water" as (1) "spirits" and (2) water that is "strong smelling, rank"—from a stinking ditch nearby. Similarly, at 4.2.29–30 he instructs his mate to ensure that the dead cat "that lyes a distance off | Be flead for supper." While this is again a joke, on the incongruity of flaying a cat rather than a larger and more edible beast, it is possible that both jokes have an element of seriousness, and that "1" is in fact departing from "2" for a short period to get a drink of one kind or another. Equally, when they say, on seeing Minutius arrive, that they'll "give him place", there is no requirement for an exit in order to "get out of his way" (see *OED,* "place," 23).

Thus we decided the matter, and we believe we have solved everything that was previously a problem. But the implications are more significant for the approach taken than for the solution. First, we took the time to think of the instructions to individual actors that are both explicit and implied by stage directions, and, equally, by the absence of directions. Then, having decided that the scene really was unplayable if we followed the quarto's stage directions strictly, we had to resolve to add one or more directions to allow the scene to happen. We had to determine what was most likely to have occurred within a Jacobean/Caroline acting company. Was regarding the soldiers *en bloc* as mutinous a view we might reasonably suppose Webster and Heywood to have held? And having come to a decision on "the characters' comings and goings," we had to decide on what textual intervention was justified. In this case, it was to depart from previous editorial tradition, and to emend the text by adding a necessary exit for a single actor only.

This small emendation was more significant than it may appear. Part of the textual justification for emendation was the knowledge that there are other places in the text where stage directions are inadequate. As Mac Jackson says, "the main contribution of the present text lies in its clarification of the characters' comings and goings and their interactions on stage." An inadequacy in a certain category of textual material, in this case missing entries and exits, therefore demanded reinvestigation of the text with an eye to dealing with any other such cases that we might previously have overlooked. This turned out to be a necessary and rewarding second look.

Shouts [within]

The end of 2.2 was of particular interest. 2.2 is Bradley's second "limiting scene," a scene in which the "*six Souldiers*" use up all the hired men, creating an immediate problem of who plays the two petitioners who appear at the start of 2.3, and a possible problem of at least two more soldiers needing to change costume in a short space of time in order to appear as lictors at 2.3.30.[11] If getting those six hired men off the stage sooner solves the casting problem, as it does, why didn't Webster and Heywood—experienced professional writers both—do that? Given the absence of a necessary exit direction in 4.2, discussed above, might there be another missing exit direction for the "*six Souldiers*"?

The "*six Souldiers*" enter at the start of 2.2 complaining that while Rome under Appius is surfeiting they, denied food, pay, and clothing, are left to sleep in the open and die of famine and disease. They determine to mutiny. Their general, Minutius, is not only unable to quell this mutiny, but is in effect taken captive while the soldier denominated as "1" in the speech prefixes relates "the grievances / Of the whole Regiment" (2.2.15–16). The soldiers frankly disbelieve Minutius's statement that their captain, Virginius, is imminently expected back from Rome with fresh supplies which he has gone to beg of Appius, and utter lurid threats about what they will do if Virginius ever returns. The sequel is impressive, though with comic overtones. Virginius enters into the midst of the threatening circle of pikes, and faces down the soldiers one by one. They abjectly swear eternal loyalty to him. His success in bringing them under control is visually evident when they immediately obey his order to "Advance your pikes" (2.2.112), a drill movement whose execution brings the threatening tips away from his chest and up to vertical. Then, in disgust, Virginius orders them to lay down their pikes and cashiers them on the spot as cowards. Only sixty lines of desperate pleading by Minutius and the soldiers brings Virginius to relent and sardonically agree to accept them under his leadership again. His final speech to the soldiers, in response to them begging for "Your pardon noble Captaine" (2.2.185), concludes with a rhyming couplet:

> Take up your armes and use them, doe, I pray,
> Ere long youle take your legs to run away.
>
> (2.2.190–91)

This is followed, to the end of the scene, by about twenty-five more lines in which Virginius responds to questions from Minutius by pretending that he was generously and respectfully received in Rome by Appius and the senate. The audience, however, has already witnessed in 1.3 what really happened: Appius using him with gross disrespect, and withholding supplies from the army as a deliberate ploy to undermine Virginius so that he, Appius, may seduce Virginius's beautiful but virtuous daughter Virginia. At one point in his misleading reply to Minutius, Virginius announces that "There's promis'd the souldier / Besides their corne a bounteous donative" (2.2.199–200; a "donative" was an occasional bounty paid by the Roman state to the army). In the right margin (2.2.200) appears the stage direction

"*A shout,*" and at the end of the scene, about fifteen lines on, is printed a general "*Exeunt.*"

The question exercising us was whether or not an exit for the soldiers earlier than the "*Exeunt*" at the end of the scene might be intended. At first glance the evidence was mixed. In favor of an earlier exit was the rhymed couplet quoted above with which Virginius in effect both takes them back and dismisses them. The scathing reference to their use of their legs would be typically double-edged if delivered as the soldiers are leaving. It should also be noted that although "Take up your arms" does not sound like a direct order, "Take up your pike" was a drill movement, and the soldiers would need to pick up the pikes they were previously ordered to "lay down" at 2.2.118 (another drill movement). It is an appropriate and ideal time for them to leave. Furthermore, the whole of the rest of the scene is between Minutius and Virginius, and the political dangers around the latter, with his stoic *romanitas,* are much more intensely demonstrated if he decides that not even his general, Minutius, should be allowed to hear how despicably Appius has behaved. In other words, the last twenty-five lines of the scene are more dramatically effective if private between the two men, with the soldiers gone. And textually, the scene already has some elements of confusion in its stage directions: a "Lieutenant" is called for at 2.2.93, but quarto provides no entry for him (a much rarer problem than the lack of an exit).[12] Furthermore, quarto's speech prefix "*Val.*" for the Lieutenant is dramatically unlikely, since Valerius is everywhere else in the play part of the civilian party of Rome, not the military party of the camp. Overall, then, an early exit for the soldiers appears dramatically effective, textually defensible and theatrically desirable.

On the other hand, the "*shout*" at 2.2.200 with which the news of the "donative" is greeted seems to render all the other arguments—critical, textual, and theatrical—irrelevant, for this stage direction apparently requires the soldiers on stage to hear the news about the donative, and to cheer that news. How could they react to the news if they were not on stage to hear it? It would appear to defy logic.

What seems at first, however, a decisive textual and theatrical indication that the soldiers stay on stage turns out to be the reverse. We decided on a more rigorous investigation of the theatrical context of shouts in the drama of the period. This led us eventually to a previously unconsidered category of stage directions. And, on the way to this discovery, the progress of our editorial deliberations is significant for the light it sheds on the uses of two research resources only recently available.

The first resource we turned to was Alan C. Dessen and Leslie Thomson's *Dictionary of Stage Directions.*[13] Reference to the entry for "shout" results in the information that "the roughly 130 examples almost always signal a ***sound*** from ***within.***" This in itself was surprising. It was not enough to justify us rejecting the possibility that our "*shout*" was one of the small category that occur on stage rather than within, but it was enough to encourage further investigation. The problem appeared to be one of logic: the soldiers need to hear the information if they are to cheer in reaction to it. Therefore we needed to examine closely our assumptions about that logic, and seek further evidence of the stagecraft of the period, if we were to resolve the apparent contradictions in our evidence.

Hence our resort to the second research resource mentioned above, the search capabilities of the "English Drama" section of the Chadwyck-Healey electronic database Literature Online (LION). As Mac Jackson, who was himself on the Advisory Board for Lion, has pointed out, "at the click of a mouse one can obtain a list of the number of instances of a particular word, phrase, or collocation within each of the [663] plays" of the period.[14] Mac and I were, in our editing of *Appius and Virginia,* able to enter a search for occurrences of "shout" (under its various spellings and forms) as a stage direction. What follows in this paper is an expansion of that work.

A search of "LION" for "shout" and its variants throws up over one hundred plays containing more than 150 shouts. (The counts are given as approximate figures because of ambiguities about whether to include, e.g., court masques, and uncertainties of some dating.) Stage directions for shouts may be divided into three main categories for our current purposes: those clearly onstage; those offstage for which entirely logical explanations are offered in the dialogue or action; and those offstage in situations apparently counter to simple logic.

1. A small number of directions are for onstage shouts, with about ten unambiguous examples, such as the "*Shout*" by the onstage spectators when Charles is thrown in the wrestling match in *As You Like It* (1.2.215), or the response in *Coriolanus* of Caius Martius' troops: "*They all shout and wave their swords, take him up in their arms, and cast up their caps*" (1.6.75.1–75.2).[15] There are a few other examples in which it is impossible to be sure whether the shouts are offstage or on, but that uncertainty does not affect the current discussion.

2. The vast majority of directions are, as Dessen and Thomson indicate, for offstage shouts. And in most cases playwrights provide what we might call realistic motivation: either dialogue to explain the reason for the shouts, or a dramatic situation in which the shouts are instantly explicable. For instance, a shout frequently heralds the entry of a character who immediately provides both explanation of the shout and advance warning to those on stage of an imminent entry. *Appius and Virginia* provides just such a typical example in the final scene of the play:

A shout.

Minutius. He speaks but Law and Justice.
Make good the streets, with your best men at arms:

> *Valerius* and *Horatio,* know the reason
> Of this loud uproar, and confused noise. [*Exeunt Valerius and Horatio.*]
> Although my heart be melting at the fall
> Of men in place and Office, we'l be just
> To punish murdrous Acts, and censure Lust.
> *Enter* VALERIUS *and* HORATIO.
> *Valerius.* *Icilius,* worthy Lord, bears through the street
> The body of *Virginia* towards this prison;
> Which when it was discovered to the people,
> Mov'd such a mournful clamour, that their cryes
> Pierc'd heaven, and forc'd tears from their sorrowing eyes.
> *Enter* ICILIUS *with the body of* VIRGINIA.
> (5.3.74–86.1)

Another common occurrence of shouts is as part of the noise of offstage battle, itself sufficient realistic motivation for them, as in Chapman's *The Revenge of Bussy D'Ambois: "Shouts within. Alarum still, and Chambers shot off. Then enter Aumall."* (4.1.10.1–10.2).[16]

3. The final category—the one that interested us—is of a small number of directions for shouts that are offstage, but appear to lack any realistic motivation. These seem to operate on a different set of dramaturgical principles. Six plays contain such directions, and they deserve detailed consideration.

The first is Heywood's *The Iron Age, Part 1,* in which stage directions for offstage shouts appear twice. In act 5 a great debate takes place between Ajax and Ulysses in front of the rest of the Greek princes over who is entitled to the dead Achilles' armor. Ajax finishes his speech thus:

> To conclude,
> Go beare these Armes for which we two contend
> Into the mid-ranks of our enemies,
> And bid vs fetch them thence, and he to weare them
> By whom this royall Armour can be wonne,
> I had rather fight then talke, so I haue done.
>
> *A loud shout within crying Aiax, Aiax:* (5.115–120.1)[17]

Ulysses' speech in reply also results in shouting: "*A shout within Vlisses, Vlisses.*" (5.208.1). This is immediately followed by Agamemnon's verdict:

> Such is the clamour of the multitude,
> And such *Ulisses* are your great deserts
> That those rich Armes are thine, the prize inioy.
> (5.209–11)

That "the multitude" is the Greek soldiers is confirmed by two comments during the debate. Diomed says at 5.83–84, during Ajax's speech, that

"*Aiax* preuailes much with the multitude, / The generall murmur doth accord with him" (though there is no indication of any such murmur on stage); and Menelaus parallels this comment at 5.180–82 as the debate swings the other way:

> Now sure the prise will to *Vlisses* fall,
> The murmuring souldiers mutter his deserts,
> Preferring him fore *Aiax:*

The two shouts within, therefore, are from Greek soldiers not present at the debate, but portrayed as reacting to its progress. The question is whether they are in any realistic sense conceived as being within earshot of the debate. The danger of this kind of realist dramatic logic—of hypothesizing, for instance, that the Greek soldiers are to be imagined as all crowded round the doorway of the generals' tent, just out of sight, and that Ajax and Ulysses both raise their voices enough for us to accept that the soldiers outside ("*within*" in theatrical terms) would be able to hear—is that we fall into the trap of what Alan Dessen has usefully identified as the "generic expectations supplied by the devotee of Agatha Christie . . . the logic of naturalism."[18] Is it not more likely that these shouts are examples of Dessen's "presentational logic": that they are nonmotivated amplifications of the moment, serving the needs of a nonrealist dramaturgy. They enlarge the emotion of the immediate situation in the way more akin to the music of opera than the causality of Ibsen.

The second sample play, *The Golden Age,* is also by Heywood. At the beginning of a new scene in act 1, Saturn enters "*with wedges of gold and siluer, models of ships, and buildings, bow and arrowes, &c. His Lords with him*" (1.210.1).[19] He proceeds to explain to his amazed courtiers that he is providing them with the arts of building, agriculture, metallurgy, navigation, and archery. Then, hearing "*A lowd shout within,*" he demands "What meanes this acclamation?"[20] The First Lord replies:

> Tis thy people
> Deuinest *Saturne* furnisht with these vses,
> (More then the Gods haue lent them) by thy meanes.
> Proclaime to thee a lasting deity.
> And would haue *Saturne* honoured as a God.
>
> (1.236–40)

Again, realist logic does not apply: Saturn has just completed telling his courtiers for the first time about wonderful new gifts for mankind, and before he can draw breath he is interrupted by an offstage shout indicating that not only have the people now been "furnisht with these vses," but have also gathered to proclaim his deity. Quick work indeed, if one were imposing the logic of naturalism. In fact, realism is even further undercut by the fact that in the previous scene the Clown already knows about these inventions of Saturn's, and tells the Nurse about them, thereby preparing us for what we are about to see when Saturn enters with his models of them all.

The third example is from Chapman's *The Tragedie of Chabot Admirall of France.* Again, a shout is heard from, in dramatic terms, outside the room where the trial of the Admiral takes place:

> *No*[*tary*]. We by his sacred Majestie appointed Judges, upon due triall, and examination of *Philip Chabot* Admirall of *France* declare him guiltie of high treasons, etc.
> *Cha*[*ncellor*]. Now Captaine of the guard,
> Secure his person, till the King signifie
> His pleasure for his death. This day is happy
> To *France,* thus reskued from the vile devourer.
>
> *A shoute within.*
>
> Harke how the votes applaud their blest deliverance!
>
> (3.2.261–69)

As in the previous examples, this "*shoute within*" appears to be an amplification of the moment: a kind of simultaneous or compressed chronology (in that the people—"the votes"—here know immediately what in reality they would know only in the future). The shout is not the result of a chain of causation.

The fourth play, also by Chapman, is *Caesar and Pompey,* in which Caesar announces his intended battle dispositions to Anthony:

> [*Caes.*] . . . Hang out of my tent
> My Crimsine coat of armes, to giue my souldiers
> That euer-sure signe of resolu'd-for fight.
> *Crass.* These hands shall giue that signe to all their longings. *Exit. Crass.*
> *Caes.* [*To Anthony.*] My Lord, my army, I thinke best to order
> In three full Squadrons: of which let me pray
> Your selfe would take on you the left wings charge;
> My selfe will lead the right wing, and my place
> Of fight elect in my tenth legion:
> My battell by *Domitius Calvinus*
> Shall take direction.
>
> *The Cote of Armes is hung out, and the Souldiers shoute within.*
>
> *Ant.* Heark, your souldiers shoute
> For ioy to see your bloody Cote of Armes
> Assure their fight this morning.
>
> (3.2.97–109)

Whereas previous examples have been of shouts triggered by a speech or an announcement, in this case the signal is visual rather than verbal. Nevertheless, the dramaturgical principle is the same: a stimulus onstage is received offstage in a manner that serves presentational logic rather than naturalist logic. The soldiers are perhaps regarded as imaginatively able to see the coat of arms, even though in theatrical terms they cannot.

The fifth play is D'Avenant's *The Unfortunate Lovers,* where late in act 1 the general Altophil, after a discussion with his supporters, determines not to revolt, but to accompany his unjustly shamed mistress Arthiopa to the church to marry her. He demands of his followers:

> [*Altoph.*] . . . you that
> Affect your Generall, follow, and afford
> Me streight your shouts of joy, not wealth,
> Wisdome nor honour, is to me above
> *(Severall shouts are heard within.*
>
> The fame and resolution of my Love.—
> *Exeunt omne, and streight several shouts etc.*
> (1.419–23.1)[21]

The "*shouts*" after the exeunt can clearly be sourced, if realist causation be needed, to Altophil's request that his followers afford him their "shouts of joy." However, the "*Severall shouts*" that interrupt his final couplet occur before his onstage followers have responded, and before anyone offstage could realistically have heard the request. As in the example from *Chabot,* therefore, we have a direction that either anticipates what is about to occur, or is a nonrealist amplification of the resonance of the moment.

The sixth and final play is the anonymous *The Costlie Whore* (1633). In act 3, while the Duke is in presence with his courtiers, an argument erupts over his intention to place a courtesan on the throne as his consort. His son Frederick and other courtiers announce that they will pull her down or forswear their allegiance:

> *Fred.*
> Will you dismisse this Strumpet to the stewes,
> Or our allegance in this act refuse.
> *Duke.*
> Doe what you dare, the election still shall stand.
> *Fred.*
> Woe and destruction then must rule the land.
> Come Lord *Rinaldo,* valiant *Alberto* come,
> We haue friends enough to grace a warlike Drum.
> *A shout within.*
> Hearke how the Commons doe applaud our cause,

Lascivious Duke, farewell father, oh vilde,
Where Queanes are mothers, *Fredericke* is no child.
Exeunt.

(3.144–52.1)[22]

Like all the other examples, the "*shout within*" follows so hard on the heels of the three lines in which Frederick announces his intention to revolt that no naturalistic explanation of how "the Commons" could react so quickly is plausible. Rather, we have again a presentational dramaturgy that compresses cause and effect into a nonrealist amplification of the immediate dramatic moment.

The examples in these six plays of stage directions for offstage shouts are not identical in their implications. For instance, the visual signal of the coat of arms hung out in *Caesar and Pompey* may be linked more to the conception of an expansive imaginative locale within the neutral architecture of the English Renaissance playhouse stage than to the logic of narrative event that is raised by the plays with verbal signals. In several cases it is just possible, by invoking the detective-story logic that Dessen derides, to posit vast crowds eavesdropping at an imaginary doorway in order to digest and broadcast the news almost before the speaker has finished a sentence.

The overwhelming evidence, however, is that a consistent and significant use of shouts within occurs as part of a "presentational logic" in which the amplification of the moment takes dramaturgical precedence over "the logic of naturalism." For this sense of a "dramaturgy of the moment" one might compare the Folio entry direction for *Twelfth Night* at 2.2.0.1: "*Enter Viola and Maluolio, at seuerall doores.*"[23] Nineteenth-century editions of Shakespeare, and countless more recent stage, film, and television presentations, have followed naturalist logic by altering the direction to "*Enter Viola, Malvolio following,*" on the basis that the plot requires Malvolio to set out in pursuit of Viola after she has already left Olivia. What this misses, of course, is the dramaturgy of a confrontational moment; the spatial logic of an onstage meeting is more important than spatial logic of a merely fictional environmental reality. Similarly, offstage shouts may evidently be designed, counter to realist expectations, to reinforce the dramaturgy of the moment.

The *Appius and Virginia* example that set us off on this investigation appears to fit precisely into this category of stage directions. Despite the critical, textual, and theatrical arguments in favor of providing an early exit for the soldiers, our first reaction was to retain them on stage because commonsense logic seemed to require them to hear the news of the donative. It is now clear, however, on the basis of comparison with other plays of the period, that the direction for "*A shout*" at 2.2.200 is overwhelmingly likely to be a call for "*A shout* [*within*]."

With a new "*Exeunt*" provided for the soldiers immediately following Virginius's dismissal of them, and the "*shout*" now "[*within*]," the scene has a significantly different emotional structure. Virginius enters into the midst of the mutiny, quells it, cashiers the soldiers, and is eventually persuaded to take them back into service. In doing so he has demonstrated his courage and leadership, and also his adherence to the traditional Roman ideals of service, sacrifice, and loyalty. He ultimately allows his tolerant understanding of his troops to show through, though this is largely masked by his sardonic dismissal of them. Once they have gone Minutius inquires "How for your owne particular?" (2.2.202). Virginius's lying response, in which he falsely tells his general how well he was received by Appius, is of a piece with his earlier *romanitas*. The loyalty of Virginius to Rome (as opposed to Appius) is reason to conceal information that might otherwise induce mutiny and civil war. The "*shout*" now acts dramaturgically as amplification of his accurate judgment of the temper of the troops, and as a validation of his decision to raise the money himself while pretending it is a donative. The scene has moved from the public camp and confrontation with the army to a much more intense scene with only two men on the stage. And even in this virtually private space, Virginius must still conceal the truth about how badly Appius treated him. He finishes the scene with another couplet (either aside to the audience, or with Minutius already leaving the stage):

> Thus men must slight their wrongs, or else conceal them,
> When generall safety wills us not reveale them.
>
> (2.2.214–15)

Clearly the added stage direction for the soldiers to exit early not only solves problems of theatrical doubling and textual interpretation, but provides a powerful dramatic close to the scene.

There are wider issues, however, than simply the resolution of particular pragmatic editing problems, or even the identification of a significant category of non-realist stage directions for shouts within.

The first question, about the precise identification of "*the first mutinous souldier*," and his relationship to "2 *Sold*," emphasizes the need for consideration of specific theatrical conditions of performance as well as textual and critical concerns. The resolution of such textual issues within a theatrical context draws attention to such matters as the likely pairing of the two hired men. It is plausible to consider that the same two actors probably played not only 1 and 2 Soldier, including the sardonic comedy of 4.2.1–35, but also the comedy of 1 and 2 Lictor in 3.2 and of 1 and 2 Serving-man in 3.5. The audience would see a pair of comic actors switching within rather similar roles, and the personalities of the actors would presumably become as significant as the characters they impersonate.

This theatrically-supported solution to the initial textual uncertainty between "1" and "2" in 4.2.1–35 and "*first mutinous souldier*/1 *Sould*" and "2 *Sold*" later in the scene also serves to reinforce the previously-published authorship study of *Appius and Virginia* by Mac Jackson, in which he identified 2.2 and 4.2.1–35 as likely to be by Webster, and noted the difference between the use of unaccompanied numerals in those sections and the generic "*Sould*" or "*Sold*" later in 4.2 in sections associated more with Heywood.[24] What is now apparent is that if Webster wrote the comic duologue for the two soldiers at 4.2.1–35, and Heywood's section started with "*Enter Minutius with his souldiers*" at (in quarto) 4.2.35.1, it is entirely explicable that Heywood's direction "*Enter the first mutinous Souldier*" would refer to the role intended by both collaborators to be played by the leading hired man. Nor would it be Heywood's concern where "2 *Sold*" had been prior to his speech at 4.2.137. And, while there is a danger of circularity of argument here, since we earlier approached the problem of specific identification with an a priori assumption of a shared conception of "*mutinous*" soldiers, the apparent solution to the problem implies that the collaborating playwrights shared a common assumption about the primary generic attributes of this particular group of characters.

To conclude: the relationship of the first questions, about stage direction identification of characters and the form of speech prefixes of mutinous soldiers, to the second major question, about offstage shouts, confirms the interdependence of evidence about stage directions, and underlines the need for wider debate about both the editorial treatment and the dramatic understanding of stage directions. New resources for this debate, such as Dessen and Thomson's *Dictionary of Stage Directions* and the Chadwyck-Healey electronic database Literature Online, enormously expand the possibilities for examining specific categories of direction, as the discussion above about shouts demonstrates. Above all, we need to be always on our guard against naive assumptions about what constitutes dramaturgical logic. Our modern realist common sense may well blind us to questions we can pertinently ask about early modern dramaturgy. The editing of Webster with Mac Jackson has been a valuable collaborative exercise in the virtues of combining theatrical and critical analysis with the widest range of textual inquiry.

Notes

1. In David Gunby, David Carnegie, and MacDonald P. Jackson, eds., *The Works of John Webster,* vol. 2 (Cambridge: Cambridge Univ. Press, 2003, 500).

2. Antony Hammond, "Encounters of the Third Kind in Stage-Directions in Elizabethan and Jacobean Drama," *Studies in Philology* 89 (1992): 71–99: 73.

3. The term "presentational logic" is drawn from Alan C. Dessen, *Elizabethan Stage Conventions and Modern Interpreters* (Cambridge: Cambridge Univ. Press, 1984), 2, and is discussed later in this essay in the section on "Shouts [within]."

4. Citations are from the Cambridge Webster text except where, as here, quarto is specified. Heywood's share of the authorship was argued by Rupert Brooke in "The Authorship of the Later *Appius and Virginia,*" *Modern Language Review* 8 (1913): 433–53, and by F. L. Lucas in his edition of *The Complete Works of John Webster,* vol. 3 (London: Chatto and Windus, 1927), 134–35, and confirmed by MacD. P. Jackson in "John Webster and Thomas Heywood in *Appius and Virginia:* A Bibliographical Approach to the Problem of Authorship," *Studies in Bibliography* 38 (1985): 217–35. For dating of composition and performance, see Lucas, pp. 121–30, Charles R. Forker, *Skull Beneath the Skin: The Achievement of John Webster* (Carbondale and Edwardsville: Southern Illinois Univ. Press, 1986), 200–202, and David Gunby and Hester Lees-Jeffries, "George Villiers, Duke of Buckingham and the Dating of Webster and Heywood's *Appius and Virginia,*" *Notes and Queries,* n.s. 49 (Sept. 2002): 324–27. Dr. Lees-Jeffries also made a valuable contribution to our deliberations about the doubling pattern for the soldiers.

5. Charles Wentworth Dilke, ed., *Old English Plays,* 6 vols. (London: John Martin, 1814–15); Alexander Dyce, ed., *The Works of John Webster,* 4 vols. (London, 1830; 2nd ed., 1857); William Hazlitt, ed., *The Dramatic Works of John Webster,* 4 vols. (London, 1857); Ashley H. Thorndike, ed., *Webster and Tourneur* (New York, 1912); F. L. Lucas, op. cit.

6. See David Bradley, *From Text to Performance in the Elizabethan Theatre: Preparing the Play for the Stage* (Cambridge: Cambridge Univ. Press, 1992), and T. J. King, *Casting Shakespeare's Plays: London Actors and Their Roles, 1590–1642* (Cambridge: Cambridge Univ. Press, 1992). For specific application of these principles, especially those of Bradley, to Webster's practice, see David Gunby, David Carnegie and Antony Hammond, eds., *The Works of John Webster,* vol. 1 (Cambridge: Cambridge Univ. Press, 1995), 98–100 and 426–27.

7. See Bradley, *From Text to Performance,* 20.

8. Bradley himself estimates a minimum adult cast of twenty-one, but seems not to have considered all the doubling possibilities; for a fuller discussion, see the Theatrical Introduction to *Appius and Virginia* in *The Works of John Webster,* ed. Gunby et al., vol. 2, 488–90.

9. See Bradley, *From Text to Performance,* 42, for discussion of this practice.

10. See Samuel R. Gardiner, *History of England from the Accession of James I to the Outbreak of the Civil War 1603–1642,* 10 vols. (London: Longmans, 1883–84), 5:265–67, 282–90, 335–36, and Gunby and Lees-Jeffries, "George Villiers," passim.

11. It may well be that thirty-odd lines was regarded as ample time by playwrights for hired men to change costume and character; its significance here is not that it is an impossibly short time, but that the need for doubling focused our attention on this particular scene transition.

12. Antony Hammond correctly notes the greater occurrence of entry directions: "entrances are usually given with relative accuracy (no matter what the nature of the manuscript, or source of the printed text) and exits often so," and comments that "prompt-books, while more scrupulous than other classes of manuscript in specifying entrances" are "much more casual about exits (after all, once the actor was on stage, there wasn't much the prompter could do to get him off again)" ("Encounters," 77, 79).

13. Alan C. Dessen and Leslie Thomson, *A Dictionary of Stage Directions in English Drama 1580–1642* (Cambridge: Cambridge Univ. Press, 1999).

14. MacD. P. Jackson, "Editing, Attribution Studies, and 'Literature Online': A New Resource for Research in Renaissance Drama," *Research Opportunities in Renaissance Drama* 37 (1998): 1–15: 3.

15. This and future citations are from *The Riverside Shakespeare,* ed. G. Blakemore Evans et al. (Boston: Houghton Mifflin, 1974), unless otherwise specified.

16. This and future citations from Chapman are from *The Plays of George Chapman: The Tragedies,* gen. ed. Allan Holaday (Cambridge: D. S. Brewer, 1987).

17. Thomas Heywood, *The Iron Age, Part 1* (1632), published electronically in the English Verse Drama Full-Text Database (Chadwyck-Healy, 1994). All citations are from this edition.

18. Dessen, *Conventions,* 2–3.

19. Thomas Heywood, *The Golden Age* (1611), published electronically in the English Verse Drama Full-Text Database (Chadwyck-Healy, 1994). All citations are from this edition.

20. 1.224 (text) and 224.1 (stage direction).

21. William D'Avenant, *The Unfortunate Lovers* (1643), published electronically in the English Verse Drama Full-Text Database (Chadwyck-Healy, 1994).

22. Anon., *The Costlie Whore* (1633), published electronically in the English Verse Drama Full-Text Database (Chadwyck-Healy, 1994).

23. *The First Folio of Shakespeare,* ed. Charlton Hinman, The Norton Facsimile (New York: Norton, 1968).

24. MacD. P. Jackson, "John Webster and Thomas Heywood," 222–23.

1620s: Middleton, Rowley, Ford, and Dekker

Thomas Middleton, *The Spanish Gypsy,* and Collaborative Authorship

Gary Taylor

The Collected Works of Thomas Middleton is founded upon, and was enabled by, the revolution in attribution studies that redefined the Middleton canon between 1920 and 1980.[1] The substantial agreement of independent investigations by David Lake (1975) and MacD. P. Jackson (1979) left few problems unsolved, and most of those remainders have been mopped up in subsequent work by MacD. P. Jackson, R. V. Holdsworth, John Jowett, Paul Mulholland, and myself.[2] The most important remaining mystery is *The Spanish Gypsy:* Middleton's presence was absolutely denied by Lake (who attributed the play to Thomas Dekker and John Ford) and doubted by Jackson. Editors and critics of Middleton cannot avoid making a decision, positive or negative, about Middleton's part-authorship of *The Spanish Gypsy.* But the dilemma the play creates for Middletonians cannot be separated from the issues it raises for attribution studies more generally. If previous investigations of dramatic authorship have left the problem of *The Spanish Gypsy* unsolved, that failure must derive from one or more procedural weaknesses. The specifics of *The Spanish Gypsy* are unique, but the procedural weaknesses are not. At the end of this essay I will summarize those weaknesses, and their implications for other works of disputed authorship—including, especially, collaborative works. But first we must immerse ourselves in the particulars of this author and this text.

The External Evidence

The external evidence for Middleton's part-authorship of this play is exceptionally strong. *The Spanish Gypsy* was first published, by Richard Marriot, in 1653.[3] The play is specifically and unambiguously attributed to Thomas Middleton and William Rowley on the title page of that edition. This fact puts it in a quite different category than two attributions (of *The Family of Love* and *Blurt Master Constable*) in Edward Archer's notoriously unreliable play lists, where Middleton's authorship has been rejected by modern scholarship.[4] In the case of *The Widow* (1652), the title page attribution to "Ben: Johnson / John Fletcher / Tho: Middleton" was contested by at least two seventeenth-century owners of the only edition, who altered the title-page by hand to eliminate Fletcher and Jonson; likewise, contemporaries explicitly denied that Francis Beaumont and John Fletcher had written all of the works attributed to them by the folio of 1649, and consequently it should surprise no one that Middleton wrote one of the plays included in that volume (*The Nice Valour)* or that Middleton and Rowley together wrote another (*Wit at Several Weapons*). By contrast, no owner or reader of any exemplar of either seventeenth century edition of *Gypsy* questioned its attribution to Middleton and Rowley.[5] Moreover, one of those exemplars—the Dyce copy of the first edition now in the Victoria and Albert Museum library—includes many handwritten annotations and additions evidently taken from some other manuscript source; but it does not question the attribution. Edmund Malone, in copying the Revels Office entry for the play onto his copy of Q1, did not question the attribution, either. Of course, all this "passive" evidence might be explained away by saying that none of the other early sources contained any evidence of authorship, but the fact remains that none of the many early readers/sources of this particular work questions the attribution.

Even more striking is the Lord Chamberlain's manuscript of 1639, listing plays owned by the theatrical entrepreneur Christopher Beeston. After groups of plays by Fletcher (five), then Massinger (five), then Shirley (thirteen), comes the following sequence: "All's Lost by Lust: The Changeling: A fayre quarrel: The spanish gipsie: The World: The Sunnes Darling: Loues Sacrifice: Tis pitty shee's a Whore."[6] This certainly looks like Rowley (*All's Lost by Lust*), Rowley and Middleton (four plays), then John Ford (three). The only known play with a title which could be abbreviated "The World" is *The World Tossed at Tennis,* apparently owned by Beeston's company. In other words, the Beeston list of 1639 by its groupings apparently provides independent confirmation of the 1653 title page. One might claim that the "error" originated in 1639, in the company that owned the play, and that the publisher's error derived from theirs. But authorship studies do not normally assume that the acting companies themselves did not know who wrote their plays. After all, since the companies paid for the plays, they had to know who to pay.

The conjecture that the publisher of the 1653 edition would have attributed the play to Middleton and Rowley because of their greater popularity is equally difficult to swallow.[7] After 1630, the only quartos published with Middleton's name on the title page had been the apologetic 1640 reprint of *Mad World* and the 1652 edition of *The Widow* (which added the names of Fletcher and Jonson in order to make the play saleable).[8] Moreover, the composition of *Spanish Gypsy* is twenty years closer to its first attribution than the two plays Archer had misattributed to Middleton. By contrast, seven plays by Ford were published between 1633 and 1653; he also published three signed commendatory poems between 1632 and 1638. Three works by Dekker were published in 1630 (against Middleton's one) and—in addition to reprints of the two parts of *The Honest Whore* published under his name in the 1630s—two plays, a pamphlet, and a commendatory poem by Dekker appeared between 1631 and 1636, with another play under his initials in 1639. Both Ford and Dekker were more visible on bookstalls than either Middleton or Rowley in the years between Middleton's death and publication of *The Spanish Gypsy.*

The evidence of the 1653 title page is also reinforced by three explicit pieces of evidence within the play itself. First, the conversation in which Alvarez and Pretiosa discuss whether she should "play the changeling" (2.1.103–12); second, the character named "Lollio" in the play-within-the-play (4.2, 4.3); third, the mistaken locale, in the Dramatis Personae list ("The Scene, Allegant"). Critics all agree that the first two features of *The Spanish Gypsy* explicitly allude to, and capitalize upon, Middleton and Rowley's *The Changeling,* written thirteen months earlier. Middleton advertises his own plays elsewhere. For instance, *The Widow* claims that a song from *More Dissemblers Besides Women* ("Come, my dainty doxies") is being sung "all the country over . . . There's scarce a gentlewoman but has that pricked" (3.1.18–20). Other authors also sometimes advertised their own earlier plays: the epilogue to Shakespeare's *Henry V* looks forward to the reign of Henry VI, a story "which oft our stage hath shown," in plays written wholly or at least in large part by Shakespeare himself. But why should Ford or Dekker go out of their way to advertize, or allude to, a play by Middleton and Rowley? Admittedly, both plays were owned by the same company. But at the time *The Spanish Gypsy* was written, *The Changeling* was hardly that company's most recent play; indeed, Dekker and Ford's own *The Sun's Darling* was performed by the same company only a couple months before *Gypsy,* much more recently than *The Changeling. The Changeling,* though, was the last play on which Middleton and Rowley had collaborated. If Middleton and Rowley were involved with *Gypsy,* it would be both typical and logical for them to refer to their most recent co-production. And this association would also account for the mistake in the Dramatis Personae list, which assigns to *Gypsy* (set in Madrid) the locale of *The Changeling.* Lake conjectures that *Gypsy* was mistakenly attributed to Middleton and Rowley "at the time when the copy for *Gypsy* was so closely associated with that for *The Changeling* that it attracted the mistaken place-specification" (217). But Lake fails to explain the crucial fact behind his conjecture: *why* were *Gypsy* and *The Changeling* ever so closely associated? That association did not begin with their publication in 1653, or even their placement in the 1639 Beeston repertoire list; nor did it begin at an unspecified time when the dramatis personae list was added to the manuscript. It began with the composition of *Gypsy,* which explicitly links itself to *The Changeling,* another play independently attributed to the same authors.

The external evidence for Middleton and Rowley's authorship of *The Spanish Gypsy* is exceptionally strong for a posthumously published play. It is much stronger than in any other case where Lake or Jackson challenged a traditional attribution on the basis of internal evidence. It is also much harder to dismiss than previous investigators (who have concentrated on the 1653 title page alone) have realized or acknowledged. To the extent that *The Spanish Gypsy* pits strong external evidence against internal evidence, it might seem to call into question the reliability of the very kinds of data upon which the canon of *The Collected Works of Thomas Middleton* has been constructed. But both the nature of the problem and the nature of the internal evidence in *Gypsy* differ fundamentally from the problem and the evidence in other texts where the Lake-Jackson synthesis of internal evidence has proven so compelling and successful. In evaluating the internal evidence for attribution of *Gypsy,* we have to ask the following question: is this evidence so unequivocally negative that it can override strong external evidence that Middleton had some part in writing the play?

The Chronological Problem

We know exactly when composition of *Spanish Gypsy* was completed: the play was licensed for performance on 9 July 1623.[9] For any evaluation of the internal evidence for authorship, this date has important consequences, which have not always been fully appreciated in previous investigations.

Certain linguistic preferences used to distinguish Middleton from his contemporaries changed over time. Middleton's *Nice Valour* (now dated in the autumn of 1622) contains only two of the eleven most distinctive Middleton oaths, and only a dozen of the less distinctive twenty-eight.[10] The parallels for such low totals are all late plays: *Hengist* (1) and *Women Beware* (2) are the only plays with two or fewer of the most distinctive oaths, and the only play with a lower total for the less distinctive oaths is *A Game at Chess* (7). Likewise, the only Middleton plays in which the affirmative *yes* strongly predominates over the synonym *ay* (usually spelled "I") are all late: *Women Beware Women* (21/17), the collaborative *Anything for a Quiet Life* (35/6) and *A Game at Chess* (14/10). Even if we restrict ourselves to the scenes in *Anything* which Lake attributes to Middleton, the preference for *yes* remains intact (13/6). Thus, in the four uncollaborative Middleton plays attributable to 1621–24, *yes* predominates 63/42. Middleton's late plays also prefer *betwixt* (26) over *between* (2): Lake notes *Women Beware Women* (10/1), but he could also have cited *A Game at Chess* (4/1) and *Nice Valour* (8/0). Lake also notices some rare oaths in *Valour* for which there are Middleton parallels only in his late plays (194). In all these features, there is a chronological pattern to Middleton's language.

This fact has significant consequences for authorship problems in the late Middleton canon. The security of the Lake/Jackson canon has been its statistical foundation in a combination of (1) linguistic minutiae with (2) demonstrably rare expletives and oaths. But Middleton's most distinctive expletives become less common in his later work, making it more difficult to distinguish him from other playwrights on that basis. At the same time, a few of his linguistic preferences shift. Such instability does not materially weaken the case for Middleton's authorship of *Nice Valour* (because the prologue and epilogue establish that the play was written by a single author, and because the linguistic pattern so overwhelmingly identifies Middleton as the only conceivable candidate). But it does weaken Jackson's case against Middleton's presence in *Spanish Gypsy,* where among the features he cited was the paucity of Middleton's most characteristic oaths and the play's strong preference for *yes* (133–34).

What if Middleton's linguistic preferences were further obscured by (1) collaboration, and/or (2) a sophisticating scribe? In the case of *The Spanish Gypsy,* the title page claims collaboration, and internal evidence has forced investigators to assume the presence of more than one author. Collaboration would have reduced the total number of distinctive features that might help us identify Middleton (if he were present); very few of his most distinctive oaths could be expected to appear. George Price, David Lake, and Shanti Padhi all agree that the first quarto of *Gypsy* was probably set from scribal copy; indeed, that conclusion seems inescapable, to anyone who examines the 1653 text closely.[11] The interference of a scribe had until recently obscured Middleton's part-authorship of *The Bloody Banquet;* but most of the extant text of that play was written by Middleton, and the pattern of expletives in an early play is distinctive enough to isolate his work from that of any of his contemporaries. But if *The Bloody Banquet* had been written in the third decade of the seventeenth century, instead of the first, we could not expect so many unusual oaths to signal Middleton's hand—especially if Middleton were a subordinate rather than dominant partner in the collaboration.[12] A play partly written by Middleton in the 1620s, which only survives in a text with scribally sophisticated linguistic features—that is, a play like *The Spanish Gypsy*—could easily not be caught by the expletives net or by the linguistic features net.

In evaluating the internal evidence for authorship, and whether it is sufficient to overrule the strong external evidence for Middleton's presence, we must make allowances for the chronological evolution of Middleton's own linguistic practices, and for the possibility that those preferences might have been overriden and obscured by a scribe, copying the play at some time between its completion in 1623 and its publication in 1653.

Linguistic Evidence: Against Middleton and Rowley

The strongest case for "the absence of Middleton and Rowley" from *The Spanish Gypsy* was made by Lake. In his summary of the incriminating evidence (pp. 219–20), Lake cited first the absence of typical Middleton oaths; but that is itself typical of late Middleton, and if he were collaborating in 1623 we could expect very few, if any, such oaths to appear in the printed text. Lake next cited the low frequency of the word *why* (8). But *A Game at Chess* has only sixteen examples of *why,* in an uncollaborative play; for a late collaborative play, the eight found in *Gypsy* are well within Middleton's range. The ratio of *ay* to *yes* is also compatible with Middleton's late preference for the latter.

Lake next cited the absence of the spellings/contractions *t'as* and *t'ad* as evidence against Middleton/Rowley. This is perverse. In the first place, there is only one example of either spelling in Lake's three unassisted Rowley texts; Lake actually uses it as a discriminant between Rowley and Middleton, so its absence hardly tells against Rowley. Moreover, eleven of the plays in the Middleton canon do not contain *any* examples of those particular spellings of the contraction.[13] The absence of the spelling *t'as* or *t'ad* is atrociously bad evidence for "the absence of Middleton and Rowley." Meanwhile, Lake ignored the fact that the contraction itself, however spelled, tells against attribution of the play to Dekker-Ford, and in favor of attribution to Middleton (see below). In fact, in his own analysis of *The Roaring Girl,* Lake had himself used the contraction (in the spellings *'thas/'thad*) as a Middleton marker, against attribution to Dekker.[14]

Other "absences" cited by Lake are equally suspect. *I've* does not appear in any unassisted Rowley play, and so its absence here hardly constitutes evidence against Rowley. It also does not appear in seven Middleton plays (*A Yorkshire Tragedy, The Puritan, A Trick to Catch the Old One, The Bloody Banquet, Hengist King of Kent, Women Beware Women, Anything for a Quiet Life*); in five of these seven exceptions, Middleton was the sole author, so the absence of *I've* in a collaborative work—where Middleton would have been responsible for fewer scenes—is hardly remarkable. Likewise, the absence of *sh'as/sh'ad* is not evidence against Rowley, who never used it in his unassisted plays; in fact, he is the only one of the four authors under consideration who never used it. Neither form appears in *The Changeling,* the "normal Middleton-Rowley collaboration" closest in date to *Gypsy;* Lake also listed none in *Wit at Several Weapons, The Old Law,* or *The World Tossed at Tennis.* In the five accepted Middleton-Rowley collaborations, there is only a single example of *sh'as* (in *A Fair Quarrel*). It would in fact be more accurate to say that the *presence* of this contraction in this spelling would tell against a Middleton-Rowley collaboration, more than its absence. As for Middleton without Rowley, these two contractions are also completely missing from six plays (*Your Five Gallants, The Roaring Girl, A Chaste Maid in Cheapside, Hengist King of Kent, The Nice Valour, Anything for a Quiet Life*). There are similar problems with the contraction spelled *we're* or *w'are:* it never appears in Rowley's unassisted work, and is not present in two Middleton-Rowley collaborations (*A Fair Quarrel* and *The World Tossed at Tennis*). Elsewhere in the Middleton canon, it is entirely absent from five plays (*A Yorkshire Tragedy, Your Five Gallants, A Chaste Maid in Cheapside, Anything for a Quiet Life, The Bloody Banquet*). Most astonishingly of all is the alleged evidence of the absence of the contraction *i'*. Again, this is not in any unassisted Rowley play. This is a clean sweep for Rowley: none of the items in this list of absent contractions tells against Rowley, and indeed in each case the linguistic absence supports his authorial presence. As for Middleton, the elision appears in only seven of his plays (*The Widow, Wit at Several Weapons, The Nice Valour, Anything for a Quiet Life, The World Tossed at Tennis, The Old Law, The Changeling*). It does not appear in the Middleton-Rowley *Fair Quarrel,* or in eighteen other plays in the Middleton canon.

Perhaps one might object that, individually, these contractions and elisions are not good evidence, but that collectively they become good evidence, because if Middleton does not use one of them in a given play he is likely to use another. But not a single one of these forms appears in *The Bloody Banquet* or *Anything for a Quiet Life.* Both these texts, noticeably, were—like *Gypsy*—printed long after Middleton's death; both were—like *Gypsy*—collaborative works; one was—like *Gypsy*—written in the early 1620s; one was—like *Gypsy,* according to Lake—a play in which Dekker had a hand. Even collectively, therefore, these "absences" do not provide convincing internal evidence against the external evidence of Middleton's presence as part-author.

"Nor are there," Lake noted, "any spellings which suggest Rowley or Middleton." But earlier, in defining the ground rules of his investigation, Lake himself had admitted that "spelling evidence . . . is hardly available for texts printed after the closing of the theatres (1642), since by that time modernization had set in" (16). By his own rules, Lake should never have expected any Middleton and Rowley spellings in a text printed in 1653. Of his three examples of spelling evidence, *'um* never appears in Middleton's unassisted work, and is a Rowley marker—but it does not appear in two of Rowley's three unassisted works, or in two Middleton-Rowley collaborations (*The Old Law* and *The World Tossed at Tennis*). Clearly, while the occasional presence of this spelling suggests Rowley rather than Middleton, its absence is poor evidence of anything. On the other hand, the spellings *you're* and *they're* are Middleton preferences; the first does not appear in two of three Rowley plays, and the second does not appear in any of them. But in both cases even Middleton's usage is inconsistent. The spelling *you're* does not appear in *A Yorkshire Tragedy, Hengist King of Kent, The World Tossed at Tennis,* or *The Bloody Banquet;* it only occurs once in *The Nice Valour* (1622) and *The Changeling* (1622). Likewise, the Middletonian spelling *they're* does not appear in *A Yorkshire Tragedy, Anything for a Quiet Life, The Changeling,* or *The Bloody Banquet.* It's also worth noting that the alternative spelling of this contraction, *th'are,* only occurs once in *Gypsy;* we are not dealing with a large number of options. Moreover, of the six plays that lack one or both of these contractions, one (*A Yorkshire Tragedy*) is unusually short, constituting only one part of four-plays-in-one; the other five were—like *Gypsy*—posthumously printed. As we should expect, Middletonian spellings tend not to survive in plays printed later in the seventeenth century, when orthographical normalization was further advanced.

So far, none of the evidence presented by Lake is truly anomalous, given the play's date and its collaborative status. Lake's only two pieces of good evidence are also mentioned by Jackson, so before I consider them let me first winnow Jackson's evidence against Middleton's authorship. There is much less special pleading in Jackson's discussion. Like Lake, Jackson did mention *I've* and *yes,* two categories of evidence I have already considered and dismissed. Jackson (p. 132) cited the low frequency of *ne'er* (7); but that is exactly the number found in *A Game at Chess,* written a year later, so this figure is well within Middleton's late range, especially in a collaborative play. Likewise with the low frequency (4) of *I'd:* that contraction does not appear at all in *The World Tossed at Tennis,* and appears four or fewer times in *Michaelmas Term, A Chaste Maid in Cheapside,* and Rowley's *A Shoemaker a Gentleman.* Again, *Gypsy* is within the Middleton-Rowley range.

There do remain, however, a number of convincing anomalies in the internal evidence, which contradict the attribution on the 1653 title page. For convenience in the subsequent discussion, I will list and number these anomalies.

1. The unparallelled low frequency of *I'm.*
2. The anomalously low frequency of *on't* (2). There are only three possible parallels for this low number in the Middleton canon. *A Yorkshire Tragedy* (1) is an unusually short text. *Anything for a Quiet Life* (6) is a collaboration with Webster (which nevertheless has three times as many examples of the contraction as *Gypsy*). *The Bloody Banquet* (0) is a collabo-

ration with Dekker, which has suffered scribal interference; the seven examples of *of't* in the printed text were almost certainly originally *on't.* Assuming that to be true, only the one-act *Yorkshire Tragedy* has a number comparable to *Gypsy.*

3. The complete absence of *e'en.* There is only one example of this contraction in *Hengist King of Kent,* only two in *The World Tossed at Tennis,* and only three in *The Bloody Banquet;* so this evidence is not watertight. But there are no parallels in the Middleton canon for complete absence of this contraction.

4. The high frequency of *hath* (16). This is higher than any play in the Middleton canon except *The Bloody Banquet* (23)—an early collaboration with Dekker, who used *hath* a good deal at a time when Middleton was more tolerant of it; moreover, that text has suffered scribal interference. The other plays in the Middleton canon that come closest to this total for *hath* also have higher totals for *has* (*Chaste Maid* 14/35, *Old Law* 14/40). The ratio for *Gypsy* is unquestionably anomalous.

5. "There are only 27 *'t* contractions, far too few for a Middleton-Rowley play" (Jackson, 132). There are only 34 *'t* contractions in *Banquet,* a Middleton-Dekker collaboration; although the total for *Gypsy* rules out Middleton-Rowley as sole collaborators, it does not rule out Middleton's presence in a play where Dekker is also present. The totals of *'t* contractions in the Middleton-Rowley collaborations are: 80, 77, 32, 133, 83.[15] There are only 32 examples in *World Tossed,* but that theatrical masque is less than half the length of a normal Middleton-Rowley play (or *Gypsy*). Middleton's half of *World Tossed* contains 25 of the contractions, Rowley's only 7. Besides, Holdsworth has shown that Middleton was unusual in his preference for *'t* contractions with prepositions, rather than with verbs. He gave figures for every unaided Middleton play (including those that Lake and Jackson add to the canon), and showed that the preference was consistent. The combined total is 1017 non-verb, 543 verb.[16] For *World Tossed*—the collaboration which has the lowest number of *'t* contractions generally—the figures are 5 verb to 2 non-verb for Rowley, and 4 verb to 21 non-verb for Middleton. *Gypsy,* by contrast, has a mere 8 *'t* contractions with pronouns, as against 19 with verbs. This ratio is demonstrably un-Middletonian. One might imagine a scribe expanding *'t* contractions, but one would not expect a scribe to discriminate between those attached to verbs and those attached to pronouns, and the like. Holdsworth gave figures for one play by Dekker and one by Ford: in *The Shoemaker's Holiday* there are 8 non-verb to 14 verb, while *'Tis Pity She's a Whore* contains 23 non-verb to 45 verb. The figures in *Gypsy* fit Dekker, Ford, or Rowley much better than they fit Middleton.

6. The high frequency of *'ee* (6). There are only three examples in the whole Middleton canon, and only two in Rowley; in both authors, never

more than one per play. *Gypsy* contains more than the whole canon of both authors combined.[17]

7. The high frequency of *whiles* (2). This form appears only four times in the Middleton-Rowley canon: once each in four different Middleton texts (*The Lady's Tragedy, Anything for a Quiet Life, Roaring Girl, The Owl's Almanac*). It is common in Ford—although no Ford play has so few examples.

8. The speech prefix *Omnes* (18). This total is acceptable for Rowley, but not Middleton, who uses it only three times (once each in *Hengist King of Kent, Women Beware Women,* and *The Nice Valour*). All of these Middleton examples come from the early 1620s. In *Bloody Banquet* the speech prefix form generic-noun-followed-by-number (equally anomalous for Middleton, and equally consistent in that play) seems due to scribal interference, and that might also be true here. (I discuss this feature at greater length in section 4, below.)

9. *deed la.* Not elsewhere in Middleton or Rowley.[18]

10. Contraction totals. Throughout *Studies in Attribution* Jackson demonstrated that the combined total for *I'm, I'd, I've, on't, ne'er,* and *e'en* is a specially good indicator of Middleton. *Gypsy* contains only fifteen. The totals for the undisputed Middleton-Rowley collaborations are *Fair Quarrel* 69, *Changeling* 74, *World Tossed* 27, *Wit at Several Weapons* 142, *Old Law* 89. Despite the diverse textual histories of these Middleton-Rowley collaborations, the late printing of *Weapons* (1647) and *Old Law* (1656), the presence of Heywood in one scene of *Old Law,* and the fact that Rowley's share is larger than Middleton's in each work except *World Tossed* (where the shares are roughly even), the totals are high in every collaboration except *World Tossed,* a text only half the length of the others. Even there, Rowley contributes only one example to the total, which is nearly double that for *Gypsy.*

11. *Gypsy* is also anomalous, as a Middleton/Rowley collaboration, in its expletives. Even *Tennis* has one instance of Rowley's *tush; Quarrel* has six, *Changeling* five, *Weapons* six, and *Old Law* four. *Gypsy* has none. Of Middleton's eleven most distinctive expletives, *Changeling* has *puh* once, *push* five times, *cuds* once, and *beshrew . . . heart* once; *Weapons* has three examples of *puh, push* once, *a my troth* twice, *cuds me* once, *cuds* once, *(a) pox* twice, and *shrew . . . heart* once; *Old Law* has *push* twice, *a pox* three times, *cuds* once, *a my troth* once, and *my life for yours* once. None of the most distinctive Middleton expletives appears in *Gypsy. Gypsy* was written within a year or so of *Changeling,* and yet *Changeling,* fairly evenly divided between the two playwrights, has thirteen instances of the Middleton or Rowley expletives, while *Gypsy* has none. The features that prove *Weapons* to belong with the undoubted Middleton-Rowley collaborations put *Gypsy* into a different category. Middleton used such expletives much

more sparingly in 1623 than in 1613, but there is no sign of a similar chronological decline in Rowley's favored expletives.

Some of these categories are stronger than others. In no. 10, for instance, the deficiency in the total can be accounted for by the low totals for *I'm, on't,* and *e'en,* already listed above (no. 1, 2, 3); so to count the low total would be, in effect, to double-count the same evidence. No. 9 depends upon a single instance. Some of the anomalies might be scribal in origin (no. 1, 4, 8).

We are nevertheless left with six categories of indisputable evidence which rule out a Middleton-Rowley two-author collaboration: 2 (*on't*), 3 (*e'en*), 5 (*'t*), 6 (*'ee*), 7 (*whiles*), 11 (expletives). These categories—which combine anomalously low figures for some features, and anomalously high figures for others—seem to me sufficient to warrant the conclusion that "*Gypsy* is not a normal Middleton/Rowley collaboration."

The Linguistic Evidence: Against Dekker and Ford

But the play is not a normal Ford-Dekker collaboration either. Indeed, Lake admits that *Gypsy* is linguistically anomalous, as a Dekker-Ford collaboration (p. 227). The virtual absence of *I'm* and *i'th'* is as anomalous in late Dekker as in Middleton. Moreover, although *I'm* is used less often by Ford on his own, only *Broken Heart* and *'Tis Pity She's a Whore* have frequencies this low; there is nothing this low in Dekker after *Satiromastix,* twenty years earlier. The complete absence of *doth* is equally anomalous for Ford. The *I'm* evidence, in particular, is used by Lake to discredit Middleton's presence; but it could equally be used to discredit Dekker's. We can only explain this linguistic feature of the play, on either hypothesis, by presuming scribal interference.

Lake tries to justify these anomalies by appeal to other Ford-Dekker collaborations, particularly *Sun's Darling.* But *Darling* does not provide the parallel Lake wants. The rate of *i'th'* in that text is double the rate in *Gypsy;* the rate of *I'm* in that text is also double the rate in *Gypsy.* Because Lake attributes to Dekker twice as many lines in *Gypsy* as in *Darling,* these statistical differences are significant; even the lowest possible figure that Lake can find in Dekker is, proportionally, four times what Lake can find for Dekker in *Gypsy.* The evidence from *Darling* is equally unhelpful in relation to Ford. Lake claims that "Ford's *does:doth* ratio in the masque (7:3) suggests that 4:0, as in *Gypsy,* would be a perfectly possible ratio for him" (228). But the ratio in *Darling* is 2.3/1; the ratio in *Gypsy* is 4.0/0. Moreover, Lake is fudging the figures here, because he does not attribute one scene section (V.a) in *Darling* to either of the two authors; *Darling* as a whole has five instances of *doth,* whereas *Gypsy* has none. The figures for

Darling make sense, because—as Lake neglects to mention—Ford's own fondness for *doth* is reinforced by Dekker's occasional use of it; there is not a single Dekker play which does not contain at least one example. The relevant figure for *Gypsy,* therefore, is not just the figure for the Ford scenes, but for the whole play (11:0). Lake also treats the *I'm* problem as though it only applied in the Dekker scenes, whereas the rest of the Ford canon demonstrates that we should expect some *I'm* from Ford, too. Indeed, in *Darling* there are more instances of *I'm* outside the scenes Lake attributes to Dekker, than in them. The overall ratio for *I'm:I am* in *Darling* is 5:31, whereas in *Gypsy* it is 2:70. In other words, the ratio is more than five times higher in *Darling!* Lake also admits that the figures for *i'th'* and *I'm* in *The Welsh Ambassador* "are very different from those in" *Gypsy* (230). He might have added that the evidence from Ford in that play is equally damaging to the case for *Gypsy,* since even in a single scene of *Ambassador* Ford uses *I'm* and *doth* once each. Lake cannot cite a single text in which Ford had even a small share that does not contain at least one instance of *doth.* In relation to three crucial pieces of linguistic evidence, *Gypsy* is anomalous as a Ford-Dekker collaboration.

These discrepancies might be explained away by various kinds of special pleading. First, there is the small sample of Ford/Dekker collaborations (two), as opposed to the larger number of Middleton/Rowley collaborations (five): a wider sample might provide a wider range of figures. But although the paucity of the sample in one respect protects the Dekker/Ford hypothesis from criticism, in another respect it weakens it: the small sample size makes it difficult to provide linguistic evidence for Dekker-and-Ford convincing enough to override the external evidence for Middleton-and-Rowley. The bulk of the case for Dekker and Ford is based upon the uncollaborative plays of each; if evidence from that database is satisfactory when it supports attribution to Dekker and Ford, why does it suddenly become unsatisfactory when it undercuts attribution to Dekker and Ford? Lake cannot have it both ways.

One might also object that *Darling* is linguistically anomalous because it belongs to a different genre ("theater masque" instead of "play"). But *Tennis* is also a "theater masque," and it fits the Middleton/Rowley pattern well enough; indeed, there is no evidence that this generic distinction (if it is one) affects the linguistic evidence—and no obvious reason why it should. The two playwrights, in either case, were writing a dramatic script for the same actors and the same theatrical space for which they wrote plays. Moreover, *Darling* was written within weeks of *Gypsy,* whereas the Middleton-Rowley collaborations were scattered anywhere from ten years to one year earlier.

Alternatively, one might point to the relatively low numbers involved here: the lower the numbers, the harder it is for any discrepancy to attain statistical significance. After all, with such small totals, one or two extra examples of *doth* or *I'm* might significantly change the overall ratios. But in each case, Lake takes the lowest figures he can find anywhere in the Dekker or Ford canon, and then extrapolates from them the possibility of *even lower figures,* to account for the pattern of *Gypsy.* Lake claims that "Collaboration sometimes produces unexpected results." Certainly, the interaction of two authors may produce results that would not have been produced by either in isolation; for instance, each may adopt habits normally characteristic of the other. But if both playwrights, when working independently, display a certain tendency, there is no reason to suppose that, when working together, they will both suddenly and simultaneously abandon that shared habit.

Finally, and more convincingly, one might object that the linguistic pattern in *Sun's Darling* has been affected by scribal interference. For instance, *Darling* is anomalous, as a Ford-Dekker collaboration, in its low frequency of parentheses (11). Dekker averages 126 per play; Ford averages 100 per play. Dekker's lowest recorded figure is 36 (in the early *Shoemaker's Holiday*); his fondness for this punctuation increased chronologically. The lowest recorded Ford figure is 67. On the basis of this evidence, we would have to conclude that *Darling* was not written by Ford and Dekker. The more reasonable conclusion is that the extant text, published in 1656, was printed from a scribal transcript, which had removed most of the parentheses; this assumption also fits with the evidence, assembled by Fredson Bowers and Julia Gasper, that the extant text of *Darling* was altered years after its first performances. The same explanation—scribal interference—would also account for the anomalously low number of parentheses in *Gypsy* (34).

If a scribe interfered with parentheses in *Darling* and *Gypsy,* then a scribe—or even the same scribe, because both texts belonged to the same company—might also have interfered with other features, like the frequency of *I'm* in *Gypsy.* But, of course, once we accept this hypothesis, then the same scribal interference that can be used to explain linguistic anomalies that contradict the Dekker/Ford hypothesis can also be used to explain linguistic anomalies that contradict the Middleton/Rowley hypothesis.

In addition to these high-frequency figures, a significant number of individual linguistic anomalies contradict the Ford-Dekker attribution. Again, for convenience, I will number the separate items of evidence, beginning with four categories I have already discussed in detail.

1. The unparallelled low frequency of *I'm.*
2. The complete absence of *doth.*
3. The anomalously low frequency of parentheses (34).

4. The low frequency of *i'th'*.

5. *i'the* (1): fourteen examples in Middleton, none in Dekker, Ford, or Rowley.[19]

6. *gi'n't* (1). This double contraction of "given it" is normally regarded as convincing evidence for Middleton's authorship. The comprehensive database of "English Drama" in Literature Online identifies examples in five Middleton plays: *A Mad World My Masters* (gi'nt), *Inner Temple Masque, Mad World, Wit at Several Weapons* (gin't), and *The Revenger's Tragedy* (gint). The only other recorded instances are one in the anonymous *Nobody and Somebody* (1606) and one in Heywood's *A Challenge for Beauty* (1636). Since both these exceptions are spelled in the same way (gin't), only the Middleton canon provides a parallel for placement of the apostrophe after the second letter (in *Mad World*), and only the Middleton canon provides more than one example. Moreover, since no one has attributed *Spanish Gypsy* to Heywood or to the anonymous author of *Nobody and Somebody*—it would, in fact, be impossible to do so—Middleton is the only candidate for the play's authorship who provides parallels for this very rare contraction.

7. The three occurrences of the contraction *'thas/'thad* in 1.5 of *Gypsy* fit the Middleton canon (which has twenty total) rather than Rowley, Ford, or Dekker. There are as many examples in this one scene as in the whole of the Ford canon; Dekker uses it, apparently, only in collaborations with Middleton. By contrast, four Middleton plays (*No Wit No Help like a Woman's, More Dissemblers Besides Women, Women Beware Women, The Widow*) have three or more examples each. This evidence is even more striking if we look at the contraction, rather than its spelling; everyone agrees that *Spanish Gypsy* was set from scribal copy, and therefore the scribe might be responsible for spelling *thad* rather than *tad* (just as, noticeably, the other examples of the "th" spelling of both contractions occur in plays apparently set from scribal copy). Scribal manuscripts of *A Game at Chess,* for instance, sometimes expand Middleton's autograph *tad.*[20] If we look at examples of both contractions, in either possible spelling, the totals for Ford and Dekker do not change, but the total for Middleton increases by forty-one, giving Middleton a total (including the single occurrence in a Middleton scene of *Bloody Banquet*) of sixty, against only three for Ford; also, in this tabulation there are eleven Middleton plays with three or more examples. Whether we look at the contraction or its spelling, these three linguistic markers contradict the Dekker-Ford hypothesis.

8. *y'ad* (2.2.168). Eleven examples in Middleton.[21] Lake (p. 223) uses this as a Ford indicator, on evidence of a single *y'had* in *Love's Sacrifice* ($K1^v$). But it is much better evidence for Middleton than for Ford, both because of the number of occurrences in Middleton (eleven, to Ford's one), and the spelling (paralleled in Middleton, but not Ford).[22] The spelling dif-

ference could be scribal or compositorial, but the contraction itself is much more probable in Middleton than Ford. Lake presumably took it as evidence of Ford because he could find one (inexact) parallel in Ford, but none in Dekker. But that reasoning puts the cart before the horse. There are no parallels for this in Ford or Dekker, unless we presume that there has been scribal interference in *Gypsy;* even under that presumption, the contraction is less likely in Ford or Dekker than in Middleton.

9. The figure for *them* (13) is anomalously low for a Dekker-Ford collaboration. Dekker's lowest figure elsewhere is thirty; he averages fifty-nine per play. Ford, by contrast, has one play with a total of twelve, and one with a total of thirteen; but *Spanish Gypsy* cannot be entirely by Ford, and Lake assigns him only one-third of it. Ford averages twenty per play. *Gypsy* is thus significantly below the average for either of the putative collaborators, far below the combined average, and farthest below the low range of the alleged chief collaborator. Moreover, *Gypsy* has many more examples of *'em* (29) than any play by Ford (who never rises above seventeen), and more than all but one play by Dekker (*If This Be Not a Good Play, the Devil is in it*). The Middleton canon, by contrast, contains fourteen plays with a higher total. Middleton is one of the few writers working in the theatre in 1623 to whom the frequency of *'em* in *Gypsy* could be attributed; it falls in the middle of the range for other Middleton-Rowley collaborations.[23] The ratio of *'em/them* in *Sun's Darling* (11:20) is in line with what we might expect from a Ford-Dekker collaboration, but the ratio in *Gypsy* (29:13) inverts the Ford-Dekker pattern.

10. Holdsworth has noted that Middleton's fondness for "interrogative repetition" distinguishes him from all his contemporaries.[24] Applying Holdsworth's very strict rules for definition of this trait further undermines Lake's attribution of the play to Dekker and Ford alone. Ford averages 23 per 1000 speeches; the scenes in *Gypsy* attributed to him by Lake have 27 per 1000, higher than any of the five Holdsworth checked. Dekker averages 29 per 1000 speeches; the scenes in *Gypsy* attributed to him by Lake have 41 per 1000 (much higher than any of the five plays Holdsworth checked, and much higher than Dekker's later plays). Thus, for both Dekker and Ford the incidence of interrogative repetition is too high. This excess cannot be attributed to Rowley, who used this formal device less than either Ford or Dekker, averaging only 21 per 1000 speeches. In the corpus of 112 plays checked by Holdsworth, only Middleton plays exceed 40 per 1000. Middleton, on this criterion, is a much more likely candidate for Lake's "Dekker" scenes than is Dekker (or anyone else).

In at least ten respects, then, *Gypsy* is anomalous as the work of Dekker and Ford. Some of these are more serious than others, of course. For instance, the low figure for parentheses (no. 3) could be due to scribal interference. But if we are forced to invoke scribal interference in order to justify the Dekker-Ford hypothesis (for which there is no external evidence), then we must also be allowed to invoke scribal interference in order to justify attribution to Middleton and Rowley (for which there is very strong external evidence). Once an interfering scribe is postulated, it becomes harder to make a convincing case *against* external evidence.[25] Dismissing any of these anomalies by invoking "scribal interference" thus produces a Catch-22 for defenders of the Dekker-Ford hypothesis.

Of the remaining evidence, some (no. 5, 6, 8) might be dismissed on the grounds that each depends upon a single occurrence. But some of the Dekker-Ford evidence cited by Lake also depends upon a single occurrence: not only *Deed la* (which I include among the anti-Middleton evidence in section 3, no. 9), but also *wou't, mumble-crust, oyster/open, parrot=woman, stile/style, float of, undertake a voluntary exile.* Noticeably, most of these Dekker-Ford items dependent upon a single occurrence are really verbal parallels, not "linguistic" evidence. (I will return to that distinction, below.) For the moment, it will help to confine ourselves to the high-frequency features that distinguish Lake's and Jackson's linguistic analysis from the collection of verbal parallels. In considering evidence that depends upon a single occurrence in the target text, an asseveration like *deed la* is much less strong, as evidence for Ford, than contractions like *gi'n't* or *i'the,* where there is a higher frequency of examples in the Middleton canon, and a stronger statistical correlation with one dramatist. At the very least, if we are going to dismiss *any* discrepancies in the Dekker-Ford evidence on the grounds that they depend upon a single occurrence, then we must also dismiss any similar discrepancies in the Middleton-Rowley evidence. This strategy, again, creates a Catch-22 for defenders of the Dekker-Ford hypothesis, by removing from consideration some of the internal evidence for a theory entirely dependent on internal evidence to overturn strong external evidence. Moreover, the Ford-Dekker hypothesis now depends upon *two* forms of special pleading: first, dismissing anything that might be due to scribal interference, and then, dismissing all single-instance anomalies (even when there are three of them).

The question now becomes: how do the anomalies which stand in the way of assuming "a normal Dekker-Ford collaboration" stack up against the anomalies which stand in the way of "a normal Middleton-Rowley collaboration"? After every allowance has been made, we are still left with seven discrepancies that seem to rule out a Middleton-Rowley two-author collaboration: the anomalously low numbers of *I'm, on't, e'en, 't,* and characteristic expletives, and the anomalously high numbers of *'ee* and *whiles.* Likewise, using the same criteria, we are left with six discrepancies which seem to rule out a Dekker-Ford two-author collaboration: the anomalously low numbers of *I'm, i'th', doth,* and *them,* the anomalously high numbers (or presence) of *'thad/'thas,* and the anomalous high incidence of interrogative repetition. In the case of the low frequency of *I'm,* we must presume scribal interference, whichever hypothesis we adopt. This evidence (of anomalously low frequency of *I'm*) should therefore be completely removed from consideration, in arbitrating between the Dekker-Ford and the Middleton-Rowley claims.

Only one conclusion seems possible. Neither the Ford/Dekker hypothesis, nor the Middleton/Rowley hypothesis, satisfactorily explains the pattern of linguistic evidence.

The Logical Problem

Since the internal evidence is contradictory, we might be justified in rejecting it entirely, and falling back upon the strong external evidence for Middleton/Rowley, which is completely consistent and uncontradicted historically. But this solution would in fact imply the general unreliability of internal evidence. There is a simpler and more satisfactory solution, with no such implications. *The anomalies in the internal evidence can be explained by postulating a Ford/Dekker/Middleton/Rowley collaboration.* This hypothesis also explains the external evidence. Partially unreliable title pages are much more common than wholly unreliable title pages. Lake and Jackson—and *The Collected Works of Thomas Middleton*—have already postulated that title pages failed to mention collaborators in *Patient Man and Honest Whore, Anything for a Quiet Life, Timon of Athens,* and *The Bloody Banquet*—not to mention examples in other canons. All the external evidence can be explained by postulating that Middleton and Rowley collaborated on the play, but were not the only collaborators. This hypothesis therefore enables us to reconcile the strong external evidence with the contradictory internal evidence.

There is an absolutely crucial logical point here, which has been ignored in previous analysis of the play, and which has accordingly undermined all previous analysis. Having established that there are anomalies in the internal evidence which rule out a two-man Middleton/Rowley collaboration, it has been assumed that the burden of proof rests upon those who would identify Middleton or Rowley anywhere in the play. That is not true. It is never true, logically, but it is especially not true where there is strong external evidence for Middleton/Rowley. Having proved that "SG ≠ M+R alone" does not prove that "SG = D+F alone." In *The Family of Love* we could rule out Middleton because we had strong contemporary external evidence that the play was written by a single playwright; we have no such evidence that *Gypsy* was written by only two playwrights—because the only evidence that could be cited in support of that hypothesis is the very title page, which the Dekker/Ford hypothesis has to jettison. Because we knew that *Family* had only one author, we could rule out Middleton by showing that there was cumulatively overwhelming internal evidence for Lording Barry and against Middleton; it was a simple binary problem and a simple binary choice. But we have no *a priori* evidence of only two authors in *Gypsy.* We therefore cannot assume that presenting some evidence for Dekker and Ford, and against Middleton and Rowley, proves that Dekker and Ford were the only authors. It proves that Middleton and Rowley were not the only authors, and it proves that Dekker and Ford contributed, but it does not establish Dekker and Ford's responsibility for the entire play. It certainly does not create a presumption of Ford's and Dekker's authorship of the whole.

One cannot defend the Dekker-Ford hypothesis by resort to Occam's razor. In the historical circumstances of the early modern London theater, a two-author collaboration is not intrinsically more likely than a four-author collaboration. Dekker, Ford, Rowley, and Middleton all participated in collaborations involving more than two authors. That historical fact may create more complex mathematical problems for modern investigators, but one cannot avoid those problems by proclaiming that they do not exist. Indeed, the Ford/Dekker hypothesis was itself constructed by the same process I am advocating here. In 1924, H. Dugdale Sykes conjectured that the title page was wrong, and that the play was "substantially, if not wholly, from the pen of John Ford."[26] Then, in 1929, accepting the claim of Ford's presence, but recognizing that it did not account for inconsistencies in the internal evidence, E. H. C. Oliphant complicated the Ford hypothesis by adding Dekker, a suggestion more fully developed by M. Joan Sargeaunt in 1935, and by Lake and others since.[27] The initial logical error was committed by Sykes, who took his own evidence of Ford's presence as evidence for the complete absence of Middleton and Rowley. That binary assumption is unwarranted. The presence of Ford in some parts of the play should never have been taken as evidence of anyone else's absence. But those who have subsequently sophisticated the Ford hypothesis, by adding Dekker, have inherited from Sykes—along with his convincing evidence for Ford's presence—the logical error at the foundation of his argument, the assumption that proving the presence of one author in parts of a text proves the complete absence of another author from any part of that text.

The Middleton/Rowley two-man hypothesis is at least logical: it is based upon the external evidence. By contrast, the Dekker/Ford two-man hypothesis is foundationally illogical; it presumes that it knows the number of authors, when it has no right to do so. It is also terminally flawed by inconsistencies in the very evidence that gave it birth. The Middleton-Rowley two-man hypothesis could rest (as in Bentley, for instance, or Schoenbaum) upon the conservative claim that internal evidence is intrinsically unreliable, and that one must therefore depend upon external evidence.[28] But the Dekker-Ford hypothesis depends entirely on internal evidence; it therefore cannot sustain or explain inconsistencies in the internal evidence.

What precisely does the most reliable internal evidence against Middleton/Rowley, and for Ford/Dekker, *prove?* That evidence falls into two categories, negative and positive, and those two categories have distinct logical consequences. The negative evidence of the anomalously low figures for *on't, e'en, 't* and certain characteristic expletives establish, beyond doubt, that Middleton and Rowley cannot have written *the entire play;* therefore, either Middleton and Rowley had additional collaborators, or the entire play was written by someone else. We have, intrinsically, no way of judging, from the low totals themselves, which of these two explanations is correct. The positive evidence of the anomalously high figures for *'ee* and *whiles,* by contrast, establishes that Middleton and Rowley did not write those parts of the text in which those specific features appear. But those features are concentrated in a very small part of the play: *whiles* in 3.3 and the middle of 5.1 (5.1.39–128), *'ee* in 3.3, the middle of 5.1 (5.1.39–128), and the beginning of 5.3 (5.3.1–64). The middle of 5.1 also contains anomaly no. 9, the single occurence of *deed la,* also pointing to Ford (and incidentally perhaps demonstrating that single occurrences of anomalies are significant after all). All three of these scenes/sections, in which positive anomalies occur, involve Clara and the rape plot. There is a logical, narrative, and dramaturgic connection between the three scenes; moreover, these scenes/sections contain no examples of *on't* or *e'en* or non-verb thereby contributing to the low totals for these features in the play as a whole. We are accordingly forced to conclude that Ford—not Rowley, or Middleton—wrote at least three passages in the play, amounting to 260 lines, or almost 12 percent of the text.

Obviously, this evidence does not prove that Ford wrote the other 88 percent, or even all the scenes involving the Clara plot. It does not create a presumption of his authorship of all those other scenes in the play; if anything, the concentration of the evidence for Ford in a few places creates a presumption that he did *not* write much of the rest of the play, and at the same time his presence helps to account for the low gross totals of certain features we would expect to find more frequently in a play wholly authored by Middleton/Rowley. Having established Ford's presence as part-author, we are now justified in looking at individual scenes/sections, weighing the local evidence for Ford against the local evidence for Middleton or Rowley; but the burden of proof still rests upon anyone who wants to prove Ford's presence in other parts of the play, and not vice versa.

Now, look at the most reliable internal evidence against a Dekker/Ford collaboration, following the same procedure adopted in looking at the most reliable evidence against a Middleton/Rowley collaboration. Again, that evidence falls into two categories. The anomalously low numbers of *i'th'*, *doth* and *them,* and the anomalously high numbers for interrogative repetition, demonstrate that the play cannot have been written by Ford and Dekker alone (just as the anomalously low figures for *on't, e'en,* and *'t* demonstrated that it could not have been written by Middleton and Rowley alone). By contrast, the anomalously high numbers of *thad/thas* (3) establish that Ford and Dekker did not write the specific passage in which those features appear: the end of 1.5. Notably, there is no overlap between the scenes/sections identified as not-Middleton/Rowley and the scenes/sections identified as not-Ford/Dekker; also notably, this positive evidence against Dekker-Ford falls in a scene/section involving the gypsy plot, rather than the rape plot. The positive linguistic evidence that this scene/section is not plausibly attributable to Ford/Dekker coincides with negative evidence to the same effect: there are no parentheses at the end of 1.5, and no instances of *doth* or *them.*

Also, since the single-occurrence linguistic evidence in favor of Ford fell in a scene identified as Ford's on other grounds, it is worth noticing that a piece of single-occurrence linguistic evidence in favor of Middleton/Rowley (*i'the'*) also occurs at the end of 1.5 (for which there are already three pieces of positive evidence for Middleton/Rowley and against Ford/Dekker). Again, this distribution tends to confirm that single-occurrence linguistic evidence is probably reliable, both when it is arguing against Middleton/Rowley and when it is arguing for them.

In short, there is nothing in the internal or external evidence which the Dekker/Ford/Middleton/Rowley hypothesis will not explain.[29] Moreover, the most reliable linguistic evidence clusters in a contrasting pattern, which separates [scenes/sections anomalous on the Middleton/Rowley hypothesis] from [scenes/sections anomalous on the Ford/Dekker hypothesis]. This is exactly the kind of contrasting pattern that establishes collaborative authorship when there are only two authors; in this case, by combining Middleton-with-Rowley and Ford-with-Dekker in our overall analysis, we have created a comparable binary, which is equally reliable for analytic purposes. Having established by such means that the combination Ford-Dekker cannot account for all the linguistic evidence any more successfully than the combination Middleton-Rowley, we have also established that the combination Ford-Dekker is concentrated in some parts of the text, while the combination Middleton-Rowley is concentrated in other parts.

Much of the play remains unattributed by this analysis, precisely because in order to establish authorship by more than two men we had to create two pairs, and restrict our global assessment to only the most reliable evidence which could not be explained by the presence of either author in a pairing: for the purposes of the four-author problem, we had to establish not-Middleton-or-Rowley and not-Ford-or-Dekker. But once we have established that neither two-author hypothesis is satisfactory, we have to look at particular unattributed scenes of the play with all four potential candidates in mind. The problem then becomes, not "can one pairing or another explain all of this play?" but "now that we know four authors are involved, which of the four is most likely to have written this particular scene section?" In such detailed scene attribution, we will obviously have to use evidence that could not be used in solving the global problem, evidence of relative probabilities rather than absolute impossibilities. We may also be able to eliminate one author or another, and then look at all of the evidence for the remaining candidates, recognizing that we may in some cases be dealing with mixed writing or with mere probabilities, enabling us to say for a certain scene only "not x" or "a or b." Even in plays with only two authors, certain scenes remain contested, and we should expect even more such uncertainties, when dealing with four authors.

However, those uncertainties about individual scenes or scenelets do not in any way disturb the global conclusion. Nothing in the internal evidence logically or historically supports the claim that the play was entirely written by Dekker and Ford only; instead, the most reliable internal evidence rules out authorship by Dekker/Ford alone, just as it rules out authorship by Middleton/Rowley alone. This is true, even if we do not take account of the external evidence for Middleton/Rowley. But that very strong external evidence supports the same conclusion: it is compatible with the four-author hypothesis, and very difficult to explain on the two-man Ford/Dekker hypothesis.

The Dekker Problem

One problem with attributing the play to Dekker and Ford, and ruling out Middleton and Rowley, is that late Dekker is, linguistically, almost impossible to distinguish from late Middleton-Rowley. This is noticeable in Lake's case for Dekker. His first move is structural and impressionistic, not linguistic: "A conviction of Dekker's presence is most easily attained in the manner outlined by Sargeant: if one accepts that the main author, or the author of the main plot, is Ford, then it becomes obvious that he had a collaborator for the gypsy scenes" (221). There are three problems with this sentence. First, as Lake's self-correction demonstrates, the author of "the main plot" is not "the main author," because the so-called "main plot" does not constitute most of the play (or give the play its title). Secondly, proving that Ford wrote certain scenes of the play, and not others, does *not* prove that the non-Ford scenes were written by "a collaborator" (singular) rather than "collaborators" (plural). Thirdly, the play cannot be neatly divided into "the main plot" and "the gypsy scenes," because the play contains at least three plots, based upon three different sources: the rape plot (based on Cervantes's "The Force of Blood"), the Don John-Pretiosa plot (based on Cervantes's "The Little Gypsy Girl"), and the Lewis-Alvarez plot (based on "The Tale of Don Luys de Castro and Don Rodrigo" in Matteo Aleman's *The Rogue,* published in 1622 in a translation by James Mabbe).[30] Indeed, even this is not an accurate description of the literary genetics of the play, because to these sources must be added Jonson's masque *Gypsies Metamorphosed* (1622), which supplies the crucial factors of (a) a troupe of "gypsies" that does not contain a single genuine gypsy, but is entirely composed of aristocrats in disguise, (b) a series of ironic prophecies, given by the fake gypsies to various real aristocrats, whose identities they already know, and (c) the idea of topical connections between gypsy stories and Anglo-Hispanic diplomacy of the early 1620s. The fact that the play had four main sources does not mean it had four authors, but Lake's description of the play's structure creates a false binary opposition, upon which he constructs a binary theory of authorship.

"A conviction of Dekker's presence is most easily attained," therefore, by illogical and unwarranted assumptions. Lake then proceeds, in his next sentence, to claim that "Dekker's style . . . first becomes unmistakable in II.i." First of all, this sentence immediately and silently abandons the logic of the very binary Lake had just constructed—because 2.1 is not the first appearance in the play of the gypsy plot. The Don John-Pretiosa plot "first" surfaces in 1.3.17–22 and 1.5.73–123 (neither of which Lake attributes to Dekker). Lake gives four reasons for assigning 2.1 to Dekker; three are linguistic features ("*ha', Omnes,* the spelling *wud*"). But none of these three is specific to Dekker. *Ha'* appears often in Middleton, and occasionally in Ford and Rowley; it occurs once in *Gypsy* in a scene Lake himself attributes to Ford (5.3). The spelling *wud* occurs only once elsewhere in Middleton, but occurs thirty-three times in Rowley's *All's Lost by Lust* (twice as many examples as in any Dekker play), and four times in Rowley's *Shoemaker a Gentleman;* it also occurs occasionally in Ford.[31] Finally, although *Omnes* is uncharacteristic of Middleton, it too is paralleled in Rowley and Ford.

In short, although two of these three features tell against Middleton, none is good evidence against Rowley. And the two features that tell against Middleton are both vulnerable to transmissional interference. One is a spelling, and spellings are demonstrably more subject to scribal or compositorial sophistication than are oaths, contractions, and variant forms. Moreover, as Lake acknowledges elsewhere, "positive spelling evidence is not, strictly speaking, proof of authorship as such; especially in collaborate plays, it may happen that one author has copied out a text composed by another" (16). That scenario—of one author copying out another's work—is particularly likely when there are four different authors, and where accordingly there is more need to tie up loose ends. The second anti-Middleton marker is a speech prefix, and prefixes are demonstrably subject to scribal sophistication. This is particularly true of *Omnes,* in this particular play. *Omnes* first appears in 2.1—which is also the first appearance in the play of a character named Alvarez. The speech prefix *Al.* (for Alvarez) has occurred twenty-one times in the scene (C2–C4^{v}), before the first *Omnes* (C4^{v}); that prefix *Omnes* is immediately followed, in the next speech and the next line, by the abbreviated prefix *Al.,* which also occurs two lines above the second appearance of *Omnes* (C4^{v}). In these circumstances, it would be intolerably ambiguous for an author or scribe—or even compositor!—to use "*All*" as a prefix for a group speech. The prefix *Omnes* again occurs in 3.1, again in a scene section where Alvarez is present, and has just been given the prefix *Al.* (sig. D4^{v}). One might continue this analysis throughout the play, but from the point of view of a scribe the pattern would already have been set by this point: *All* should be avoided, even when it is found in the copy, because of potential confusion with *Al.* Indeed, all of the remaining scenes which contain the prefix *Omnes* also contain Alvarez, and speech prefixes *Al.* (3.1, 3.2, 4.1, 4.3, 5.3). In these circumstances, *Omnes* cannot be taken as reliable evidence of authorship.

Neither Lake, nor anyone else, can make a case for Dekker's part-authorship of *Gypsy* on the basis of linguistic evidence. This fact perhaps accounts for the reluctance of both Hoy and Padhi to concede his presence at all.[32] I believe he did write parts of the play, but his part-authorship is demonstrated, not by linguistic evidence, but by the fourth category cited by Lake: "phrases" (221). For instance, quoting the line "Farewell old Gray-beard, adue Mother mumble-crust" (2.1.225–26), Lake points out that "mother Mumble-crust" occurs in *Satiromastix* and "Madge-mumble-crust" in *The Shoemaker's Holiday* and "mumble crust lord" in a Dekker scene of *The Welsh Ambassador.* We can now test the reliability of the verbal parallels cited by Lake, using the comprehensive database of English plays assembled in Literature OnLine. As Jackson has demonstrated, LION enables us to put the despised "verbal parallels" of earlier attribution studies on a sound statistical basis.[33] The whole database affords only one additional parallel for "mumble crust": the phrase "Iacke-mumble-crust" in *Patient Grissel,* by Dekker and Chettle. Moreover, juxtaposed to the Dekkerian "mumble-crust" is the noun "Gray-beard." LION yields no Middleton, Rowley, or Ford examples, but that noun appears in Dekker's *2 Honest Whore* and in a Dekker scene of Dekker and Webster's *Northward Ho.*

But although an impersonally searchable database thus confirms that Dekker is indeed virtually certain to have written the line cited by Lake (though not necessarily all 270 lines of the scene), it does not support Lake's method for isolating and evaluating phrasal evidence. Lake's approach to verbal parallels is anecdotal: he seizes a phrase that strikes him as characteristic of a given author, then cites parallels from that author for that phrase. Literature Online provides a control for such claims, but checking anecdotal evidence does not alter the essentially subjective character of the initial selection process. A more reliable procedure for determining authorship by means of verbal parallels would be to use the electronic database to check a given passage or scene, systematically, for verbal parallels. This is a daunting task, which cannot be undertaken in this short essay.[34]

Any approach to the problem of attribution in *Gypsy* must begin with the recognition that it will be impossible to discredit the Middleton-Rowley title-page attribution by means of the combination of expletive and linguistic evidence that Lake and Jackson so successfully used to solve other problems in the Middleton canon. Such evidence can help identify a few scenes/sections of the play as Ford's work, but it cannot reliably differentiate Middleton and Rowley from Dekker in the great bulk of the play. This fact places a daunting burden of proof on any investigator seeking to discredit the external evidence.

The burden of proof, and the analytical problem, is multiplied by the complexity of the plot, and the potential complexity of any collaboration involving four authors. Every act, and virtually every scene, contains material from more than one strand of the densely intertwined narrative. One therefore cannot reasonably assume that a single author was responsible for any whole act, or any whole scene. The first quarto is not even divided into scenes; the scene divisions provided by editors are based on the logic of a cleared stage and a change of locale, but that logic need not govern collaboration in a play as complex as this, especially if we have to consider the possibility of four different authors. The more reliable divisions, for the purpose of authorship analysis, would be into scene sections, marked by the entrance or exit of a character or group of characters (as in the French neoclassical system of scene numbering). Indeed, even Lake had to acknowledge the significance of such divisions, when he attributed the first part of 3.2 to Dekker (up to *Exit Gipsies Dancing*) and the remainder to Ford. Even an unjustifiably simplified binary account of the play's authorship requires such divisions of scenes into scenelets. It is noticeable, for instance, that in act 1 the only two anticipations of the Don John-Pretiosa plot occur in stylistically distinct material at the end of two scenes (1.3, 1.5). In each cases, the ending could have been added, later or by another hand, to a scene that makes perfect sense without it.

Given this complexity of distribution, all four authors would have to be working closely together, and sometimes one might copy out work originally written by someone else, or need to provide linking material between separately written scenelets. In these circumstances, it would not be surprising—it might indeed be inevitable—that even some scenelets included mixed writing. Rowley might well have written or rewritten material for his own role, even in scenes basically composed by someone else. Indeed, one effect of the work of Holdsworth and Gossett has been to demonstrate that there is some mixed writing in some scenes of other Middleton-Rowley plays (where we have to deal with only two authors). Given such complexities, it is not surprising that Lake's linguistic evidence cannot make much headway in distributing the scenes of *The Witch of Edmonton* to its various known authors (Dekker, Ford, Rowley, and "etc."): linguistic evidence alone, which works by statistical accumulation, generally becomes less effective as the field of analysis shrinks.

Middleton's Presence

Our global consideration of the linguistic evidence has already isolated the end of 1.5 as a section of the play which contradicts the Dekker-Ford two-author hypothesis. Since we need only establish that a single section of the play was written by Middleton in order to explain the title-page attribution, it seems sensible to concentrate on this scene, and in particular on the end of the scene (1.5.73–123). Lake and others have attributed the whole scene to Ford, and his authorship of its first half seems certain. But a division of the scene into two parts makes obvious sense. The beginning deals entirely with the already launched tragic rape plot; the ending develops a new comic subplot, introducing the subject of Don John's relationship to the gypsies.

In the last fifty lines of the scene we find *'thad* (twice), *'thas, has, hath, does, i'th, I'd, i'the, prithee, ye, 'em* (four times), *a* (meaning "he"), *y'are* (twice), and one of only eight instances in the whole play of the Middletonian interjection *why.* Of these, all but two are compatible with attribution to Middleton. Of the two exceptions (*hath* and *a*), the pronoun in particular tells against Middleton, because *a* in that sense occurs only eleven times elsewhere in his uncollaborative canon, all in plays written by 1613; it is demonstrably uncharacteristic of Middleton's late work. However, these two anomalies both occur in the first speech after Diego's entrance, which might therefore be the end of Ford's section of the scene (1.5.73–76), or might be a linking speech, or even the beginning of a linking speech (since both occur in line 74), transcribed by Ford to link his material to Middleton's.

If we ignore as intrinsically uncertain this single bridging speech, the rest of the scene would never be attributed to Ford on linguistic grounds. A number of the linguistic markers are indifferent, in arbitrating between Middleton and Ford: *I'd, why, y'are, prithee.* Likewise, although *ye* is more characteristic of Ford than Middleton, and the eight examples in the play as a whole exceed the total in any Middleton play, that total is also far lower than in any Ford play: Ford's lowest total for *ye* is eleven, and lowest total for *ye* plus *'ee* is thirty-seven—in contrast to the fourteen in *Spanish Gypsy.* Thus, *ye* may be evidence of Ford's presence in the play overall, but it does not demonstrate his authorship of the whole play, or of this subscene. The single occurrence of *ye* here (1.5.114) is certainly possible for Middleton; that form occurs sixty-one times overall in his canon. Likewise, the two occurences of *yes* are perfectly compatible with Middleton's late preference for that form of affirmation.[35]

When the evidence is not neutral, it tells strongly against Ford. Ford prefers both *hath* and *doth;* the preference in 1.5.75–123 is three *has, does*/0 *hath, doth.* No play of Ford prefers *'em* to *them,* and no Ford play has more than seventeen examples of *'em* in total. The total in these fifty lines is 4 *'em*/0 *them,* which would be anomalous for either Ford or Dekker. Indeed, Middleton is the only one of the four collaborators with a consistent strong preference for *'em.* And, as I have already noted, *i'the, 't(h)ad, 't(h)as* and the absence of parenthesis are excellent evidence for Middleton and against Ford or Dekker.

The subscene also has two other contractions, not discussed by Lake or Jackson, which strongly suggest Middleton. The contraction *may't* at 1.5.94 does not appear anywhere else in *The Spanish Gypsy,* and does not appear even once in the canon of either Ford or Dekker.[36] It appears six or seven times in material written by Middleton (all in dramatic texts of 1616–23).[37] Of playwrights alive in 1623, only Heywood used the contraction as many times as Middleton, and the Heywood examples are not chronologically bunched, as Middleton's are. Middleton's writing also provides an exact parallel for the whole phrase in which this contraction appears ("much good may't do").[38] This contraction therefore seems to provide excellent evidence that Middleton wrote this scenelet. Moreover, the contraction *to th'* appears twice here; there are at least fifty-seven examples in Middleton, including "to th' city" (*Gypsy* 1.5.98; *The Lady's Tragedy* 1.1.91 and *The Nice Valour* 5.1.70). More generally, most of the Middleton examples occur before consonants; the elision then works backwards, the preceding "to" forming a syllable with the truncated "th" (as in both examples in this scene). Only ten of the fifty-seven Middleton examples I have identified were written before 1611; Middleton used this elision more frequently in the second half of his career. By contrast, Ford seldom used the contraction *to 'th.*[39] He never used it more than three times in any play; here, there are two examples in a single scene. When he did use it, he overwhelmingly preferred to do so before vowels. There is no Ford parallel for the specific phrase "to th' city."

But we are now moving from "linguistic evidence," proper, to parallels of phrasing, which should be considered globally, not individually—a task too big to attempt here. But even without such a study, it is already apparent that the cumulative and interlocking linguistic evidence for attribution of 1.5.75–123 to Middleton rather than Ford is strong and consistent in its own right, as strong and consistent as the evidence that Ford wrote at least three passages in the play. The internal evidence in 1.5.75–123 amply supports the title-page attribution of a part of this play to Thomas Middleton.

Conclusions

My interest in *The Spanish Gypsy* was driven by an entirely pragmatic imperative: as general editor, I had to decide whether or not to include it in *The Collected Works of Thomas Middleton.* But, as MacD. P. Jackson's career amply demonstrates, one cannot pursue attribution problems in the Middleton canon without confronting, at a practical and theoretical level, broader issues about the nature of authorship and the logic of attribution.

One lesson we should take away from *The Spanish Gypsy* is the unreliability of generalizations about external evidence. The Shakespeare canon, for example, has remained relatively stable for centuries, because the external evidence defining that canon is, overall, exceptionally strong. Shakespeareans are therefore particularly prone to generalize that external evidence should outweigh internal evidence. In the Middleton canon, by contrast, the external evidence is often weak, and Middletonians are therefore particularly prone to generalize that internal evidence should always outweigh external evidence. Having spent much of a big book overturning weak external evidence with strong internal evidence, the usually logical and meticulous David Lake minimized the strength of the external evidence for Middleton and Rowley's presence in *The Spanish Gypsy,* and exaggerated the internal evidence for Dekker's and Ford's presence. The methods of Lake and Jackson were and are so useful precisely because they analyzed the internal evidence of individual texts against a global background of data from many early modern authors; but the external evidence for the authorship of any given text derives from a specific document, or documents, and is therefore always particular, individual, historical. We cannot generalize about external evidence, even within a single canon, but must analyze independently the credentials of the external evidence for any given work.

Secondly, no investigation of a text of uncertain authorship among the plays of the early modern theater should begin with an assumption about the number of writers involved. Commercial plays almost never seem to have been written by more than five authors, but any number between one and five is historically plausible. Title pages, when they are wrong, almost always err by minimizing the number of collaborators; on the rare occasions when they add names—as in the case of *The Widow*—the added names are always prestigious ones (Beaumont, Fletcher, Jonson, or Shakespeare).[40] Analytically, one must begin an investigation of the internal evidence for the authorship of a disputed text by determining whether the author(s) to whom the play is attributed could be responsible for all its features. The process is thus intrinsically binary: one sets a given text against the pattern established by a given canon. Set against the Middleton canon, or the Rowley canon, or the combined Middleton-Rowley canon, *The Spanish Gypsy* is anomalous; set against the Shakespeare canon, *Henry the Sixth, Part One* is anomalous.[41] But that does not mean we should conclude that Shakespeare wrote none of the text of *Henry the Sixth, Part One,* or that Middleton and Rowley wrote none of the text of *The Spanish Gypsy.* Having isolated, by the initial binary investigation, features or passages that cannot reasonably be attributed to the proposed author(s), we must then examine whether those other features or passages can themselves be attributed to the work of a single author. This involves another, essentially binary process. (If anything, this process will tend to underestimate the number of actual authors, because in small patches of text the idiosyncracies of a particular contributor may not be sufficiently frequent to differentiate him from some other author already identified in the text.) From the perspective of a modern investigator, it is easiest to assume there is just one author; if that hypothesis fails, it is then easiest to assume there were only two. But what is easiest for us bears no necessary relationship to what was easiest, or common, for them.

Third, different kinds of internal evidence are most useful at different stages of this investigative process. High-frequency features like those analyzed by Hoy, Lake, and Jackson should identify whether a text is or is not homogeneous, and if it is not, they should narrow the range of plausible candidates for the role of collaborator. When only two authors are involved, high frequency features may be able to identify both, and provide a general map of which parts of the play each is most likely to have written. But the greater the heterogeneity in the high-frequency features of the target text, or the greater the number of known or probable collaborators, the less useful the high-frequency features become, in identifying which collaborators wrote which parts of the text. High-frequency features have established that Ford wrote a few passages of *The Spanish Gypsy,* and that Middleton wrote at least one. But high-frequency features cannot, in themselves, prove that Dekker or Rowley wrote parts of *The Spanish Gypsy,* though such features can establish the possible presence of both. My own investigation, in this essay, cannot be said to have proven, beyond contradiction, that Rowley and Dekker collaborated with Middleton and Ford on this play. For Rowley, I am at this point relying on external evidence (which seems to be reliable in general, and which also seems supported by internal evidence for the other named author). For Dekker, I am at this point relying on strong and interlocking verbal parallels in one line of the text. But with the exception of that one line, I cannot claim, here, to have demonstrated Dekker's presence, and I have not attempted to demonstrate Rowley's authorship of any particular speech or scene. For both authors, absolute proof could only be provided by large numbers of low-frequency features ("verbal parallels"), systematically collected and evaluated.

Fourth, solutions to the most important problems often depend on an understanding of the least important authors. In *The Spanish Gypsy,* Rowley is more difficult to identify than Middleton or Ford, because so many of his plays were undoubtedly written in collaboration; he also shared with Dekker most of the few high-frequency features of his work that readily differentiate him from Middleton. Serious investigation of authorship problems in the Renaissance dramatic canon began with efforts to resolve certain anomalies in the Shakespeare canon. Lake's book, like Jackson's, had implications for Shakespeare, but was primarily dedicated to defining the Middleton canon. These procedures have, in fact, been successful in mapping most of the Shakespeare and the Middleton canons. But the few remaining problems in both canons—and in Fletcher's—will almost certainly require sustained investigation of less glamorous figures, the less talented but no less individual workmen who kept the early modern theatrical machine running. As Arthur Miller wrote at the end of *The Death of a Salesman,* "Attention must be paid to such a person."

Notes

1. *The Collected Works of Thomas Middleton,* gen. ed. Gary Taylor (Oxford: Oxford Univ. Press, forthcoming). In what follows I will take for granted the canon, chronology, and titles defined by that edition. For details, see the Middleton website at www.as.ua.edu/english/strode/middleton.

2. David Lake, *The Canon of Thomas Middleton's Plays* (Cambridge: Cambridge Univ. Press, 1975); MacD. P. Jackson, *Studies in Attribution: Middleton and Shakespeare,* Salzburg Studies in English Literature 79 (Salzburg: Institut für Anglistik und Amerikanistik, 1979); R. V. Holdsworth, "Middleton and Shakespeare: The Case for Middleton's Hand in Timon of Athens," unpublished Ph.D. thesis (Univ. of Manchester, 1982), and "Middleton's Authorship of *A Yorkshire Tragedy,*" *Review of English Studies,* n.s. 45 (1994): 1–25; Gary Taylor, MacD. P. Jackson, and Paul Mulholland, "Thomas Middleton, Lording Barry, and *The Family of Love,*" *Papers of the Bibliographical Society of America* 93 (1999): 213–42; Gary Taylor and John Jowett, *Shakespeare Reshaped 1606–1623* (Oxford: Clarendon, 1993); Taylor, "Thomas Middleton, Thomas Dekker, and *The Bloody Banquet,*" *Papers of the Bibliographical Society of America* 94 (2000): 197–233; Taylor, "Middleton and Rowley—and Heywood: *The Old Law* and New Technologies of Attribution," *Papers of the Bibliographical Society of America* 96 (2002): 165–217.

3. For a bibliographical description see W. W. Greg, *A Bibliography of the English Printed Drama to the Restoration,* 4 vols. (London: Bibliographical Society, 1939–59), no. 717.

4. For Archer's unreliability, see W. W. Greg, "Authorship Attributions in the Early Play-lists," *Edinburgh Bibliographical Society Transactions* 2 (1946): 305–26. Since 1946

a number of additional Archer attributions have been questioned. For a summation of much of the evidence for Dekker's sole authorship of *Blurt,* see *A Critical Old-Spelling Edition of Thomas Dekker's "Blurt, Master Constable,"* ed. Thomas Leland Berger, Salzburg Studies in English Literature, 83 (Salzburg: Institut für Anglistik und Amerikanistik, 1979); Berger did not include Jackson's evidence against the Middleton attribution, published the same year.

5. All surviving copies of the first edition were examined for press variants and manuscript annotations by Shanti Padhi in "A Critical Old-spelling Edition of *The Spanish Gipsie* by Middleton, Rowley (and possibly Ford)," unpub. D.Phil. thesis (Oxford Univ., 1984). She makes the point that the corrector does not alter the title-page attribution (p. lxxii).

6. E. K. Chambers, ed., "Dramatic Records: The Lord Chamberlain's Office," in *Collections,* vol. 2. part 3, gen. ed. W. W. Greg (Oxford: Malone Society, 1931), 389–90 (reproducing Public Record Office xii:5/134, p. 337). W. J. Lawrence, in *Pre-Restoration Stage Studies* (Cambridge, Mass., 1927), noted that "The plays are enumerated in groups according to their authors . . ." and identified "The World" as *The World Tost at Tennis* (337).

7. H. J. Oliver, in *The Problem of John Ford* (Melbourne: Melbourne Univ. Press, 1955), objected that a play by Dekker and Ford would have sold better or as well as one by Middleton and Rowley (34).

8. The 1653 edition of *The Changeling,* published at about the same time as *The Spanish Gypsy,* was not reprinted, and not a great seller (since the unsold stock was reissued with a new title page in 1668).

9. Nigel Bawcutt, ed., *The Control and Censorship of Caroline Drama: The Records of Sir Henry Herbert, Master of the Revels 1623–73* (Oxford: Clarendon, 1996), 141.

10. Jackson, *Studies in Attribution,* 141. For the date, see Gary Taylor, "Thomas Middleton, *The Nice Valour,* and the Court of James I," *The Court Historian* 6 (2001): 1–36.

11. Lake, 215; Padhi, xxvi; George R. Price, "The Quartos of *The Spanish Gypsy* and Their Relation to *The Changeling,*" *Papers of the Bibliographical Society of America* 52 (1958): 111–25. I provide a good deal of additional evidence for scribal copy behind the 1653 edition in the Textual Introduction to *The Spanish Gypsy* in *Thomas Middleton and Early Modern Textual Culture: A Companion to The Collected Works,* gen. ed. Gary Taylor (Oxford: Oxford Univ. Press, forthcoming).

12. On the authorship problem, see Taylor, *"Bloody Banquet";* on the date, see Gary Taylor, "Gender, Hunger, Horror: The History and Significance of *The Bloody Banquet,*" *Journal of Early Modern Cultural Studies* 1 (2001): 1–45.

13. The contractions do not occur in *The Patient Man and the Honest Whore, A Chaste Maid in Cheapside, The Witch, Hengist King of Kent, Women Beware Women, Wit at Several Weapons, Anything for a Quiet Life, The Bloody Banquet, A Fair Quarrel, The Changeling, or The World Tossed at Tennis.*

14. Lake, *Canon,* 54.

15. Jackson has informed me that the total for *World Tossed at Tennis* given in *Studies in Attribution* accidentally omitted the eight instances of *on't* (which were included in the overall *'t* totals for the other plays) and that he also overlooked one Rowley instance of *'t* in the Rowley portion of *Tennis.* I give in the text the corrected total.

16. *A Yorkshire Tragedy* is the only play in which non-verbal "*'t*" contractions do not predominate, and there the figure is four to nine: the totals for this very short play are too low to have much meaning, and, as Holdsworth points out, five of the verbal "*'t*" contractions occur within the three lines of a single speech in which Husband is extremely agitated: "where ist, powr't down, down with it, downe with it, I say powr't oth ground lets see't, let's see't."

17. The eight instances of *ye* are also a bit high, but Middleton has two plays with seven, and Rowley two plays with ten and fourteen; so only *'ee* is undeniably reliable evidence against a Middleton-Rowley collaboration.

18. Literature Online (for 1576–1642) shows this occurring only in Ford's *Fancies* (twice), Dekker and Ford's *Welsh Ambassador* (once), and Marston's *Dutch Courtesan* (once). Of playwrights active in 1623, only Ford used this rare contraction.

19. Figures for *i'th'* in the Middleton canon: *Puritan* 1, *Phoenix* 1, *Chaste Maid* 8, *Widow* 1, *Wit at Several Weapons* 3. The high total in *Chaste Maid* may itself be scribal; Lake notes other evidence of scribal interference in that play (27). But there is at least one example in five different Middleton plays.

20. See *A Game at Chess* 1041 (autograph Trinity manuscript *t'ad,* scribal Archdale manuscript *'t'had,* scribal Rosenbach manuscript *th'ad*), 1315 (Trinity *tad;* but *it had* in the Archdale and Lansdowne scribal manuscripts, and in Q3, clearly set from a scribal manuscript). Line numbers cite T. H. Howard-Hill's transcript of the Trinity manuscript in *A Game at Chess by Thomas Middleton 1624,* ed. Howard-Hill (Oxford: Malone Society, 1990).

21. Compare *Hengist* 5.1.252, 256, and 1.2.37; *No Wit* C1v; *Dissemblers* E7, F8; *Women Beware Women* 3.3.286; *Fair Quarrel* 2.1.192, 5.1.9; *Old Law* 4.2.237, 5.1.271 (both in passages assigned to Middleton).

22. Literature Online gives the following parallels in plays of the period. For *y'ad,* there are only twenty-nine instances in twenty-six 1576–1642 plays, including none by Ford or Dekker. The *Gypsy* example is paralleled by two examples in *Old Law.* For *ye'ad* there are only five total instances in five plays, three of them in the Middleton canon: *Widow, Fair Quarrel* (5.1, usually assigned to Rowley; but patches of Middleton writing are suspected), and *Wit at Several Weapons* (2.1, assigned to Middleton). For *y'had,* there are Middleton examples in *Hengist* (2), *Dissemblers* (2), *Women Beware* (1), and *No Wit* (1); one in *A Match at Midnight* (perhaps by Rowley), and one in Ford's *Love's Sacrifice.* There is also one in *The Witch of Edmonton* (1.2), but this is a play of little use in relation to *The Spanish Gypsy;* since it was attributed on the title page of the first edition to Dekker, Ford, Rowley, "etc.," it represents a collaboration by at least three, and possibly four, of the authors at issue in *Gypsy,* and—since any division of shares in *Edmonton* is necessarily conjectural, and indeed more conjectural than usual—the play cannot reliably be used to arbitrate between the rival claims in *Gypsy.*

23. Fletcher wrote or co-wrote thirty plays with a total for *'em* greater than *Gypsy,* but by 1623 he was working exclusively for the King's Men. Among other playwrights working in 1623, Massinger would be the likeliest alternative, with six uncollaborative plays exceeding the *Gypsy* figure. However, both Fletcher and Massinger seem ruled out by the external evidence, since the 1639 play list had already grouped their plays, by author, earlier in the sequence. Chapman and Day would be possible, on the basis of one unassisted early play; but although both were alive in 1623, neither was very active in the theater, and Chapman's very distinctive individual style is certainly nowhere present in *Gypsy.* Webster wrote two collaborative plays—*Westward Ho* with Dekker, *A Cure for a Cuckold* with Rowley and Heywood—which qualify. But Middleton (or Middleton with Rowley) is easily the author with the most internal evidence for such a preference who also fits the external evidence. I include *The Patient Man and the Honest Whore* and *The Roaring Girl* among Middleton examples, since the high figures are due to his presence, rather than Dekker's.

24. Holdsworth, "Timon," 236–67.

25. In *Bloody Banquet,* for instance, the evidence for scribal interference reinforces the title-page attribution to "T.D."

26. H. Dugdale Sykes, *Sidelights on Elizabethan Drama* (1924), 183.

27. Oliphant, *Shakespeare and His Fellow Dramatists,* 2 vols. (1929), II, 18 ("certainly seems in the main to be from the workshop of Ford and Dekker"); Sargeaunt, *John Ford* (1935), 41–52.

28. G. E. Bentley, *The Jacobean and Caroline Stage,* 7 vols. (Oxford: Clarendon Press, 1941–68), IV, 893. Alfred Harbage, *Annals of English Drama 975–1700,* rev. S. Schoenbaum (London: Methuen, 1964).

29. The low totals for *I'm* must be scribal. The only alternative to this explanation would be to identify another author, of the whole play, who seldom used *I'm* but who otherwise mixed features favored by Middleton, Rowley, Ford, and Dekker. No author of the period fits that profile, and postulating the existence of such an author would still not explain the external evidence for Middleton and Rowley.

30. Padhi, cxxix–cxxxi (citing parallels in part 2, book 1, chapter 4 of Guzman).

31. Lake's tables do not distinguish between *wud* and *woud,* presumably because he regards the significant feature as the absence of the medial l.

32. Cyrus Hoy, *Introductions, Notes, and Commentaries to Texts in "The Dramatic Works of Thomas Dekker,"* 4 vols. (Cambridge: Cambridge Univ. Press, 1980), III, 234 ("the case for Ford's presence in the play is a good deal stronger than the one that Lake is able to make for Dekker").

33. MacD. P. Jackson, "Editing, Attribution Studies, and 'Literature Online': A New Resource for Research in Renaissance Drama," *Research Opportunities in Renaissance Drama* 37 (1998): 1–15; Jackson, "Late Webster and His Collaborators: How Many Playwrights Wrote *A Cure for a Cuckold?*" *Publications of the Bibliographical Society of America* 95 (2001): 295–313; Taylor, "*Old Law* and New Attribution Technologies." The value of a comprehensive check of all verbal or phrasal parallels in the canons of the candidate authors had earlier been demonstrated by Holdsworth ("Timon," 1982) and by Taylor and Jowett (1993), but those earlier studies had been based on manual searches of only two authors, one (Shakespeare) already digitally concorded. It was Jackson who pointed out to me the support LION afforded for Dekker's authorship of this line in 2.1.

34. I and MacD. P. Jackson have in fact drafted an initial report of an investigation of several extended passages of the play, using this method; we hope to publish it soon.

35. Another detail that might appear to favor Ford is not reliable: "on my life" (1.5.92). There are no exact parallels for this asseveration in Middleton. But Middleton does have "a my life" (=o' my life) elsewhere (*Phoenix* 15.159, *Trick* 5.2.30, *Weapons* 3.1.71); since *Gypsy* is a late printing of a scribal text, we cannot be certain that "on" is not here a scribal expansion of authorial "a," as happens for instance at *Bloody Banquet* 1.4.9, where Middleton's "a purpose" becomes "on purpose" (also 2.3.7). There are several examples of such expansion in scribal texts of *A Game at Chess,* and in folio texts of Shakespeare, where the quartos have "a." If this were an early quarto apparently printed from authorial papers, the difference between *a* and *on* would have evidentiary value; here, it does not.

36. The significance of this contraction was first noticed by Padhi, "Critical Edition," xcix, who contrasted Middleton's practice with Ford's. I have verified and retabulated her evidence, using Literature Online and the draft texts of the Middleton edition. She did not notice the absence of the contraction from Dekker's canon, or the chronological pattern in Middleton's.

37. See *Widow* 2.2, 3.2 (1616?), *Old Law* 4.2 (1618–19?), where it appears twice, *World Tossed at Tennis* (front matter, perhaps by Rowley), *Women Beware Women* 2.2.462 (1621?), *Triumphs of Integrity* (1623). It also appears in *Old Law* 5.1, but in the first part of the scene, now attributed to Heywood (who used *may't* six times in other plays); I have therefore not counted this as a Middleton example.

38. *Old Law* 4.2.26, "much good mayt do".

39. I have found only eleven parallels in Ford's unassisted work: *Broken Heart* 2, *Fancies* 1, *Love's Sacrifice* 1, *Lover's Melancholy* 1, *Perkin Warbeck* 2, *Queen* 1, *'Tis Pity* 3. Only two of these occur before consonants. It also occurs seven times in collaborative works: *Sun's Darling* 3 (Dekker and Ford), and *Witch of Edmonton* 4 (all in 4.1 and 4.2).

40. Shakespeare's name was added to Rowley's on the title page of *The Birth of Merlin;* Beaumont's was added to the title page of the Fletcher folio, though he collaborated on very few of the texts in that volume. Since I am here concerned with the problem of the number

of collaborators, the addition of names needs to be distinguished from the substitution of a relatively famous name for an unfamiliar one, or the provision of a well-known name in a case where the publisher has no idea of the real author.

41. See Gary Taylor, "Shakespeare and Others: The Authorship of *1 Henry VI*," *Medieval and Renaissance Drama in England* 7 (1995): 145–205; I conclude that the play was written by Shakespeare, Thomas Nashe, and two as yet unidentified others.

MacDonald P. Jackson: Bibliography

Brian Boyd

Most reviews are omitted.

1961 "The Visionary Moment: An Essay on the Poetry of A. R. D. Fairburn." *Kiwi 1961* (Auckland Univ. Students' Association): 22–31.

1962[a] "Affirmative Particles in *Henry VIII.*" *Notes and Queries* 206: 372–74.

1962[b] "A Shakespearian Quibble." *Notes and Queries* 207: 331–32.

1963[a] "Material for an Edition of *Arden of Feversham.*" Unpub. BLitt thesis, Oxford Univ. v + 338pp.

1963[b] "Anthony Mundy and *Sir Thomas More.*" *Notes and Queries* 208: 96.

1963[c] "'The Gods Deserve Your Kindness!': *King Lear,* III.vi.5." *Notes and Queries* 208: 101.

1963[d] "Love's Labours Lost?" *Times Literary Supplement,* 12 July: 509.

1963[e] "The Cult of Hughes and Gunn." *Poetry Review* 54 (autumn): 247–48.

1963[g] "Shakespeare and *Edmund Ironside.*" *Notes and Queries* 208: 331–32.

1963[h] "An Emendation to *Arden of Faversham.*" *Notes and Queries* 208: 410.

1964[a] "Edward Archer's Ascription of *Mucedorus* to Shakespeare." *AUMLA* 22: 233–48.

1964[b] "Dekker's Back-Door'd Italian." *Notes and Queries* 209: 37.

1964[c] "Langbaine and the Memorial Versions of *Henry VI, Parts II and III.*" *Notes and Queries* 209: 134.

1964[d] "Entangled by Locks—Entangled by Looks." *English Studies* 45: 43–44.

1965[a] *Shakespeare's "A Lover's Complaint": Its Date and Authenticity.* Auckland: University of Auckland, Bulletin 72, English Series 13. 39 pp.

1965[b] "*Edward III,* Shakespeare, and Pembroke's Men." *Notes and Queries* 210: 329–31.

1966[a] Editor, *Poetry Australia: New Zealand Issue.* Sydney: South Head Press. 48 pp.

1966[b] "*Henry V,* III.vi.181: An Emendation." *Notes and Queries* 211: 133–34.

1966[c] "Drama in Auckland." *Landfall* 80 (December): 385–91.

1967[a] "Suggestions for a Controlled Experiment to Test Precognition in Dreams." *Journal of the American Society for Psychical Research* 61: 346–53.

1968[a] "Annual Bibliography of Commonwealth Literature, 1967: New Zealand." *The Journal of Commonwealth Literature* 6 (January): 81–88.

1969[b] "Annual Bibliography of Commonwealth Literature, 1968: New Zealand." *The Journal of Commonwealth Literature* 8 (December): 66–74.

1970[a] "Annual Bibliography of Commonwealth Literature, 1969: New Zealand." *The Journal of Commonwealth Literature* 10 (December): 102–9.

1971[a] "Three Old Ballads and the Date of *Doctor Faustus*." *AUMLA* 36: 187–200.

1971[b] "A Note on the Text of *Edward III*." *Notes and Queries* 216: 453–54.

1971[c] "A Non-Shakespearian Parallel to the Comic Mispronunciation of 'Ergo' in Hand D of *Sir Thomas More*." *Notes and Queries* 216: 139.

1971[d] "Annual Bibliography of Commonwealth Literature, 1970: New Zealand." *The Journal of Commonwealth Literature* 6.2 (December): 90–99.

1972[a] "Shakespeare's *Sonnets, Parthenophil and Parthenophe,* and *A Lover's Complaint*." *Notes and Queries* 217: 125–26.

1972[b] "Annual Bibliography of Commonwealth Literature, 1971: New Zealand." *The Journal of Commonwealth Literature* 7.2 (December): 118–26.

1973[a] "Conversation with Allen Curnow." *Islands* 4 (winter): 142–63.

1973[b] "Three Unidentified Play Titles of the Early Seventeenth Century." *Notes and Queries* 218: 465–66.

1973[c] "Annual Bibliography of Commonwealth Literature, 1972: New Zealand." *The Journal of Commonwealth Literature* 8.2 (December): 124–33.

1974[a] "Compositor C and the First Folio Text of *Much Ado About Nothing*." *Papers of the Bibliographical Society of America* 68: 414–18.

1974[b] "Annual Bibliography of Commonwealth Literature, 1973: New Zealand." *The Journal of Commonwealth Literature* 9.2 (December): 115–22.

1975[a] "Punctuation and the Compositors of Shakespeare's *Sonnets,* 1609." *The Library,* 30: 1–24.

1975[b] "North's Plutarch and the Name 'Escanes' in Shakespeare's *Pericles*." *Notes and Queries* 220: 173–74.

1975[c] *Punctuation and the Compositors of Shakespeare's "Sonnets," 1609.* London: Oxford Univ. Press for the Bibliographical Society. 24 pp. Reprinted from 1975[a].

1975[d] with Peter Alcock. "Annual Bibliography of Commonwealth Literature, 1974: New Zealand." *The Journal of Commonwealth Literature* 10.2 (December): 125–36.

1976[a] Review of *The Canon of Thomas Middleton's Plays,* by David J. Lake. *Journal of English and Germanic Philology* 75: 414–17.

1978[a] "[New Zealand] Creative Writing [1952–1977]." In *Thirteen Facets,* edited by Ian Wards. Wellington: Government Printer: 275–302.

1978[b] "The Printer of the First Quarto of *Astrophil and Stella* (1591)." *Studies in Bibliography* 31: 201–03.

1978[c] "Linguistic Evidence for the Date of Shakespeare's Additions to *Sir Thomas More*." *Notes and Queries* 223: 154–56.

1978[d] "Compositors B, C, and D, and the First Folio Text of *Love's Labour's Lost*." *Papers of the Bibliographical Society of America* 72: 61–65.

1979[a] *Studies in Attribution: Middleton and Shakespeare.* Salzburg: Institut für Anglistik und Amerikanistik, Univ. of Salzburg, Jacobean Drama Studies 79, 1979. x, 228 pp.

1979[b] "Extraversion, Neuroticism, and Date of Birth: A Southern Hemisphere Study." *Journal of Psychology* 101: 197–98.

1979[c] "A Hint for Investigators of Authorship." *Shakespeare Newsletter* 29: 43–44.

1979[d] "Compositorial Practices in Tourneur's *The Atheist's Tragedy*." *Studies in Bibliography* 32: 210–15.

1980[a] "'A Curious Typesetting Characteristic' in Some Elizabethan Quartos." *The Library,* 6th series, 2: 70–72.

1981[a] "Compositorial Practices in *The Revenger's Tragedy,* 1607–08." *Publications of the Bibliographic Society of America* 75: 157–70.

1981[b] "Hand D of *Sir Thomas More.*" *Notes and Queries* 225: 146.

1982[a] "Two Shakespeare Quartos: *Richard III* (1597) and *1 Henry IV* (1598)." *Studies in Bibliography* 25: 173–90.

1982[b] "An Allusion to Marlowe's *The Jew of Malta* in an Early Seventeenth-Century Pamphlet Possibly by Thomas Middleton." *Notes and Queries* 226: 132–33.

1983[a] Editor, *"The Revenger's Tragedy": Attributed to Thomas Middleton: A Facsimile of the 1607/8 Quarto.* East Brunswick: Associated Univ. Presses. 114 pp.

1983[b] and Vincent O'Sullivan. Editors, *The Oxford Book of New Zealand Writing Since 1945.* Auckland: Oxford Univ. Press. xxxvi, 680 pp.

1983[c] "A Contribution to the *Lear* Revolution." Review of *The Textual History of "King Lear,"* by P. W. K. Stone. *Shakespeare Quarterly* 34: 121–26.

1983[d] "Fluctuating Variation: Author, Annotator, or Actor?" In *The Division of the Kingdoms: The Two Texts of "King Lear,"* edited by Gary Taylor and Michael B. Warren. Oxford: Clarendon Press: 313–49.

1984[a] "Anthony Mundy and The Play of Thomas More." *Moreana* 22:85: 83–84.

1984[b] "The Year's Contributions to Shakespearian Study: Editions and Textual Studies." *Shakespeare Survey* 37 (Cambridge: Cambridge Univ. Press): 202–19.

1984[c] "Renaissance Drama Productions (1984): *Arden of Faversham,* Little Theatre, Auckland." *Research Opportunities in Renaissance Drama* 27: 127–29.

1985[a] "John Webster and Thomas Heywood in *Appius and Virginia:* A Bibliographical Approach to the Problem of Authorship." *Studies in Bibliography* 38, 217–35.

1985[b] "The Year's Contributions to Shakespearian Study: Editions and Textual Studies." *Shakespeare Survey* 38 (Cambridge: Cambridge Univ. Press), 238–54.

1985[c] "Renaissance Drama Productions (1985): *The Duchess of Malfi,* Lyttelton Theatre, London, National Theatre Company." *Research Opportunities in Renaissance Drama* 28: 169–71.

1986[a] "The Manuscript Copy for the Quarto (1598) of Shakespeare's 1 Henry IV." *Notes and Queries* 231: 353–54.

1986[b] and Michael Neill. Editors, *The Selected Plays of John Marston.* Cambridge: Cambridge Univ. Press. xxxvi, 535 pp.

1986[c] "The Transmission of Shakespeare's Text." In *The Cambridge Companion to Shakespeare Studies,* edited by Stanley Wells. Cambridge: Cambridge Univ. Press, 163–85.

1986[e] with Gary Taylor. Editors, *Pericles.* In *William Shakespeare: The Complete Works,* general editors Stanley Wells and Gary Taylor. Oxford: Oxford Univ. Press, 1167–98.

1986[f] with Gary Taylor. Editors. *Pericles.* In *William Shakespeare: The Complete Works: Original-Spelling Edition,* general editors Stanley Wells and Gary Taylor. Oxford: Oxford Univ. Press, 1169–1200.

1986[g] "Ursula Bethell." *Landfall* 158: 269–70.

1986[h] "The Year's Contributions to Shakespearian Study: Editions and Textual Studies." *Shakespeare Survey* 39 (Cambridge: Cambridge Univ. Press), 236–52.

1987[a] "Compositors' Stints and the Spacing of Punctuation in the First Quarto (1609) of Shakespeare's *Pericles.*" *Publications of the Bibliographic Society of America* 81: 17–23.

1987[b] with Gary Taylor. Textual Notes on *Pericles.* In *William Shakespeare: A Textual Companion,* edited by Stanley Wells, Gary Taylor, John Jowett, and William Montgomery. Oxford: Oxford Univ. Press, 556–92.

1987[c] "Printer's Copy for the First Folio Text of *Othello:* The Evidence of Misreadings." *The Library* 9: 262–67.

1987[d] "Conversation with Allen Curnow." In Allen Curnow, *Look Back Harder: Critical Essays 1935–1984,* edited by Peter Simpson. Auckland: Auckland Univ. Press, 245–65. Reprinted from 1973[a].

1987[e] "The Year's Contributions to Shakespearian Study: Editions and Textual Studies." *Shakespeare Survey* 40 (Cambridge: Cambridge Univ. Press): 224–36.

1988[a] "Interview with Kendrick Smithyman." *Landfall* 168: 403–20.

1988[b] "India and Indian or Judea and Judean? Shakespeare's *Othello,* V.ii.356, and Peele's *Edward I,* scene i, line 107." *Notes and Queries* 233: 479–80.

1988[c] "The Year's Contributions to Shakespearian Study: Editions and Textual Studies." *Shakespeare Survey* 41 (Cambridge: Cambridge Univ. Press): 228–45.

1989[a] "Editing *Hamlet* in the 1980s: Textual Theories and Textual Practices." *Hamlet Studies* 11: 60–72.

1989[b] "*Titus Andronicus:* Play, Ballad, and Prose History." *Notes and Queries* 234: 325–27.

1989[c] "*The Wars of the Roses:* The English Shakespeare Company on Tour." *Shakespeare Quarterly* 40: 208–12.

1990[a] "The Year's Contributions to Shakespearian Study: Editions and Textual Studies." *Shakespeare Survey* 42 (Cambridge: Cambridge Univ. Press): 200–13.

1990[b] "*Pericles,* Acts I and II: New Evidence for George Wilkins." *Notes and Queries* 235: 192–96.

1990[c] "Echoes of Spenser's *Prothalamion* as Evidence against an Early Date for Shakespeare's *A Lover's Complaint.*" *Notes and Queries* 235: 180–82.

1990[d] "How Many Horses Has Sonnet 51? Textual and Literary Criticism in Shakespeare's Sonnets." *English Language Notes* 27: 10–19.

1990[e] "The Additions to *The Second Maiden's Tragedy:* Shakespeare or Middleton?" *Shakespeare Quarterly* 41: 402–5.

1991[a] "Poetry: Beginnings to 1945." In *The Oxford History of New Zealand Literature in English,* edited by Terry Sturm. Auckland: Auckland Univ. Press, 335–86, 723–25.

1991[b] "The Year's Contributions to Shakespearian Study: Editions and Textual Studies." *Shakespeare Survey* 43 (Cambridge: Cambridge Univ. Press), 255–70.

1991[c] "George Wilkins and the First Two Acts of *Pericles:* New Evidence from Function Words." *Literary and Linguistic Computing* 6: 155–63.

1992[a] "Kendrick Smithyman." In *In the Same Room: Conversations with New Zealand Writers,* edited by Elizabeth Alley and Mark Williams. Auckland: Univ. of Auckland Press, 121–39.

1993[a] "Rhyming in *Pericles:* More Evidence of Dual Authorship." *Studies in Bibliography* 46: 239–49.

1993[b] "The Authorship of *Pericles:* The Evidence of Infinitives." *Notes and Queries* 238: 197–200.

1993[c] "Shakespearean Features of the Poetic Style of *Arden of Faversham.*" *Archiv für das Studium der neueren Sprachen und Literaturen* 230: 273–304.

1994[a] Entries on Arthur H. Adams, Fleur Adcock, Blanche Baughan, Ruth Dallas, Anne French, and Charles Spear. In *The Oxford Companion to Twentieth-Century Poetry in English,* edited by Ian Hamilton. Oxford: Oxford Univ. Press, 3, 4, 31–32, 114, 172, 510.

1994[b] "Another Metrical Index for Shakespeare's Plays: Evidence for Chronology and Authorship." *Neuphilologische Mitteilungen* 95: 453–58.

1995[a] Editor. *A. R. D. Fairburn: Selected Poems.* Wellington: Victoria Univ. Press, 152 pp.

1995[b] "Function Words in *The Funeral Elegy.*" *Shakespeare Newsletter* 45. 4: 74–78.

1995[c] Review of *Shakespeare Reshaped, 1606–1623,* by Gary Taylor and John Jowett. *Yearbook of English Studies* 25: 274–76.

1996[a] "Stage Directions and Speech Headings in Act 1 of *Titus Andronicus* Q (1594): Shakespeare or Peele?" *Studies in Bibliography* 49: 134–48.

1997[a] "Shakespeare's Brothers and Peele's Brethren: *Titus Andronicus* Again." *Notes and Queries* 242: 494–95.

1997[b] "Phrase Lengths in *Henry VIII:* Shakespeare and Fletcher." *Notes and Queries* 242: 75–80.

1997[c] Review of *Titus Andronicus* (Arden Shakespeare), edited by Jonathan Bate and *Titus Andronicus* (New Cambridge Shakespeare), edited by Alan Hughes. *Modern Language Review* 92: 946–48.

1997[d] with Diana Harris. "Stormy Weather: Derek Jarman's *The Tempest.*" *Literature/Film Quarterly* 25: 90–98.

1998[a] "Editing, Attribution Studies, and 'Literature Online': A New Resource for Research in Renaissance Drama." *Research Opportunities in Renaissance Drama* 12: 1–15.

1998[b] "Indefinite Articles in *Titus Andronicus,* Peele, and Shakespeare." *Notes and Queries* 243: 308–10.

1998[c] "New Work on the Compositors of Shakespeare's Sonnets (1609)." *Shakespeare Newsletter* 48: 31–34.

1998[d] "Poetry: Part One: Beginnings to 1945." In *The Oxford History of New Zealand Literature in English, Second Edition,* edited by Terry Sturm. Auckland: Oxford Univ. Press, 394–446.

1998[f] "Petruchio's Barber's Shop: *The Taming of the Shrew,* IV.iii.91." *English Language Notes* 36: 15–19.

1998[g] "The Compositors of *Appius and Virginia* (1654)." *Publications of the Bibliographic Society of America* 92: 535–40.

1998[h] Review of *Shakespeare's Earliest Tragedy: Studies in 'Titus Andronicus,'* by Harold Metz. *Publications of the Bibliographic Society of America* 92: 90–94.

1998[i] Entries on J. R. Hervey, Bill Manhire, W. H. Oliver, Vincent O'Sullivan, *The Butcher Papers, Shuriken.* In *The Oxford Companion to New Zealand Literature,* edited by Roger Robinson and Nelson Wattie. Auckland: Oxford Univ. Press, 81, 235, 335–36, 414, 418–21, 494.

1998[j] Review of *Shakespeare's Edward III,* edited by Eric Sams. *Shakespeare Quarterly* 49: 91–93.

1998[k] with Michael Neill. “Morphew, Leprosy, Melancholy and the Date of Marston’s *Antonio and Mellida.*” *Notes and Queries* 243: 358–60.

1998[l] Review of *The Texts of “Othello” and Shakespearian Revision,* by E. A. J. Honigmann. *Shakespeare Studies* 26: 364–72.

1998[m] Review of *The Art of Shakespeare’s Sonnets,* by Helen Vendler. *AUMLA* 89: 124–25.

1999[a] with Gary Taylor and Paul Mulholland. “Thomas Middleton, Lording Barry and *The Family of Love.*” *Publications of the Bibliographic Society of America* 93: 213–41.

1999[b] “*Titus Andronicus* and Electronic Databases: A Correction and a Warning.” *Notes and Queries* 244: 209–10.

1999[c] “‘Censor’ in *The Taming of the Shrew,* IV.iii.91.” *Notes and Queries* 244: 211–12.

1999[d] “Rhymes in Shakespeare’s ‘Sonnets’: Evidence of Date of Composition.” *Notes and Queries* 244: 213–19.

1999[e] “Shakespeare’s Sonnets: Rhyme and Reason in the Dark Lady Series.” *Notes and Queries* 244: 219–23.

1999[f] “John Webster’s *The Devil’s Law-Case,* I.ii.27–29: An Emendation.” *Notes and Queries* 244: 258–60.

1999[g] “Latin Formulae for Act Endings in Early Modern English Plays.” *Notes and Queries* 244: 262–65.

1999[e] “‘A Wood Near Monte Athena’: Michael Hoffman’s *A Midsummer Night’s Dream.*” *Shakespeare Newsletter* 49: 29–48.

1999[f] Review of *Shakespeare’s Sonnets* (Arden Shakespeare), edited by Katherine Duncan-Jones, *The Sonnets* (Cambridge School Shakespeare), edited by Rex Gibson. *Shakespeare Quarterly* 50: 368–72.

1999[g] with Diana Harris. “Stormy Weather: Derek Jarman’s *The Tempest.*” *Shakespearean Criticism Yearbook 1997,* 42: 339–45. Reprinted from 1997[e].

1999[h] “A Statistical Study of the Phaistos Disc.” *Kadmos: Zeitschrift für vor- und frühgriechische Epigraphik* 38: 19–30.

1999[i] “A Man’s Life and a Woman’s Death: Arthur H. Adams’s Female Writer of Genius.” *Kotare: New Zealand Notes and Queries* 2: 20–24.

1999[j] Review of *Text: An Interdisciplinary Annual of Textual Studies, 10. Bibliographical Society of Australia and New Zealand Bulletin* 24: 182–85.

2000[a] “Aspects of Organization in Shakespeare’s *Sonnets* (1609).” *Parergon* 17: 109–34.

2000[b] “Bottom’s Entry-Line: *A Midsummer Night’s Dream,* III.i.98.” *Notes and Queries* 245: 69–70.

2000[c] “Foreword.” In *Nga Waiata Aroha a Hekepia: Love Sonnets by Shakespeare,* trans. Merimeri Penfold. Auckland: Holloway Press, Univ. of Auckland: [iii–iv].

2001[a] “‘But with just cause’: *Julius Caesar,* III.i.47.” *Notes and Queries* 246: 282–84.

2001[b] “Spurio and the Date of *All’s Well That Ends Well.*” *Notes and Queries* 246: 298–99.

2001[c] “Finding the Pattern: Peter Short’s Shakespeare Quartos Revisited.” *Printers and Readers: Special Issue of Bibliographical Society of Australia and New Zealand Bulletin* 25: 67–86.

2001[d] “Late Webster and His Collaborators: How Many Playwrights Wrote *A Cure for a Cuckold?*” *Publications of the Bibliographic Society of America* 95: 295–313.

2001[e] Editor, *The Selected Poems of Eugene Lee-Hamilton (1845–1907): A Victorian Craftsman Rediscovered.* Lampeter and New York: Edwin Mellen Press. 228 pp.

2001[f] "Vocabulary and Chronology: The Case of Shakespeare's Sonnets." *Review of English Studies* 52: 59–75.

2001[g] "Structural Parallelism on the Phaistos Disc: A Statistical Analysis." *Kadmos: Zeitschrift für vor- und frühgriechische Epigraphik* 39: 57–71.

2001[h] "Preface." In Jan Kemp, *Only One Angel.* Otago: Otago Univ. Press: [7–8].

2001[i] "Translating Shakespeare's Sonnets into Maori: An Interview with Merimeri Penfold." *Shakespeare Quarterly* 52: 492–98.

2001[j] with David Carnegie. "The Crux in *A Cure for a Cuckold:* A Cryptic Message, a Doubtful Intention, and Two Dearest Friends." *Modern Language Review* 96: 14–20.

2001[k] "Shakespeare's *Richard II* and the Anonymous *Thomas of Woodstock.*" *Medieval and Renaissance Drama in England* 14: 17–65.

2002[a] "Dating Shakespeare's Sonnets: Some Old Evidence Revisited." *Notes and Queries* 248: 237–41.

2002[b] "Determining Authorship: A New Technique." *Research Opportunities in Renaissance Drama* 41: 1–14.

2002[c] "Pause Patterns in Shakespeare's Verse: Canon and Chronology." *Literary and Linguistic Computing* 17: 37–46.

2002[d] "The Distribution of Pronouns in Shakespeare's Sonnets." *AUMLA* 97: 22–38.

2002[e] "All Our Tribe." Review of *Te Tangata Whai Rawi o Weneti (The Maori Merchant of Venice),* directed by Don Selwyn. *Landfall* 204 (spring 2002), 155–63.

2003[a] with David Gunby and David Carnegie. Editors, *The Works of John Webster,* vol. 2: *The Devil's Law-Case, A Cure for a Cuckold and Appius and Virginia.* Cambridge: Cambridge Univ. Press. xxxi + 644 pp.

2003[b] *Defining Shakespeare: Pericles as Test Case.* Oxford: Oxford Univ. Press. xiv + 250 pp.

2003[c] Review of *Attributing Authorship,* by Harold Love. *Shakespeare Quarterly* 54: 314–16.

FORTHCOMING

"Francis Meres and the Cultural Contexts of Shakespeare's Rival Poet Sonnets." *Review of English Studies.*

with Gary Taylor. "Thomas Middleton and *The Spanish Gypsy:* Protocols for Attribution in Cases of Multiple Collaborators."

with David Gunby and David Carnegie. Editors, *Works of John Webster,* vol. 3. Cambridge: Cambridge Univ. Press.

"Early Modern Authorship: Canons and Chronologies." In *Early Modern Authorship: A Textual Companion to the Oxford Middleton,* edited by Gary Taylor. Oxford: Oxford Univ. Press.

Editor, *The Revenger's Tragedy.* In *The Complete Works of Thomas Middleton.* Gen. ed. Gary Taylor. Oxford: Oxford Univ. Press.

"James Shirley, John Webster, and the Melbourne Manuscript." *Medieval and Renaissance Drama in England.*

"*A Lover's Complaint* Revisited." *Shakespeare Studies.*

Contributors

BRIAN BOYD, University Distinguished Professor, Department of English, University of Auckland, arrived at Auckland as a postdoctoral fellow in New Zealand literature, working under Mac Jackson on novelist Maurice Gee. He has published widely on Vladimir Nabokov, including the biography *Vladimir Nabokov: The Russian Years* and *Vladimir Nabokov: The American Years* (1990, 1991), but has also taught early modern drama with Mac at Auckland and published on Shakespeare, the novel, and evolution and literary, art and play theory. He is currently at work on a book on cognition, evolution, and fiction and a biography of Karl Popper.

DAVID CARNEGIE is Reader and Programme Director, Theatre, at Victoria University of Wellington. He has co-edited with David Gunby and Mac Jackson the Cambridge *Works of John Webster* (volume 3 forthcoming). He publishes on Elizabethan stagecraft, and has edited three plays for the Malone Society. Recent articles include "The Crux in *A Cure for a Cuckold:* A Cryptic Message, a Doubtful Intention, and Two Dearest Friends" (2001), written jointly with Mac Jackson.

WARD E. Y. ELLIOTT, Burnet C. Wohlford Professor of American Political Institutions at Claremont McKenna College, Claremont, California, was co-adviser, with Robert J. Valenza, to the Claremont Shakespeare Clinic and co-author, with Valenza, of many articles on Shakespeare authorship. His field is American constitutional law. Among his writings are *The Rise of Guardian Democracy,* a history of voting rights disputes in the U.S. Supreme Court, and articles on smog, transportation, and population policy.

DAVID GUNBY, Professor of English at the University of Canterbury, Christchurch, New Zealand, is co-editor (with David Carnegie and Mac Jackson) of the Cambridge edition of *The Works of John Webster,* the second volume of which appeared in 2003. His publications include *John Webster: Three Plays, Webster: The White Devil,* and forthcoming *New DNB* and *Cambridge Bibliography of English Literature* entries on Webster, Cyril Tourneur, and William Rowley.

ANDREW GURR, educated at Auckland and Cambridge, is now Professor and Director of the Renaissance Texts Research Centre at the University of

Reading, and Director of Globe Research at the International Globe Research Centre in London. Among his books are *The Shakespearean Stage 1574-1642, Playgoing in Shakespeare's London, The Shakespearian Playing Companies,* and editions of *Richard II* and *Henry V,* and *Philaster.*

JOHN JOWETT is Reader in Shakespeare Studies at the Shakespeare Institute, University of Birmingham, and a General Editor of Arden Early Modern Drama. He edited plays in the Oxford Shakespeare *Complete Works* (1986), in which Mac Jackson co-edited *Pericles,* and Thomas Middleton's *Collected Works* (forthcoming), for which he and Jackson are Associate General Editors. Publications include the Oxford edition of *Richard III* (2000). He is currently editing *Timon of Athens* and *Sir Thomas More.*

JOHN KERRIGAN is Professor of English 2000 at the University of Cambridge and Fellow of St John's College. He has published editions of Shakespeare's *Sonnets and A Lover's Complaint* (1986), an anthology of female-voiced laments, *Motives of Woe* (1991), that puts *A Lover's Complaint* in context, and articles on Renaissance textual and editorial problems—examples of which are reprinted in his *On Shakespeare and Early Modern Literature* (2001). Beyond the Renaissance, he has chiefly published on comparative literature, Romanticism, and modern British and Irish poetry.

MICHAEL NEILL is Professor of English at the University of Auckland, and a colleague of Mac Jackson's for thirty-six years. He cut his editorial teeth with Mac on *The Selected Plays of John Marston* (1986); he has since edited *Anthony and Cleopatra* (1994) for the Oxford Shakespeare, and will soon complete *Othello* for the same series. His publications include *Issues of Death* (1997), and *Putting History to the Question* (2000). His contribution to the present volume is part of a larger project on ideas of service in early modern drama.

MARINA TARLINSKAJA, trained in the sophisticated Russian tradition of metrical analysis, is a research professor in the Department of Linguistics, University of Washington. Among her books are *English Verse: Theory and History* (1976), *Shakespeare's Verse: Iambic Pentameter and the Poet's Idiosyncracies* (1987), *Strict Stress-Meter in English Poetry Compared with German and Russian* (1993) and the forthcoming *English Versification: Meters, Rhythms, Grammar, Semantics.*

GARY TAYLOR, Director of the Hudson Strode Program in Renaissance Studies at the University of Alabama, has served as general editor of the works of Shakespeare (Oxford, 1986) and Middleton (Oxford, forthcoming), has written the introductory survey of chronology and authorship for *William Shakespeare: A Textual Companion* (Oxford, 1987), and has written extensively on problems of attribution and editing in Renaissance drama and poetry.

ROBERT J. VALENZA, Keck Professor of Mathematics and Computer Science at Claremont McKenna College, was co-adviser to the Claremont Shakespeare Clinic and co-author of many articles on Shakespeare authorship. He wrote the text analysis program, INTELLEX, and was the first to apply modal and hyperspherical analysis to authorship studies. Among his books are: *Linear Algebra: An Introduction to Abstract Mathematics, Abstract Algebra,* and *Fourier Analysis on Number Fields.* He has written on Alfred North Whitehead's mathematics and metaphysics, defined the notion of elasticity of factorization in number fields, and done much simulation modeling and signal processing. He was lead engineer for software for RCA communications satellites, and guided six satellite launches. He has never lost a spacecraft.

BRIAN VICKERS is Professor of English Literature and director of the Centre for Renaissance Studies at the ETH (Eidgenössiche Technische Hochschule) Zürich. He describes MacDonald Jackson's contribution to authorship studies as having been indispensable in his own work in this field over the last five years, which has resulted in two books, *"Counterfeiting" Shakespeare: Evidence, Authorship, and John Ford's* A Funerall Elegye, and *Shakespeare, Co-Author: A Historical Study of Five Collaborative Plays.*

Index

Since the authorship of many of the works discussed has been established, if at all, with difficulty, works are indexed under title, with the best current attribution indicated in brackets afterward.